Lecture Notes in Computer Science 1657
Edited by G. Goos, J. Hartmanis and J. van Leeuwen

Springer
*Berlin*
*Heidelberg*
*New York*
*Barcelona*
*Hong Kong*
*London*
*Milan*
*Paris*
*Singapore*
*Tokyo*

Thorsten Altenkirch Wolfgang Naraschewski
Bernhard Reus (Eds.)

# Types for Proofs and Programs

International Workshop, TYPES'98
Kloster Irsee, Germany, March 27-31, 1998
Selected Papers

Springer

Series Editors

Gerhard Goos, Karlsruhe University, Germany
Juris Hartmanis, Cornell University, NY, USA
Jan van Leeuwen, Utrecht University, The Netherlands

Volume Editors

Thorsten Altenkirch
Bernhard Reus
Ludwig-Maximilians-Universität, Institut für Informatik
Oettingenstr. 67, D-80538 München, Germany
E-mail: {alti,reus}@informatik.uni-muenchen.de

Wolfgang Naraschewski
Technische Universität München, Institut für Informatik
Arcisstr. 21-1528, D-80290 München, Germany
E-mail: narasche@informatik.tu-muenchen.de

Cataloging-in-Publication data applied for

Die Deutsche Bibliothek - CIP-Einheitsaufnahme

**Types for proofs and programs** : international workshop, types '98, Kloster Irsee, Germany, March 27 - 31, 1998 ; selected papers / Thorsten Altenkirch ... (ed.). - Berlin ; Heidelberg ; New York ; Barcelona ; Hong Kong ; London ; Milan ; Paris ; Singapore ; Tokyo : Springer, 1999
(Lecture notes in computer science ; Vol. 1657)
ISBN 3-540-66537-4

CR Subject Classification (1998): F.4.1, F.3.1, D.3.3, I.2.3

ISSN 0302-9743
ISBN 3-540-66537-4 Springer-Verlag Berlin Heidelberg New York



Typesetting: Camera-ready by author
SPIN: 10704119 06/3142 – 5 4 3 2 1 0 Printed on acid-free paper

# Preface

This book contains a selection of papers presented at the second annual workshop held under the auspices of the Esprit Working Group 21900 Types. The workshop took place in Irsee, Germany, from 27 to 31 of March 1998 and was attended by 89 researchers.

Of the 25 submissions, 14 were selected for publication after a regular refereeing process. The final choice was made by the editors.

This volume is a sequel to the proceedings from the first workshop of the working group, which took place in Aussois, France, in December 1996. The proceedings appeared in vol. 1512 of the LNCS series, edited by Christine Paulin-Mohring and Eduardo Giménez.

These workshops are, in turn, a continuation of the meetings organized in 1993, 1994, and 1995 under the auspices of the Esprit Basic Research Action 6453 *Types for Proofs and Programs.* Those proceedings were also published in the LNCS series, edited by Henk Barendregt and Tobias Nipkow (vol. 806, 1993), by Peter Dybjer, Bengt Nordström and Jan Smith (vol. 996, 1994) and by Stefano Berardi and Mario Coppo (vol. 1158, 1995). The Esprit BRA 6453 was a continuation of the former Esprit Action 3245 *Logical Frameworks: Design, Implementation and Experiments.* The articles from the annual workshops organized under that Action were edited by Gerard Huet and Gordon Plotkin in the books *Logical Frameworks* and *Logical Environments*, both published by Cambridge University Press.

## Acknowledgments

We would like to thank Irmgard Mignani and Agnes Szabo-Lackinger for helping us with processing the registrations, and Ralph Matthes and Markus Wenzel for organizational support during the meeting. We are indebted to the organizers of the Working Group Types and also to Peter Clote, Tobias Nipkow and Martin Wirsing for giving us the opportunity to organize this workshop and for their support. We would also like to acknowledge funding by the European Union. This volume would not have been possible without the work of the referees. They are listed on the next page and we thank them for their invaluable help.

June 1999

Thorsten Altenkirch
Wolfgang Naraschewski
Bernhard Reus

## List of Referees

Peter Aczel
Thorsten Altenkirch
Gilles Barthe
Henk Barendregt
Uli Berger
Marc Bezem
Venanzio Capretta
Mario Coppo
Catarina Coquand
Roberto Di Cosmo
Gilles Dowek
Marc Dymetman
Jean-Christophe Filliâtre
Neil Ghani
Martin Hofmann
Furio Honsell
Paul Jackson
Felix Joachimski
Florian Kammüller
James McKinna
Simão Melo de Sousa
Thomas Kleymann
Hans Leiss
Petri Mäenpää
Ralph Matthes
Michael Mendler
Wolfgang Naraschewski
Tobias Nipkow
Sara Negri
Christine Paulin-Mohring
Henrik Persson
Randy Pollack
David Pym
Christophe Raffalli
Aarne Ranta
Bernhard Reus
Eike Ritter
Giovanni Sambin
Monika Seisenberger
Anton Setzer
Jan Smith
Sergei Soloview
Makoto Takeyama
Silvio Valentini
Markus Wenzel
Benjamin Werner

# Table of Contents

# On Relating Type Theories and Set Theories *

Peter Aczel

Departments of Mathematics and Computer Science
Manchester University
petera@cs.man.ac.uk

## Introduction

The original motivation[1] for the work described in this paper was to determine the proof theoretic strength of the type theories implemented in the proof development systems Lego and Coq, [12, 4]. These type theories combine the impredicative type of propositions[2], from the calculus of constructions, [5], with the inductive types and hierarchy of type universes of Martin-Löf's constructive type theory, [13]. Intuitively there is an easy way to determine an upper bound on the proof theoretic strength. This is to use the 'obvious' **types-as-sets** interpretation of these type theories in a strong enough classical axiomatic set theory. The elementary forms of type of Martin-Löf's type theory have their familiar set theoretic interpretation, the impredicative type of propositions can be interpreted as a two element set and the hierarchy of type universes can be interpreted using a corresponding hierarchy of strongly inaccessible cardinal numbers. The assumption of the existence of these cardinal numbers goes beyond the proof theoretic strength of ZFC. But Martin-Löf's type theory, even with its W types and its hierarchy of universes, is not fully impredicative and has proof theoretic strength way below that of second order arithmetic. So it is not clear that the strongly inaccessible cardinals used in our upper bound are really needed. Of course the impredicative type of propositions does give a fully impredicative type theory, which certainly pushes up the proof theoretic strength to a set theory[3], $\mathsf{Z}^-$, whose strength is well above that of second order arithmetic. The hierarchy of type universes will clearly lead to some further strengthening. But is it necessary to go beyond ZFC to get an upper bound?

* This paper was written while on sabbatical leave from Manchester University. I am grateful to my two departments for making this possible. I am also grateful to Nijmegen University Computer Science Department for supporting my visit there. Some of the ideas for this paper were developed during that visit.

[1] The same motivation may be found in [15]. More or less the same tools are used there as here; i.e. the types-as-sets and sets-as-trees interpretations. But that paper focuses on slightly different results to the ones obtained here.

[2] Here we will ignore the use of any rules for putting types other than $\Pi$ types into the impredicative type of propositions.

[3] The theory $\mathsf{Z}^-$ is obtained from Zermelo set theory, Z, by only using formulae with restricted quantifiers in the separation axiom scheme

Surprisingly perhaps, the types-as-sets interpretation[4] has hardly been studied systematically[5]. So it is the main aim of this paper to start such a systematic study. In section 2 we first present some of the details of the TS interpretation of a type theory $\mathsf{MLW}^{\mathsf{ext}}$ that is a reformulation of Martin-Löf's extensional type theory with $W$ types but no type universes. This interpretation is carried out in the standard axiomatic set theory ZFC and so gives a proof theoretic reduction of $\mathsf{MLW}^{\mathsf{ext}}$ to ZFC. Of course this result is much too crude and we go on in section 2 to describe two approaches to getting a better result.

The first approach is to make the type theory classical by adding the natural formulation of the law of excluded middle. It turns out that to carry through the interpretation we need to strengthen the set theory by adding a global form of the axiom of choice and we get a proof theoretic reduction of $\mathsf{MLW}^{\mathsf{ext}} + \mathsf{EM}$ to ZFGC. Fortunately it is known that the strengthened set theory is not proof theoretically stronger, so that we do get a reduction of $\mathsf{MLW}^{\mathsf{ext}} + \mathsf{EM}$ to ZFC.

Section 2 ends with the second approach, which is to replace the classical set theory by a constructive set theory, $\mathsf{CZF}^+$, that is based on intuitionistic logic rather than classical logic. So we get a reduction of $\mathsf{MLW}^{\mathsf{ext}}$ to $\mathsf{CZF}^+$.

In section 3 we extend the results of section 2 by adding first a type universe reflecting the forms of type of $\mathsf{MLW}^{\mathsf{ext}}$ and then an infinite cumulative hierarchy of such type universes. To extend the TS interpretation to the resulting type theories we use, in classical set theory, strongly inaccessible cardinal numbers for the type theories with EM, and in constructive set theory, *inaccessible sets* as introduced in [11]. Finally in section 3, we formulate type theories having rules for the impredicative type of propositions of the calculus of constructions and formulate corresponding axioms of constructive set theory and again describe how each of these type theories has a TS interpretation into a corresponding set theory.

In section 4 we briefly describe how the **sets-as-trees** interpretation[6] of CZF into the type theory MLWU, first presented in [1] and then developed further in [2, 3, 10, 11], extends to the other set theories, giving reductions to the corresponding type theories with an extra type universe. Fortunately each type theory with an infinite hierarchy of type universes is proof theoretically as strong as the type theory with a type universe added on top, so that we end up with results stating that to each of the type theories we consider that have an infinite hierarchy of type universes there is a corresponding set theory of the same proof theoretic strength. In particular the type theory $\mathsf{MLWPU}_{<\omega}$, that is our aproximation to the type theories implemented in Lego and Coq, has the same proof theoretic strength as the set theory $\mathsf{CZF}^+\mathsf{pu}_{<\omega}$. This last result does not solve the original problem motivating our work as the set theory is unfamiliar. Nevertheless I think that it does give a new handle on the problem. The new set theory is an interesting one and I plan to present some results about it on a future occasion.

---

4 Here abbreviated TS interpretation.
5 But see [6–8, 15].
6 Here abbreviated ST interpretation.

In section 1 we set up our particular approach to the syntax of our type theories and the TS interpretation of them. We have tried to make this as simple as possible. We have preferred to focus on extensional Martin-Löf type theories having extensional equality types $Eq(A, a_1, a_2)$ for the TS interpretation, as the rules for these types are easily seen to be sound. We have also added equality types $EQ(A_1, A_2)$ for the same reason. For the reverse ST interpretation these equality types are not needed, but nor are any intensional equality types needed, so we can simply drop the extensionality rules.

In this paper we claim various results about proof theoretic reductions between formal systems. When we have reductions both ways we write that the formal systems have the same proof theoretic strength. What do we mean by such claims? Here I will only be concerned with the relatively weak notion of reduction given by a finitistic relative consistency proof. It is standard practice to take the quantifier free theory PRA of primitive recursive arithmetic to codify finitistic mathematics. A more convenient, but essentially equivalent theory is the formal system $\Sigma^0_1$-IA. This is the subsystem of Formal Arithmetic, PA, in which the induction scheme is restricted to $\Sigma^0_1$ formulae. For each type theory or set theory, $\Sigma$ that we will be interested in there will be a standard $\Pi^0_1$ sentence $Con(\Sigma)$ of Formal Arithmetic, that naturally expresses the formal consistency of $\Sigma$. For formal systems, such as the set theories, that use a first order language, the system is understood to be consistent if there is no proof of a contradiction $A \wedge \neg A$. In the case of the type theories considered here, where there is an empty type, $\mathbf{0}$, we will call the type theory consistent if there is no derivation in the type theory of a judgement of the form $\Rightarrow a : \mathbf{0}$, for some $a$. Given two formal systems $\Sigma_1$ and $\Sigma_2$, $\Sigma_1$ is defined to be proof theoretically reducible to $\Sigma_2$ if the sentence $Con(\Sigma_2) \to Con(\Sigma_1)$ can be proved in $\Sigma^0_1$-IA. In this paper we generally obtain such a reduction via an explicit interpretation that allows any derivation of a theorem of $\Sigma_1$ to determine a corresponding derivation in $\Sigma_2$, in such a way that $Con(\Sigma_2) \to Con(\Sigma_1)$ easily follows. The interpretations can probably be used to give proof theoretic reductions in a stronger sense than used here.[7] But we leave such strengthenings for others. We say that two formal systems are of the same proof theoretic strength if each is proof theoretically reducible to the other.

# 1 The General Form of the Syntax and Set Theoretical Semantics of Our Type Theories

## 1.1 Syntax

We give the general form of the syntax of the type theories we will consider.

**The Pseudoterms.** These are expressions, $M$, given by the following abstract syntax.

$$M ::= x \mid c_0 \mid c_1(M) \mid c_2(M, M) \mid c_3(M, M, M) \mid (Qx : M)M$$

[7] See [9] and [14] for more discussion of the concepts of proof theoretic reduction.

where $x : VAR$, $c_0 : C_0$, $c_1 : C_1$, $c_2 : C_2$, $c_3 : C_3$ and $Q : QUANT$. Here $VAR$ is an infinite set of variables and the sets $C_i$, for $i = 0, 1, 2, 3$, and $QUANT$ are finite sets of symbols that will depend on the type theory.

Each $Q$ operates as a variable binder so that free occurrences of $x$ in $M'$ get bound in $(Qx : M)M'$. The notions of free and bound occurrences of variables and the substitution operation are defined in the standard way. We write $M[M_1, \ldots, M_n/x_1, \ldots x_n]$ for the result of simultaneously substituting $M_i$ for $x_i$ in $M$, for $i = 1, \ldots n$, relabelling bound variables in the usual way so as to avoid variable clashes. For this we assume that the variables $x_1, \ldots, x_n$ are pairwise distinct. In general we will not distinguish between pseudoterms that only differ in a suitable relabelling of the bound variables.

### The Pseudojudgements and Formal Judgements of a Type Theory.

**Definition 1** *A* **pseudojudgement** *has the form* $\Gamma \Rightarrow \mathsf{B}$ *where* $\Gamma$ *is a pseudocontext and* $\mathsf{B}$ *is a pseudobody, as defined below.*

- *A* **pseudocontext** *is a finite sequence* $x_1 : M_1, \ldots, x_n : M_n$ *of* **pseudodeclarations,** $x_i : M_i$ *for* $i = 1, \ldots, n$ *where each* $M_i$ *is a pseudoterm and each* $x_i : VAR$ *and, for* $1 \leq j < i$, $x_i$ *is distinct from* $x_j$ *and is not free in* $M_j$.
- *A* **pseudobody** *has one of the following four forms.*

$$\begin{array}{ll} M \ \mathsf{type}, & M_1 = M_2, \\ M_0 : M, & M_1 = M_2 : M \end{array}$$

*When the pseudocontext is the empty sequence then we get a pseudojudgement* $\Rightarrow \mathsf{B}$ *which will usually simply be written* $\mathsf{B}$.

If $\Gamma$ is a pseudocontext $x_1 : M_1, \ldots, x_n : M_n$ then a variable $y$ is **new to** $\Gamma$ if $y$ is distinct from each $x_i$ and not free in any $M_i$.

**Note:** If $\Gamma$ is a pseudocontext $x_1 : M_1, \ldots, x_n : M_n$, the variable $x$ is distinct from each $x_i$ and $M$ is a pseudoterm that has no free occurrences of any $x_i$ then $x_1 : M_1[M/x], \ldots, x_n : M_n[M/x]$ is also a pseudocontext that we will abbreviate $\Gamma[M/x]$. Also we can define the result $\mathsf{B}[M/x]$ of substituting $M$ for $x$ in a pseudobody $\mathsf{B}$ in the obvious way. For example $(M_1 = M_2)[M/x]$ is defined to be $M_1[M/x] = M_2[M/x]$.

The rules of inference of the type theories that we will consider will be given schematically and will have **instances** of the following form.

$$\frac{J_1 \quad \cdots \quad J_k}{J}$$

where $k \geq 0$ and $J_1 \cdots J_k$ are the **premisses** and $J$ is the **conclusion** of the instance, both the premisses and the conclusion being pseudojudgements. When $k = 0$, so that there are no premisses then the line above the conclusion will be omitted in writing the inference.

The schemes presenting the rules will have the abbreviated form

$$\frac{\Gamma_1 \Rightarrow \mathsf{B}_1 \quad \cdots \quad \Gamma_k \Rightarrow \mathsf{B}_k}{\Delta \Rightarrow \mathsf{B}},$$

which is unabbreviated by making explicit an implicit pseudocontext metavariable $\Gamma$ of the scheme by adding it to the front of the left hand side of each premiss and the conclusion to get the scheme

$$\frac{\Gamma, \Gamma_1 \Rightarrow \mathsf{B}_1 \quad \cdots \quad \Gamma, \Gamma_k \Rightarrow \mathsf{B}_k}{\Gamma, \Delta \Rightarrow \mathsf{B}}.$$

Note that an unabbreviated scheme will generally involve metavariables and an instance of the scheme will be obtained by substituting for the metavariables, provided that the side conditions of the scheme hold.

A pseudojudgement is a theorem and so a **formal judgement** of the type theory, if it is in the smallest class of pseudojudgements that includes the conclusion whenever it includes the premisses of any instance of a rule of the type theory. Whenever a pseudocontext $\Gamma$ appears in a formal judgement $\Gamma \Rightarrow \mathsf{B}$ then we call $\Gamma$ a **context**.

All our type theories will have a common list of general rules of inference. These come under three headings, assumption rules, equality rules and substitution rules.

### General Rules

**Assumption Rules** In these rules the variable $x$ must be new to the implicit context $\Gamma$; i.e. not appear in $\Gamma$. Also, in the second assumption rule, the variable $x$ must not be declared in $\Delta$.

$$\frac{A \ \mathsf{type}}{x : A \Rightarrow x : A} \qquad \frac{\Delta \Rightarrow \mathsf{B} \qquad A \ \mathsf{type}}{x : A, \Delta \Rightarrow \mathsf{B}}$$

**Equality Rules**

$$\frac{A \ \mathsf{type}}{A = A} \qquad \frac{A_1 = A_2}{A_2 = A_1} \qquad \frac{A_1 = A_2 \qquad A_2 = A_3}{A_1 = A_3}$$

$$\frac{a : A}{a = a : A} \qquad \frac{a_1 = a_2 : A}{a_2 = a_1 : A} \qquad \frac{a_1 = a_2 : A \qquad a_2 = a_3 : A}{a_1 = a_3 : A}$$

$$\frac{a : A_1 \qquad A_1 = A_2}{a : A_2} \qquad \frac{a_1 = a_2 : A_1 \qquad A_1 = A_2}{a_1 = a_2 : A_2}$$

**Substitution Rule**

$$\frac{x : A, \Delta \Rightarrow \mathsf{B} \qquad a : A}{\Delta[a/x] \Rightarrow \mathsf{B}[a/x]}$$

**Congruence Rules**

$$\frac{x : A, \Delta \Rightarrow C \ \mathsf{type} \qquad a_1 = a_2 : A}{\Delta[a_1/x] \Rightarrow C[a_1/x] = C[a_2/x]} \qquad \frac{x : A, \Delta \Rightarrow c : C \qquad a_1 = a_2 : A}{\Delta[a_1/x] \Rightarrow c[a_1/x] = c[a_2/x] : C[a_1/x]}$$

## 1.2 Types-as-Sets

We now assume given a fixed type theory T and a fixed set theory S. We will work informally in the set theory S.

A types-as-sets interpretation (TS interpretation) of T in S is determined by the following set theoretic data.

- For each $c_0$, a set $c_0^\natural$
- For each $c_n$, where $n = 1, 2, 3$, a definable $n$-place operation $c_n^\natural$ assigning a set $c_1^\natural(A_1, \ldots, A_n)$ to each $n$-tuple $A_1, \ldots, A_n$ of sets.
- For each $Q$, a definable operation $Q^\natural$ that assigns to each set $B$ that is a function a set $Q^\natural(B)$. In practice, if $A$ is a set and $F$ is a definable unary operation on sets then, using the Replacement Axiom Scheme, that will be available in our set theory, we may form the set $B = \{(a, F(a)) \mid a \in A\}$ which is a function defined on $A$. The result of applying $Q^\natural$ to this set $B$ will be written $(Q^\natural a \in A)F(a)$.

**The Interpretation Functions.** By a **variable assignment** we mean a set theoretic function that assigns a set $\xi(x)$ to each variable $x$. We can define the interpretation function mapping each variable assignment $\xi$ to the interpretation $[[M]]_\xi$ of $M$, for each pseudoterm $M$. The definition is by structural induction on the formation of the pseudoterm $M$, using the variable assignment when $M$ is a variable and using the corresponding operation on sets, as illustrated earlier, for each other form of expression. In the following $n = 1, 2$ or $3$.

$$\begin{aligned} [[x]]_\xi &= \xi(x) \\ [[c_0]]_\xi &= c_0^\natural \\ [[c_n(M_1, \ldots, M_n)]]_\xi &= c_n^\natural([[M_1]]_\xi, \ldots, [[M_n]]_\xi) \\ [[(Qx : M)M']]_\xi &= (Q^\natural a \in [[M]]_\xi)[[M']]_{\xi(a/x)} \end{aligned}$$

Here $\xi(a/x)$ is the variable assignment $\xi'$ that is like $\xi$ except that $\xi'(x) = a$.

The following lemmas are proved by a routine induction on the structure of the pseudoterm $M$.

**Lemma 2** *If the variable $x$ is not free in the pseudoterm $M$ and $\xi, \xi'$ are variable assignments that agree except possibly at $x$ then $[[M]]_\xi = [[M]]_{\xi'}$.*

**Lemma 3 (Substitution Lemma)** $[[M[M'/x]]]_\xi = [[M]]_{\xi([[M']]_\xi/x)}$ *for all pseudoterms $M$, $M'$, all variables $x$ and all variable assignments $\xi$.*

**Definition 4** *If $\Gamma$ is a pseudocontext $x_1 : M_1, \ldots, x_n : M_n$ then let $\xi \models \Gamma$ if*

$$\xi(x_i) \in [[M_i]]_\xi \text{ for } i = 1, \ldots n.$$

**Lemma 5** *If $\Gamma$ is a pseudocontext $x_1 : M_1, \ldots, x_n : M_n$, $x$ is a variable distinct from each $x_i$ and $M$ is a pseudoterm that has no free occurrences of any $x_i$ then $\xi \models \Gamma[M/x] \iff \xi([[M]]_\xi/x) \models \Gamma$ for each variable assignment $\xi$.*

**Definition 6** *We define* $\xi \models \mathsf{B}$ *for each form of pseudobody* $\mathsf{B}$.

- $\xi \models M$ type *for any pseudoterm* $M$,
- $\xi \models M_1 = M_2$ *if* $[[M_1]]_\xi = [[M_2]]_\xi$,
- $\xi \models M : M'$ *if* $[[M]]_\xi \in [[M']]_\xi$,
- $\xi \models M_1 = M_2 : M'$ *if* $[[M_1]]_\xi = [[M_2]]_\xi \in [[M']]_\xi$,

**Lemma 7** $\xi \models \mathsf{B}[M/x] \iff \xi([[M]]_\xi/x) \models \mathsf{B}$.

**Definition 8** *A pseudojudgement* $\Gamma \Rightarrow \mathsf{B}$ *is* **valid**, *written* $\models \Gamma \Rightarrow \mathsf{B}$ *if, for all variable assignments* $\xi$, $\xi \models \Gamma$ *implies* $\xi \models \mathsf{B}$.

**Definition 9 (Soundness)** *A rule of inference is* **sound** *if, for every instance* $\frac{J_1 \cdots J_k}{J}$ *of the rule, if the premisses are valid then so is the conclusion; i.e.* $[\models J_1 \,\&\cdots\&\, \models J_k]$ *implies* $\models J$. *A type theory* $\mathsf{T}$ *is* **sound** *if each of its rules is sound. When we have a sound TS interpretation of a type theory* $\mathsf{T}$ *in a set theory* $\mathsf{S}$ *we will write* $\mathsf{T} \leq_{\mathrm{TS}} \mathsf{S}$.

The following result is by structural induction following the inductive definition of the formal judgements of a type theory.

**Lemma 10** *If the type theory* $\mathsf{T}$ *is sound then every formal judgement of* $\mathsf{T}$ *is valid.*

**Proposition 11** *Each general rule is sound. Moreover, for each quantifier* $Q$ *of the type theory the following congruence rule is sound.*

$$\frac{x : M \Rightarrow M_1 = M_2}{(Qx : M)M_1 = (Qx : M)M_2}$$

The proof of this result is straightforward. The assumption and equality rules are trivial. The substitution and congruence rules make use of previously stated lemmas.

## 2 The Theory $\mathsf{MLW}^{\mathsf{ext}}$

We will start with the theory MLW. The abstract syntax of the theory is determined by the following syntax equations.

$$c_0 ::= \mathbf{0} \mid \mathbf{1} \mid \mathbf{2} \mid * \mid 1 \mid 2, \qquad c_1 ::= R_0 \mid \pi_1 \mid \pi_2,$$
$$c_2 ::= R_1 \mid pair \mid sup \mid app \mid rec, \qquad c_3 ::= R_2, \qquad Q ::= \Pi \mid \Sigma \mid W \mid \lambda.$$

### 2.1 Some Defined Forms of Pseudoterm

$$(M_1 \to M_2) = (\Pi\_ : M_1)M_2 \qquad (M_1 \times M_2) = (\Sigma\_ : M_1)M_2$$
$$(M_1 + M_2) = (\Sigma x : \mathbf{2})R_2(M_1, M_2, x) \qquad \mathbb{N} = (Wx : \mathbf{2})R_2(\mathbf{0}, \mathbf{1}, x)$$

Note that the underscore, _, in the first two definitions represents a vacuous variable; i.e. a variable that is being bound by $\Pi$ and $\Sigma$ but does not occur in $M_2$.

## 2.2 Special Rules for MLW

### Type Formation Rules

$$c \text{ type} \qquad (c \in \{0, 1, 2\}) \qquad\qquad \frac{A_1 \text{ type} \quad A_2 \text{ type} \quad c : 2}{R_2(A_1, A_2, c) \text{ type}}$$

$$\frac{x : A \Rightarrow B \text{ type}}{(Qx : A)B \text{ type}} \qquad (Q \in \{\Pi, \Sigma, W\})$$

Using the definitions above we have the following derived type formation rules.

$$\mathbb{N} \text{ type} \qquad\qquad \frac{A_1 \text{ type} \quad A_2 \text{ type}}{(A_1 \# A_2) \text{ type}} \qquad (\# \in \{\rightarrow, \times, +\})$$

### Introduction Rules

$$* : 1 \qquad 1 : 2 \qquad 2 : 2 \qquad\qquad \frac{x : A \Rightarrow b : B}{(\lambda x : A)b : (\Pi x : A)B}$$

$$\frac{x : A \Rightarrow B \text{ type} \quad a : A \quad b : B[a/x]}{pair(a, b) : (\Sigma x : A)B}$$

$$\frac{x : A \Rightarrow B \text{ type} \quad a : A \quad f : (B[a/x] \rightarrow (Wx : A)B)}{sup(a, f) : (Wx : A)B}$$

### Special Congruence Rules

$$\frac{x : A \Rightarrow B_1 = B_2}{(Qx : A)B_1 = (Qx : A)B_2} \qquad (Q \in \{\Pi,\ \Sigma,\ W\})$$

$$\frac{x : A \Rightarrow b_1 = b_2 : B}{(\lambda x : A)b_1 = (\lambda x : A)b_2 : (\Pi x : A)B}$$

### Elimination Rules

$$\frac{x : 0 \Rightarrow C \text{ type} \quad a : 0}{R_0(a) : C[a/x]} \qquad\qquad \frac{x : 1 \Rightarrow C \text{ type} \quad a : 1 \quad c : C[*/x]}{R_1(c, a) : C[a/x]}$$

$$\frac{x : 2 \Rightarrow C \text{ type} \quad a : 2 \quad c_1 : C[1/x] \quad c_2 : C[2/x]}{R_2(c_1, c_2, a) : C[a/x]}$$

$$\frac{x : A \Rightarrow B \text{ type} \quad f : (\Pi x : A)B \quad a : A}{app(f, a) : B[a/x]}$$

$$\frac{x : A \Rightarrow B \text{ type} \quad c : (\Sigma x : A)B}{\begin{cases} \pi_1(c) : A \\ \pi_2(c) : B[\pi_1(c)/x] \end{cases}}$$

$$\frac{\begin{cases} x : A \Rightarrow B \text{ type} \quad z : W \Rightarrow C \text{ type} \\ b : (\Pi x : A)(\Pi u : B \rightarrow W)D(x, u) \quad e : W \end{cases}}{rec(b, e) : C[e/z]}$$

In the last rule we used $W$ to abbreviate $(Wx : A)B$ and $D(x,u)$ to abbreviate $(\Pi y : B)C[app(u,y)/z] \to C[sup(x,u)/z]$.

**Computation Rules**

$$\frac{A_1 \text{ type} \quad A_2 \text{ type}}{\begin{cases} R_2(A_1, A_2, 1) = A_1 \\ R_2(A_1, A_2, 2) = A_2 \end{cases}} \qquad \frac{x : \mathbf{1} \Rightarrow C \text{ type} \quad c : C[*/x]}{R_1(c, *) = c : C[*/x]}$$

$$\frac{x : \mathbf{2} \Rightarrow C \text{ type} \quad c_1 : C[1/x] \quad c_2 : C[2/x]}{\begin{cases} R_2(c_1, c_2, 1) = c_1 : C[1/x] \\ R_2(c_1, c_2, 2) = c_2 : C[2/x] \end{cases}}$$

$$\frac{x : A \Rightarrow b : B \quad a : A}{app((\lambda x : A)b, a) = b[a/x] : B[a/x]}$$

$$\frac{x : A \Rightarrow B \text{ type} \quad a : A \quad b : B[a/x]}{\begin{cases} \pi_1(pair(a,b)) = a : A \\ \pi_2(pair(a,b)) = b : B[a/x] \end{cases}}$$

$$\frac{\begin{cases} x : A \Rightarrow B \text{ type} \quad z : W \Rightarrow C \text{ type} \\ b : (\Pi x : A)(\Pi u : B \to W)D(x,u) \quad a : A \quad f : B[a/x] \to W \end{cases}}{rec(b, sup(a,f)) = app(app(app(b,a),f),g) : C[sup(a,f)/z]}$$

In this last rule we used the following abbreviations.

$$\begin{aligned} W &\text{ for } (Wx : A)B, \\ D(x,u) &\text{ for } (\Pi y : B)C[app(u,y)/z] \to C[sup(x,u)/z], \\ g &\text{ for } (\lambda y : B[a/x])rec(b, app(f,y)). \end{aligned}$$

### 2.3 Extending to MLW$^{\text{ext}}$

We first extend the syntax equations using $c_2 ::= \cdots \mid EQ$ and $c_3 ::= \cdots \mid Eq$. We add the rules of inference given by the following schemes in abbreviated form.

$$\frac{A \text{ type} \quad a_1 : A \quad a_2 : A}{Eq(A, a_1, a_2) \text{ type}} \qquad \frac{A_1 \text{ type} \quad A_2 \text{ type}}{EQ(A_1, A_2) \text{ type}}$$

$$\frac{a_1 = a_2 : A}{* : Eq(A, a_1, a_2)} \qquad \frac{A_1 = A_2}{* : EQ(A_1, A_2)}$$

$$\frac{c : Eq(A, a_1, a_2)}{\begin{cases} a_1 = a_2 : A \\ c = * : Eq(A, a_1, a_2) \end{cases}} \qquad \frac{c : EQ(A_1, A_2)}{\begin{cases} A_1 = A_2 \\ c = * : EQ(A_1, A_2) \end{cases}}$$

## 2.4 The TS Interpretation of $\mathsf{MLW}^{\mathsf{ext}}$ in ZFC

We will work informally in the set theory ZFC. We use the usual von Neumann definition of the natural numbers; i.e. $0 = \emptyset$, $1 = \{0\}$, $2 = \{0, 1\}$, etc .... Ordered pairs are defined as usual; i.e. for sets $a, b$ we define $(a, b) = \{\{a\}, \{a, b\}\}$. As usual functions are single valued sets of ordered pairs. For any set $b$, its **domain** and **range** are the sets $dom(b) = \{x \mid \exists y\ (x, y) \in b\}$ and $ran(b) = \{y \mid \exists x\ (x, y) \in b\}$.

If $a$ is a set and $B$ is a definable operation that assigns a set $B(x)$ to each $x \in a$ then we let $\Pi_{x \in a} B(x)$ be the set of all the functions $f$, with domain $a$, such that $f(x) \in B(x)$ for all $x \in a$. Also, we let $\Sigma_{x \in a} B(x)$ be the set of all pairs $(x, y)$ such that $x \in a$ and $y \in B(x)$.

A **function coding** in set theory consists of a pair of definable operations APP, LAM on sets, APP being binary and LAM being unary, such that if $f$ is a function and $a \in dom(f)$ then

$$\mathrm{APP}(\mathrm{LAM}(f), a) = f(a).$$

The standard example of a function coding is given by the definitions

$$\begin{aligned} \mathrm{APP}(a, b) &= \{x \in \bigcup\bigcup\bigcup a \mid \exists y[x \in y \ \&\ (b, y) \in a]\}, \\ \mathrm{LAM}(a) &= a \end{aligned}$$

for all sets $a, b$. Later it will be convenient to use a non-standard function coding. In the following we assume given some function coding. Given sets $a, b, c, d$ let

$$\begin{aligned} \mathrm{EXP}(a, b) &= \{\mathrm{LAM}(f) \mid f : a \to b\} \\ \mathrm{PI}_{x \in a} B(x) &= \{\mathrm{LAM}(f) \mid f \in \Pi_{x \in a} B(x)\} \text{ if } B(x) \text{ is a set for each } x \in a \\ \mathrm{APP}_2(a, b, c) &= \mathrm{APP}(\mathrm{APP}(a, b), c) \\ \mathrm{APP}_3(a, b, c, d) &= \mathrm{APP}(\mathrm{APP}(\mathrm{APP}(a, b), c), d) \end{aligned}$$

We now present the set theoretic interpretations of the syntactic operations of $\mathsf{ML}^{\mathsf{ext}}$, leaving the interpretations for the $W$ rules til later.

$$\mathbf{0}^\natural = 0,\ \mathbf{1}^\natural = 1,\ \mathbf{2}^\natural = 2,\ *^\natural = 0,\ 1^\natural = 0,\ 2^\natural = 1$$

$$R_0^\natural(a) = a,\ \pi_1^\natural(a) = \{x \mid \exists y\ (x, y) = a\},\ \pi_2^\natural(a) = \{y \mid \exists x\ (x, y) = a\}$$

$$R_1^\natural(a, b) = a,\ pair^\natural(a, b) = (a, b),\ app^\natural(a, b) = \mathrm{APP}(a, b)$$

$$R_2^\natural(a, b, c) = \{x \mid (c = 1^\natural \ \&\ x \in a) \vee (c = 2^\natural \ \&\ x \in b)\}$$

$$EQ^\natural(a, b) = \{x \mid x = 0 \ \&\ a = b\},\ Eq^\natural(a, b, c) = \{x \mid x = 0 \ \&\ b = c \ \&\ b \in a\}$$

If $b$ is a function with domain $a$ let

$$\lambda^\natural(b) = \mathrm{LAM}(b) \qquad \Pi^\natural(b) = \mathrm{PI}_{x \in a} b(x) \qquad \Sigma^\natural(b) = \Sigma_{x \in a} b(x)$$

To deal with the $W$ rules we will need the following result.

**Theorem 12**

1. *For each set* $b$ *there is a smallest set* $W$ *such that if* $(x, y) \in b$ *and* $f \in \mathrm{EXP}(y, W)$ *then* $(x, f) \in W$. *We write* $\mathcal{W}(b)$ *for this set* $W$.
2. *Given a set* $g$ *let* $Y(g) = \Sigma_{x \in dom(g)} \Sigma_{u \in dom(\mathrm{APP}(g,x))} dom(\mathrm{APP}_2(g, x, u))$ *and if* $(x, (u, v)) \in Y(g)$ *then let* $X_{u,v} = \{(\mathrm{APP}(u, y), \mathrm{APP}(v, y)) \mid y \in dom(u)\}$. *There is a smallest set* $f$ *such that if* $(x, (u, v)) \in Y(g)$ *and* $X_{u,v} \subseteq f$, *then* $((x, u), \mathrm{APP}_3(g, x, u, v)) \in f$. *We write* $\mathcal{R}(g)$ *for this set* $f$.
3. *Let* $a, b, c$ *be sets such that* $b, c$ *are functions with* $dom(b) = a$ *and* $dom(c) = \mathcal{W}(b)$ *and let* $W = \mathcal{W}(b)$. *Let* $g \in \mathrm{PI}_{x \in a} \mathrm{PI}_{u \in \mathrm{EXP}(b(x), W)} d((x, u))$ *where* $d(w) = \mathrm{EXP}(\mathrm{PI}_{y \in b(x)} c(\mathrm{APP}(u, y)), c(w))$ *for* $w = (x, u) \in W$. *Then* $\mathcal{R}(g)$ *is the unique function* $f \in \Pi_{w \in W} c(w)$ *such that if* $w = (x, u) \in W$ *then*

$$f(w) = \mathrm{APP}_3(g, x, u, \mathrm{LAM}(H(f, u))).$$

*Here* $H(f, u)$ *is the function* $h \in \Pi_{y \in b(x)} c(\mathrm{APP}(u, y))$ *such that*

$$h(y) = f(\mathrm{APP}(u, y)) \text{ for } y \in b(x).$$

**Proof of the Theorem in ZFC.**

The first two parts of this theorem are applications of the following result.

**Lemma 13** *Let* $\Theta$ *be a definable operation on sets such that, for some set* $B$, *whenever* $X$ *is a set such that* $\Theta(X)$ *has an element then there is a surjective function* $f : b \to X$ *for some* $b \in B$. *Then there is a smallest class* $I$ *such that*

$$X \subseteq I \implies \Theta(X) \subseteq I.$$

*Moreover* $I$ *is a set.*

To prove part 1 of the theorem, using this lemma, it suffices to let

$$\Theta(X) = \bigcup_{(x,y) \in b} \{(x, \mathrm{LAM}(f)) \mid f : y \to X \text{ is onto } X\},$$

and choose $B = ran(b)$. For part 2 we let

$$\Theta(X) = \{((x, u), \mathrm{APP}_3(g, x, u, v)) \mid (x, (u, v)) \in Y(g) \;\&\; X = X_{u,v}\},$$

and choose $B = \{X_{u,v} \mid (x, (u, v)) \in Y(g)\}$. For part 3 of the theorem, first observe that, by an easy induction following the inductive definition of $\mathcal{R}(g)$, $dom(\mathcal{R}(g)) \subseteq W$. Now, by another easy induction, this time on the inductive definition of $W$, observe that, for each $w = (x, u) \in W$, $\mathrm{APP}_3(g, x, u, LAM(H(f, u)))$ is the unique $z$ such that $(w, z) \in \mathcal{R}(g)$ and moreover $z \in c(w)$. All this shows that $\mathcal{R}(g)$ is an $f$ satisfying the desired conditions. Finally, another proof by induction on $W$ will show that $\mathcal{R}(g)$ is the unique $f$ satisfying these conditions.

We now turn to the proof of the lemma. Let $\Gamma$ be the operation on sets given by

$$\Gamma(Y) = \bigcup_{X \in Pow(Y)} \Theta(X),$$

for each set $Y$. The operation $\Gamma$ is monotone and we must show that it has a least fixed point. By transfinite recursion on ordinals we can define sets $I^\alpha$, for ordinals $\alpha$, so that $I^\alpha = \Gamma(I^{<\alpha})$, where $I^{<\alpha} = \bigcup_{\beta<\alpha} I^\beta$. Let $\kappa$ be an infinite regular ordinal such that $card(b) < \kappa$ for all $b \in B$.

We now claim that $I^\kappa \subseteq I^{<\kappa}$. To see this, let $a \in I^\kappa$. Then $a \in \Theta(X)$ for some set $X \subseteq I^{<\kappa}$. For each $x \in X$ let $h(x)$ be the least ordinal $\gamma < \kappa$ such that $x \in I^\gamma$. By the assumption on $\Theta$ there is $b \in B$ and a function $f : b \to X$ that is onto $X$. If $\alpha = card(b)$ then $\alpha < \kappa$ and there is a function $g : \alpha \to b$ that is onto $b$. It follows that $h \circ f \circ g : \alpha \to \kappa$. As $\kappa$ is regular there is $\beta < \kappa$ such that $h \circ f \circ g : \alpha \to \beta$. As $f \circ g$ is onto $X$ it follows that $h : X \to \beta$ so that $X \subseteq I^{<\beta}$ and hence $a \in I^\beta \subseteq I^{<\kappa}$.

It is a standard consequence of this claim that $I^\kappa$ is the least fixed point of $\Gamma$ and so is the desired set $I$ of the lemma.[8]

To interpret the extra syntax needed for the $W$ rules we use $sup^\natural(a,b) = (a,b)$, $rec^\natural(a,b) = \mathcal{R}(a)(b)$ and if $b$ is a function we use $W^\natural(b) = \mathcal{W}(b)$.

**Theorem 14** (ZFC) *The type theory* $\mathsf{MLW}^{\mathsf{ext}}$ *is sound.*

This result gives a proof theoretic reduction of the type theory $\mathsf{MLW}^{\mathsf{ext}}$ to the set theory ZFC. We write $\mathsf{MLW}^{\mathsf{ext}} \leq_{\mathsf{TS}} \mathsf{ZFC}$ to express this reduction. The type theory is constructive in the sense that when the propositions-as-types idea is used to represent logic then intuitionistic logic is represented and the law of excluded middle is not justified. On the other hand the set theory is classical. In the following two subsections we improve on the result by first making the type theory classical and second by making the set theory constructive.

## 2.5 Adding Excluded Middle

Recall that the logical notions are represented in MLW by using the propositions-as-types idea. In particular the operation + on types represents disjunction and negation is represented by the operation that maps a type $A$ to the type $A \to \mathbf{0}$. So to add the law EM of excluded middle to the type theory we extend the syntax $c_1 ::= \cdots \mid cl$ and add the following rule.

$$\frac{A \ \mathsf{type}}{cl(A) : A + (A \to \mathbf{0})}.$$

We call the resulting theory MLW + EM.

[8] This proof of the lemma uses the classical theory of cardinal numbers and uses AC. I do not think that AC can be avoided. Instead of AC it may be possible to use the axiom that there are unboundedly many regular ordinals.

We need to extend the TS interpretation by having an equation for the new form of pseudoterm. To do so we strengthen the axiom system ZFC by adding a one-place function symbol $CH$ to the language of ZFC and adding the following global form of the axiom of choice.

$$\forall x[x \neq \emptyset \to CH(x) \in x].$$

The axiom schemes of ZFC should be extended to the extended language. We call the resulting axiom system ZFGC. Working in this axiom system we can define an operation $CL$ where, for each set $a$,

$$CL(a) = \begin{cases} (\emptyset, CH(a)) & \text{if } a \neq \emptyset \\ (\{\emptyset\}, \emptyset) & \text{if } a = \emptyset \end{cases}$$

We can now let $cl^\natural = CL$. It is easy to check that $\xi \models [cl(A) \in A + (A \to \mathbf{0})]$ for each pseudoterm $A$ and each variable assignment $\xi$. So we get the result that $\mathsf{MLW}^{\mathsf{ext}} + \mathsf{EM} \leq_{\mathrm{TS}} \mathsf{ZFGC}$.

## 2.6 Reduction to a Constructive Set Theory

We now follow the other strategy to improve on the result $\mathsf{MLW}^{\mathsf{ext}} \leq_{\mathrm{TS}} \mathsf{ZFC}$. This is to weaken ZFC to a constructive set theory. In [1] a constructive set theory CZF was introduced that is a subtheory of ZF whose logic is intuitionistic. This set theory was shown to have the property that when excluded middle is added to the logic then a theory CZF + EM is obtained that has the same theorems as ZF. Here we will consider the extension $\mathsf{CZF}^+ = \mathsf{CZF} + \mathsf{REA}$ of CZF obtained by adding to CZF the following axiom, that was first introduced in [3]. First we define a transitive set $A$ to be a **regular set** if, for every $a \in A$ and every set $R \subseteq a \times A$ such that $\forall x \in a \exists y \in A[(x, y) \in R]$ there is a set $b \in A$ such that $\forall x \in a \exists y \in b[(x, y) \in R]$ and $\forall y \in b \exists x \in a[(x, y) \in R]$.

**Regular Extension Axiom** (REA) Every set is a subset of a regular set.

The construction, in subsection 2.4, of the TS interpretation of $\mathsf{MLW}^{\mathsf{ext}}$ was carried out in the set theory ZFC. It is straightforward to show that the construction can be carried through in $\mathsf{CZF}^+$. In fact it can all be carried through in CZF, except for the proof of Lemma 13 The proof in ZFC that was given here of that lemma used the power set axiom and some of the classical theory of cardinal numbers and needed the axiom of choice. Instead we can apply Theorem 5.2 of [3] to see that the lemma is provable in $\mathsf{CZF}^+$.[9] So we now have the following result.

**Theorem 15** ($\mathsf{CZF}^+$) *The type theory* $\mathsf{MLW}^{\mathsf{ext}}$ *is sound.*

This can be expressed as $\mathsf{MLW}^{\mathsf{ext}} \leq_{\mathrm{TS}} \mathsf{CZF}^+$.

---

[9] The status of $\mathsf{CZF}^+ + \mathsf{EM} \equiv \mathsf{ZF} + \mathsf{REA}$ is unclear. Every theorem is a theorem of ZFC. But it is probable that REA is not provable in ZF.

# 3 Adding Type Universes

In this section we consider natural ways of extending the type theory MLW with one or more type universes; i.e. types of types. In each case we define a corresponding way of extending set theory so that the TS interpretation extends to include the type universes.

## 3.1 Adding a Single Reflecting Type Universe, U

We extend the type theory MLW to MLWU by adding a type U of types that has rules that reflect the type forming rules of MLW. First we extend the syntax with $c_0 ::= \cdots \mid \mathsf{U}$. Next we add the rules given by the following schemes in abbreviated form.

$$\mathsf{U}\ \mathsf{type} \qquad \frac{A : \mathsf{U}}{A\ \mathsf{type}} \qquad c : \mathsf{U} \qquad (c \in \{\mathbf{0},\ \mathbf{1},\ \mathbf{2}\})$$

$$\frac{A : \mathsf{U} \qquad x : A \Rightarrow B : \mathsf{U}}{(Qx : A)B : \mathsf{U}} \qquad (Q \in \{\Pi,\ \Sigma,\ W\})$$

When extending $\mathsf{MLW}^{\mathsf{ext}}$ to $\mathsf{MLW}^{\mathsf{ext}}\mathsf{U}$ we also need rules for U to reflect $Eq$ and $EQ$; i.e.

$$\frac{A : \mathsf{U} \qquad a_1 : A \qquad a_2 : A}{Eq(A, a_1, a_2) : \mathsf{U}} \qquad \frac{A_1 : \mathsf{U} \qquad A_2 : \mathsf{U}}{EQ(A_1, A_2) : \mathsf{U}}$$

In order to extend the TS interpretation to $\mathsf{MLW}^{\mathsf{ext}}\mathsf{U} + \mathsf{EM}$ it suffices to add to ZFGC the axiom that there is a strongly inaccessible cardinal and interpret U as the set $\mathsf{U}^\natural$ of all sets of set theoretic rank less than the least strongly inaccessible cardinal. If we call the resulting set theory $\mathsf{ZFGC}_1$ then we get the reduction $\mathsf{MLW}^{\mathsf{ext}}\mathsf{U} + \mathsf{EM} \leq_{\mathrm{TS}} \mathsf{ZFGC}_1$. To extend the TS interpretation of $\mathsf{MLW}^{\mathsf{ext}}$ in $\mathsf{CZF}^+$ we add to $\mathsf{CZF}^+$ an individual constant u and axioms expressing that u is an inaccessible set in the sense of [11][10]. We write $\mathsf{CZF}^+\mathsf{u}$ for the resulting theory. Now it suffices to take $\mathsf{U}^\natural = \mathsf{u}$ and we get the reduction $\mathsf{MLW}^{\mathsf{ext}}\mathsf{U} \leq_{\mathrm{TS}} \mathsf{CZF}^+\mathsf{u}$.

## 3.2 Adding an Infinite Hierarchy, $\mathsf{U}_0, \mathsf{U}_1, \ldots$, of Reflecting Type Universes

This time we extend the syntax using $c_0 ::= \cdots \mid \mathsf{U}_n \qquad (n = 0, 1, \ldots)$ and add rules given by the following schemes for $n = 0, 1, \ldots$.

$$\mathsf{U}_n\ \mathsf{type} \qquad \frac{A : \mathsf{U}_n}{A\ \mathsf{type}} \qquad c : \mathsf{U}_n \qquad (c \in \{\mathbf{0},\ \mathbf{1},\ \mathbf{2}\})$$

$$\frac{A : \mathsf{U} \qquad x : A \Rightarrow B : \mathsf{U}_n}{(Qx : A)B : \mathsf{U}_n} \qquad (Q \in \{\Pi,\ \Sigma,\ W\})$$

[10] i.e. a regular set that is a transitive model of $\mathsf{CZF}^+$.

$$U_n : U_{n+1} \qquad \frac{A : \mathsf{U}_n}{A : \mathsf{U}_{n+1}}$$

In the case of $\mathsf{MLW}^{\mathsf{ext}}$ we also need the obvious rules for reflecting $Eq$ and $EQ$. We get the resulting type theories $\mathsf{MLWU}_{<\omega}$ and $\mathsf{MLW}^{\mathsf{ext}}\mathsf{U}_{<\omega}$. To extend the TS interpretation we need to extend the classical and intuitionistic set theories in the following way. We add an infinite sequence $\mathsf{u}_n$ for $n = 0, 1, \ldots$ of individual constants to the set theoretical language and add axioms $\mathsf{u}_n \in \mathsf{u}_{n+1}$ for $n = 0, 1, \ldots$. In the classical case we also add axioms that express that each $\mathsf{u}_n$ is the set of sets of rank less than a strongly inaccessible cardinal number and in the constructive case we add axioms that express that each $\mathsf{u}_n$ is an inaccessible set. We write $\mathsf{ZFGCu}_{<\omega}$ and $\mathsf{CZF}^{+}\mathsf{u}_{<\omega}$ for the resulting extensions. We extend the TS interpretation by taking $\mathsf{U}_n^{\natural} = \mathsf{u}_n$ for each $n$ and get the reductions $\mathsf{MLW}^{\mathsf{ext}}\mathsf{U}_{<\omega} + EM \leq_{\mathsf{TS}} \mathsf{ZFGCu}_{<\omega}$ and $\mathsf{MLW}^{\mathsf{ext}}\mathsf{U}_{<\omega} \leq_{\mathsf{TS}} \mathsf{CZF}^{+}\mathsf{u}_{<\omega}$.

### 3.3 Adding an Impredicatively *Π*-closed Type Universe P

We extend the syntax with $c_0 ::= \cdots \mid \mathsf{P}$ and add rules given by the schemes

$$\mathsf{P}\ \mathsf{type} \qquad \frac{A : \mathsf{P}}{A\ \mathsf{type}} \qquad \frac{A : \mathsf{P} \qquad a_1 : A \qquad a_2 : A}{a_1 = a_2 : A}$$

$$\mathbf{0} : \mathsf{P} \qquad \frac{x : A \Rightarrow B : \mathsf{P}}{(\Pi x : A)B : \mathsf{P}} \qquad \frac{x : A \Rightarrow B_1 = B_2 : \mathsf{P}}{(\Pi x : A)B_1 = (\Pi x : A)B_2 : \mathsf{P}}$$

With these rules the type P behaves like the impredicative type of propositions of the calculus of constructions, with the additional properties that $\mathbf{0} : \mathsf{P}$ and all the propositions in P are proof-irrelevant. Adding these rules we get the type theories MLWP and $\mathsf{MLW}^{\mathsf{ext}}\mathsf{P}$. To get the type theories MLWPU and $\mathsf{MLW}^{\mathsf{ext}}\mathsf{PU}$ we need to add the previously given rules for U and also the following rules so that U reflects P.

$$\mathsf{P} : \mathsf{U} \qquad \frac{A : \mathsf{P}}{A : \mathsf{U}}$$

Similarly we can define the type theories $\mathsf{MLWPU}_{<\omega}$ and $\mathsf{MLW}^{\mathsf{ext}}\mathsf{PU}_{<\omega}$.

We show how to extend the TS interpretation so as to interpret the type P and justify its rules. In classical set theory we can interpret P as the set $2 = \{0, 1\}$. But to do so we need to use a non-standard function coding. Recall that our TS interpretation uses an arbitrary function coding and so far the standard one has been good enough. But to justify the rules for P we use the following non-standard function coding.

$$\mathrm{APP}(a, b) = \{y \mid (b, y) \in a\},$$
$$\mathrm{LAM}(a) = \bigcup_{(x,z) \in a}(\{x\} \times z).$$

The advantage of this function coding over the standard one is that we can prove the following result, which we express in a form that still usefully holds in constructive set theory. Recall that $1 = \{0\}$.

**Proposition 16** *For any set $a$, if $B(x) \subseteq 1$ for each $x \in a$ then*

$$\mathrm{PI}_{x \in a} B(x) = \{y \in 1 \mid \forall x \in a(B(x) = 1)\} \subseteq 1$$

*so that* $\mathrm{PI}_{x \in a} B(x) = 1 \iff \forall x \in a(B(x) = 1)$.

Note that in classical set theory the subsets of 1 are just the elements of $2 = \{0, 1\}$. In constructive set theory the subsets of 1 play the role of the *small extensional propositions* and the above result expresses that the PI operation behaves like universal quantification on such propositions.

Using this result we get the soundness of the rules for P and hence the reductions $\mathsf{MLW^{ext}P + EM} \leq_{\mathrm{TS}} \mathsf{ZFGC}$, $\mathsf{MLW^{ext}PU + EM} \leq_{\mathrm{TS}} \mathsf{ZFGC_1}$ and $\mathsf{MLW^{ext}PU_{<\omega} + EM} \leq_{\mathrm{TS}} \mathsf{ZFGCu_{<\omega}}$. In constructive set theory we cannot use $Pow(1) = \{x \mid x \subseteq 1\}$ to interpret the type P as the class $Pow(1)$ cannot be shown to be a set in CZF or its constructive extensions. Instead we will here simply extend the theory to give us what we want. So we add a new individual constant p to the language and add the following axioms.

1. $0 \in \mathsf{p}$,
2. $\forall x \in \mathsf{p}\ x \subseteq 1$,
3. If $B$ is a function with domain the set $a$ such that $\forall x \in a\ B(x) \in \mathsf{p}$ then $\mathrm{PI}_{x \in a} B(x) \in \mathsf{p}$.

This gives us the extension $\mathsf{CZF^+p}$. For the theories $\mathsf{CZF^+pu}$, $\mathsf{CZF^+pu_{<\omega}}$ we also need the axioms $\mathsf{p} \in \mathsf{u}$, $\mathsf{p} \in \mathsf{u_0}$ respectively.

Of course in the TS interpretations in our constructive set theories we let $\mathsf{P}^\natural = \mathsf{p}$ and get the reductions: $\mathsf{MLW^{ext}P} \leq_{\mathrm{TS}} \mathsf{CZF^+p}$, $\mathsf{MLW^{ext}PU} \leq_{\mathrm{TS}} \mathsf{CZF^+pu}$ and $\mathsf{MLW^{ext}PU_{<\omega}} \leq_{\mathrm{TS}} \mathsf{CZF^+pu_{<\omega}}$.

## 4 Interpreting Set Theories in Type Theories

We now explore to what extent the proof theoretic reductions we have obtained using the TS interpretation can be reversed using what we will here call the ST interpretation. This is the **sets-as-trees** interpretation that was introduced and developed in [1–3] and has also been used in [10, 11]. It is used to interpret a set theory in a type theory. The idea for the original interpretation, in [1], of *CZF* in MLWU was to interpret the sets of CZF as the well-founded trees of the type $V = (Wx : \mathsf{U})x$, the membership and equality relations of CZF being interpreted as terms $\epsilon_V$, $=_V$ of type $V \to (V \to \mathsf{U})$. Using the propositions-as-types idea each sentence of CZF was interpreted as a type of MLWU and it was shown that each theorem of CZF is an inhabited type of MLWU; i.e. a type $A$ such that $a : A$ can be derived in MLWU for some term $a$. In this way a proof theoretic reduction of CZF to MLWU is obtained that will be expressed as [11]

[11] Notice that the ST interpretation does not use any kind of equality types, neither intensional nor extensional, so that we have stated the stronger result of a reduction to MLWU rather than to $\mathsf{MLW^{ext}U}$.

CZF $\leq_{ST}$ MLWU. In fact, as shown in [3], we get CZF$^+$ $\leq_{ST}$ MLWU. Also, it is easy to see that, using the rule EM of MLWU + EM we can justify both the law of excluded middle and global choice for the set theory so as to get the reduction ZFGC $\leq_{ST}$ MLWU + EM. Unfortunately this and the previous reduction do not match up exactly with our earlier TS reductions. The trouble is the need to use a type universe U in our ST interpretation. In order to interpret the type universe in set theory we need to strengthen the set theory with a set theoretic version; i.e. an inaccessible set in the constructive set theory case and a strongly inaccessible cardinal in the classical set theory case. Now, if we wish to extend the ST interpretation of CZF$^+$ to an interpretation of CZF$^+$u, we need to use two of the type universes $\mathsf{U}_0$, $\mathsf{U}_1$ of MLWU$_{<\omega}$ and their rules and use the type $V_1 = (Wx : \mathsf{U}_1)x$ to interpret the universe of sets of CZF$^+$u. The inaccessible set u of CZF$^+$u can be modelled by $\mathsf{v}_0 = sup(V_0, (\lambda x : V_0)h(x)) : V_1$ where $V_0 = (Wx \in \mathsf{U}_0)x : \mathsf{U}_1$ and $h(x) : V_1$ is defined by transfinite recursion on $x : V_0$ so that

$$h(sup(a, f)) = sup(V_0, (\lambda x : a)h(app(f, x)))$$

for $a : \mathsf{U}_0$ and $f : a \to V_0$; i.e. $h(x)$ is the term $rec(b, x)$ where $b$ is the term $(\lambda x : \mathsf{U}_0)(\lambda y : x \to V_0)(\lambda z : x \to V_1)sup(x, z)$.

We can extend these ideas to more universes, a set theory with $n$ inaccessibles being given an ST interpretation in a type theory with $n + 1$ type universes, $\mathsf{U}_0, \ldots, \mathsf{U}_n$, with the universe of sets of the set theory being interpreted as the type $V_n = (Wx : \mathsf{U}_n)x$.

Fortunately we do get a matching of a set theory with a type theory of the same proof theoretic strength when we go to the limit. First consider the type theory MLWU$_{<\omega}$U that is obtained from MLWU$_{<\omega}$ by adding the type universe U at the top reflecting all the rules of MLWU$_{<\omega}$ so that in particular we have the rules

$$\mathsf{U}_n : \mathsf{U} \qquad\qquad \frac{A : \mathsf{U}_n}{A : \mathsf{U}}$$

for $n = 0, 1, \ldots$. As above we get an ST interpretation of CZF$^+_\omega$ into this theory, using $V = (Wx \in \mathsf{U})x$ to interpret the universe of sets of the set theory, giving us CZF$^+_\omega$ $\leq_{ST}$ MLWU$_{<\omega}$U. Now observe that we have a proof theoretic reduction MLWU$_{<\omega}$U $\leq$ MLWU$_{<\omega}$. The idea for this is that any derivation in the left hand type theory can only involve finitely many of the type universes $\mathsf{U}_i$ and so can be translated into a derivation in the right hand type theory by replacing the symbol U everywhere by $\mathsf{U}_n$, where $n$ is chosen large enough so that $n > i$ whenever $\mathsf{U}_i$ occurs in the derivation. Using a previous TS reduction, we get the next result.

**Theorem 17** *The following theories are of the same proof theoretic strength:* CZF$^+$u$_{<\omega}$, MLWU$_{<\omega}$U, MLWU$_{<\omega}$, MLW$^{\mathsf{ext}}$U$_{<\omega}$.

We have the same situation for classical set theory so that, using the fact that global choice does not increase the proof theoretic strength, we get the next result.

**Theorem 18** *The following theories are of the same proof theoretic strength:* $\mathsf{ZFCu}_{<\omega}$, $\mathsf{ZFGCu}_{<\omega}$, $\mathsf{MLWU}_{<\omega}\mathsf{U} + \mathsf{EM}$, $\mathsf{MLWU}_{<\omega} + \mathsf{EM}$, $\mathsf{MLW}^{\mathsf{ext}}\mathsf{U}_{<\omega} + \mathsf{EM}$.

Finally we observe that the ST interpretation carries over to the set theory $\mathsf{CZF}^{+}\mathsf{p}$ to give the reduction $\mathsf{CZF}^{+}\mathsf{p} \leq_{\mathrm{ST}} \mathsf{MLWUP}$ and, as above, the reduction $\mathsf{CZF}^{+}\mathsf{pu}_{<\omega} \leq_{\mathrm{ST}} \mathsf{MLWPU}_{<\omega}$. This, with a previous reduction gives us the following result.

**Theorem 19** *The following theories are of the same proof theoretic strength:* $\mathsf{CZF}^{+}\mathsf{pu}_{<\omega}$, $\mathsf{MLWPU}_{<\omega}$, $\mathsf{MLW}^{\mathsf{ext}}\mathsf{PU}_{<\omega}$.

## References


1. Peter Aczel, The Type Theoretic Interpretation of Constructive Set Theory, in: MacIntyre, A., Pacholski, L., Paris, J. (eds), *Logic Colloquium '77*, (North Holland, Amsterdam, 1978).
2. Peter Aczel, The Type Theoretic Interpretation of Constructive Set Theory: Choice Principles, in: Troelstra, S.S., van Dalen, D. (eds), *The L.E.J. Brouwer Centenary Symposium*, (North Holland, Amsterdam, 1982).
3. Peter Aczel, The Type Theoretic Interpretation of Constructive Set Theory: Inductive Definitions, in: Marcus, R.B. et al. (eds), *Logic, Methodology and Philosophy of Science VII*, (North Holland, Amsterdam, 1986).
4. Barras et al. *The Coq Proof Assistant Reference Manual*, Version 6.1 INRIA Technical Report, 1996.
5. Thierry Coquand, Metamathematical Investigations of a Calculus of Constructions. In P. Oddifredi (editor), *Logic and Computer Science*. Academic Press, 1990.
6. Peter Dybjer, Inductive sets and families in Martin-Löf's type theory and their set-theoretic semantics. In Gerard Huet and Gordon Plotkin (editors), *Logical Frameworks*, pp 280-306, Prentice Hall, 1991.
7. Peter Dybjer, A general formulation of simultaneous inductive-recursive definitions in type theory. To appear in *The Journal of Symbolic Logic*, 1999?
8. Peter Dybjer and Anton Setzer, A finite axiomatization of inductive-recursive definitions. To appear in *Proceedings of TLCA 1999*, LNCS.
9. Solomon Feferman, Hilbert's Program Relativised: Proof-Theoretical and Foundational Reductions, *Journal of Symbolic Logic, Vol 53*, (1988) 364-384.
10. Ed. Griffor and Michael Rathjen, The Strength of some Martin-Löf type theories, *Archiv for Mathematical Logic 33* (1994) 347-385.
11. Ed. Griffor and Michael Rathjen, Inaccessibility in Constructive Set Theory and type theory, Technical Report U.U.D.M. 1996:20, Department of Mathematics, Uppsala University.
12. Zhaohui Luo and Randy Pollack, *LEGO Proof Development System: User's Manual*, Edinburgh University Computer Science Department Technical Report, ECS-LFCS-92-211, 1992.
13. Per Martin-Löf, *Intuitionistic type Theory*. Studies in Proof Theory, Bibliopolis, 1984.
14. Michael Rathjen, The Realm of Ordinal Analysis, To appear in S.B. Cooper, J.K. Truss (eds.): *Sets and Proofs*, Proceedings of the Logic Cooloquium '97, Cambridge University Press.
15. Benjamin Werner, Sets in Types, Types in Sets, *TACS '97*, LNCS 1281.

# Communication Modelling and Context-Dependent Interpretation: An Integrated Approach*

René Ahn and Tijn Borghuis

Eindhoven University of Technology, P.O.Box 513, 5600 MB Eindhoven, The Netherlands. Email: e-mail: `rahn@ipo.tue.nl`, e-mail: `tijn@win.tue.nl`

**Abstract** In this paper we present a simple model of communication. We assume that communication takes place between two agents. Each agent has a private and subjective knowledge state. The knowledge of both agents is partial, finite, and represented in a computational way. We investigate how ideas can be transferred from one agent to the other one, in spite of the subjective nature of the knowledge of both participants. Posing the problem in this way, it can be seen that mechanisms for context-dependent interpretation are a prerequisite for succesfull communication.

## 1 Introduction

Language solves a problem. It helps people to exchange ideas, even if these people come from different backgrounds, know different concepts and individuals, and have wildly diverging views in many different matters. Ideas that are privately known to one agent, are transformed into a public message and subsequently decoded by another agent, who interpretes this message, and reacts on it. We model this proces, starting from subjective knowledge states, and show how content which is meaningful in the subjective knowledge state of one agent can be transferred to the subjective knowledge state of another agent by means of a common language.

Throughout this paper we concentrate on the simple case where two agents communicate about their common (physical) environment. Specifically, we use examples in which two agents discuss an electron-microscope, a situation taken from the 'DenK-project' ([2]). In this project we constructed a man-machine interface based on the approach to communication sketched in this paper.

## 2 Formalising Knowledge States

In this section, we show how an agent's subjective knowledge state can be formalized by means of type theoretical contexts. First, however, we explain what we mean by knowledge.

* This research was sponsored by the Organization for Inter-university Cooperation between the universities of Tilburg and Eindhoven (SOBU).

## 2.1 Knowledge

Each person understands the world in terms of his own concepts. Which concepts a person has formed at a given moment in time is obviously dependend on many factors, like his physical and cultural environment, personal history, etc. Although we are not concerned with the formation of concepts here, we assume that concepts pertaining to an agents physical environment are somehow inspired by his sense impressions: a human interacting with his environment experiences these impressions as an organised whole, in which various familiar phenomena interact in more or less predictable ways. These correlations between sense impressions somehow allow concepts to be formed that are subsequently used to 'understand' the diverse experiences from which they have arisen. Some of these concepts are 'inhabitable', i.e. they may have instances. The person which is familiar with a specific inhabitable concept will recognise an instance of this concept, whenever he runs into it[1]. In this way he is able to connect his raw experience with the subjective concepts that he uses to classify it. As a consequence, each agent has its own concepts, often similar to, but not necessarily identical with, those of his fellow-agents.

An agent's conscious knowledge[2] about the world will be formulated entirely in terms of the concepts that he recognises. This knowledge is not static, but can grow as a result of communication, observation and inference processes. The resulting body of knowledge, the *knowledge state*, will not be a bare set of facts, but a structured conglomerate of justified beliefs, where each new item must be embedded in the knowledge which is already present. Thus, this body of knowledge is:

*Subjective*: It is formulated in terms of personal concepts, it will be partial, and it may even be incorrect.
*Incremental*: The ways in which this body of knowledge can be extended depend on what is already present.
*Justified*: Knowledge is not a collection of bare facts, but will be justified in terms of other, more basic knowledge.

## 2.2 Knowledge States as Contexts

How can these 'subjective', 'incremental', and 'justified' knowledge states be formalised? Fortunately, a similar problem arises in mathematics. The main concern of mathematicians is to show which consequences follow from certain assumptions. On the one hand this activity is virtually unconstrained: new concepts may be developed, and assumptions can be freely made, independent from external reality. On the other hand the mathematician has to adhere to a strong kind of

[1] How this happens is irrelevant here, an obvious possibility is through neural networks.
[2] Here we take knowledge in the everyday sense of the word. We quote the definition in Webster's new dictionary of synonyms (p. 481): 'Knowledge applies not only to a body of facts gathered by study, investigation, or experience but also to a body of ideas acquired by inference from such facts or accepted on good grounds as truths.'

mental hygiene: concepts can only be formed if they fit into existing categories, assumptions can only be made if they are meaningful in the context of that which is already given, and all conclusions have to be thoroughly justified. Pure Type Systems (PTSs, [3]) are typed-lambda calculi that can be used to record such mathematical activity in a formal and machine-readable format. In this paper, we assume that a person that tries to understand the outside world is, in many respects, comparable to a mathematician. However, the concepts that this person develops will be inspired by his sense data, and the assumptions that he makes are assumptions about the outside world, and are (one hopes) supported by what he sees. In other words, the 'body of hypotheses' that this person develops will be grounded in the external world.

A PTS-context $\Gamma$ can represent the 'body of hypotheses' of a mathematician. We propose to use such a context to represent the knowledge state of an agent. To reflect the assumptions of an agent about the real world, this context has to be partially grounded in its sense-impressions. This can be achieved if some inhabitable terms $T$ in the context have an *observational interpretation*. This interpretation is the personal ability of the agent to judge whether something which is perceived is an inhabitant of $T$ or not. A typical PTS may have the sorts $*_s$ and $*_p$, where the sort $*_p$ corresponds to the type containing all possible propositions, and the sort $*_s$ to the type containing all possible categories of objects. For all types $T$ for which the agent has an interpretation, either $\Gamma \vdash T : *_s$ or $\Gamma \vdash T : *_p$.

Combining sense-impressions and interpretations, the agent takes certain types to be inhabited. This is expressed by judgements that contain atomic justifications, i.e. justifications which do not admit analysis. These correspond to perceived objects, or direct physical evidence for a certain proposition. Though an agent is only able to recognize types, he can nevertheless deal with individual objects: if the agent knows a certain type $T$ to have exactly one inhabitant[3], it will interpret all terms in $T$ as denoting the same individual. In cases where such a type $T$ has an observational interpretation, the agent is able to *recognise* this individual in the outside world.

### 2.3 Growth of Knowledge

An agent's knowledge can grow. In our formalization, this knowledge growth corresponds to an extension of the context representing the agent's knowledge state.

Reasoning is one possible mechanism for knowledge growth. The reasoning of an agent is modelled by the construction of new statements out of those occuring in the context representing his knowledge state. Derivability on this context ($\Gamma \vdash E : T$) reflects the agent's ability to find rational evidence ($E$) for an assertion ($T$) in his current knowledge state. We assume that the derivation rules

[3] Technically, this might be expressed by an axiom stating that all inhabitants of $T$ are Leibniz-identical

are the same for all agents; knowledge states differ in content, but all agents 'use the same logic'.

After deriving a new statement $(E : T)$, the knowledge state $(\Gamma)$ should be updated by somehow appending this statement. To allow this kind of recording of conclusions, De Bruijn ([5]) proposed to enrich the notion of context with 'definitions'. Using this idea, the context can be extended with a *definition* $x = E : T$[4] whenever a judgement $\Gamma \vdash E : T$ is derived in which $E$ is a complex expression. This definition expresses that the variable $x$ of type $T$ may be used to refer to the complex term $E$ in further derivations: $\Gamma, x = E : T \vdash x : T$. In other words, the definition 'abbreviates' the complex term with a fresh variable. At any point in time a definition can be 'unfolded' again, replacing the abbreviation $(x)$ with the complex term $E$. In the presence of definitions, a well-formed context will look like this: $x_1 : T_1, x_2 : T_2, x_3 = E_3 : T_3, x_4 : T_4, \ldots, x_n = E_n : T_n$. It represents a structured collection of assumptions (atomic justifications), intermingled with conclusions (complex justifications) that have been drawn on the basis of these assumptions.

At first sight, recording the results of reasoning in the knowledge state may seem to be a mere ergonomical device: although the definition saves the trouble of going through the derivation of $E$ again, the statement $E : T$ can be reconstructed on any context $\Gamma'$ containing $\Gamma$ $(\Gamma \subseteq \Gamma')$. However, in practice agents have limited deductive powers, allowing them only to oversee the more or less obvious consequences of their knowledge; conclusions which can be derived with a reasonable amount deductive work. For such agents storing conclusions in the knowledge state literally broadens their horizon, by bringing consequences into view that were unreachable before.

Whereas the reasoning process extends an agent's knowledge state from within, knowledge can also be obtained from external sources through communication and observation. This kind of information is represented by a pseudo-context $y_1 : T_1, \ldots, y_m : T_m$, where $y_1, \ldots, y_m$ are fresh variables. In general, if one appends a pseudo-context $\Delta$ to a well-formed context $\Gamma$, the result $(\Gamma, \Delta)$ is not a well-formed context. In order to ensure the well-formedness of the result, we require that $\Delta$ is an *extending segment* of $\Gamma$:

**Definition 1.** *A pseudo-context $\Delta$ is an* extending segment *of a well-formed context $\Gamma$ iff $\Gamma, \Delta$ is a well-formed context.*

On the one hand this is just a technical requirement. On the other hand, given that types represent concepts in the agent's knowledge state, it captures the intuition that an agent can only extend its knowledge state with information that is *meaningful* to it, i.e. expressed in terms of familiar concepts.

### 2.4 Common versus Private Knowledge

The backbone of a communication process between (two) agents is the continous extension of their common knowledge. To model this process adequately, we need

[4] This is shorthand for: $x = E$ and $E : T$ which together imply that $x : T$

to distinguish within the knowledge state of each agent that part of its knowledge which it *assumes* to be shared. So for each agent $p$ we have a context $\Gamma_p$ which contains all of its knowledge, within which we can distinguish a (sub)context $\Psi_p$, with $\Psi_p \subseteq \Gamma_p$, which contains all knowledge that, *according to* $p$, is shared.

Both $\Gamma_p$ and $\Psi_p$ are well-formed type theoretical contexts in their own right. The common context $\Psi_p$ is 'a part of' the private context $\Gamma_p$, and this relation can be defined in a straightforward way:

**Definition 2.** *Given two legal contexts $\Gamma$ and $\Gamma'$, $\Gamma$ is* a part of *$\Gamma'$, notation $\Gamma \sqsubseteq \Gamma'$, iff*

*1 for all statements of the form $x : T$ occurring in $\Gamma$ either:*
*$x : T$ or a definition $x = E : T$ occurs in $\Gamma'$,*
*2 all statements of the form $x = E : T$ occurring in $\Gamma$ occur also in $\Gamma'$.*

Under this 'part of'-relation, every definition in $\Gamma$ must occur in $\Gamma'$ (*2*), but declarations in $\Gamma$ may be replaced by definitions in $\Gamma'$ (*1*). This will be of use in Sect. 5, where it allows us to 'link' shared information in $\Psi_p$ to private information in $\Gamma_p$.

The distinction between common and private knowledge gives rise to a somewhat more fine-grained account of reasoning. Since both $\Gamma_p$ and $\Psi_p$ are legal contexts, new statements can be constructed on either context using the derivation rules. Hence we can model the agent reaching 'private conclusions' in reasoning with private information ($\Gamma_p$) and 'common conclusions' in reasoning with common information ($\Psi_p$). Information that is shared with another agent is also privately available, as reflected in the inclusion $\Psi_p \subseteq \Gamma_p$. This inclusion guarantees that any statement derivable on an agent's common context ($\Psi_p$) is also derivable on his private context ($\Gamma_p$), but not the other way around.

# 3 Communicable Content

The previous section shows how the knowledges states of communicating agents are modelled by means of type theoretical contexts. In this section, we extend the model with a formal account of communicable content: first the relation between the subjective knowledge states and the common language in which the agents communicate is discussed, then we characterize communicable content.

## 3.1 Concepts and the Common Language

One the one hand, each agent has its own knowledge state, built on concepts which are meaningful only to himself. On the other hand, the agents speak a common language in which they communicate. Hence each agent somehow connects its subjective concepts to words in this language. For instance, each of the agents will recognise a certain class of objects that are used by people to sit on. There is a word to describe this class in the language; in English objects in this class are called 'chairs'. There may be certain differences in interpretation, i.e. one agent may recognise an object as a chair that the other would call otherwise, but on the whole the two categories will match quite well. This is the case, because the use of all words is constantly being gauged by the language community.

If a word in a given language corresponds to a concept, this concept is neccessarily common to a rather large group, i.e. the speakers of the language in question. The specific individual objects that we encounter in our daily life, such as 'my chair', are not commonly known among all speakers. Accordingly there exist no words that directly refer to these objects. This means we have to refer to these objects as instances of a certain class, and try to point out the particular object through a description of characteristic properties that are accessible to the dialogue partner.

For the purposes of this paper it is not neccesary to elaborate the mapping between language and Type Theory. We simply assume that for each agent ($p$) there exists a partial mapping $T_p \leftrightsquigarrow W$ between type variables in its knowledge state and words in the vocabulary of the shared language. How this mapping was formed (when the language was learned) is also outside the scope of our model. Though the mapping between the knowledge states and the language in our model is rather crude it still reflects the fact that words must necessarily refer to general concepts, which are meaningful to the language community as a whole: the mapping does not extend to the level of particular individuals and proofs, i.e. the inhabitants of inhabitants of $*_p$ or $*_s$.

### 3.2 Messages

Against the background of our unsophisticated account of the relation between the knowledge states and the language spoken by the agents, we wish to understand how information can be exchanged between private type theoretical knowledge states, using expressions in some public language. These expressions, which we call 'messages', will somehow have to be meaningfully related to the knowledge states of *both* agents; they express content that an agent can communicate to his dialogue partner.

We assume that there are two agents, $A$ and $B$, that both have a subjective knowledge state. If communication is to be possible, they must share a common vocabulary $W$. To communicate the speaker ($A$) must encode a segment $\Delta_A$ which is meaningful within its own knowledge state into a public message, using this vocabulary. This message is sent to the hearer, ($B$) which subsequently decodes it. If the communication is to be succesful, the result of decoding must be meaningful to $B$, i.e. it must be an extending segment of $B$'s context.

How can segments be encoded and decoded? Obviously, both encoding and decoding have to be based on the common vocabulary. The agent $A$ uses the mapping $T_A \leftrightsquigarrow W$ to encode a segment $\Delta_A$. Given the mapping , it simply substitutes in the segment $\Delta_A$ the words of the vocabulary for the types they are related to. However, not every meaningful segment $\Delta_A$ can be encoded succesfully. Obviously, we must ensure that the result of encoding, which is to be a public message, does not contain any privately bound variables. Segments that meet this requirement we call *codeable.*

All this is expressed formally in the following definitions:

**Definition 3.** *A variable* $z$ occurs free in a segment $\Delta$, $\Delta \equiv x_1 : T_1, \ldots, x_n : T_n$, *iff* $z$ *occurs free in* $T_i$ $(1 \leq i \leq n)$ *and there is no statement* $x_j : T_j$ *with* $1 \leq j < i$ *such that* $z \equiv x_j$.

**Definition 4.** *A segment* $\Delta_A$ *is* codeable *if for all variables* $z$ *occuring free in* $\Delta_A$ *there is a word* $w$ *in* $W$ *such that* $z \leftrightsquigarrow w$.

**Definition 5.** *A message* $\mu$ *is the result of coding a codable segment* $\Delta_A$. *I.e. the result of replacing all variables that occur free in* $\Delta_A$ *by the corresponding words from the mapping* $T_A \leftrightsquigarrow W$

Thus, coding a codable segment yields a public message. Upon receiving such a message, the recipient ($B$) can try to decode it. Basically, decoding is the inverse of encoding, using the recipients mapping, $T_B \leftrightsquigarrow W$, in the direction from words to types [5]. Note that, if a non-codable segment were encoded, subsequent decoding would yield a pseudo-context which contains unbound variables and hence cannot be an extending segment of any context.

### 3.3 Example

Take a simple situation where the agents $A$ and $B$ assume that they share all concepts related to their common vocabulary. This means that in the knowledge state of each agent $p$, all types related to a word in the vocabulary (by $T_p \leftrightsquigarrow W$) are declared in their common context ($\Psi_p$). We assume that the common vocabulary consists of English words[6], hence messages appear in a sort of 'toy English'; as segments where words have been substituted for some of their variables, e.g. $b$ : *bundle*, $p$ : *primary*$(b)$. In the table below, which only lists the shared knowledge of $A$ and $B$, we see that agents $A$ and $B$ have a shared vocabulary that contains at least the words 'bundle','lens', 'primary' and 'enter'. The type variables corresponding to these words are declared in their common contexts $\Psi_A$ and $\Psi_B$. Note that $A$ and $B$ have different type variables that correspond to the same word: in $A$'s knowledge state the concept 'lens' is mapped to by the type $x_3$, in $B$'s knowledge state it is mapped to the type $y_5$.

[5] Here we assume that the mapping is one to one, and that this is a simple matter. In a more realistic setting, using natural language, such an assumption is no longer justified as words can be ambiguous. But, even then, the requirement that the result of decoding must be an extending segment of the receiver's context can often be used to disambiguate the message succesfully, see [6]

[6] To construct a more realistic mapping, not only the vocabulary but the whole language should be taken into account. For a mapping from type theory to English, see ([7]).

| $\Psi_A$ | $T_A \leftrightsquigarrow W$ | $\Psi_B$ | $T_B \leftrightsquigarrow W$ |
|---|---|---|---|
| $x_1 : *_s,$ | $x_1 \leftrightsquigarrow \mathit{bundle}$ | $\ldots,$ | |
| $x_2 : x_1 \to *_p,$ | $x_2 \leftrightsquigarrow \mathit{primary}$ | $y_5 : *_s,$ | $y_5 \leftrightsquigarrow \mathit{lens}$ |
| $x_3 : *_s,$ | $x_3 \leftrightsquigarrow \mathit{lens}$ | $y_6 : y_5,$ | |
| $x_4 : x_1 \to x_3 \to *_p,$ | $x_4 \leftrightsquigarrow \mathit{enter}$ | $\ldots,$ | |
| $x_5 : x_1,$ | | $y_{17} : *_s,$ | $y_{17} \leftrightsquigarrow \mathit{bundle}$ |
| $x_6 : x_3,$ | | $y_{18} : y_{17}$ | |
| $\ldots$ | | $y_{19} : y_{17} \to y_5 \to *_p,$ | $y_{19} \leftrightsquigarrow \mathit{enter}$ |
| | | $\ldots,$ | |
| | | $y_{32} : y_{17} \to *_p,$ | $y_{32} \leftrightsquigarrow \mathit{primary}$ |
| | | $\ldots$ | |

In this setting $A$ can, for instance, encode the segment: $u : x_1, v : x_3, z : x_4(uv)$ (with $z, u, v$ $\Psi_A$-fresh). This segment meaning 'there is a bundle and there is a lens, and the bundle enters the lens' to $A$, encodes into the message: $u : \mathit{bundle}, v : \mathit{lens}, z : \mathit{enter}(uv)$. If the agent $B$ decodes this, it ends up with the segment: $u : y_{17}, v : y_5, z : y_{19}(uv)$ which is meaningful to it. The segment can be shown to extend $B$'s common context as $\Psi_B \vdash y_{17} : *_p$, $\Psi_B, u : y_{17} \vdash y_5 : *_s$, and $\Psi_B, u : y_{17}, v : y_5 \vdash y_{19}(uv) : *_p$.

## 4 Polarity and Information Flow

Depending on the situation, $A$ and $B$ may share more than just their vocabulary, even at the beginning of a dialogue. There may be certain general knowledge which they can correctly assume to share with their partner, or they may share certain information as a result of a previous conversation. This information will then also be represented in their common contexts. In our example, this is in fact the case: apart from the types related to the vocabulary, each agent has a representation for a particular bundle ($x_5$ and $y_{18}$ respectively) and a particular lens ($x_6$ and $y_6$ respectively). In their messages, both agents need to be able to refer to these individuals. To do so, they must make descriptions of these objects that can be understood by their dialogue partners. Thus we also need a mechanism that provides this possibility.

So far we have described only one way of dealing with extending segments (Sect. 2.2): the agent simply appends the extending segment to his knowledge state. This is passive in the sense that the agent makes no effort whatsoever to connect the new information represented by the extending segment to the information already present in his knowledge state. The new information is simply stored as a set of additional 'hypotheses' or 'assumptions' (all justifications in the segment are atomic). However, the receiving agent can also digest a decoded segment in a different, more active way by trying to find justifications (objects and proofs) in his own current contexts to replace the dummy inhabitants of the statements in the extending segment. In doing so, we say that the agent constructs a 'realization' for the extending segment in his original context.

**Definition 6.** *let $\Delta \equiv x_1 : T_1, ..., x_n : T_n$ be an extending segment of $\Gamma$, and let*
$\Gamma \vdash D_1 : T_1$ *and*
$\Gamma \vdash D_2 : T_2[x_1 := D_1]$, *and*
$\Gamma \vdash D_3 : T_3[x_1 := D_1, x_2 := D_2]$, *and*
... *and*
$\Gamma \vdash D_n : T_n[x_1 := D_1, ..., x_{n-1} := D_{n-1}]$ *then we call*
$\Delta^* \equiv x_1 = D_1 : T_1, ..., x_n = D_n : T_n$ a realization *of $\Delta$ in $\Gamma$ under the substitution* $[x_1 := D_1, ..., x_n := D_n]$.

Processing a segment actively, the agent appends the realization $\Delta^*$ to its context instead of the extending segment $\Delta$. The point is that segments when used in this way, act as selective 'hooks' with which the rest of the message is connected to particular inhabitants in the knowledge state of the hearer. In fact, an actively processed segment does not provide the hearer with new information. Formally, this fact is reflected by the following proposition[7], which shows that realizations can be eliminated:

**Proposition 1.** *Assume $\Gamma, \Delta \vdash B : C$ Let $\Delta^*$ be a realization of $\Delta$ in $\Gamma$ under the substitution $[S]$, then $\Gamma, \Delta^* \vdash B : C$ and $\Gamma \vdash B[S] : C[S]$.*

Thus, an extending segment $\Delta$ of a context $\Gamma$ can be used in two quite different ways: either as *hypothesis* extending the current knowledge state, or as a *requirement* for which a realization is to be constructed in the current knowledge state. We call the former use of segments 'positive', the latter 'negative'. These two *polarities* determine the direction of the flow of information in our communication model.

# 5 Communication

The previous sections have shown how content that is privately meaningful to agent $A$ can be encoded in a public message which can subsequently be decoded by agent $B$. If this process is succesful, the result of this decoding is meaningful to $B$; a segment extending its knowledge state. As we have seen, $B$ can process this segment in different ways ('passive' or 'active'), and $B$'s knowledge state has two parts (common context, and private context). In communication, the various possibilities the receiving agent has for processing a message can be used by the agent sending the message to achieve its communicative goals. By labelling (parts of) the message with tags stating where and how it should be processed, the sending agent can control the way the message is received by the other agent. As a consequence, the expressions exchanged between two communicating agents in our model are *labeled messages*, rather than just messages. Using more traditional terminology, we could say that a labeled message is the unit corresponding to an utterance, where the message carries the content of the utterance and the labels its pragmatic force.

[7] This is simply an iterated version of the 'Substitution Lemma' for PTSs, see ([3]).

The following definition introduces notation for the two pairs of epistemically motivated labels we have encountered sofar, and describes their use:

**Definition 7.** *If a (part of a) message* $\mu \equiv z_i : w_i, ..., z_j : w_j$ *(where* $w_i, \ldots, w_j$ *are words from* $W$*, possibly followed by a number of arguments) is labelled*

- positive, *notation:* $z_i : w_i, ..., z_j : w_j\ [z_i, \ldots, z_j]^+$, *the receiving agent has to* append *the segment resulting from decoding* $\mu$ *to one of the contexts representing its knowledge state.*
- negative, *notation:* $z_i : w_i, ..., z_j : w_j\ [z_i, \ldots, z_j]^-$, *the receiving agent has to* construct a realization *for the segment resulting from decoding* $\mu$ *on one of the contexts representing its knowledge state.*
- common, *notation:* $z_i : w_i, ..., z_j : w_j\ [z_i, \ldots, z_j]_\Psi$, *the* location *where the receiving agent has to process the segment resulting from decoding* $\mu$ *is its* common context.
- private, *notation:* $z_i : w_i, ..., z_j : w_j\ [z_i, \ldots, z_j]_\Gamma$, *the* location *where the receiving agent has to process the segment resulting from decoding* $\mu$ *is its* private context.

As we will see, tags can apply to different variables within one message, specifying for each part of this message on which location and with what polarity it is to be processed by the receiving agent.

In the next subsections we show how the ingredients presented sofar can be used by the agents in our model to perform two basic acts of communication: providing information, and obtaining information.

## 5.1 Providing Information

Suppose that agent $A$ wants to provide information to agent $B$. In fact, $A$ wants to tell $B$ that the commonly known bundle,to which $A$ itself refers as $x_5$, enters a lens, which at present $A$ does not assume to be shared. In English, $A$ might express this by the sentence 'The primary bundle enters a lens[8]'. Using labeled messages, $A$ can express this information as follows:

$$b : bundle, p : primary(b), l : lens, q : enter(b, l)\ [b, p]^-_\Psi\ [l, q]^+_\Psi \quad (1)$$

This message ($\mu$) is an encoding of the segment $b : x_1, p : x_2(b), l : x_3, q : x_4(b, l)$. The tags show that it has a positive and a negative part. The first, negative, part ($\mu_1$) corresponds to description of the primary bundle:

$$b : bundle, p : primary(b)\ [b, p]^-_\Psi \quad (2)$$

It instructs $B$ to find a realization for $b$ and $p$ on its common context $\Psi_B$ for the segment ($\Delta_{B1}$) resulting from decoding $\mu_1$. Assuming that $A$'s use of the description was appropriate, $B$ will find an object, say $y_{34}$, representing the

[8] Note that in this sentence the commonly known bundle is referred to by a definite, and the privately known lens by an indefinite.

bundle in its common context along with a proof that it is the primary bundle, say $N$. Agent $B$ extends its common context with this realization, $b = y_{34} : y_{17}, p = N : y_{32}(b)$, and proceeds by processing the second part of the message. This part ($\mu_2$) contains the proposition asserted by $A$ that for some lens $l$ the primary bundle enters $l$:

$$l : lens, q : enter(b, l)\ [l, q]^{+}_{\Psi} \tag{3}$$

Note that the $b$ that occurs free in $\mu_2$ is now bound in the extended common context by the definition $b = y_{34} : y_{17}$. The second part of the message is tagged positively; $B$ is supposed to 'absorb' the information in the segment ($\Delta_{B2} \equiv l : y_5, q : (y_{19}(b, l)$ resulting from decoding $\mu_2$, i.e. add the statements in $\Delta_{B2}$ to its common context. The first statement in $\Delta_{B2}$ introduces a new lens ($l$) into $B$'s common context. The second statement introduces a new 'piece of evidence' into the common context, a proof object ($q$) for the proposition that $b$ enters $l$.

The processing of the entire tagged message therefore updates the common context of $B$ in two steps: $\Psi_B \Rightarrow \Psi'_B$ with $\Psi'_B \equiv \Psi_B, \Delta^*_{B1}$ where $\Delta^*_{B1}$ is a realization of $\Delta_{B1}$ in $\Psi_B$ under substitution $[S]$, followed by $\Psi'_B \Rightarrow \Psi''_B$ with $\Psi''_B \equiv \Psi'_B, \Delta_{B2}$. According to proposition 1, $\Delta^*_{B1}$ can be eliminated in favour of $[S]$ yielding $\Psi''_B \equiv \Psi, \Delta_{B2}[S]$ (where $\Delta_{B2}[S]$ abbreviates the application of $[S]$ to the statements in $\Delta_{B2}$). From this point of view the net effect of the entire message on the common context of $B$ is an update with evidence for the proposition that for some lens ($l$) the primary bundle ($y_{34}$) enters that lens.

It should be noted that the reaction of agent $B$ in this example is the simplest or 'most cooperative' one possible; it adds the information provided by $A$ without questioning it in any way. Depending on factors in the dialogue situation not considered here, this reaction could be more 'cautious'[9].

The succesful sending of labeled message by $A$ not only affects the knowledge state of $B$, but also that of $A$ itself. The message was sent in public, and hence affects the common context of $A$ in the same way as the common context of $B$. As we described above for $B$, this results in an extension of the common context: $\Psi_A \Rightarrow \Psi''_A$ with $\Psi''_A \equiv \Psi_A, \Delta^*_{A1}, \Delta_{A2}$, or equivalently $\Psi''_A \equiv \Psi_A, \Delta_{A2}[S]$ (where $[S]$ substitutes $A$'s representation of the primary bundle for $b$).

Privately agent $A$ will know more, we assumed it had some justification for its message. In particular, $A$ must have 'evidence' for the proposition expressed by the positively tagged part of the message, $\mu_2$. The least we can assume about this evidence is that there exists a realization of $\Delta_{A2}$ on its private context $\Gamma_A$, e.g.: $\Delta^*_{A2} \equiv l = x_{35} : x_3, q = M : x_4(b, l)$. This realization shows in which respects $A$ can know more in its private context than in its common context: in $\Gamma_A$ it knows which lens the bundle enters ($x_{35} : x_3$), rather than just 'a lens' ($l$) in $\Psi_A$. Moreover, in $\Gamma_A$ it has a structured proof ($M$) for this rather than a 'dummy' ($q$) in $\Psi_A$. Agent $A$ can connect its 'private' justifications to

[9] For instance, the DenK-system will not accept all assertions made by the user, because it is an expert on the domain whereas the user is a novice.

its 'common' justifications by updating its private context with the realization: $\Gamma_A \Rightarrow \Gamma'_A$ with $\Gamma'_A \equiv \Gamma_A, \Delta^*_{A2}$. By adding these definitions, $x_{35}$ is linked to $l$ and $M$ to $q$ ($b$ was already linked to $A$'s representation of the primary bundle by the update of $\Psi_A$ with $\Delta^*_{A1}$). Without this link, $A$ would be unable to combine information about $l$ and $x_{35}$ in its private context.

## 5.2 Obtaining Information

Alternatively, one might suppose that $A$ wants to obtain information from $B$. If $A$ did not know which the lens primary bundle enters, he might ask in English 'Which lens does the primary bundle enter?'. To do this, $A$ can use the same message as in the previous case but tagged differently:

$$b : bundle, p : primary(b, l) : lens, q : enter(b, l)\ [b, p]^-_{\Psi}\ [l, q]^-_{\Gamma} \tag{4}$$

The first part of the message ($\mu_1$) is tagged as before:

$$b : bundle, p : primary(b)\ [b, p]^-_{\Psi} \tag{5}$$

Hence it will be processed by $B$ in the previously described way yielding an update of $\Psi_B$ with $\Delta^*_{B1}$; a realization for the primary bundle. The tags for the second part of the message ($\mu_2$) differ from those in the previous example two ways:

$$l : lens, q : enter(b, l)\ [l, q]^-_{\Gamma} \tag{6}$$

Firstly, $\mu_2$ now has a negative polarity, instructing agent $B$ to view it as requirement. Secondly, $\mu_2$ has to be processed on the *private* context. In other words, $B$ is required to construct a realization on $\Gamma_B$ for the segment ($\Delta_{B2}$) resulting from decoding $\mu_2$; it has to find a lens and construct a proof that the primary bundle enters this lens[10]. We assume that $B$ is able to construct such a realization, say $l = y_{79} : y_5, q = M : y_{19}(l, b)$. At least one of the items in this realization must be 'strictly private' in the sense that it is available on $\Gamma_B$ but not on the subcontext $\Psi_B$, for the reason mentioned above: if the entire realization could be constructed on $\Psi_B$, a realization could also be constructed on $\Psi_A$ and then $A$'s request for information would be superfluous. In this particular case, the lens ($y_{79}$) could be in $\Psi_B$ but the proof object cannot be derived on $\Psi_B$. The update of its private context with the realization, $\Gamma_B \Rightarrow \Gamma'_B$ with $\Gamma'_B \equiv \Gamma_B, \Delta^*_{B2}$, brings $B$ in a position where it (privately) posseses all information needed to answer $A$'s question.

Since the identity of objects cannot be communicated directly, $B$ will have to describe the lens $y_{79}$ to $A$ using common resources. For instance, if it is commonly known among $A$ and $B$ that the microscope contain a number of condensor lenses

[10] Type theoretically this requirement is well-formed, $\Delta_{B2}$ is an extending segment of $\Gamma_B$: the variable $b$ occurring free in $\Delta_{B2}$ is bound in $\Gamma_B$ after the update of $\Psi_B$ with $\Delta^*_{B1}$ because of the inclusion $\Psi_B \subseteq \Gamma_B$.

which are arranged in some order, $B$ could send a labeled message to expressing that the primary bundle enters the first condensor lens to describe the lens to $A$. This labeled message, which again *provides* information, will update the common contexts of both $A$ and $B$, in the way described in Sect. 5.1, with the information $A$ wanted to obtain.

## 6 Conclusions

We have presented a simple model of communication for cases where two participants exchange information about a shared environment. The model is based on an explicit type-theoretical formalization of the knowledge states of the communicating agents, which stresses the subjective nature of these states. This formalization of knowledge states by type theoretical contexts has an inherent notion of meaningfulness: not only do these contexts show which propositions and categories of objects an agent takes to be inhabitated at a given time, but also which types are well-formed for this agent given its knowledge state, i.e. what information is meaningful to it.

In the model, we show how an agent can communicate content which is meaningful to itself to another agent by means of a shared (public) language, despite the subjective nature of its knowledge state. The fact that the agents share a language implies that each agent has an personal mapping between some of the types in its knowledge state and the constructs in the shared language. We show how an agent can encode content which is meaningful in its knowledge state in a public message, and how the agent receiving this message can decode it (using its own mapping) into information which is meaningful in its own knowledge state. As the examples show, information can be exchanged between agents and subsequently shared.

Our approach to communication is not centered around the notion of truth, but tries to show how personal information becomes shared. Accordingly, it emphasizes information *flow*. This is reflected in the notion of polarity, which specifies the direction of the flow, and also in the importance that we attach to the various locations where the information can reside. It seems that such emphasis helps to get a computational understanding of various phenomena in dialogue. In fact, the direction of information flow underlies the distinction between questions and assertions, as well as that between definite and indefinite descriptions.

Although the model is hardly elaborated here, we do show how utterances can be interpreted within the knowledge of the receiver, and how communication really leads to progress through an *extension* of that which is commonly known. In our model all information is distributed over the participants, even if a part of it is assumed to be shared. This realistic feature of the approach brings out the difficulties involved in referring, even when referring to commonly known objects. In fact, we do not see how such reference would be possible without a context-dependent interpretation mechanism involving the construction of realizations, similar to the one sketched here. Interestingly, type theory offers the possibility to use this same mechanism to refer to reasons, i.e. justifications, as well. This provides a direct handle on the argumentive structure of the dialogue.

A different matter is how all this works out in practice: actual agents in actual dialogues. In the Denk-project we constructed a man-machine interface based on the approach to communication sketched in this paper. The interface contains an artificial agent that reasons in type theory and interprets the utterances of user in a context-sensitive way ([2]). This shows that at least for a given domain and a small fragment of English our approach is feasible ([6]).

We feel that our model could provide a point of departure for a computational theory of dialogue. We are strengthened in this conviction by the mutually compatible theories of various linguistic phenomena that have already been formulated in this framework, such as: presuppositions ([8]), the resolution of definite descriptions (including anaphora and uses of deixis, ([4])) and question/answer relations ([8]).

## References


1. Ahn, R.: 1994, Communicating contexts: A pragmatic approach to information exchange, in P. Dybjer, B. Nordström, and J. Smith (eds.), *The proceedings of the BRA workshop: Types of Proofs and Programs*, Vol. 996 of *Springer Lecture Notes in Computer Science*, Springer Verlag, Berlin
2. Ahn, R. et al.: 1994, The denk-architecture: A fundamental approach to user-interfaces, *Artificial Intelligence Review* 5(8)
3. Barendregt, H.: 1992, Lambda calculi with types, in S. Abramsky, D. Gabbay, and T. Maibaum (eds.), *Handbook of Logic in Computer Science*, Oxford University Press, Oxford
4. Beun, R. and Kievit, L.: 1996, Resolving definite expressions in DenK, in *Proceedings of the 5th International Pragmatics Conference*, Mexico City
5. De Bruijn, N.: 1980, A survey of the project automath, in J. Seldin and J. Hindley (eds.), *To H.B. Curry: Essays on Combinatory Logic, Lambda Calculus and Formalisms*, pp 589–606, Academic Press
6. Kievit, L.:1998, *Context-driven Natural Language Interpretation*, Ph.D. thesis, Tilburg University, Tilburg
7. Mäenpää, P. and Ranta, A.: 1990, An implementation of intuitionistic categorial grammar, in L. Kálmán and L. Pólos (eds.), *Papers from the Second Symposium on Logic and Language*, Akademiai Kiado, Budapest
8. Piwek, P.: 1998, *Logic, Information & Conversation*, Ph.D. thesis, Eindhoven University of Technology, Eindhoven

# Gröbner Bases in Type Theory

Thierry Coquand and Henrik Persson

Department of Computing Science,
Chalmers University of Technology and University of Göteborg,
S-412 96 Göteborg, Sweden

**Abstract.** We describe how the theory of Gröbner bases, an important part of computational algebra, can be developed within Martin-Löf's type theory. In particular, we aim for an *integrated* development of the algorithms for computing Gröbner bases: we want to prove, constructively in type theory, the existence of Gröbner bases and from such proofs extract the algorithms. Our main contribution is a reformulation of the standard theory of Gröbner bases which uses generalised inductive definitions. We isolate the main non-constructive part, a minimal bad sequence argument, and use the open induction principle [Rao88,Coq92] to interpret it by induction. This leads to short constructive proofs of Dickson's lemma and Hilbert's basis theorem, which are used to give an integrated development of Buchberger's algorithm. An important point of this work is that the elegance and brevity of the original proofs are maintained while the new proofs also have a direct constructive content. In the appendix we present a computer formalisation of Dickson's lemma and an abstract existence proof of Gröbner bases.

## 1 Introduction

This work is part of a project to develop computational algebra completely within Martin–Löf's type theory [NPS90], in an integrated fashion. Since the birth of the subject, algorithms in computational algebra have usually been *externally* developed: an algorithm is given and its correctness and termination is proved using classical logic. A possible reason for this approach is that classical abstract algebra is inherently non–constructive; e.g. existence–proof of primitive objects like prime and maximal ideals require Zorn's lemma, a highly non–constructive principle. This makes the other approach difficult, the *integrated* development, where an algorithm is extracted from a constructive existence proof. The notion of integrated and external programming logics was introduced by Girard [Gir86], for a comparison between the integrated and external approach to program development, see [Dyb90].

Gröbner bases together with an algorithm for computing them, was introduced by Buchberger [Buc65,Buc85]. It can be seen as a generalisation of the Euclidian algorithm for computing the greatest common divisor (gcd) of polynomials in several variables. In the case of polynomials in one variable, one can easily decide whether a polynomial $f$ is in the ideal generated by the set of polynomials $F = \{f_1, \ldots, f_n\}$: just compute the gcd of $F$, since it generates the ideal of $F$, it is enough to check whether it divides $f$. This gives many algorithmic solutions to problems concerning polynomials in one variable.

However, in the case of polynomials in several variables, this technique does not work. One problem is that $F$ may not have a single generator of its ideal; hence one needs to define when a polynomial is divided by a set of polynomials. Another more important problem is that this technique is not complete: if $F$ divides $f$ then $f$ is in the ideal of $F$, but $f$ might be in the ideal of $F$ even though $F$ does not divide $f$. This is where Gröbner bases come into play; a Gröbner basis $G$ of $F$ is a finite set of polynomials which generates the same ideal and divides $f$ if and only if $f$ is in the ideal of $F$.

There are several thorough presentations of Gröbner bases and their applications [Buc85,Buc98,BW93,CLO97,Frö97]. However, these proofs are in general not constructive, which makes their development hard to translate into type theory. Our main contribution is a reformulation of the standard theory of Gröbner bases which replaces the non–constructive arguments by the use of generalised inductive definitions [Acz77]. A natural question is then whether the original elegant arguments are lost forever in this constructive framework? We show that this is not so by isolating the main non–constructive principle, a minimal bad sequence argument, and use the open induction principle [Rao88,Coq92] to interpret it by induction. This leads to short constructive proofs which follow the original arguments, and which have been formalised on computer.

In Section 2, we present a constructive existence proof of Gröbner bases for polynomial rings with field–coefficients. This proof uses a short constructive proof of Dickson's lemma [Dic13] which was extracted from a classical proof using open induction. During this work, we became aware of the work in [Thé98], where Théry presents a formal verification in Coq [HKPM97] of Buchberger's algorithm for computing Gröbner bases for polynomial rings with field coefficients. This formal proof is constructive, except for a classical proof of Dickson's lemma [Pot96]. A difference is that Théry's development is external; he starts with a program for Buchberger's algorithm and proves that it computes Gröbner bases, whereas we prove the existence of Gröbner bases constructively in such a way that Buchberger's algorithm is contained in the proof.

In Section 3, we present a short constructive proof of Hilbert's basis theorem, also extracted from a classical proof using open induction. This theorem can be used to prove termination of generalisations of Buchberger's algorithm for computing Gröbner bases for polynomials over principal ideal domains [BW93] and other algebraic structures [JL91]. Another approach was taken by Jacobsson and Löfwall [JL91] who proved constructively Hilbert's basis theorem by using Gröbner bases and a different definition of Noetherian.

This work is similar in spirit to Berger and Schwichtenberg [BS96], where an algorithm for computing the gcd of natural numbers is extracted from a classical existence proof. A difference is that they extract the proof automatically from a formal classical proof, whereas we manually rephrase an informal classical proof.

## 2 Gröbner Bases for Fields

In this section we assume $K$ to be an arbitrary field with a decidable equality, e.g. the rationals $\mathbb{Q}$. We will consider the polynomial ring $K[X_1, \ldots, X_m]$, i.e. the set of polynomials in $m$ variables with coefficients in $K$. A good suggestion on how to define polynomial rings in type theory can be found in [Jac95], where a formalisation in Nuprl [Con86] is described. We abbreviate monic monomials $X_1^{k_1} \cdots X_m^{k_m}$ as $X^\alpha$, where $\alpha = (k_1, \ldots, k_m)$. We say that that $X^\alpha$ *divides* $X^\beta$ if $\alpha \leq^m \beta$, where $(k_1, \ldots, k_m) \leq^m (l_1, \ldots, l_m) = k_1 \leq l_1 \,\&\cdots\&\, k_m \leq l_m$. When the $m$ is clear from the context, we will omit it and write $\leq$. Note that $X^\alpha \cdot X^\beta = X^{\alpha+\beta}$, where $\alpha + \beta = (k_1 + l_1, \ldots, k_m + l_m)$, and $\frac{X^\alpha}{X^\beta} = X^{\alpha-\beta}$, where $\alpha - \beta = (l_1 - k_1, \ldots, l_m - k_m)$ if $X^\beta$ divides $X^\alpha$. We define the *least common multiple of* $\alpha$ *and* $\beta$, $lcm(\alpha, \beta)$, as $(\max(k_1, l_1), \ldots, \max(k_m, l_m))$, if $\alpha = (k_1, \ldots, k_m)$ and $\beta = (l_1, \ldots, l_m)$.

We assume a total *compatible* well–founded order $\succ$ on the monomials, that is an order where $\alpha_1 \succ \alpha_2$ implies $\alpha_1 + \beta \succ \alpha_2 + \beta$. One possible order is: first order in terms of total degree, then monomials with equal total degree are ordered lexicographically. If $f$ is a polynomial, $c_1 \neq 0$ and $c_1 X^{\alpha_1}$ is the highest monomial in $f$ w.r.t. this order, we define $hd\ f = c_1 X^{\alpha_1}$. We define the *multi–degree* of such $f$, $mdeg(f)$, to be $\alpha_1$.

Next, we define a reduction algorithm in the ring $K[X_1, \ldots, X_m]$:

**Definition 1.** *A* reduction *of $f$ after reducing by a set of non-zero polynomials $G = \{g_1, \ldots, g_n\}$, $RED(f; G)$, is defined by $\succ$-recursion on* mdeg($f$)*:*

$$RED(0; G) = 0,$$

$$RED(f; G) = \begin{cases} RED(f - \frac{hd\ f}{hd\ g_i} g_i; G), & \text{if } \exists g_i \in G.\, \mathrm{mdeg}(g_i) \leq \mathrm{mdeg}(f), \\ f, & \text{otherwise.} \end{cases}$$

To make *RED* into a deterministic algorithm, one must decide on a strategy to choose the $g_i$ in the above clause; for example to try $g_1$ first, then $g_2$, and so on. One problem is that the choice of this strategy might affect the result; consider e.g. $f = XY^2 + Y^2 + X$, $g_1 = XY - 1$ and $g_2 = Y^2 - 1$: if we always try to reduce by $g_1$ first, $RED(f; g_1, g_2) = X + Y + 1$, whereas if we always try $g_2$ first, $RED(f; g_1, g_2) = 2X + 1$. Another problem is that *RED* does not give a decision procedure for membership in ideals; e.g. $RED(X; Y^2 + X, Y) = X \neq 0$ for any strategy but $X \in Idl(Y^2 + X, Y)$, where $Idl(a_1, \ldots, a_n)$ is the ideal generated by $a_1, \ldots, a_n$. We say that a finite set is a Gröbner basis, if we can use *RED* as a decision procedure to decide the ideal it generates:

**Definition 2.** *$G$ is a* Gröbner basis *(for the ideal it generate), if $RED(f; G) = 0$ whenever $f \in Idl(G)$.*

One can prove that $RED(f; G)$ is unique and independent of strategy when $G$ is a Gröbner basis, see e.g. [BW93].

## 2.1 Construction of Gröbner Bases

Rather than first giving an algorithm which constructs Gröbner bases for ideals and then prove it correct, we will give a direct and *constructive* proof that for any finitely generated ideal, there exists a corresponding Gröbner basis. Since this proof is constructive, it will in particular contain an algorithm for constructing Gröbner bases.

To motivate the development, consider the example set $\{Y^2 + X, Y\}$; this is not a Gröbner basis as explained above, since $X \in \mathit{Idl}(Y^2 + X, Y)$, but $\mathit{RED}(X; Y^2+X, Y) \neq 0$. The first step is to find a systematic method to generate all such possible counter–examples.

**Definition 3.** *Given two polynomials $f$ and $g$, their* S-polynomial, spol$(f, g)$, *is defined as*

$$\mathrm{spol}(f,g) = \frac{X^\alpha}{hd\ f} \cdot f - \frac{X^\alpha}{hd\ g} \cdot g$$

*where* $\alpha = \mathrm{lcm}(\mathrm{mdeg}(f), \mathrm{mdeg}(g))$.

S-polynomials give a practical characterisation of Gröbner bases:

**Theorem 4.** $G = \{g_1, \ldots, g_t\}$ *is a Gröbner basis if* $\mathit{RED}(\mathrm{spol}(g_i, g_j); G) = 0$ *for all* $i < j \leq t$.

*Proof.* In this case we prove that the set of elements $f$ such that $\mathit{RED}(f; G) = 0$ is closed by addition. Since this set is clearly closed by multiplication by monomials, this will imply that we have $\mathit{RED}(f; G) = 0$ for all $f$ in $\mathit{Idl}(G)$, as desired.

We prove that if $\mathit{RED}(f; G) = \mathit{RED}(g; G) = 0$ then $\mathit{RED}(f + g; G) = 0$ by induction on $\mathit{mdeg}(f)$ and $\mathit{mdeg}(g)$. The only case which is not direct is if we have $\mathit{mdeg}(f) = \mathit{mdeg}(g)$, $\mathit{RED}(f; G) = \mathit{RED}(f - m_i g_i; G)$, $\mathit{RED}(g; G) = \mathit{RED}(g - m_j g_j; G)$, where $m_i = r_i X^{\alpha_i}, m_j = r_j X^{\alpha_j}$ are suitable monomials, and $\mathit{mdeg}(f - m_i g_i) \prec \mathit{mdeg}(f)$, $\mathit{mdeg}(g - m_j g_j) \prec \mathit{mdeg}(g)$. We can write

$$g_i = s_i X^{\beta_i} + h_i, \; g_j = s_j X^{\beta_j} + h_j$$

with $\mathit{mdeg}(h_i) \prec \mathit{mdeg}(g_i)$ and $\mathit{mdeg}(h_j) \prec \mathit{mdeg}(g_j)$. We have then

$$f + g - (r_i + \frac{r_j c_j}{c_i}) X^{\alpha_i} g_i = m\mathit{spol}(g_i, g_j) + f - m_i g_i + g - m_j g_j$$

for a suitable monomial $m$. By induction hypothesis the right hand side reduces to 0, hence so does $f + g$.

A naive approach to compute a Gröbner basis for a set is to add counter–examples (S-polynomials) to it until it satisfies the condition in Theorem 4. Quite surprisingly, this process will always terminate. The proof of this relies on a non–trivial combinatorial result known as *Dickson's lemma*: for any sequence of monic monomials $X^{\alpha_1}, X^{\alpha_2}, \ldots$, there will eventually be $i < j$ such that $X^{\alpha_i}$ divides $X^{\alpha_j}$.

## 2.2 A Constructive Proof of Dickson's Lemma

In this subsection, we present a constructive proof of Dickson's lemma. The proof is a translation of the classical proof in Appendix A; the main non-constructive part, a minimal bad sequence argument, have been replaced by the open induction principle [Rao88,Coq92]. Dickson's lemma says that for any infinite sequence of $n$-tuples of natural numbers $\sigma_1, \sigma_2, \ldots$, there exists $i < j$ such that $\sigma_i \leq^n \sigma_j$, where $(a_1, \ldots, a_n) \leq^n (b_1, \ldots, b_n)$ if $\forall 0 < i \leq n.\, a_i \leq b_i$. Classically, a relation is called *well*[1] if it satisfies the condition above.

*Remark 5.* The proofs in this section only require $<$ to be a decidable relation which is well-founded on its underlying set $A$, with $a \leq b$ defined as $\neg(b < a)$. However, we will only instantiate the theorems for $<$ being the less-than relation on $\mathbb{N}$.

We want to express in type theory, extended with inductive definitions, what it means for a relation $R$ over a set $B$ to be well. To this end, we define $Good_R(b_0 \cdots b_m)$ to be $\exists i < j \leq m.\, b_i \, R \, b_j$. We use an inductive definition of *bar* [ML68] to express that for any infinite sequence $b_0 b_1 \cdots$, $Good_R(\sigma)$ will eventually hold for an initial segment $\sigma$ of $b_0 b_1 \cdots$.

**Definition 6.** *Given a set $B$ and a predicate $P$ over the lists of $B$, we define inductively when the predicate $P$* bars *$\sigma$, written $P \mid \sigma$:*

$$\frac{P(\sigma)}{P \mid \sigma} \qquad\qquad \frac{\forall b.\, P \mid \sigma.b}{P \mid \sigma}$$

*This is a generalised inductive definition [Acz77], which comes with a transfinite induction principle:*

$$\frac{\begin{array}{c}\forall \rho.\, P(\rho) \Rightarrow \Psi(\rho),\\ \forall \rho.\, (\forall b.\, P \mid \rho.b) \;\Rightarrow\; (\forall b.\, \Psi(\rho.b)) \;\Rightarrow\; \Psi(\rho)\end{array}}{P \mid \sigma \;\Rightarrow\; \Psi(\sigma)}$$

Here $\sigma.b$ is the list $\sigma$ extended with the element $b$. Intuitively, $P \mid \sigma$ means that $P$ will eventually hold for any extension of $\sigma$. Classically, assuming the axiom of dependent choices, $Good_R \mid []$ is provable iff $R$ satisfies the classical definition of well. This justifies us to define $R$ to be well iff $Good_R \mid []$ is provable.

**Lemma 7.** *If $\forall \sigma, \rho, \gamma.\, P(\sigma\rho) \Rightarrow P(\sigma\gamma\rho)$, then $\forall \sigma, \rho, \gamma.\, P \mid \sigma\rho \;\Rightarrow\; P \mid \sigma\gamma\rho$.*

*Proof.* Immediate by induction on the proof of $P \mid \sigma\rho$.

Given two relations $R$ and $S$ over sets $A$ and $B$ respectively, the product relation, $R \times S$, over $A \times B$ is defined as $(a, b)\,(R \times S)\,(a', b') = a\,R\,a' \;\&\; b\,S\,b'$. Following [Coq92], we define a predicate $M(\sigma)$, expressing that an initial sequence $\sigma$ of pairs in $A \times B$ is *minimal w.r.t.* $<$, by recursion on $\sigma$:

$$\begin{aligned} M([]) &= \top,\\ M(\sigma.(x, b)) &= M(\sigma) \;\&\; \forall y.\, y < x \Rightarrow \forall b.\, Good_{\leq \times R} \mid \sigma.(y, b). \end{aligned}$$

[1] in previous work, the relation was required to be a quasi-order (well-quasi order).

The predicate $M$ will play the rôle of the minimal bad sequence in Appendix A.1; if $M(\sigma)$ holds, and $\rho$ has a lexicographically smaller sequence of first components, then $Good_{\leq \times R} \mid \rho$ should hold.

Raoult's open induction principle can be expressed using these definitions:

**Theorem 8 (Open Induction).** *For any finite sequence $\sigma$ of pairs in $A \times B$, if $M(\sigma)$ and $\forall a, b.\, M(\sigma.(a,b)) \Rightarrow Good_{\leq \times R} \mid \sigma.(a,b)$, then $Good_{\leq \times R} \mid \sigma$.*

*Proof.* Assume $\sigma$ to be a finite sequence such that $M(\sigma)$ and $\forall a, b.\, M(\sigma.(a,b)) \Rightarrow Good_{\leq \times R} \mid \sigma.(a,b)$. We prove $\forall x. \forall b.\, Good_{\leq \times R} \mid \sigma.(x,b)$ by induction on $x$: Assume $\forall y.\, y < x \Rightarrow \forall b.\, Good_{\leq \times R} \mid \sigma.(y,b)$. From this we directly obtain $M(\sigma.(x,b))$, and by hypothesis, $Good_{\leq \times R} \mid \sigma.(x,b)$.

This theorem is a simplification of that in [Coq92] but it uses only generalised inductive definitions iterated once [Acz77]. It will interpret the argument: if $Good_{\leq \times R} \mid \sigma$ holds under the assumption that $\sigma$ starts a minimal bad sequence, then $Good_{\leq \times R} \mid \sigma$ holds without this assumption as well. Therefore, the classical proof of Dickson's lemma in Appendix A can be interpreted as:

**Lemma 9.** *If $Good_R \mid b_1 \cdots b_m$ holds, then*

$$\forall x_1, \ldots, x_m.\, M((x_1,b_1)\cdots(x_m,b_m)) \Rightarrow Good_{\leq \times R} \mid (x_1,b_1)\cdots(x_m,b_m).$$

*Proof.* By induction on the proof of $Good_R \mid b_1 \cdots b_m$:

$Good_R(b_1 \cdots b_m)$: Then there exists a $i < j \leq m$ such that $b_i \, R \, b_j$. Now, by cases on the decidable $<$, we have either $\neg(x_i > x_j)$, that means $x_i \leq x_j$ so $(x_i, b_i)\,(\leq \times R)\,(x_j, b_j)$ holds, hence $Good_{\leq \times R}((x_1,b_1)\cdots(x_m,b_m))$. Otherwise, $x_i > x_j$, and since $M((x_1,b_1)\cdots(x_m,b_m))$ implies $M((x_1,b_1)\cdots(x_i,b_i))$, we get $Good_{\leq \times R} \mid (x_1,b_1)\cdots(x_{i-1},b_{i-1})(x_j,b_j)$, and by Lemma 7, we are done.

$\forall b.\, Good_R \mid (b_1 \cdots b_m b)$: Immediate by Theorem 8 and IH.

**Corollary 10 (Dickson's lemma).** *For all $n \in \mathbb{N}$, $Good_{\leq^n} \mid []$.*

*Proof.* By induction on $n$: the case $n = 0$ is trivial. Otherwise, $n = m + 1$, and $Good_{\leq^m} \mid []$ holds. We instantiate the development above with $R$ being $\leq^m$, and by Lemma 9 we are done.

Dickson's lemma implies the existence of Gröbner bases for any finitely generated (f.g.) ideal in $K[X_1, \ldots, X_m]$:

**Theorem 11.** *Every f.g. ideal $F = Idl(f_1, \ldots, f_n)$ has a Gröbner basis $G$.*

*Proof.* We prove this using Dickson's lemma. Let $m_i = mdeg(f_i)$. Define $Bad(\sigma)$ as $\neg Good(\sigma)$. We can assume that $Bad(m_1 \cdots m_n)$ holds; if $m_i \leq m_j$ for $i < j$, we repeatedly reduce $F$ by dividing $f_j$ by $f_i$. The result follows from Dickson's lemma and the following lemma:

$$\begin{aligned} Good_{\leq} \mid m_1 \cdots m_k \;\Rightarrow\; & \forall f_1, \ldots, f_k.\, (\forall i.\, m_i = mdeg(f_i)) \Rightarrow \\ & Bad(m_1 \cdots m_k) \Rightarrow \exists G.\, G \text{ is a Gröbner basis for } f_1, \ldots, f_k, \end{aligned}$$

which is proved by induction on the proof of $Good_{\leq} \mid m_1 \cdots m_k$:

*Good*$(m_1 \cdots m_k)$: This contradicts with *Bad*$(m_1 \cdots m_k)$.

$\forall m.\, Good_{\leq} \mid m_1 \cdots m_k m$: Assume $f_1, \ldots, f_k$ with $mdeg(f_i) = m_i$ for all $i$. Consider $RED(spol(f_i, f_j); f_1, \ldots, f_k)$ for $i \neq j$. If all are zero, $\{f_1, \ldots, f_k\}$ is already a Gröbner basis by Theorem 4. Otherwise, let $f_{k+1}$ be the first $RED(spol(f_i, f_j); f_1, \ldots, f_k) \neq 0$. Then $m_l \not\leq mdeg(f_{k+1})$ for all $l \leq k$, so if $Bad(m_1 \cdots m_k)$, then $Bad(m_1 \cdots m_k mdeg(f_{k+1}))$. Hence, by IH, we have a Gröbner basis for $F \cup \{f_{k+1}\}$, and since $f_{k+1}$ is in $Idl(F)$, this is a Gröbner basis for $F$. □

This is an integrated version of Buchberger's algorithm: while $F$ is not a Gröbner basis, add normalised S-polynomials to $F$. Optimisations of the algorithm can be made by changing the proof, e.g. the order in which to compute the S-polynomials.

## 3 Hilbert's Basis Theorem

In this section we prove constructively Hilbert's Basis Theorem (HBT). This is used to prove termination of generalisations of Buchberger's algorithm for computing Gröbner bases for polynomials over principal ideal domains [BW93] and other algebraic structures [JL91].

In these more general cases, there are similar notions of reductions and ways of generating counter–examples and to decide whether the set is a Gröbner basis. As in the previous section, we need to prove that the process of adding counter–examples to the ideal ends. This follows from HBT, which concerns *Noetherian* rings. There are several classically equivalent definitions of Noetherian:

**Definition 12.** *A ring $R$ is* Noetherian, *if either of the following classically equivalent conditions holds:*

1. *every ideal in $R$ is finitely generated,*
2. *there exists no infinite strictly increasing sequence of ideals,*
3. *for every infinite sequence $a_0, a_1 \ldots$ of elements in $R$, there exists an $m$ such that $a_m \in Idl(a_0, \ldots, a_{m-1})$.*

HBT says that if $R$ is a Noetherian ring, so is $R[X_1, \ldots, X_m]$.

### 3.1 A Constructive Proof of Hilbert's Basis Theorem

In this subsection, we present a constructive proof of HBT. Again, the proof is a translation of the classical proof in Appendix A; as in the previuos section, the open induction principle [Rao88,Coq92] can be used to replace the minimal bad sequence argument. Contrary to the constructive proofs of HBT previously known to us [Ric74,MRR88,JL91], the proof extracted does not require decidability of the equality in the ring or its ideals.

We want to express in type theory, extended with inductive definitions, the notion of Noetherian rings. To this end, we define $Good_R(a_0 \cdots a_m)$ to be $\exists k \leq$

$m. a_k \in Idl(a_0, \ldots, a_{k-1})$ for any ring $R$. The inductive definition of bar gives a good constructive definition of Noetherian: classically, assuming the axiom of dependent choices, $Good_R \mid []$ is provable iff $R$ satisfies the second condition in Definition 12. This justifies us to define a ring $R$ to be Noetherian iff $Good_R \mid []$ is provable.

**Lemma 13.** *If $Good_R \mid a_0 \cdots a_k\sigma$, then $Good_R \mid a_0 \cdots a_{k-1}(a_k + \sum_{i=0}^{k-1} r_i a_i)\sigma$.*

*Proof.* By induction on the proof of $Good_R \mid a_0 \cdots a_k\sigma$: If $Good_R(a_0 \cdots a_k\sigma)$, then it is direct since any $\sum_{i=0}^{k-1} r_i a_i$ is in $Idl(a_0, \ldots, a_{k-1})$. Otherwise, we have $\forall a.\, Good_R \mid a_0 \cdots a_k\sigma a$, and the result follows by IH.

To prove HBT, it is enough to prove that for any finitely generated $R$-module $R[X]$, if $R$ is Noetherian, then $R[X]$ is Noetherian. In the rest of this section, we assume $R[X]$ to be a finitely generated $R$-module. To interpret the minimal bad sequence argument in Appendix A.2, we define a predicate $M(\sigma)$, expressing that the finite sequence $\sigma$ of lists of $R$ is *minimal*, and prove a corresponding open induction principle for it.

$$M([]) = \top$$
$$M(\sigma.f) = M(\sigma)\ \&\ \forall g.\, |g| < |f| \Rightarrow P(\sigma.g)$$

where $|f|$ is the length of the list $f$, and $P(f_1 \cdots f_k) = Good_{R[X]} \mid \varphi(f_1) \cdots \varphi(f_k)$ where $\varphi(a_0 \cdots a_k) = a_0 + a_1 X + \cdots + a_k X^k$. If we write $\delta f = 0.f$, where $0.f$ is the list $f$ with 0 put in front, then $\varphi(\delta f) = X\varphi(f)$. We use lists here rather than elements of $R[X]$ to avoid a decidable equality in $R$ in the proof of HBT.

**Theorem 14 (Open Induction).** *For any sequence $\sigma$ of lists of $R$, if $M(\sigma)$ and $\forall f.\, M(\sigma.f) \Rightarrow P(\sigma.f)$, then $P(\sigma)$.*

*Proof.* Assume $\sigma$ such that $M(\sigma)$ and $\forall f.\, M(\sigma.f) \Rightarrow P(\sigma.f)$. We prove $\forall f.\, P(\sigma.f)$ by induction on the degree of $f$: Assume $\forall g.\, |g| < |f| \Rightarrow P(\sigma.g)$. This directly implies $M(\sigma.f)$, and by hypothesis, $P(\sigma.f)$.

The classical proof of Hilbert's Basis Theorem in Appendix A.2 becomes:

**Lemma 15.** *Given $a_0, \ldots, a_m$ of $R$ such that $Good_R \mid (a_0 \cdots a_m)$ holds, and a sequence $f_0, \ldots, f_m$ of lists of $R$, $M((f_0.a_0) \cdots (f_m.a_m)) \Rightarrow P((f_0.a_0) \cdots (f_m.a_m))$.*

*Proof.* By induction on the proof of $Good_R \mid a_0 \cdots a_m$:

$Good_R(a_0 \cdots a_m)$: Then there exists a $k \leq m$ such that $a_k \in Idl(a_0, \ldots, a_{k-1})$, hence $a_k = r_0 a_0 + \cdots + r_{k-1} a_{k-1}$ for $r_0, \ldots, r_{k-1} \in R$. Let $g_i = f_i.a_i$. Either there exists $0 \leq i < k$ such that $|g_i| > |g_k|$. In that case, since we have $M(g_0 \cdots g_i)$, we obtain $P(g_0 \cdots g_{i-1} g_k)$ and by Lemma 7 repeatedly, $P(g_0 \cdots g_{i-1} g_i \cdots g_k \ldots g_m)$. In the other case, $|g_i| \leq |g_k|$ for all $i < k$, and we construct

$$g^* = g_k - \sum_{i=0}^{k-1} r_i (\delta^{|g_k| - |g_i|} g_i),$$

where summation of lists of equal lenght are just pointwise addition, and scalar multiplication is taken pointwise. Since $|g^*| < |g_k|$ and $M(g_0 \cdots g_k)$, we have $P(g_0 \cdots g_{k-1} g^*)$. Note that $\varphi(g^*) = \varphi(g_k) - \sum_{i=0}^{k-1} r_i(X^{|g_k|-|g_i|}\varphi(g_i))$, so by Lemma 13, $P(g_0 \cdots g_{k-1} g_k)$, and by Lemma 7, we are done.

$\forall a.$ $Good_R \mid a_0 \cdots a_m a$: By IH, we get for any $a \in R$ and sequence $f_0, \ldots, f_m, f$ of lists of $R$, $M((f_0.a_0)\cdots(f_m.a_m)(f.a)) \Rightarrow P((f_0.a_0)\cdots(f_m.a_m)(f.a))$. This also holds if $f.a$ is replaced by the empty list, so by Theorem 14, $P(f_0 \cdots f_m)$.

**Corollary 16 (Hilbert's Basis Theorem).** *$Good_R \mid [] \Rightarrow Good_{R[X_1,\ldots,X_m]} \mid []$.*

*Proof.* By induction on $m$ and Lemma 15, since $R[X]$ is a ring if $R$ is.

# 4 Conclusions

This work shows how a non–trivial part of classical mathematics can be translated into constructive type theory by using the open induction principle. The constructive proofs share the elegance and brevity of the original proofs, and has a direct formalisation in type theory. This is shown in Appendix B below, where a computer formalisation of Dickson's lemma and an abstract existence proof of Gröbner bases is presented.

This can be seen as a general and integrated development of Buchberger's algorithm in a functional language. To be able to execute this program, one needs to formalise a polynomial ring over a field, the reduction function, and Theorem 4. For the remaining formalisation, one should be able to use the already existing work of Jackson [Jac95] and Théry [Thé98].

# A Classical Proofs

## A.1 A Classical Proof of Dickson's Lemma

Dickson's lemma has a short classical proof which uses a *minimal bad sequence argument* [NW63]:

**Proposition 17 (Dickson's lemma).** *For all $n \in \mathbb{N}$, $\leq^n$ is well.*

*Proof.* By induction on $n$: If $n = 0$, it is trivial, so assume $n = m + 1$ and $\leq^m$ is well. We prove that if $<$ is well-founded and $R$ is well, then $\leq \times R$ is also well, where $a \leq b$ is defined as $\neg(b < a)$. The proof is by contradiction: if $\leq \times R$ is not well, then there exists an infinite sequence $u_1, u_2, \ldots$ which is *bad*, i.e. for no $i < j$, $u_i \,(\leq \times R)\, u_j$. Using the axiom of dependent choices, we can construct a minimal bad sequence $v_1, v_2, \ldots$ in the following way: choose $v_1 = (x_1, w_1)$ with $x_1$ minimal among the first components of those pairs which starts a bad sequence. When $v_1, \ldots, v_k$ has been chosen, choose $v_{k+1} = (x_{k+1}, w_{k+1})$ with $x_{k+1}$ minimal among the first components of those tuples continuing a bad sequence from $v_1, \ldots, v_k$. The existence of such minimal bad sequence is the main non-constructive part of the proof.

Since $R$ is well by assumption, there exists $i < j$ such that $w_i \, R \, w_j$. But by construction, we must have $x_i \leq x_j$, otherwise $x_j w_i$ would continue a smaller bad sequence. Hence $(x_i, w_i) \, (\leq \times R) \, (x_j, w_j)$, which contradicts that $v_1, v_2, \ldots$ is a bad sequence.

### A.2 A Classical Proof of Hilbert's Basis Theorem

We give a short classical proof of HBT taken from [BW93], which uses two of the equivalent conditions in Definition 12:

**Proposition 18.** *If $R$ is a noetherian ring, then so is $R[X_1, \ldots, X_n]$.*

*Proof.* Since $R[X]$ is a ring if $R$ is, it is enough to consider the case $n = 1$, the other cases follow by induction. Assume for a contradiction that $I$ is an ideal of $R[X]$ and $I$ is not finitely generated. Then $I$ is not the zero ideal. We construct an infinite sequence $(f_i)_{i \in \mathbb{N}}$ of polynomials in $I$ using the axiom of dependent choices:

1. $f_0$ is a non-zero polynomial in $I$ of minimal degree.
2. $f_{i+1}$ is a polynomial in $I \setminus Idl(f_0, \ldots, f_i)$ of minimal degree.

It is clear that $\deg f_j \leq \deg f_k$ if $j < k$. We denote the (non-zero) head coefficient of $f_i$ by $a_i$. Since $R$ is noetherian, there exists an $m$ such that $a_m \in Idl(a_0, \ldots, a_{m-1})$, i.e. $a_m = r_0 a_0 + \cdots + r_{m-1} a_{m-1}$ where $r_0, \ldots, r_{m-1} \in R$. But then the polynomial

$$f^* = f_m - \sum_{i=0}^{m-1} X^{\deg f_m - \deg f_i} r_i f_i$$

must be in $I \setminus Idl(f_0, \ldots, f_{m-1})$ since otherwise $f_m \in Idl(f_0, \ldots, f_{m-1})$. But $\deg f^* < \deg f_m$, contradicting the minimality of $f_m$.

## B Formal Proofs in Agda

Here we present some formal proofs in Agda [Coq98], a type-checker in the ALF-family for a variant of Martin-Löf's type theory. This type theory is very similar to Cayenne [Aug98], a functional programming language with dependent types.

### B.1 Dickson's lemma in Agda

```
-- Theory of Dickson's lemma, takes a wellfounded relation gt and a well relation R
-- and proves leq x R (product of the two relations) to be a well relation.
--
package thDickson (A,B::Set)(gt::Rel A)(R::Rel B)
                  (wfgt::WF A gt)(dgt::decRel A gt)(gR::WR B R) =
```

```
let
 leq (a,b::A) :: Set = Not (gt a b)
 leqxR (x,y::A*B) :: Set = (leq x.fst y.fst) & (R x.snd y.snd)

 GBarlR :: Pred (List (A*B)) = GRBar (A*B) leqxR
in
open OpenIndGoodRel (A*B) (fstR A B gt) leqxR (WFlem1 A gt wfgt (A*B) (fstR A B gt)
                   (Fst A B) (\(x,y::A*B) -> \(h::gt x.fst y.fst) -> h))
    use Min, open_ind
in
struct
(:) (x::A*B)(l::List (A*B)) :: List (A*B) = @Cons x l
sndL :: Fun (List (A*B)) (List B) = let {f (a::A*B) :: B  = a.snd} in map (A*B) B f

lem0 (l::List (A*B))(a::A*B)(h1::ExistsL B (\(x::B) -> R x a.snd) (sndL l))(h::Min l)
  :: GBarlR (a:l) =
 let lem (vs::List (A*B))(h::ExistsL B (\(x1::B) -> R x1 a.snd) (sndL vs))(h1::Min vs)
        :: GBarlR (a:vs) =
      case vs of
       (Nil)  -> case h of { }
       (Cons a1 as) -> case h of
                    (Inl x) -> case dgt a1.fst a.fst of
                             (No no) ->  @Base (@Inl (@Inl
                                    (struct{fst :: leq a1.fst a.fst = no;
                                            snd :: R a1.snd a.snd = x })))
                             (Yes a') -> GRBarmon (A*B) leqxR (a:@Nil) as
                                            (h1.fst a a') (a1:@Nil)
                    (Inr y) -> GRBarmon (A*B) leqxR (a:@Nil) as
                                  (lem as y h1.snd) (a1:@Nil)
 in lem l h1 h

lem1 (us::List (A*B))(h1::GoodR B R (sndL us))(h::Min us) :: GBarlR us =
 case us of
  (Nil) ->  case h1 of { }
  (Cons a as) -> case h1 of
              (Inl x) -> case as of
                       (Nil) ->  case x of { }
                       (Cons a' as') -> lem0 (a':as') a x h.snd
              (Inr y) -> GRBarmon (A*B) leqxR @Nil as
                             (lem1 (append (A*B) @Nil as) y h.snd) (a:@Nil)

keylem (us::List (A*B))(h::GRBar B R (sndL us)) :: (h1::Min us)-> GBarlR us =
 case h of
   (Base h1) -> lem1 us h1
   (Ind f) -> \(h1::Min us)->open_ind us h1 (\(u::A*B) -> keylem (u:us) (f u.snd))

keylem_cor :: WR (A*B) leqxR = keylem @Nil gR @tt

-- This is the general version of Dickson's lemma.
--
Dickson (A::Set)(gt::Rel A)(wfgt::WF A gt)(dgt::decRel A gt)(n::Nat)
 :: WR (Vec A n) (VecRel A (NotR A gt) n) =
 case n of
  (Zero)  -> @Ind (\(a::Vec A @Zero)->
                 @Ind (\(a1::Vec A @Zero)-> @Base (@Inl (@Inl @tt))))
  (Succ n1) -> let package thD = thDickson A (Vec A n1) gt (VecRel A (NotR A gt) n1)
                                   wfgt dgt (Dickson A gt wfgt dgt n1)
            in thD.keylem_cor
```

## B.2 Abstract Existence proof of Gröbner bases

Below is a formal proof of the existence of Gröbner bases for ideals in an arbitrary polynomial ring (`Poly`). We do not need to assume any properties of a polynomial ring at this level. The development is general and captures the reasoning in Section 2; for instance the assumption `bars::GBar @Nil` can be instantiated by the formal proof of Dickson's lemma above. Some parts of the proof terms were omitted to improve the presentation, these are denoted by "...".

```
package GB0  (Poly::Set)
             (Z::Poly)
             (plusP, timesP::BinOp Poly)
             ((==)::Rel Poly)
             (P::Poly->Pred (List Poly)) =
 let LP :: Set = List Poly
     ForallLP :: Pred Poly -> Pred LP = ForallL Poly
     ExistsLP :: Pred Poly -> Pred LP = ExistsL Poly
     Good::Pred (List Poly) = GoodP Poly P
     GBar :: Pred LP = Bar Poly Good
     Bad :: Pred LP = NotP LP Good
     (:) (f::Poly)(fs::LP) :: LP = @Cons f fs
 in
 open pkIdeal Poly (==) plusP timesP Z use Ideal, eqI, eqvI, congI, ilem1, ilem2
 in
 struct
 package GB1 (spols::LP -> LP)
             (GB::Pred LP)
             (RED::Poly -> LP -> Poly)
             (deceq::decRel Poly (==))
             (ispol::(fs::LP)->ForallLP (\(g::Poly)-> Ideal fs g) (spols fs))
             (iRED::(f::Poly)->(fs::LP)->Ideal (f:fs) (RED f fs))
             (iREDP::(g::Poly)->(gs::LP)->P (RED g gs) gs -> RED g gs == Z)
             (Pprop::(f::Poly)->(fs::LP)->Exists Poly (\(g::Poly) ->
                                         eqI (f:fs) (g:fs) & Not (P g fs)))
             (gbchar::(gs::LP)->ForallLP (\(g'::Poly) -> RED g' gs == Z)
                                  (spols gs) -> GB gs)
             (bars::GBar @Nil)
  = open eqvI use ire, isy, itr
    in
    struct
    lem1 (fs::LP) :: Or (ExistsLP (\(h :: Poly) -> Not (RED h fs == Z)) (spols fs))
                        (ForallLP (\(h :: Poly) ->  RED h fs == Z) (spols fs))
          = existsLlem1 Poly (\(h :: Poly) -> RED h fs == Z)
                             (\(x :: Poly) -> deceq (RED x fs) Z) (spols fs)

    badlem (gs::LP)(g::Poly)(h1::Not (RED g gs == Z))(b::Bad gs)::Bad ((RED g gs):gs) =
     \(x :: Good ((RED g gs):gs)) -> case x of
                                       (Inl x') -> h1 (iREDP g gs x')
                                       (Inr y) -> b y

    remEq1 (fs::LP)::ForallLP (\(g' :: Poly) -> eqI ((RED g' fs):fs) fs) (spols fs) =
     let l1 (sfs::LP)
            (f1::ForallLP (\(g::Poly)-> Ideal fs g) sfs)
          :: ForallLP (\(g'::Poly) -> eqI ((RED g' fs):fs) fs) sfs =
          case sfs of
           (Nil) -> @tt
           (Cons a as) -> ...
     in l1 (spols fs) (ispol fs)

    GBof (F,G::LP) :: Set = eqI G F & GB G

    thm (fs::LP)(gb::GBar fs)(b::Bad fs) :: Exists LP (GBof fs) =
     case gb of
      (Base h) ->  elimNO (Exists LP (GBof fs)) (b h)
      (Ind f) ->
        case lem1 fs of
          (Inl x) ->  let l1 (sgs::LP)
                             (f2::ExistsLP (\(g'::Poly) -> Not (RED g' fs == Z)) sgs)
                             (f3::ForallLP (\(g'::Poly) -> eqI ((RED g' fs):fs) fs) sgs)
                             :: Exists LP (GBof fs) =
                                case sgs of
                                  (Nil) ->  case f2 of { }
                                  (Cons a as) -> ...
                      in l1 (spols fs) x (remEq1 fs)
```

```
      (Inr y) ->  struct fst :: LP = fs
                         snd :: GBof fs fs = struct fst :: eqI fs fs = ire fs
                                                    snd :: GB fs = gbchar fs y

badprop (f::Poly)(fs::LP)(b::Bad fs)(np::Not (P f fs)) :: Bad (f:fs) =
   \(x :: Good (f:fs)) -> case x of
                            (Inl x') -> np x'
                            (Inr y) -> b y

exbad (fs::LP) :: Exists LP (\(gs::LP) -> Bad gs & eqI fs gs)
   = case fs of
      (Nil) ->  struct fst :: LP = @Nil
                         snd :: Bad fst & (eqI @Nil fst) = ...
      (Cons a as) ->  ...

cor (fs::LP) :: Exists LP (GBof fs) =  let gs :: LP = (exbad fs).fst
                                           bad :: Bad gs = (exbad fs).snd.fst
                                           eq :: eqI fs gs = (exbad fs).snd.snd
                                           th :: Exists LP (GBof gs) = ...
                                       in ...
```

# References


[Acz77] P. Aczel. An Introduction to Inductive Definitions. In J. Barwise, editor, *Handbook of Mathematical Logic*, pages 739–782. North-Holland Publishing Company, 1977.

[Aug98] L. Augustsson. Cayenne - a language with dependent types. Technical report, Department of Computing Science, Chalmers University of Technology, 1998. Homepage: http://www.cs.chalmers.se/~augustss/cayenne/.

[BS96] U. Berger and H. Schwichtenberg. The greatest common divisor: a case study for program extraction from classical proofs. In *Proceedings of the Workshop TYPES '95, Torino, Italy, June 1995*, number 1158 in Lecture Notes in Computer Science. Springer-Verlag, 1996.

[Buc65] B. Buchberger. *An Algorithm for Finding a Basis for the Residue Class Ring of a Zero-Dimensional Polynomial Ideal (German)*. PhD thesis, University of Innsbruck, 1965.

[Buc85] B. Buchberger. Gröbner bases: An algorithmic method in polynomial ideal theory. In N. K. Bose, editor, *Multidimensional systems theory*, pages 184–232. Reidel Publ. Co., 1985.

[Buc98] B. Buchberger. Introduction to Gröbner bases. In B. Buchberger and F. Winkler, editors, *Gröbner bases and applications*, pages 3–31. Cambridge University Press, 1998.

[BW93] T. Becker and V. Weispfenning. *Gröbner bases*, volume 141 of *Graduate Texts in Mathematics*. Springer-Verlag, New York, 1993. In cooperation with H. Kredel.

[CLO97] D. Cox, J. Little, and D. O'Shea. *Ideals, varieties, and algorithms*. Undergraduate Texts in Mathematics. Springer-Verlag, New York, second edition, 1997.

[Con86] R. L. Constable et al. *Implementing Mathematics with the NuPRL Proof Development System*. Prentice-Hall, Englewood Cliffs, NJ, 1986.

[Coq92] Th. Coquand. Constructive topology and combinatorics. In *proceeding of the conference Constructivity in Computer Science, San Antonio, LNCS 613*, pages 28–32, 1992.

[Coq98] C. Coquand. The homepage of the Agda type checker. Homepage: http://www.cs.chalmers.se/~catarina/Agda/, 1998.

[Dic13] L. E. Dickson. Finiteness of the odd perfect and primitive abundant numbers with $n$ distinct prime factors. *Am. J. Math.*, 35:413–422, 1913.

[Dyb90] P. Dybjer. Comparing integrated and external logics of functional programs. *Science of Computer Programming*, 14:59–79, 1990.

[Frö97] R. Fröberg. *An introduction to Gröbner bases.* John Wiley & Sons, 1997.

[Gir86] J-Y Girard. Linear logic and parallelism. In M. Venturini Zilli, editor, *Mathematical Models for the Semantics of Parallelism*, number LNCS 280, pages 166–182. Springer-Verlag, September 1986.

[HKPM97] G. Huet, G. Kahn, and C. Paulin-Mohring. The Coq proof assistant: A tutorial. Technical report, Rapport Technique 204, INRIA, 1997.

[Jac95] P. B. Jackson. *Enhancing the Nuprl proof development system and applying it to computational abstract algebra.* PhD thesis, Cornell University, 1995.

[JL91] C. Jacobsson and C. Löfwall. Standard bases for general coefficient rings and a new constructive proof of Hilbert's basis theorem. *J. Symbolic Comput.*, 12(3):337–371, 1991.

[ML68] P. Martin-Löf. *Notes on Constructive Mathematics.* Almqvist & Wiksell, 1968.

[MRR88] R. Mines, F. Richman, and W. Ruitenburg. *A course in constructive algebra.* Universitext. Springer-Verlag, New York, 1988.

[NPS90] B. Nordström, K. Petersson, and J. M. Smith. *Programming in Martin-Löf's Type Theory. An Introduction.* Oxford University Press, 1990.

[NW63] C. Nash-Williams. On well-quasi-ordering finite trees. *Proceedings of the Cambridge Philosophical Society*, 59:833–835, 1963.

[Pot96] Loïc Pottier. Dixon's lemma. URL: ftp://www.inria.fr/safir/pottier/MON, 1996.

[Rao88] J-C. Raoult. Proving open properties by induction. *Information processing letters*, 29:19–23, 1988.

[Ric74] F. Richman. Constructive aspects of noetherian rings. In *Proc. AMS 44*, pages 436–441, 1974.

[Thé98] L. Théry. Proving and computing: A certified version of the Buchberger's algorithm. In *proceeding of the 15th International Conference on Automated Deduction, Lindau, Germany, LNAI 1421*, 1998.

# A Modal Lambda Calculus with Iteration and Case Constructs

Joëlle Despeyroux and Pierre Leleu

INRIA
2004 Route des Lucioles, B.P. 93
F-06902 Sophia-Antipolis Cedex, France.
Joelle.Despeyroux@sophia.inria.fr, LeleuP@wanadoo.fr

**Abstract.** An extension of the simply-typed $\lambda$-calculus, allowing iteration and case reasoning over terms of functional types that arise when using higher order abstract syntax, has recently been introduced by F. Pfenning, C. Schürmann and the first author. This thorny mixing is achieved thanks to the help of the operator '$\Box$' of modal logic S4. Here we give a new presentation of their system, with reduction rules, instead of evaluation judgments, that compute the canonical forms of terms. Our presentation is based on a modal $\lambda$-calculus that is better from the user's point of view. Moreover we do not impose a particular strategy of reduction during the computation. Our system enjoys the decidability of typability, soundness of typed reduction with respect to typing rules, the Church-Rosser and strong normalization properties and it is a conservative extension over the simply-typed $\lambda$-calculus.

## 1 Introduction

Higher order abstract syntax ([PE88]) is a representation technique which proves to be useful when modelizing in a logical framework a language which involves bindings of variables. Thanks to this technique, the formalization of an (object-level) language does not need definitions for free or bound variables in a term. Nor does it need definitions of notions of substitutions, which are implemented using the meta-level application, i.e. the application available in the logical framework. Hypothetical judgments are also directly supported by the framework.

On the other hand, inductive definitions are frequent in mathematics and semantics of programming languages, and induction is an essential tool when developing proofs. Unfortunately it is well-known that a type defined by means of higher order abstract syntax cannot be defined as an inductive type in usual inductive type theories (like CCI [Wer94], [PM92], or Martin-Löf's Logical Framework [NPS90] for instance).

In a first step towards the resolution of this dilemma, Frank Pfenning, Carsten Schürmann and the first author have presented ([DPS97]) an extension of the simply-typed $\lambda$-calculus with recursive constructs (operators for iteration and case reasoning), which enables the use of higher order abstract syntax in an inductive type. To achieve that, they use the operator '$\Box$' of modal logic IS4 to distinguish the types '$A \to B$' of the functional terms well-typed in the simply-typed $\lambda$-calculus from the types '$\Box A \to B$' of the functional terms possibly containing recursive constructs.

In this paper, we present an alternative presentation of their system that we claim to be better in several aspects. We use the same mechanism as theirs to mix higher order abstract syntax and induction but our typing and reduction rules are quite different. Indeed there are several presentations of modal $\lambda$-calculus IS4 ([BdP96], [PW95], [DP96]). We have chosen the variant by Frank Pfenning and Hao-Chi Wong ([PW95]), which has context stacks instead of simple contexts. This peculiarity creates some difficulties in the metatheoretical study but the terms generated by the syntax are simpler than those of [DPS97] (no 'let box' construction), and so this system is more comfortable to use.

Moreover, instead of introducing an operational semantics which computes the canonical form ($\eta$-long normal form) using a given strategy, our system has reduction rules, which allow a certain nondeterminism in the mechanism of reduction. We have been able to adapt classic proof techniques to show the important metatheoretic results: decidability of typability, soundness of typing with respect to typing rules, Church-Rosser property (CR), Strong Normalization property (SN) and conservativity of our system with respect to the simply-typed $\lambda$-calculus. The main problems we encountered in the proofs are on one hand due to the use of functional types in the types of the recursive constructors, and on the other hand due to the use of $\eta$-expansion. To solve the problems due to $\eta$-expansion, we benefit from previous works done for the simply-typed $\lambda$-calculus ([JG95]) and for system F ([Gha96]).

In the second section of the paper, we introduce our version of the modal inductive system, its syntax, its typing and reduction rules. Then in the third section, we prove its essential properties (soundness of typing, CR, SN) from which we deduce that it is a conservative extension of the simply-typed $\lambda$-calculus. Finally, we discuss related works and outline future work. A full version of this paper with complete technical developments is available in [Lel97].

## 2 The System

In this section, we present the syntax, the typing rules and the semantics of our system. First, let us briefly recall our motivations.

### 2.1 Higher-Order Abstract Syntax

The mechanics of higher order abstract syntax (HOAS) has already been exposed in many places, for example in [HHP93]. Let us introduce here a simple example of representation using HOAS, that will be useful later when we illustrate the mechanism of the reduction rules.

Suppose we want to represent the untyped $\lambda$-terms in the simply-typed $\lambda$-calculus with no extra equations. We introduce the type $L$ of untyped $\lambda$-terms together with two constructors $\texttt{lam} : (\texttt{L} \to \texttt{L}) \to \texttt{L}$ and $\texttt{app} : \texttt{L} \to \texttt{L} \to \texttt{L}$.

It is well-known ([HHP93]) that the canonical forms ($\beta$-normal $\eta$-long) of type $L$ are in one-to-one correspondence with the closed untyped $\lambda$-terms and that this correspondence is compositional. For instance the term of type $L$ (`lam` $\lambda$`x` : `L.(app x x)`) represents the untyped $\lambda$-term $\lambda x.(x\ x)$.

Now, these constructors do not define an inductive type in usual inductive type theories like the Calculus of Inductive Constructions ([Wer94]) or the Extended Calculus of Constructions ([Luo94]) because of the leftmost occurence of $L$ in the type of constructor lam. If we allowed this kind of inductive definition, we would be confronted with two serious problems. First, we would lose the one-to-one correspondence between the objects we represent and the canonical forms of type $L \to \cdots \to L$. For instance, if we have a Case construct (definition of a function by case over inductive terms), the term (`lam` $\lambda$`x` : `L.Case x of ...`) does not represent any untyped $\lambda$-term. Moreover we would lose the important property of strong normalization; more precisely we could write terms which would reduce to themselves. Our goal is to introduce a system which repairs these deficiencies.

Following [DPS97], we will use the modal operator '$\Box$' of modal logic IS4 to distinguish the types '$A \to B$' of the functional terms well-typed in the simply-typed $\lambda$-calculus from the types '$\Box A \to B$' of the functional terms possibly containing recursive contructs. For instance, in our system, a term such as '$\lambda x$ : $L$.Case $x$ of ...' will have type $\Box L \to L$ whereas constructor 'lam' will have type $(L \to L) \to L$. Thus, our typing judgment will rule out undesirable terms such as '(lam $\lambda x : L$.Case $x$ of ...)'.

## 2.2 Syntax

The system we present here is roughly the simply-typed $\lambda$-calculus extended by pairs, modality IS4 and recursion. We discuss the addition of polymorphism and dependent types in the conclusion.

**Types** To describe the types of the system, we consider a countable collection of constant types $L_j$ ($j \in \mathbb{N}$), called the *ground* types. In our approach, they play the role of *inductive* types. The *types* are inductively defined by:

$$\text{Types} : T := L_j \mid T_1 \to T_2 \mid T_1 \times T_2 \mid \Box T$$

A type is said to be *pure* if it contains no '$\Box$' operator and no product.

**Context stacks** Following the presentation of [PW95], we have *context stacks* instead of simple contexts. As usual a context $\Gamma$ is defined as a list of unordered declarations $x : A$ where all the variables are distinct. A *context stack* $\Delta$ is an ordered list of contexts, separated by semi colons $\Gamma_1; \ldots; \Gamma_n$. '.' denotes the empty context as well as the empty stack.

*Notations.* A context stack is said to be *valid* if all the variables of the stack are distinct. We call *local* context of a stack $\Delta = \Gamma_1; \ldots; \Gamma_n$ the last context of the stack: $\Gamma_n$. The notation '$\Delta, \Gamma$', where $\Delta$ is a stack $\Gamma_1; \ldots; \Gamma_n$ and $\Gamma$ is a context, is the stack $\Gamma_1;\ldots;\Gamma_n,\Gamma$. Similarly, the notation '$\Delta,\Delta'$', where $\Delta$ is the stack $\Gamma_1;\ldots;\Gamma_n$ and $\Delta'$ is the stack $\Gamma'_1;\ldots;\Gamma'_m$, is the stack $\Gamma_1;\ldots;\Gamma_n,\Gamma'_1;\ldots;\Gamma'_m$. If $\Delta$ is a valid stack of $m$ contexts $\Gamma_1;\ldots;\Gamma_m$ and $n$ is an integer, $\Delta^n$ denotes the stack $\Delta$ where the last $n$ contexts have been removed: $\Gamma_1;\ldots;\Gamma_{m-n}$ if $n < m$, and the empty stack '.' if $n \geq m$.

**Terms** We view open terms of type $L$, depending on $n$ variables of type $L$, as *functional terms* of type $L_n = L \to \cdots \to L \to L$, as in [DH94]. For example, terms in the untyped $\lambda$-calculus given in Section 2.1 will have three possible forms, involving what we called *higher-order constructors*, written with vectorial notations:

$$\begin{array}{l} \text{app} : \lambda\overrightarrow{x} : \overrightarrow{L}.(\text{app}\ P\ Q) \\ \text{lam} : \lambda\overrightarrow{x} : \overrightarrow{L}.(\text{lam}\ P) \\ \text{var} : \lambda\overrightarrow{x} : \overrightarrow{L}.x_i \end{array}$$

In general of course, the type of a constructor of a pure type $L$ contains other types than $L$. Before describing the set of the terms, we consider a finite collection of constant terms (the *constructors*) $C_{j,k}$, given with their pure type: $(B_{j,k,1} \to \cdots \to B_{j,k,n_{j,k}}) \to L_j$ , where each $B_{j,k,l}$ is a pure type and $L_j$ is a ground type. If $n_{j,k} = 0$, the type of $C_{j,k}$ is simply $L_j$.

The *terms* are inductively defined by:

$$\begin{array}{rl} \text{Terms} : M := & x \mid C_{j,k} \mid (M\ N) \mid \lambda x : A.M \mid \uparrow M \mid \downarrow M \mid \langle M_1, M_2\rangle \\ & \mid \text{fst}\ M \mid \text{snd}\ M \mid \langle\sigma\rangle\text{Case}\ M\ \text{ of }\ (M_{j,k}) \mid \langle\sigma\rangle\text{It}\ M\ \text{ of }\ ({M'}_{j,k}) \end{array}$$

where $\sigma$ is a function mapping the ground types $L_j (j \in \mathbb{N})$ to types, $(M_{j,k})$ and $({M'}_{j,k})$ are collections of terms indexed by the indexes of the constructors.

We delay till Section 2.7 the explanation of the arguments of operators 'Case' and 'It'. The modal operator '$\uparrow$' introduces an object of type $\Box A$ while the operator '$\downarrow$' marks the elimination of a term of type $\Box A$. As usual, terms equivalent under $\alpha$-conversion are identified.

## 2.3 Typing Rules for Case and It on a Simple Example

We give here the typing rules for Case and It for the untyped $\lambda$-calculus example of Section 2.1. Except for the use of the $\Box$ operator, and the use of $L_n$ instead of $L$, there are pretty standard for the app case. Note how the use of $L_n$ enables us to extend the usual case (app) to the fonctional case (lam) in an intuitive manner:

$$\frac{\Delta \vdash M : \Box L_n \qquad \Delta \vdash M_{\text{app}} : \Box L_n \to \Box L_n \to A \qquad \Delta \vdash M_{\text{lam}} : \Box L_{n+1} \to A}{\Delta \vdash \langle\sigma\rangle\text{Case}\ M \text{ of } M_{\text{app}}\ M_{\text{lam}} : A_n}$$

$$\frac{\Delta \vdash M : \Box L_n \qquad \Delta \vdash M'_{\text{app}} : A \to A \to A \qquad \Delta \vdash M'_{\text{lam}} : (A \to A) \to A}{\Delta \vdash \langle\sigma\rangle\text{It}\ M \text{ of } M'_{\text{app}}\ M'_{\text{lam}} : A_n}$$

where $A = \sigma(L)$ is the resulting type of the case or iteration process on $M$.

The Case and It functions take as arguments the resulting values for the $n$ variables of the term $M$ being analysed; hence the resulting type $A_n$ for both operators in the above rules.

### 2.4 Examples

Let us assume that we have defined the types of the integers 'Nat' by declaring two constructors '$0$ : Nat' and '$S$ : Nat $\to$ Nat'. We can informally define the function which counts the number of bound variables in an untyped $\lambda$-term by:

- $\text{Count}(\text{app } M\ N) = \text{Count}(M) + \text{Count}(N)$
- $\text{Count}(\text{lam } \lambda x : L.(M\ x)) = \text{Count}(M\ x)$, where $\text{Count}(x) = 1$

This function can be implemented in our system using the It construct, where $\sigma = \{L \mapsto Nat\}$. Count has type $\Box L \to \Box\text{Nat}$:

$$\text{Count} := (\langle\sigma\rangle\text{It}\ \ \lambda m, n : \Box\text{Nat..(plus } m\ n)\ \ \lambda p : \Box\text{Nat} \to \Box\text{Nat.}(p \uparrow (S\ 0)))$$

The function 'Form' of type $\Box(L \to L) \to \text{Nat}$, which returns 0 if its argument is a free variable, 1 if it is an abstraction term and 2 if it is an application, can be defined as follows:

$$\text{Form } M := (\langle\sigma\rangle\text{Case}\ \ M\ \ \text{of}\ \ \lambda u, v : \Box(L \to L)..2\ \ \lambda f : \Box(L \to L \to L).1\ \ \ 0)$$

### 2.5 Typing Rules

The typing rules are a combination of the rules for simply-typed $\lambda$-calculus, for pairs and projections, for modal $\lambda$-calculus IS4 ([PW95]) and the new rules for the recursive constructs 'Case' and 'It'. Due to lack of place we do not give the rules for pairs and projections in this extended abstract. The rules are written in Figure 1 with the following notations:

**Notations** $B_{j,k,1}, \ldots, B_{j,k,n_{j,k}}$ are pure types. $L_j$ is an inductive type. $(T_i)_{i=1,\ldots,p}$ is a collection, possibly empty, of pure types. Each $T_i$ can be decomposed as $T_i{}^1 \to \cdots \to T_i{}^{r_i} \to L_i$, where $L_i$ is a ground type and each $T_i{}^j$ is a pure type.

Given the types $C$, $D_1, \ldots, D_p$, we denote $D_1 \to \cdots \to D_p \to C$ by $\prod_{i=1}^{i=p} D_i.C$.

We define $T'_z$ by:

$$T'_z := \Box(T_1 \to \cdots \to T_p \to T_z^1) \to \cdots \to \Box(T_1 \to \cdots \to T_p \to T_z^{r_z}) \to \sigma(L_z)$$

The map $\sigma$ from ground types to types is extended over pure types by the equation: $\sigma(A \to B) = \sigma(A) \to \sigma(B)$.

These typing rules may seem complex at first sight but they are naturally derived from the behaviour of the Case and It operators with respect to reduction (sections 2.7, 2.8).

Although expressed differently, our typing rules are similar to those in [DPS96] (in which one can find many examples), with a more user friendly modal core.

$$\text{(Var)}\ \frac{x : A \in \text{local context of } \Delta}{\Delta \vdash x : A}\ \Delta \text{ valid}$$

$$(\lambda)\ \frac{\Delta, x : A \vdash M : B}{\Delta \vdash \lambda x : A.M\ :\ A \to B} \qquad \text{(App)}\ \frac{\Delta \vdash M : A \to B \quad \Delta \vdash N : A}{\Delta \vdash (M\ N) : B}$$

$$(\uparrow)\ \frac{\Delta ; . \vdash M : A}{\Delta \vdash \uparrow M : \Box A} \qquad (\downarrow)\ \frac{\Delta \vdash M : \Box A}{\Delta \vdash \downarrow M : A} \qquad \text{(Pop)}\ \frac{\Delta \vdash M : \Box A}{\Delta ; \Gamma \vdash M : \Box A}\ \Delta ; \Gamma \text{ valid}$$

$$(C_{j,k})\ \frac{}{\Delta \vdash C_{j,k} : B_{j,k,1} \to \cdots \to B_{j,k,n_{j,k}} \to L_j}\ \Delta \text{ valid}, n_{j,k} \in \mathbb{N}$$

$$\text{(Case)}\ \frac{\Delta \vdash M : \Box \left( \prod_{i=1}^{i=p} T_i.L_n \right) \quad \Delta \vdash M_{j,k} : \prod_{q=1}^{q=n_{j,k}} \Box \left( \prod_{i=1}^{i=p} T_i.B_{j,k,q} \right).\sigma(L_j)}{\Delta \vdash \langle \sigma \rangle \text{Case } M \text{ of } (M_{j,k}) : \prod_{z=1}^{z=p} T'_z.\sigma(L_n)}$$

$$\text{(It)}\ \frac{\Delta \vdash M : \Box \left( \prod_{i=1}^{i=p} T_i.L_n \right) \quad \Delta \vdash M'_{j,k} : \prod_{q=1}^{q=n_{j,k}} \sigma(B_{j,k,q}).\sigma(L_j)}{\Delta \vdash \langle \sigma \rangle \text{It } M \text{ of } (M'_{j,k}) : \prod_{i=1}^{i=p} \sigma(T_i).\sigma(L_n)}$$

**Fig. 1.** Typing rules

## 2.6 Basic Properties

The system allows the same basic stack manipulations as the modal $\lambda$-calculus IS4 without Case and It ([PW95]). In particular, as usual, the typing judgments are preserved by thinning and strengthening. Later, these properties will still be true for typed reduction and the interpretations of types.

The substitution rule is still admissible.

The inversion lemmas are not totally trivial because our typing rules are not syntax-driven. If we try to type a term of type $\Box A$, we can always apply rule (Pop) as well as the structural rule for $M$. Nevertheless, they remain fairly simple (see [Lel97]).

## 2.7 Reduction Rules for Case and It on a Simple Example

Now, we turn to the reduction rules of our system. They are inspired by the reduction rules for Case and It that have been suggested to us by Martin Hofmann as a means to describe the evaluation mechanism of [DPS97]. These reduction rules are also the ones underlying the terms and induction principles presented in [DH94] in the Calculus of Inductive Constructions. Indeed this research was undertaken with this main idea in mind: our approach to HOAS (i.e. considering terms in $L_n = L \to \cdots \to L$ instead of terms of type $L$ ([DH94])) should lead to a much more elegant system than the usual approach. The result seems to confirm our intuition.

First we show the reduction rules for Case and It in the simple setting of the example of Section 2.1. For the sake of simplicity we introduce some notations.

**Notations.** For any type $B$, the type $B_n$ ($n \in \mathbb{N}$) is defined by $B_0 := B$ and $B_{n+1} := B \to B_n$. We consider a map $\sigma$ from the inductive types to types such that $\sigma(L) = A$, terms $M_{\text{app}}$ of type $\Box L_n \to \Box L_n \to A$, $M_{\text{lam}}$ of type $\Box L_{n+1} \to A$, $M'_{\text{app}}$ of type $A \to A \to A$ and $M'_{\text{lam}}$ of type $(A \to A) \to A$. We define two macros 'case' and 'it' by:

$$\text{case } M := \langle\sigma\rangle\text{Case } M \text{ of } M_{\text{app}}\ M_{\text{lam}}$$
$$\text{it } M := \langle\sigma\rangle\text{It } M \text{ of } M'_{\text{app}}\ M'_{\text{lam}}$$

**Reduction rules.** In our example, the reduction rules for Case and It are the following ones:

$$(\text{case } \uparrow \lambda\vec{x} : \vec{L}.(\text{app } P\ Q)) \hookrightarrow \lambda\vec{u} : \vec{A}.(M_{\text{app}}\ \uparrow \lambda\vec{x} : \vec{L}.P\ \uparrow \lambda\vec{x} : \vec{L}.Q)$$
$$(\text{case } \uparrow \lambda\vec{x} : \vec{L}.(\text{lam } P)) \hookrightarrow \lambda\vec{u} : \vec{A}.(M_{\text{lam}}\ \uparrow \lambda\vec{x} : \vec{L}.P)$$
$$(\text{case } \uparrow \lambda\vec{x} : \vec{L}.x_i) \hookrightarrow \lambda\vec{u} : \vec{A}.u_i$$

$$(\text{it } \uparrow \lambda\vec{x} : \vec{L}.(\text{app } P\ Q)) \hookrightarrow \lambda\vec{u} : \vec{A}.(M'_{\text{app}}\ ((\text{it } \uparrow \lambda\vec{x} : \vec{L}.P)\ \vec{u})\ ((\text{it } \uparrow \lambda\vec{x} : \vec{L}.Q)\ \vec{u}))$$
$$(\text{it } \uparrow \lambda\vec{x} : \vec{L}.(\text{lam } P)) \hookrightarrow \lambda\vec{u} : \vec{A}.(M'_{\text{lam}}\ ((\text{it } \uparrow \lambda\vec{x} : \vec{L}.P)\ \vec{u}))$$
$$(\text{it } \uparrow \lambda\vec{x} : \vec{L}.x_i) \hookrightarrow \lambda\vec{u} : \vec{A}.u_i$$

The first argument of the Case and It constructs, $M$, is the inductive term to analyze (representing an untyped $\lambda$-term in our example). The second one, $M_{\text{app}}$, is the function which processes the case of constructor 'app'. The third argument, $M_{\text{lam}}$, is the function which processes the case of constructor 'lam'. Roughly speaking the 'Case' construct computes its result by applying $M_{\text{app}}$ or $M_{\text{lam}}$ to the sons of its main argument. For iteration, the mechanism of reduction is a bit different: the terms $M'_{\text{app}}$ and $M'_{\text{lam}}$ are applied to the result of 'It' on the sons of the main argument. Operationally, the effect of 'It' on a term $M$ amounts to replacing the constructors lam and app by the terms $M'_{\text{lam}}$ and $M'_{\text{app}}$ in $M$ (see [DPS97]).

Now since we want to benefit from higher order declarations, the main argument of Case/It may have a functional type. In particular we also want to be able to compute Case/It of a projection $\lambda\vec{x} : \vec{L}.x_i$ without a leftmost constructor. That is the reason for the functional type of Case/It constructs : they take as input the values of the computation for the projections (see [DPS97]).

## 2.8 Reduction Rules

Now we describe the whole set of reduction rules. Given a term of our calculus, what we want to obtain at the end of the computation is the term of the object language it represents. As we have seen earlier (Section 2.1), the canonical forms ($\beta$-normal $\eta$-long) are in one-to-one correspondence with the object terms. Thus we want the computation to return canonical forms. That means our reduction rules will incorporate $\eta$-expansion.

The $\eta$-expansion reduction rule has been thoroughly studied (see [CK93], [Aka93], [JG95]). Adopting it forces us to restrict the reduction rules in some way if we still want Strong Normalization. Thus the reduction we will consider will not be a congruence (more precisely it will not be compatible with the application) and this will induce slight changes in the usual schemes of the proofs of the Church-Rosser and Strong Normalization properties.

The choice of $\eta$-expansion also means we have to keep track of the types of the terms. Indeed a term can only be $\eta$-expanded if it has type $A \to B$. Thus we will define a notion of typed reduction.

The reduction relation is defined by the inference rules in Figures 2 (simple types and modality) and 3 (Case and It). We have omitted the product rules and the compatibility rules other than ($\mathrm{App_l}$), which are straightforward.

$$(\beta)\ \frac{\Delta \vdash (\lambda x : A.P\ \ Q) : B}{\Delta \vdash (\lambda x : A.P\ \ Q) \hookrightarrow P[Q/x] : B} \qquad (\beta\Box)\ \frac{\Delta \vdash \downarrow\uparrow M : A}{\Delta \vdash \downarrow\uparrow M \hookrightarrow M : A}$$

$$(\eta)\ \frac{\Delta \vdash M : A \to B \quad M \text{ not an abstraction} \quad x \text{ fresh}}{\Delta \vdash M \hookrightarrow \lambda x : A.(M\ x) : A \to B} \qquad (\eta\Box)\ \frac{\Delta \vdash \uparrow\downarrow M : \Box A}{\Delta \vdash \uparrow\downarrow M \hookrightarrow M : \Box A}$$

$$(\mathrm{App_l})\ \frac{\Delta \vdash M \hookrightarrow M' : A \to B\ (\neq \eta\text{-step}) \quad \Delta \vdash N : A}{\Delta \vdash (M\ \ N) \hookrightarrow (M'\ \ N) : B} \qquad (\mathrm{Pop})\ \frac{\Delta \vdash M \hookrightarrow N : \Box A}{\Delta; \Gamma \vdash M \hookrightarrow N : \Box A}$$

**Fig. 2.** Reduction rules. Simple types and modality

As usual we define the relations $\hookrightarrow_*$ and $=$ (conversion) respectively as the reflexive, transitive and the reflexive, symmetric, transitive closures of $\hookrightarrow$.

# 3 Metatheoretical Results

The classic properties of subject reduction, confluence and strong normalization have already been established for a modal $\lambda$-calculus IS4 without induction ([Lel98a]). Here we extend these results to the recursive operators Case and It.

## 3.1 First Results

First, we state soundness of typed reduction with respect to typing rules. It is easily proved by induction on the derivation of the first hypothesis.

**Theorem 1 (Soundness of reduction).**
*If $\Delta \vdash M \hookrightarrow M' : A$ then $\Delta \vdash M : A$ and $\Delta \vdash M' : A$.*

$$(\text{Case } C_{j,k})\ \frac{\Delta \vdash \langle\sigma\rangle\text{Case } \uparrow \lambda\vec{x} : \vec{T}.(C_{j,k}\ M_1 \ldots M_{n_{j,k}})\ \text{of}\ (M_{j,k}) : \prod_{z=1}^{z=p} T'_z.\sigma(L_n)}{\begin{array}{l}\Delta \vdash \langle\sigma\rangle\text{Case } \uparrow \lambda\vec{x} : \vec{T}.(C_{j,k}\ M_1 \ldots M_{n_{j,k}})\ \text{of}\ (M_{j,k}) \hookrightarrow \\ \qquad \lambda\vec{u} : \vec{T'}.(M_{j,k}\ \ \uparrow \lambda\vec{x} : \vec{T}.M_1\ \ldots\ \uparrow \lambda\vec{x} : \vec{T}.M_{n_{j,k}}) : \prod_{z=1}^{z=p} T'_z.\sigma(L_n)\end{array}}$$

$$(\text{Case } x_k)\ \frac{\Delta \vdash \langle\sigma\rangle\text{Case } \uparrow \lambda\vec{x} : \vec{T}.(x_k\ M_1 \ldots M_{r_k})\ \text{of}\ (M_{j,k}) : \prod_{z=1}^{z=p} T'_z.\sigma(L_n)}{\begin{array}{l}\Delta \vdash \langle\sigma\rangle\text{Case } \uparrow \lambda\vec{x} : \vec{T}.(x_k\ M_1 \ldots M_{r_k})\ \text{of}\ (M_{j,k}) \hookrightarrow \\ \qquad \lambda\vec{u} : \vec{T'}.(u_k\ \ \uparrow \lambda\vec{x} : \vec{T}.M_1\ \ldots\ \uparrow \lambda\vec{x} : \vec{T}.M_{r_k}) : \prod_{z=1}^{z=p} T'_z.\sigma(L_n)\end{array}}$$

$$(\text{It } C_{j,k})\ \frac{\Delta \vdash \langle\sigma\rangle\text{It } \uparrow \lambda\vec{x} : \vec{T}.(C_{j,k}\ M_1 \ldots M_{n_{j,k}})\ \text{of}\ (M'_{j,k}) : \prod_{i=1}^{i=p} \sigma(T_i).\sigma(L_n)}{\begin{array}{l}\Delta \vdash \langle\sigma\rangle\text{It } \uparrow \lambda\vec{x} : \vec{T}.(C_{j,k}\ M_1 \ldots M_{n_{j,k}})\ \text{of}\ (M'_{j,k}) \hookrightarrow \\ \quad \lambda\vec{u} : \overrightarrow{\sigma(T)}.(M'_{j,k}\ \ ((\langle\sigma\rangle\text{It } \uparrow \lambda\vec{x} : \vec{T}.M_1\ \text{of}\ (M'_{j,k})\ \ \vec{u})\ \ldots \\ \qquad\qquad ((\langle\sigma\rangle\text{It } \uparrow \lambda\vec{x} : \vec{T}.M_{n_{j,k}}\ \text{of}\ (M'_{j,k})\ \ \vec{u})) : \prod_{i=1}^{i=p} \sigma(T_i).\sigma(L_n)\end{array}}$$

$$(\text{It } x_k)\ \frac{\Delta \vdash \langle\sigma\rangle\text{It } \uparrow \lambda\vec{x} : \vec{T}.(x_k\ M_1 \ldots M_{r_k})\ \text{of}\ (M'_{j,k}) : \prod_{i=1}^{i=p} \sigma(T_i).\sigma(L_n)}{\begin{array}{l}\Delta \vdash \langle\sigma\rangle\text{It } \uparrow \lambda\vec{x} : \vec{T}.(x_k\ M_1 \ldots M_{r_k})\ \text{of}\ (M'_{j,k}) \hookrightarrow \\ \quad \lambda\vec{u} : \overrightarrow{\sigma(T)}.(u_k\ \ ((\langle\sigma\rangle\text{It } \uparrow \lambda\vec{x} : \vec{T}.M_1\ \text{of}\ (M'_{j,k})\ \ \vec{u})\ \ldots \\ \qquad\qquad ((\langle\sigma\rangle\text{It } \uparrow \lambda\vec{x} : \vec{T}.M_{r_k}\ \text{of}\ (M'_{j,k})\ \ \vec{u})) : \prod_{i=1}^{i=p} \sigma(T_i).\sigma(L_n)\end{array}}$$

**Fig. 3.** Reduction rules for Case and It

The relationship between substitution and typed reduction is not as easy as in the simply-typed $\lambda$-calculus. If $P \hookrightarrow_* P'$ and $Q \hookrightarrow_* Q'$ then we do not have any more $P[Q/x] \hookrightarrow_* P'[Q'/x]$ because of the side-conditions of reduction rules ($\eta$) and ($\text{App}_{\text{l}}$). Thus we only prove weak forms of the usual results. For instance, if $\Delta, x : A \vdash P : B$ and $\Delta \vdash Q \hookrightarrow Q' : A$, we only state that there is a term $R$ such that $\Delta \vdash P[Q/x] \hookrightarrow_* R : B$ and $\Delta \vdash P[Q'/x] \hookrightarrow_* R : B$. Nevertheless, these results enable us to prove the local confluence property:

**Lemma 1 (Local Confluence).**
*If $\Delta \vdash M \hookrightarrow N : A$ and $\Delta \vdash M \hookrightarrow P : A$ then there is a term $Q$ such that $\Delta \vdash N \hookrightarrow_* Q : A$ and $\Delta \vdash P \hookrightarrow_* Q : A$.*

### 3.2 Strong Normalization

Now we briefly sketch our proof of the Strong Normalization theorem for our system. The proof follows the idea of normalization proofs 'à la Tait' and is inspired by [Wer94] (for the inductive part) and [Gha96] (for the $\eta$-expansion part).

**Reducibility Candidates**

First we give a definition of the reducibility candidates ([GLT89]) adapted to our setting. Let us call $\Lambda$ the set of our terms, defined in Section 2.2.

**Definition 1 (Reducibility Candidates).**
*Given a type A, the* reducibility candidates $CR_A$ *are sets of pairs* $(\Delta, M)$ *of a context stack and a term. They are defined as follows:*

**CR1** $\forall(\Delta, M) \in \mathcal{C}$, *M is strongly normalizing in* $\Delta$ *(i.e. there is no infinite sequence of reductions starting from M in* $\Delta$*).*
**CR1'** $\mathcal{C} \subset \{(\Delta, M) \mid \Delta \vdash M : A\}$
**CR2** $\forall(\Delta, M) \in \mathcal{C}$ *such that* $\Delta \vdash M \hookrightarrow M' : A$, *we have* $(\Delta, M') \in \mathcal{C}$.
**CR3** *If* $M \in \mathcal{NT}$, $\Delta \vdash M : A$ *and* $\forall M'$ *such that* $\Delta \vdash M \hookrightarrow M' : A$ ($\neq$ $\eta$*-expansion*), $(\Delta, M') \in \mathcal{C}$ *then we have* $(\Delta, M) \in \mathcal{C}$.
**CR4** *If* $A = B \to C$ *and* $(\Delta, M) \in \mathcal{C}$ *then* $(\Delta, \lambda z : B.(M\ \ z)) \in \mathcal{C}$, *where z is a fresh variable.*

*where* $\mathcal{NT} = \Lambda \backslash (\{\lambda x : A.M \mid M \in \Lambda\} \cup \{\uparrow M \mid M \in \Lambda\} \cup \{\langle M, N\rangle \mid M, N \in \Lambda\})$.

Note that instead of taking sets of terms, we consider sets of pairs of a stack and a term. Indeed, since, because of $\eta$-expansion, our reduction is typed, it is convenient for the reducibility candidates to contain well-typed terms. In rule CR3, the restriction "$\Delta \vdash M \hookrightarrow M' : A$ is not an $\eta$-expansion" comes from [JG95]. It has been introduced to cope with $\eta$-expansions. The rule CR4 is also needed because of the $\eta$-expansions ([Gha96]).

As usual, if $\mathcal{C}$ and $\mathcal{D}$ belong to $\text{CR}_A$ then $\mathcal{C} \cap \mathcal{D}$ belong to $\text{CR}_A$. Thus $\text{CR}_A$ is an *inf-semi lattice*. Next, we define the sets $\mathcal{C} \to \mathcal{D}$, $\mathcal{C} \times \mathcal{D}$, $\Box\mathcal{C}$ where $\mathcal{C}$ and $\mathcal{D}$ are two reducibility candidates:

**Definition 2 ($\mathcal{C} \to \mathcal{D}$, $\Box\mathcal{C}$, $\mathcal{C} \times \mathcal{D}$).**

- $\mathcal{C} \to \mathcal{D} := \{(\Delta, M) \mid \Delta \vdash M : A \to B$ *and* $\forall \Gamma, \forall((\Delta, \Gamma), N) \in \mathcal{C}$, $((\Delta, \Gamma), (M\ \ N)) \in \mathcal{D}\}$
- $\Box\mathcal{C} := \{(\Delta, M) \mid \Delta \vdash M : \Box A$ *and* $\forall \Delta'$ *stack s.t.* $(\Delta, \Delta')$ *is valid*, $((\Delta, \Delta'), \downarrow M) \in \mathcal{C}\}$.
- $\mathcal{C} \times \mathcal{D} := \{(\Delta, M) \mid \Delta \vdash M : A \times B$ *and* $\forall \Gamma$ *context s.t.* $(\Delta, \Gamma)$ *is valid*, $((\Delta, \Gamma), \mathit{fst}\ M) \in \mathcal{C}$ *and* $((\Delta, \Gamma), \mathit{snd}\ M) \in \mathcal{D}\}$.

In the definition of $\Box\mathcal{C}$, we need to extend the stack of contexts $\Delta$ with $\Delta'$ in order to get $((\Delta, \Delta'), M) \in \Box\mathcal{C}$ whenever $(\Delta, M) \in \Box\mathcal{C}$ (similarly to the case of $\mathcal{C} \to \mathcal{D}$).

In the definition of $\mathcal{C} \to \mathcal{D}$, the context $\Gamma$ added to the stack is essential; In the intermediate lemmas, it allows us to add fresh variables to the context.

**Proposition 1.** *If* $\mathcal{C}$ *and* $\mathcal{D}$ *are C.R., then* $\mathcal{C} \to \mathcal{D}$, $\mathcal{C} \times \mathcal{D}$ *and* $\Box\mathcal{C}$ *are C.R..*

**Interpretation of types and contexts**

Following the sketch of normalization proofs 'à la Tait', we define the interpretations of types.

**Definition 3 (Interpretations of types).**

- $[\![L_j]\!] := \{(\Delta, M) \mid \Delta \vdash M : L_j$ *and* $M$ *is SN in* $\Delta\}$,
- $[\![A \to B]\!] := [\![A]\!] \to [\![B]\!]$,
- $[\![A \times B]\!] := [\![A]\!] \times [\![B]\!]$,
- *If* $A$ *is not pure,* $[\![\Box A]\!] := \Box[\![A]\!]$

All the above interpretations are obviously C.Rs., except, maybe, for the first case:

**Proposition 2 ($[\![L_j]\!]$ is a C.R.).**
*The set* $[\![L_j]\!]$ *is a reducibility candidate.*

In order to define $[\![\Box A]\!]$ in the case $A$ is pure, we have to take into account the fact that $\Box A$ may be the type of the inductive argument of Case/It. The definition of $[\![\Box A]\!]$ in this case involves the smallest fixpoint of a function we do not give here, because of space limitation (see [Lel97]).

At this point, we have defined the interpretation of type $[\![A]\!]$ for all the types $A$. The following theorem stems from the definitions of the interpretations of types.

**Theorem 2 ($[\![A]\!]$ is a C.R.).**
*Given any type* $A$*, the set* $[\![A]\!]$ *is a C.R.*

Then we define the notion of *interpretation of context stack.* Like in the classic case of the simply-typed $\lambda$-calculus, the *interpretation* $[\![\Delta]\!]_\Psi$ of stack $\Delta$ in stack $\Psi$ is a set of substitutions from $\Delta$ to $\Psi$ but the definition is a bit more complex here because we have to deal with context stacks, instead of simple contexts. Thus we use a non standard notion of substitution.

**Definition 4 (Pre-substitution).**
*A* pre-substitution $\rho$ *from a stack* $\Delta$ *to a stack* $\Psi$ *is a mapping from the set of the variables declared in* $\Delta$ *into the set of the terms with all their free variables in* $\Psi$*.*

*A* pre-substitution $\rho$ *can be applied to a term* $M$ *with all its free variables in* $\Delta$*. The result of this operation, denoted by* $\rho(M)$*, is equal to term* $M$ *where all its free variables* $x$ *have been replaced by their images under* $\rho$*,* $\rho(x)$*.*

**Notations.** Given two stacks $\Delta$ and $\Psi$, a pre-substitution $\rho$ from $\Delta$ to $\Psi$, a variable $x$ not declared in $\Delta$ and $M$ a term with all its free variables in $\Psi$, we denote by $\rho[x \mapsto M]$ the pre-substitution from $\Delta, x : A$ to $\Psi$ such that $\rho[x \mapsto M](y) = \rho(y)$ if $y$ is declared in $\Delta$ and $\rho[x \mapsto M](x) = M$.

Given a stack $\Delta'$ such that $\Delta; \Delta'$ is valid and a substitution $\rho'$ from $\Delta'$ to $\Psi$, '$\rho; \rho'$' denotes the pre-substitution from $\Delta; \Delta'$ to $\Psi$ such that $(\rho; \rho')(x) = \rho(x)$ if $x$ is declared in $\Delta$ and $(\rho; \rho')(x) = \rho'(x)$ if $x$ is declared in $\Delta'$.

**Definition 5 (Interpretation of context stack).**
*Given two stacks* $\Delta$ *and* $\Psi$, *the* interpretation *of* $\Delta$ *in* $\Psi$, $[\![\Delta]\!]_\Psi$, *is a set of pre-substitutions from* $\Delta$ *to* $\Psi$. *It is defined by induction on* $\Delta$:

- $[\![.]\!]_\Psi$ *is the singleton whose only element is the empty pre-substitution from* . *to* $\Psi$.
- $[\![\Gamma, x : A]\!]_\Psi$ *is the set of the pre-substitutions* $\rho[x \mapsto M]$, *where* $\rho$ *belongs to* $[\![\Gamma]\!]_\Psi$ *and* $(\Psi, M)$ *is in* $[\![A]\!]$.
- $[\![\Delta; \Gamma]\!]_\Psi$ *is the set of pre-substitutions* $\rho; \rho'$ *such that* $\rho$ *belongs to* $[\![\Delta]\!]_{\Psi^n}$ $(n \in I\!N)$ *and* $\rho'$ *belongs to* $[\![\Gamma]\!]_\Psi$.

*where the notation* $\Psi^n$ *has been previously defined in Section 2.2.*

In the definition of $[\![\Delta; \Gamma]\!]_\Psi$, the requirement that $\rho$ belongs to $[\![\Delta]\!]_{\Psi^n}$, more flexible than the requirement that $\rho$ belongs to $[\![\Delta]\!]_\Psi$, enables us to cope with the context stacks in the proofs. For example, we will have that $\rho$ belongs to $[\![\Delta; .]\!]_{\Psi,\Psi'}$ whenever $\rho$ belongs to $[\![\Delta]\!]_\Psi$.

**Soundness of typing** The following lemma is proved by induction on the derivation of $\Delta \vdash M : A$. The most difficult case occurs for rule ($\uparrow$). It is solved by using the typing restrictions imposed by modality (see [Lel97]).

**Lemma 2 (Soundness of Typing).**
*If* $\Delta \vdash M : A$ *and* $\rho \in [\![\Delta]\!]_\Psi$, *then* $(\Psi, \rho(M)) \in [\![A]\!]$.

The strong normalization theorem is then an easy corollary, using the fact that for any stack $\Delta$, the pre-substitution identity from $\Delta$ to $\Delta$ belongs to $[\![\Delta]\!]_\Delta$.

**Theorem 3 (Strong Normalization).**
*There is no infinite sequence of reductions.*

### 3.3 Confluence and Conservative Extension

The *confluence* property is a corollary of the strong normalization (Theorem 3) and the local confluence results (this fact is often called "Newman's Lemma", after [New42]).

**Theorem 4 (Confluence).** *If* $\Delta \vdash M \hookrightarrow_* N : A$ *and* $\Delta \vdash M \hookrightarrow_* P : A$ *then there is a term* $Q$ *such that* $\Delta \vdash N \hookrightarrow_* Q : A$ *and* $\Delta \vdash P \hookrightarrow_* Q : A$.

As usual, the 'uniqueness of normal forms' property is a corollary of the strong normalization and confluence theorems.

**Corollary 1 (Uniqueness of normal forms).**
*If* $\Delta \vdash M : A$ *then* $M$ *reduces to a unique canonical form in* $\Delta$.

The *conservative extension* property uses the strong normalization result together with a technical lemma, that defines the possible forms of a canonical term [Lel97].

**Theorem 5 (Conservative extension).**
*Our system is a* conservative extension *of the simply-typed λ-calculus, i.e. if* $\Delta \vdash M : A$ *with* $\Delta$ *pure context stack and* $A$ *pure type then* $M$ *has a unique canonical form* $N$ *which is* pure.

## 4 Related Works

Our system has been inspired by [DPS97]. The main difference is that the underlying modal λ-calculus is easier to use and seems to be better adapted to a future extension to dependent types. Splitting the context in two parts (the intuitionistic and the modal parts) would most probably make the treatment of dependent types even more difficult: how should we represent a modal type which depends on both non-modal and modal types?

We also provide reduction rules, instead of a particular strategy for evaluation. Finally, due to that latter point and the fact that we have adapted well known proof methods, our metatheoretic proofs are much more compact and easier to read.

Raymond McDowell and Dale Miller have proposed [MM97] a meta-logic to reason about object logics coded using higher order abstract syntax. Their approach is quite different from ours, less ambitious in a sense. They do not give a typing system, supporting the judgments-as-types principle, but two logics: one for each level (object and meta). Moreover they only have induction on natural numbers, which can be used to derive other induction principles via the construction of an appropriate measure.

Frank Pfenning and Carsten Schürmann have also defined a meta-logic '$\mathcal{M}_2$', which allows inductive reasoning over HOAS encodings in LF([PS98]). It was designed to support automated theorem proving. This meta-logic has been implemented in the theorem prover Twelf, which gives a logical programming interpretation of $\mathcal{M}_2$. Twelf has been used to automatically prove properties such as type preservation for Mini-ML.

¿From our definition of valid terms in an object language $L_n = L \to \cdots \to L \to L$ implemented in the Calculus of Inductive Constructions, we derived an induction principle, that we claimed to be more natural, and more powerful, than the usual ones ([DH94]). Martin Hofmann recently formalized this induction principle in a modal meta-logic, using categorical tools [Hof99]. In this paper, he very nicely formalizes and compares, on the categorical level, several representations of terms using HOAS, and several induction principles currently used, sometimes without justifications, for fonctional terms.

## 5 Conclusion and Future Work

We have presented a modal λ-calculus IS4 with primitive recursive constructs that we claim to be better than the previous proposition [DPS97]. The conservative extension theorem, which guarantees that the adequacy of encodings is preserved, is proved as well as the Church-Rosser and strong normalization properties.

Our main goal is now to extend this system to dependent types and to polymorphic types. This kind of extension is not straightforward but we expect our system to be flexible enough to allow it. We have already proposed an extension of our system to dependent types, only with a "non-dependent" rule for eliminatin for the moment [DL99,Lel98b]. A full treatment of dependent types would have given an induction principle that we did not succeed in justifying in our setting. The work by Martin Hofmann [Hof99] suggests that we should be able to go further in this direction.

Another interesting direction of research consists in replacing our recursive operators by operators for pattern-matching such as those used in the ALF [MN94] system, implementing Martin-Löf's Type Theory [NPS90]. Some hints for a concrete syntax for that extension have been given in [DPS97]. F. Pfenning and C. Schürmann are currently working on the definition of a meta-logic along these lines.

**Acknowledgments** Thanks are due to Martin Hofmann for his suggestion for reduction rules which, stengthening us in the intuitions we had in previous works, make it possible the present results. We also thank Andr Hirschowitz for many fruitful discussions.

## References

[Aka93] Y. Akama. On Mints' reduction for ccc-calculus. In *Proceedings TLCA*, pages 1–12. Springer-Verlag LNCS 664, 1993.

[BdP96] Gavin Bierman and Valeria de Paiva. Intuitionistic necessity revisited. In *Technical Report CSRP-96-10*, School of Computer Science, University of Birmingham, June 1996.

[CK93] R. Di Cosmo and D. Kesner. A Confluent Reduction for the Extensional Typed λ-calculus. In *Proceedings ICALP'93*. Springer-Verlag LNCS 700, 1993.

[DH94] J. Despeyroux and A. Hirschowitz. Higher-order syntax and induction in coq. In F. Pfenning, editor, *Proceedings of the fifth Int. Conf. on Logic Programming and Automated Reasoning (LPAR 94), Kiev, Ukraine, July 16–21, 1994*, volume 822. Springer-Verlag LNAI, 1994.

[DL99] Joëlle Despeyroux and Pierre Leleu. Primitive recursion for higher-order abstract syntax - dependant types. Draft, submitted for publication, 1999.

[DP96] Rowan Davies and Frank Pfenning. A modal analysis of staged computation. In Jr. Guy Steele, editor, *Proceedings of the 23rd Annual Symposium on Principles of Programming Languages*, pages 258–270, St. Petersburg Beach, Florida, January 1996. ACM Press.

[DPS96] Joëlle Despeyroux, Frank Pfenning, and Carsten Schürmann. Primitive recursion for higher-order abstract syntax. Technical Report CMU-CS-96-172, Carnegie Mellon University, September 1996.

[DPS97] Joëlle Despeyroux, Frank Pfenning, and Carsten Schürmann. Primitive Recursion for Higher-Order Abstract Syntax. In J.R. Hindley and P. de Groote, editors, *Int. Conf. on Typed lambda calculi and applications - TLCA'97*, pages 147–163, Nancy, France, April 1997. Springer-Verlag LNCS 1210.

[Gha96] Neil Ghani. Eta Expansions in System F. Technical Report LIENS-96-10, LIENS-DMI, Ecole Normale Superieure, 1996.

[GLT89] Jean-Yves Girard, Yves Lafont, and Paul Taylor. *Proofs and Types*. Cambridge University Press, 1989.

[HHP93] Robert Harper, Furio Honsell, and Gordon Plotkin. A framework for defining logics. *Journal of the Association for Computing Machinery*, 40(1):143–184, January 1993.

[Hof99] Martin Hofmann. Semantical analysis of higher-order abstract syntax. In IEEE, editor, *Proceedings of the International Conference on Logic In Computer Sciences, LICS*, 1999.

[JG95] C.B. Jay and N. Ghani. The Virtues of Eta-Expansion. *Journal of Functional Programming*, 5(2):135–154, April 1995.

[Lel97] Pierre Leleu. A Modal Lambda Calculus with Iteration and Case Constructs. Technical Report RR-3322, INRIA, France, December 1997. http://www.inria.fr/RRRT/RR-3322.html.

[Lel98a] Pierre Leleu. Metatheoretic Results for a Modal Lambda Calculus . Technical Report RR-3361, INRIA, France, 1998. http://www.inria.fr/RRRT/RR-3361.html.

[Lel98b] Pierre Leleu. *Syntaxe abstraite d'ordre supérieur et récursion dans les théories typées*. Phd thesis, Ecole Nationale des Ponts et Chaussées (ENPC), December 1998. In French.

[Luo94] Zhaohui Luo. *Computation and Reasoning*. Oxford University Press, 1994.

[MM97] Raymond McDowell and Dale Miller. A logic for reasoning with higher-order abstract syntax. In *Proceedings of LICS'97*, pages 434–445, Warsaw, 1997.

[MN94] Lena Magnusson and Bengt Nordström. The ALF proof editor and its proof engine. In Henk Barendregt and Tobias Nipkow, editors, *Types for Proofs and Programs*, pages 213–237. Springer-Verlag LNCS 806, 1994.

[New42] M.H.A. Newman. On theories with a combinatorial definition of 'equivalence'. *Ann. Math.*, 43(2):223–243, 1942.

[NPS90] Bengt Nordström, Kent Petersson, and Jan Smith. *Programming in Martin-Löf's Type Theory: An Introduction*. Oxford University Press, 1990.

[PE88] Frank Pfenning and Conal Elliott. Higher-order abstract syntax. In *Proceedings of the ACM SIGPLAN '88 Symposium on Language Design and Implementation*, pages 199–208, Atlanta, Georgia, June 1988.

[PM92] Ch. Paulin-Mohring. Inductive definitions in the system coq. rules and properties. In J.F. Groote M. Bezem, editor, *Proceedings of the Int. Conf. on Typed Lambda Calculi and Applications, TLCA'93*, Springer-Verlag LNCS 664, 1992.

[PS98] F. Pfenning and C. Schürmann. Automated Theorem Proving in a Simple Meta Logic for LF. In *Proceedings of the CADE-15 Conference*, Lindau - Germany, July 1998.

[PW95] Frank Pfenning and Hao-Chi Wong. On a modal $\lambda$-calculus for S4. In S. Brookes and M. Main, editors, *Proceedings of the Eleventh Conference on Mathematical Foundations of Programming Sematics*, New Orleans, Louisiana, March 1995. To appear in *Electronic Notes in Theoretical Computer Science*, Volume 1, Elsevier.

[Wer94] Benjamin Werner. *Une Théorie des Constructions Inductives*. PhD thesis, Université Paris 7, 1994.

# Proof Normalization Modulo

Gilles Dowek and Benjamin Werner

INRIA-Rocquencourt, B.P. 105, 78153 Le Chesnay Cedex, France.

**Abstract.** We consider a class of logical formalisms, in which first-order logic is extended by identifying propositions modulo a given congruence. We particularly focus on the case where this congruence is induced by a confluent and terminating rewrite system over the propositions. We show that this extension enhances the power of first-order logic and that various formalisms, including Church's higher-order logic (HOL) can be described in our framework.
We conjecture that proof normalization and logical consistency always hold over this class of formalisms, provided some minimal conditions over the rewrite system are fulfilled. We prove this conjecture for some subcases, including HOL.

## 1 Introduction

### 1.1 Motivations

A proof-system implements a given logical formalism. The choice of this formalism is important, since in the field of actually mechanically checked formal proofs, logical formalisms are required not only to be *expressive* (logical complexity), but also *practicable.* More precisely, some important issues are:

- The conciseness of proofs: in recent practical developments, it clearly appeared that the size of the proof-object and thus its handling and the practicability of proof-checking can become critical; and the formalism in which this proof is expressed is an important factor to that respect.
- A side-effect of the latter is also that smaller proofs often reflect more closely the mathematical intuition. In other words, this allows the user to better grasp the mathematical object he/she produces.
- Last but not least, automatic proof-search and more generally computer-provided user-help depend upon the chosen formalism. It is well-known that proof synthesis algorithms are expressed more or less clearly in different logics.

In this respect, a particular attention has often been given to the distinction between *calculation* and *reasoning* steps. Schematically, the first can be unambiguously and mechanically performed and reproduced; whereas the latter

Gilles.Dowek@inria.fr, http://coq.inria.fr/~dowek/
Benjamin.Werner@inria.fr, http://coq.inria.fr/~werner/

correspond to the application of a logical inference rule, whose choice is the responsibility of the author/user. As a consequence, the calculation steps can be omitted in the proof objects. A typical instance is the conversion rule of type theories; a typical application is recent work using computational reflection like, for instance, [1].

### 1.2 Systems Modulo

*Theorem proving modulo* is a way to remove computational arguments from proofs by reasoning modulo a congruence on propositions. This idea is certainly not new. For instance, in a language containing an associative binary function symbol $+$, Plotkin [11] proposes to identify propositions such as $P((a+b)+c)$ and $P(a+(b+c))$ that differ only by a rearrangement of brackets. Similarly, the *conversion rule* of type theories [9, 2, 10] a.o. identifies propositions w.r.t. generalized $\beta$-reduction: the propositions $1+1=2$ and $2=2$ are logically identical.

In [3], we have proposed to use this idea in the definition of first-order logic itself. In the simplest cases, we can define first a congruence on terms (e.g. identifying the term $(a+b)+c$ with the term $a+(b+c)$) and then extend this congruence to propositions. However, in some cases, we want to define directly the congruence on propositions. A striking point is that adding well-chosen congruences enhances the logical expressivity of the formalism; typically, it leads to a first-order and axiom-free presentation of Church's higher-order logic (HOL). A interesting application is that enforcing the distinction between calculation and reasoning leads to a very nice clarification of higher-order resolution. See [3] for details.

### 1.3 About this work

In this paper, we study theorem proving modulo from the proof-theoretic viewpoint and more particularly the properties of cut-elimination and consistency. Proof normalization for such proof systems does not always hold and we present several counter-examples below; but we conjecture that proofs always normalize for congruences that can be defined by a confluent and terminating rewrite system, which rewrites terms to terms and atomic propositions to arbitrary ones.

In this paper we show some particular cases of this conjecture: we show that proof normalization holds for our presentation of higher-order logic, for all congruences defined by a confluent and terminating rewriting system rewriting terms to terms and atomic propositions to *quantifier free* propositions and for *positive* rewrite systems i.e. ones in which the right hand side of each rewrite rule contains only positive occurrences of atomic propositions.

## 2 Deduction Modulo

As already mentioned, the class of systems we consider here, are all built on top of the logical rules of first-order logic. The actual expressive power being determined solely by the choice of the congruence. In this present version, we only consider the natural deduction presentation and restrict ourselves to intuitionistic logic; our results can be extended to classical sequent calculus, but this requires some more attention and space. We refer to [4] for extensive details as well as for detailed proofs.

## 2.1 Natural deduction modulo

We place ourselves in many-sorted first-order logic. The definitions below are well-known and thus not too detailed.

We consider a countable set of *sorts*, whose elements will be denoted by $s, s', s_1 \ldots$. The set of *object variables* is numerable, and every variable has an associated sort; we write $x^s, y^{s'} \ldots$. We give ourselves a set of function symbols and of predicate symbols. Each of these comes with its *rank*. The formation rules for objects and propositions are the usual ones:

- If $f$ is a function symbol of rank $(s_1, \ldots, s_n, s')$ and $t_1, \ldots, t_n$ are respectively objects of sort $s_1, \ldots, s_n$, then $f(t_1, \ldots, t_n)$ is a well-formed object of sort $s'$.
- If $P$ is a predicate symbol of rank $(s_1, \ldots, s_n)$ and $t_1, \ldots, t_n$ are respectively objects of sort $s_1, \ldots, s_n$, then $P(t_1, \ldots, t_n)$ is a well-formed *atomic proposition.*

Well-formed propositions are built-up from atomic propositions, from the usual connectors $\Rightarrow, \vee, \wedge, \bot$, and the quantifiers $\forall$ and $\exists$. Remark that, implicitly, quantification in $\forall x^s P$ or $\exists x^s P$ is restricted over the sort $s$.

In what follows, we will often omit the sort of variables, simply writing $x, y$, etc.

In order for proof-checking to be decidable, we assume that various relations are decidable (equality over variables, the sort of variables, the rank of symbols, etc).

Finally, let $\equiv$ be a decidable congruence on propositions.

Figure 1 gives the rules of natural deduction modulo this congruence. As mentioned above, proof checking is decidable, since we provided the necessary assumptions and the needed information in the quantifier rules.

## 2.2 Equivalence

**Proposition 1.** *(Equivalence) For every congruence $\equiv$, there exists a theory $\mathcal{T}$ such that*

$$\mathcal{T}\Gamma \vdash P \quad \textit{if and only if} \quad \Gamma \vdash_{\equiv} P$$

*Proof.* Take the theory $\mathcal{T}$ containing all the propositions $P \Leftrightarrow Q$ where $P \equiv Q$.

$$(\text{AXIOM})\ \frac{}{\Gamma \vdash_{\equiv} A'} A \in \Gamma \text{ and } A \equiv A'$$

$$(\Rightarrow\text{-INTRO})\ \frac{\Gamma, A \vdash_{\equiv} B}{\Gamma \vdash_{\equiv} C} C \equiv (A \Rightarrow B) \qquad (\Rightarrow\text{-ELIM})\ \frac{\Gamma \vdash_{\equiv} C \quad \Gamma \vdash_{\equiv} A}{\Gamma \vdash_{\equiv} B} C \equiv (A \Rightarrow B)$$

$$(\wedge\text{-INTRO})\ \frac{\Gamma \vdash_{\equiv} A \quad \Gamma \vdash_{\equiv} B}{\Gamma \vdash_{\equiv} C} C \equiv (A \wedge B)$$

$$(\wedge\text{-ELIM1})\ \frac{\Gamma \vdash_{\equiv} C}{\Gamma \vdash_{\equiv} A} C \equiv (A \wedge B) \qquad (\wedge\text{-ELIM2})\ \frac{\Gamma \vdash_{\equiv} C}{\Gamma \vdash_{\equiv} B} C \equiv (A \wedge B)$$

$$(\vee\text{-INTRO1})\ \frac{\Gamma \vdash_{\equiv} A}{\Gamma \vdash_{\equiv} C} C \equiv (A \vee B) \qquad (\vee\text{-INTRO2})\ \frac{\Gamma \vdash_{\equiv} B}{\Gamma \vdash_{\equiv} C} C \equiv (A \vee B)$$

$$(\vee\text{-ELIM})\ \frac{\Gamma \vdash_{\equiv} D \quad \Gamma, A \vdash_{\equiv} C \quad \Gamma, B \vdash_{\equiv} C}{\Gamma \vdash_{\equiv} C} D \equiv (A \vee B)$$

$$(\bot\text{-ELIM})\ \frac{\Gamma \vdash_{\equiv} B}{\Gamma \vdash_{\equiv} A} B \equiv \bot$$

$$(\forall\text{-INTRO})\ \frac{\Gamma \vdash_{\equiv} A}{\Gamma \vdash_{\equiv} B} B \equiv (\forall x\ A) \text{ and } x \text{ not free in } \Gamma$$

$$(\forall\text{-ELIM})\ \frac{\Gamma \vdash_{\equiv} B}{\Gamma \vdash_{\equiv} C} B \equiv (\forall x\ A) \text{ and } C \equiv ([t/x]A)$$

$$(\exists\text{-INTRO})\ \frac{\Gamma \vdash_{\equiv} C}{\Gamma \vdash_{\equiv} B} B \equiv (\exists x\ A) \text{ and } C \equiv ([t/x]A)$$

$$(\exists\text{-ELIM})\ \frac{\Gamma \vdash_{\equiv} C \quad \Gamma, A \vdash_{\equiv} B}{\Gamma \vdash_{\equiv} B} C \equiv (\exists x\ A) \text{ and } x \text{ is not free in } \Gamma, B$$

**Fig. 1. Natural deduction modulo**

## 2.3 Rewriting

The framework we have defined up to here is extremely general. In the following, and to study proof-theoretic properties, we mainly deal with the case where the congruence $\equiv$ is generated by a rewriting relation. The definition is straightforward.

**Definition 1.** *We say that a congruence $\equiv$ is defined by a confluent and terminating rewriting system $\mathcal{R}$ rewriting terms to terms and atomic propositions to arbitrary ones when $P \equiv Q$ if and only if $P$ and $Q$ have the same normal form for the system $\mathcal{R}$. In this case, the congruence $\equiv$ is decidable.*

*Remark 1.* The definition above can be slightly generalized allowing non-oriented equations relating terms to terms and atomic propositions to atomic propositions (for instance commutativity). To this end we consider a *class rewrite system* $\mathcal{RE}$ formed with a rewrite system $\mathcal{R}$ rewriting atomic propositions to propositions and a set $\mathcal{E}$ of equations equating atomic propositions with atomic propositions and terms with terms and defining a congruence written $=_{\mathcal{E}}$.

Given a system $\mathcal{RE}$, the term $t$ $\mathcal{RE}$*-rewrites* to $t'$, if $t =_{\mathcal{E}} u[\sigma(l)]_\omega$ and $t' =_{\mathcal{E}} u[\sigma(r)]_\omega$, for some rule $l \to r \in \mathcal{R}$, some term $u$, some occurrence $\omega$ in $u$ and some substitution $\sigma$.

## 2.4 Examples

For matters of space, we only provide two examples here.

*Example 1.* (Simplification) In an integral ring, we can use the usual simplification rules over objects like $a \times 0 \to 0, a \times (b + c) \to a \times b + a \times c$, etc. But we can also add the following rule for simplifying equalities:

$$a \times b = 0 \to a = 0 \vee b = 0$$

or the rule

$$a \times b = a \times c \to a = 0 \vee b = c$$

*Example 2.* (Higher-order logic) As mentioned above, deduction modulo allows to capture formalisms which go beyond the usual field of first-order logic; here is a faithful encoding of Church's higher-order logic.

The *sorts* are *Simple types* inductively defined by

- $\iota$ and $\mathrm{o}$ are simple types,
- if $T$ and $U$ are simple types then $T \to U$ is a simple type.

The language $\mathcal{L}$ is composed of the individual symbols

- $S_{T,U,V}$ of sort $(T \to U \to V) \to (T \to U) \to T \to V$,
- $K_{T,U}$ of sort $T \to U \to T$,
- $\dot{\Rightarrow}$, $\dot{\wedge}$, $\dot{\vee}$ of sort $\mathrm{o} \to \mathrm{o} \to \mathrm{o}$, $\dot{\bot}$ of sort $\mathrm{o}$,
- $\dot{\forall}_T$ and $\dot{\exists}_T$ of sort $(T \to \mathrm{o}) \to \mathrm{o}$,

the function symbols

- $\alpha_{T,U}$ of rank $(T \to U, T, U)$,

and the predicate symbol

- $\varepsilon$ of rank (o).

As can be guessed, $S_{T,U,V}$ and $K_{T,U}$ are typed combinators and used to represent the functions which are the objects of HOL. The objects and functions $\dot{\Rightarrow}, \dot{\wedge}, \dot{\vee}, \dot{\bot}, \dot{\forall}_T$ and $\dot{\exists}_T$ allow to represent propositions as objects of sort o. Finally, the predicate $\varepsilon$ allows to transform such an object $t$ : o into the actual corresponding proposition $\varepsilon(t)$. This typical reflection operation appears clearly in the rewrite rules:

$$
\begin{aligned}
\alpha(\alpha(\alpha(S,x),y),z) &\to \alpha(\alpha(x,z),\alpha(y,z)) \\
\alpha(\alpha(K,x),y) &\to x \\
\varepsilon(\alpha(\alpha(\dot{\Rightarrow},x),y)) &\to \varepsilon(x) \Rightarrow \varepsilon(y) \\
\varepsilon(\alpha(\alpha(\dot{\wedge},x),y)) &\to \varepsilon(x) \wedge \varepsilon(y) \\
\varepsilon(\alpha(\alpha(\dot{\vee},x),y)) &\to \varepsilon(x) \vee \varepsilon(y) \\
\varepsilon(\dot{\bot}) &\to \bot \\
\varepsilon(\alpha(\dot{\forall},x)) &\to \forall y\ \varepsilon(\alpha(x,y)) \\
\varepsilon(\alpha(\dot{\exists},x)) &\to \exists y\ \varepsilon(\alpha(x,y))
\end{aligned}
$$

## 3 Reduction and Cut-Elimination

We now turn to the study of cut-elimination. Since we here place ourselves in a natural deduction framework, this result boils down to the normalization property with respect to $\beta$-reduction. It is possible to define what is a normal (or cut-free) proof directly on the natural deduction derivations. For matters of space, we omit this here, and go directly to defining the typed $\lambda$-terms underlying proofs.

### 3.1 Proof-terms

Following Heyting semantics and Curry-Howard isomorphism we write proofs as $\lambda$-terms typed by propositions of first-order logic. These terms can contain both variables of the first-order language (written $x, y, z$...) and proof variables (written $\alpha, \beta, \ldots$). Terms of the first-order language are written $t, u, v, \ldots$ while proof-terms are written $\pi, \rho, \ldots$

**Definition 2 (Proofs).**

$$\begin{aligned}\pi ::= \quad & \alpha \\ & \mid \lambda\alpha\ \pi \mid (\pi\ \pi') \\ & \mid (\pi, \pi') \mid fst(\pi) \mid snd(\pi) \\ & \mid i(\pi) \mid j(\pi) \mid (\delta\ \pi_1\ \alpha\pi_2\ \beta\pi_3) \\ & \mid (botelim\ \pi) \\ & \mid \lambda x\ \pi \mid (\pi\ t) \\ & \mid (t, \pi) \mid (exelim\ \pi\ x\alpha\pi')\end{aligned}$$

As it is now usual, $\lambda$-abstraction models the $\forall$-intro and $\Rightarrow$-intro rule, application the corresponding elimination rules, the pair construct models the $\wedge$-introduction, etc.

Figure 2 gives the typing rules of this calculus. As can easily be seen, we have a typed $\lambda$-calculus, with dependent products. The only originality is that types are identified modulo $\equiv$.

*Remark 2.* An alternative presentation of this type system would thus be to take simply the usual $\lambda\Pi$-calculus extended with dependent pair types (or $\Sigma$-types), but with a *generalized conversion rule*:

$$\frac{\Gamma \vdash_{\equiv} t : A}{\Gamma \vdash_{\equiv} t : B} \ (\text{if } A \equiv B)$$

Obviously a sequent $A_1, ..., A_n \vdash_{\equiv} B$ is derivable in natural deduction modulo if and only if there is a proof $\pi$ such that the judgment $\alpha_1 : A_1, ..., \alpha_n : A_n \vdash_{\equiv} \pi : B$ is derivable in this system.

### 3.2 Proof reduction rules

As usual, the process of cut elimination is modeled by (generalized) $\beta$-reduction. The following reductions are usual:

**Definition 3.**

$$\begin{aligned}(\lambda\alpha\ \pi_1\ \pi_2) &\to [\pi_2/\alpha]\pi_1 \\ fst(\pi_1, \pi_2) &\to \pi_1 \\ snd(\pi_1, \pi_2) &\to \pi_2 \\ \delta(i(\pi_1), \alpha\pi_2, \beta\pi_3) &\to [\pi_1/\alpha]\pi_2 \\ \delta(j(\pi_1), \alpha\pi_2, \beta\pi_3) &\to [\pi_1/\beta]\pi_3 \\ (\lambda x\ \pi\ t) &\to [t/x]\pi \\ (exelim\ (t, \pi_1)\ \alpha x\pi_2) &\to [t/x, \pi_1/\alpha]\pi_2\end{aligned}$$

*A proof is said to be* normal *(respectively* normalizing *or* strongly normalizing*) if and only if the corresponding $\lambda$-term is normal (respectively normalizing or strongly normalizing). We write $\mathcal{SN}$ for the set of strongly normalizing proofs.*

$$\frac{}{\Gamma \vdash_{\equiv} \alpha : A'} \text{ (axiom} \quad \text{if } \alpha : A \in \Gamma \text{ and } A \equiv A')$$

$$\frac{\Gamma\alpha : A \vdash_{\equiv} \pi : B}{\Gamma \vdash_{\equiv} \lambda\alpha\ \pi : C} \text{ (}\Rightarrow\text{-intro if } C \equiv (A \Rightarrow B))$$

$$\frac{\Gamma \vdash_{\equiv} \pi : C \quad \Gamma \vdash_{\equiv} \pi' : A}{\Gamma \vdash_{\equiv} (\pi\ \pi') : B} \text{ (}\Rightarrow\text{-elim if } C \equiv (A \Rightarrow B))$$

$$\frac{\Gamma \vdash_{\equiv} \pi : A \quad \Gamma \vdash_{\equiv} \pi' : B}{\Gamma \vdash_{\equiv} (\pi, \pi') : C} \text{ (}\wedge\text{-intro if } C \equiv (A \wedge B))$$

$$\frac{\Gamma \vdash_{\equiv} \pi : C}{\Gamma \vdash_{\equiv} fst(\pi) : A} \text{ (}\wedge\text{-elim if } C \equiv (A \wedge B))$$

$$\frac{\Gamma \vdash_{\equiv} \pi : C}{\Gamma \vdash_{\equiv} snd(\pi) : B} \text{ (}\wedge\text{-elim if } C \equiv (A \wedge B))$$

$$\frac{\Gamma \vdash_{\equiv} \pi : A}{\Gamma \vdash_{\equiv} i(\pi) : C} \text{ (}\vee\text{-intro if } C \equiv (A \vee B))$$

$$\frac{\Gamma \vdash_{\equiv} \pi : B}{\Gamma \vdash_{\equiv} j(\pi) : C} \text{ (}\vee\text{-intro if } C \equiv (A \vee B))$$

$$\frac{\Gamma \vdash_{\equiv} \pi_1 : D \quad \Gamma\alpha : A \vdash_{\equiv} \pi_2 : C \quad \Gamma\beta : B \vdash_{\equiv} \pi_3 : C}{\Gamma \vdash_{\equiv} (\delta\ \pi_1\ \alpha\pi_2\ \beta\pi_3) : C} \text{ (}\vee\text{-elim if } D \equiv (A \vee B))$$

$$\frac{\Gamma \vdash_{\equiv} \pi : B}{\Gamma \vdash_{\equiv} (botelim\ \pi) : A} \text{ (}\bot\text{-elim if } B \equiv \bot)$$

$$\frac{\Gamma \vdash_{\equiv} \pi : A}{\Gamma \vdash_{\equiv} \lambda x\ \pi : B} \text{ (}\forall\text{-intro} \quad \text{if } x \text{ is not free in } \Gamma \text{ and } B \equiv (\forall x\ A))$$

$$\frac{\Gamma \vdash_{\equiv} \pi : B}{\Gamma \vdash_{\equiv} (\pi\ t) : C} \text{ ((}A, t) \ \forall\text{-elim if } B \equiv (\forall x\ A) \text{ and } C \equiv ([t/x]A))$$

$$\frac{\Gamma \vdash_{\equiv} \pi : C}{\Gamma \vdash_{\equiv} (t, \pi) : B} \text{ ((}A, t) \ \exists\text{-intro if } B \equiv (\exists x\ A) \text{ and } C \equiv ([t/x]A))$$

$$\frac{\Gamma \vdash_{\equiv} \pi : C \quad \Gamma\alpha : A \vdash_{\equiv} \pi' : B}{\Gamma \vdash_{\equiv} (exelim\ \pi\ x\alpha\pi') : B} \text{ (}\exists\text{-elim} \quad \text{if } x \text{ is not free in } \Gamma B \text{ and } C \equiv (\exists x\ A))$$

**Fig. 2.** Typing rules

**Theorem 1.** *Provided $\equiv$ is defined from a rewrite system verifying the conditions of definition 1, there is no normal proof of the sequent* $[] \vdash_{\equiv} \bot$.

*Proof.* A normal closed proof can only end by an introduction rule. Thus, we should have a congruence like $\bot \equiv A \wedge B$ of $\bot \equiv A \vee B$, which is impossible.

## 3.3 Counter-examples to termination

To illustrate the subtle link between the combinatorial properties of the rewrite system $\mathcal{R}$ (termination, confluence,...) and the logical properties of the induced formalism (consistency, cut elimination), we here provide two systems where these properties do not hold.

*Example 3.* (Russell's paradox)
Consider the following rewriting system

$$R \rightarrow R \Rightarrow S$$

Modulo this rewriting system, the proof $\lambda\alpha : R\ (\alpha\ \alpha)\ \lambda\alpha : R\ (\alpha\ \alpha)$ has type $S$. The only way to reduce this proof is to reduce it to itself and hence is not normalizable.

An instance of this rule is skolemized naive set theory. In naive set set theory we have the following axiom scheme

$$\forall x_1 \ldots \forall x_n\ \exists y\ \forall z\ (z \in y \Leftrightarrow P)$$

for any propositional expression $P$.

Skolemizing this scheme, we introduce for each proposition $P$ a symbol $f_{x_1,\ldots,x_n,z,P}$ and an axiom

$$\forall x_1 \ldots \forall x_n\ \forall z\ (z \in f_{x_1,\ldots,x_n,z,P}(x_1,\ldots,x_n) \Leftrightarrow P)$$

This axiom can be turned into the rewrite rule

$$z \in f_{x_1,\ldots,x_n,z,P}(x_1,\ldots,x_n) \rightarrow P$$

In particular, we have a rewrite rule

$$z \in f_{z,(z \in z) \Rightarrow \bot} \rightarrow (z \in z) \Rightarrow \bot$$

and hence writing $R$ for the proposition $f_{z,(z \in z) \Rightarrow \bot} \in f_{z,(z \in z) \Rightarrow \bot}$ and $S$ for the proposition $\bot$ we have

$$R \rightarrow R \Rightarrow S.$$

We thus reconstructed Russell's counter-example to consistency and cut elimination for naive set theory.

*Example 4.* (Crabbé's counter-example)

Even if Zermelo's set theory (Z) is considered to be consistent, it is well-known that cut elimination is problematic and does generally not hold. The proof of non-normalization is called Crabbé's counter-example (see [8, 5] for details). Again, it is here illustrated by the fact that the straightforward encoding of Z as a deduction modulo necessitates a non-terminating rewrite system.

Consider the following rewriting system

$$C \to E \wedge (C \Rightarrow D)$$

Modulo this rewriting system, the proof

$$\lambda\alpha : C\ (snd(\alpha)\ \alpha)\ (\beta, \lambda\alpha : C\ (snd(\alpha)\ \alpha))$$

is a proof of $D$ in the context $E$. The only way to reduce this proof is to reduce it to

$$(snd(\beta, \lambda\alpha : C\ (snd(\alpha)\ \alpha))\ (\beta, \lambda\alpha : C\ (snd(\alpha)\ \alpha)))$$

and then to itself

$$(\lambda\alpha : C\ (snd(\alpha)\ \alpha)\ (\beta, \lambda\alpha : C\ (snd(\alpha)\ \alpha)))$$

Hence it is not normalizable.

An instance of this example is skolemized set theory. In set set theory we have an axiom scheme

$$\forall x_1\ ...\ \forall x_n\ \forall w\ \exists y\ \forall z\ (z \in y \Leftrightarrow (z \in w) \wedge P)$$

skolemizing this scheme, we introduce for each proposition $P$ a symbol $f_{x_1,...,x_n,z,P}$ and an axiom

$$\forall x_1\ ...\ \forall x_n\ \forall z\ (z \in f_{x_1,...,x_n,z,P}(x_1, ..., x_n, w) \Leftrightarrow (z \in w \wedge P))$$

This axiom can be turned into the rewrite rule

$$z \in f_{x_1,...,x_n,z,P}(x_1, ..., x_n, w) \to z \in \wedge P$$

In particular, we have a rewrite rule

$$z \in f_{z,(z \in z) \Rightarrow \bot}(w) \to z \in w \wedge ((z \in z) \Rightarrow \bot$$

and hence writing $C$ for the proposition $f_{z,(z\in z)\Rightarrow\bot}(w) \in f_{z,(z\in z)\Rightarrow\bot}(w)$, $D$ for the proposition $\bot$ and $E$ for the proposition $f_{z,(z\in z)\Rightarrow\bot}(w) \in w$ we have

$$C \to E \wedge (C \Rightarrow D)$$

In these examples the rewriting system itself is not terminating, as $R$ (resp.) $C$ reduces to a proposition where it occurs. We conjecture that this non termination is responsible for the non termination of reduction of proofs.

*Conjecture 1.* If $\mathcal{R}$ is a confluent and normalizing rewrite system (resp. class rewrite system), then proof reduction modulo $\mathcal{R}$ is normalizing.

An obvious consequence is that deduction modulo $\mathcal{R}$ is consistent, by theorem 1.

# 4 Proving Normalization

Now we want to prove some particular cases of the conjecture. First that proofs normalize for the definition of higher-order logic given above. Then, that proofs normalize for all rewrite systems reducing terms to terms and atomic propositions to *quantifier-free* propositions (as in the simplification example above). At last, that proofs normalize modulo all *positive* rewrite systems i.e. ones in which the right hand side of each rewrite rule contains only positive occurrences of atomic propositions.

We first define a notion of pre-model and prove that when a congruence bears a pre-model then proofs normalize modulo this congruence. Then we shall construct premodels for our particular cases.

## 4.1 Reducibility techniques

The basic tools used hereafter are the ones of reducibility proofs, whose main concepts are due to Tait [12] and Girard [6, 7]. In particular, since we want to treat the case of higher-order logic, we need some form of reducibility candidates. We here take a definition similar to [7], but other ones like Tait's saturated sets would also apply.

**Definition 4 (Neutral proof).**
*A proof is said to be* neutral *if its last rule is an axiom or an elimination, but not an introduction.*

**Definition 5 (Reducibility candidate).**
*A set $R$ of proofs is a* reducibility candidate *if*

- *if $\pi \in R$, then $\pi$ is strongly normalizable,*
- *if $\pi \in R$ and $\pi \to \pi'$ then $\pi' \in R$,*
- *if $\pi$ is neutral and if for every $\pi'$ such that $\pi \to^1 \pi'$, $\pi' \in R$ then $\pi \in R$.*

Mostly, we follow the main scheme of reducibility proofs. That is we try, for every proposition $P$, to exhibit a set of terms $\mathcal{R}_P$ such that:

- All elements of $\mathcal{R}_P$ are strongly normalizing.
- If $\Gamma \vdash t : P$ holds, then $t \in \mathcal{R}_P$ (that is modulo some closure condition w.r.t. substitution).

The first condition is ensured by verifying that all $\mathcal{R}_P$ are reducibility candidates. The second one is proved by induction over the derivation of $\Gamma \vdash t : P$ using closure conditions due to the definition of $\mathcal{R}_P$. Typically, for instance: if $\pi \in \mathcal{R}_{A \Rightarrow B}$ then for each proof $\pi'$ element of $\mathcal{R}_A$, $(\pi\ \pi')$ is an element of $\mathcal{R}_B$.

Most important, and like for other calculi with dependent types, we will need the condition that if $A \equiv B$ then $\mathcal{R}_A = \mathcal{R}_B$.

The closure condition above for $\mathcal{R}_{A \Rightarrow B}$ can be viewed as a partial definition; the situation is similar for the other connectors and quantifiers. Thus, we understand that the crucial step will be to choose the right sets for $\mathcal{R}_A$ in the case where $A$ is an atomic proposition (that is potentially a redex w.r.t. $\mathcal{R}$). In other words, to define the family $\mathcal{R}_A$, it will be enough to define for each predicate symbol $P$ the sets $\mathcal{R}_{P(t_1,\dots,t_n)}$, or equivalently to give, for each $n$-ary predicate symbol $P$, a function $\tilde{P}$ that maps $n$-uples of terms to some well-chosen reducibility candidate.

It is well-know that a reducibility proof essentially boils down to the construction of a particular syntactical model. This comparison is particularly striking here since, in first-order logic, to define a model, we also need to provide, for each predicate symbol $P$ a function $\tilde{P}$ that maps every $n$-tuple of terms to a truth value.

We can pursue this comparison. If two terms $t_1$ and $t_1'$ are congruent then the sets $\tilde{P}(t_1, ..., t_n)$ and $\tilde{P}(t_1', ..., t_n)$ must be identical. The function $\tilde{P}$ is then better defined as a function from an abstract object (for instance, the class of $t_1$ and $t_1'$) that $t_1$ and $t_1'$ denote.

Then the condition that two congruent propositions must have the same denotation can be expressed as the fact that the rewrite rules are valid in the model.

## 4.2 Pre-model

Formalizing the discussion above, we end-up with the following notion.

**Definition 6 (Pre-model).** *Let $\mathcal{C}$ be the set of all reducibility candidates.*
*Let $\mathcal{L}$ be a (many sorted) first-order language. A* pre-model *for $\mathcal{L}$ is given by:*

- *for each sort $T$ a set $\mathcal{M}_T$,*
- *for each function symbol $f$ (of rank $(s_1, ..., s_n, s')$) a function*

$$\tilde{f} \in \mathcal{M}_{s'}^{\mathcal{M}_{s_1} \times \ldots \times \mathcal{M}_{s_n}}$$

- *for each predicate symbol $P$ (of rank $(s_1, ..., s_n)$) a function*

$$\tilde{P} \in \mathcal{C}^{\mathcal{M}_{s_1} \times \ldots \times \mathcal{M}_{s_n}}.$$

**Definition 7.** *Let $t$ be a term and $\varphi$ an assignment mapping all the free variables of $t$ of sort $T$ to elements of $\mathcal{M}_T$. We define the object $|t|_\varphi$ by induction over the structure of $t$.*

- $|x|_\varphi = \varphi(x)$,
- $|f(t_1, \ldots, t_n)|_\varphi = \tilde{f}(|t_1|_\varphi, \ldots, |t_n|_\varphi)$.

**Definition 8.** *Let $A$ be a proposition and $\varphi$ an assignment mapping all the free variables of $A$ of sort $T$ to elements of $\mathcal{M}_T$. We define the set $|A|_\varphi$ of proofs by induction over the structure of $A$.*

- *A proof $\pi$ is an element of $|P(t_1, \ldots, t_n)|_\varphi$ if it belongs to $\tilde{P}(|t_1|_\varphi, \ldots, |t_n|_\varphi)$ (and is thus strongly normalizable).*

- *A proof $\pi$ is element of $|A \Rightarrow B|_\varphi$ if it is strongly normalizable and when $\pi$ reduces to a proof of the form $\lambda\alpha\pi_1$ then for every $\pi'$ in $|A|_\varphi$, $[\pi'/\alpha]\pi_1$ is an element of $|B|_\varphi$.*
- *A proof $\pi$ is an element of $|A \wedge B|_\varphi$ if it is strongly normalizable and when $\pi$ reduces to a proof of the form $(\pi_1, \pi_2)$ then $\pi_1$ and $\pi_2$ are elements of $|A|_\varphi$ and $|B|_\varphi$.*
- *A proof $\pi$ is an element of $|A \vee B|_\varphi$ if it is strongly normalizable and when $\pi$ reduces to a proof of the form $i(\pi_1)$ (resp. $j(\pi_2)$) then $\pi_1$ (resp. $\pi_2$) is an element of $|A|_\varphi$ (resp. $|B|_\varphi$).*
- *A proof $\pi$ is an element of $|\bot|_\varphi$ if it is strongly normalizable*[1].
- *A proof $\pi$ is an element of $|\forall x\ A|_\varphi$ if it is strongly normalizable and when $\pi$ reduces to a proof of the form $\lambda x\pi_1$ then for every term $t$ of sort $T$ (where $T$ is the sort of $x$) and every element $E$ of $\mathcal{M}_T$, the proof $[t/x]\pi_1$ is an element of $|A|_{\varphi+(x,E)}$.*
- *A proof $\pi$ is an element of $|\exists x\ A|_\varphi$ if it is strongly normalizable and there exists an element $E$ of $\mathcal{M}_T$ (where $T$ is the sort of $t$) such that when $\pi$ reduces to a proof of the form $(t, \pi_1)$, then $\pi_1$ is an element of $|A|_{\varphi+(x,E)}$.*

Looking at the two last clauses of this definition, we may notice that no correlation is required between the interpretation of the proof variables $\varphi$ and the instantiations of object variables. This simplifies the proof, and is possible since instantiating object variables in proof terms does not create new (proof-)redexes. This is somewhat similar to the situation in typed $\lambda$-calculi, where the substitution of type variables does not create redexes in terms (see [7] for instance).

**Definition 9.** *A pre-model is a pre-model of $\equiv$ if when $A \equiv B$ then for every assignment $\varphi$, $|A|_\varphi = |B|_\varphi$.*

The following usual conditions are easily proved by induction over the proposition $A$; the two last ones require a little more case analysis.

**Proposition 2.** *For any proposition $A$, term $t$, variable $x$ and assignment $\varphi$:*

- $|[t/x]A|_\varphi = |A|_{\varphi+(x,|t|_\varphi)}$
- *If $\pi$ is an element of $|A|_\varphi$ then $\pi$ is strongly normalizable.*
- *If $\pi$ is an element of $|A|_\varphi$ and $\pi \to \pi'$, then $\pi'$ is an element of $|A|_\varphi$.*
- *If $\pi$ is neutral and if for every $\pi'$ such that $\pi \to^1 \pi'$, $\pi' \in |A|_\varphi$ then $\pi \in |A|_\varphi$.*

¿From the three last properties, we deduce:

**Lemma 1.** *For every proposition $A$ and assignment $\varphi$, $|A|_\varphi$ is a reducibility candidate.*

---

[1] As usual, we could chose about any other reducibility candidate for the definition of $|\bot|_\varphi$.

### 4.3 The Normalization theorem

We can now prove that if a system has a pre-model then proofs modulo this system normalize. The proofs of this section are a little long and tedious but bears no essential novelty. We omit them for matter of space and again refer to [4] for details.

**Theorem 2.** *Let $A$ be a proposition and $\pi$ a proof of $A$ modulo $\equiv$. Let $\theta$ be a substitution mapping the free variables of sort $T$ of $A$ to terms of sort $T$, $\varphi$ be an assignment mapping free variables of $A$ to elements of $\mathcal{M}_T$ and $\sigma$ a substitution mapping proof variables of propositions $B$ to elements of $|B|_\varphi$. Then $\sigma\theta\pi$ is an element of $|A|_\varphi$.*

**Corollary 1.** *Every proof of $A$ is in $|A|_\emptyset$ and hence strongly normalizable*

### 4.4 Pre-model construction

Constructing the pre-model for a given theory, is the part of the consistency proof that bears the logical complexity; i.e. it is the part of the proof that cannot be done in the theory itself. The construction for HOL follows essentially the original proof. The two other ones we present are more typical of deduction modulo.

**Proposition 3.** *Higher-order logic has a pre-model, hence proofs normalize in higher-order logic.*

*Proof.* We construct a pre-model as follows. The essential point is that we anticipate the fact that objects of sort o actually represent propositions, by interpreting them as reducibility candidates. Thus quantification over o becomes impredicative in the model.

$$\mathcal{M}_o = \mathcal{C} \qquad \tilde{S} \equiv a \mapsto (b \mapsto (c \mapsto a(c)(b(c))))$$

$$\mathcal{M}_\iota = \{0\} \qquad \tilde{K} \equiv a \mapsto (b \mapsto a)$$

$$\mathcal{M}_{T\to U} = \mathcal{M}_U^{\mathcal{M}_T} \qquad \tilde{\alpha}(a,b) = a(b)$$

$$\tilde{\varepsilon}(a) = a$$

$$\tilde{\Rightarrow}(a,b) \equiv \{\pi \in \mathcal{SN} | \pi \to^* \lambda\alpha\pi_1 \Rightarrow \forall\pi' \in a.[\pi'/\alpha]\pi_1 \in b\}$$

$$\tilde{\wedge}(a,b) \equiv \{\pi \in \mathcal{SN} | \pi \to^* (\pi_1,\pi_2) \Rightarrow \pi_1 \in a \wedge \pi_2 \in b\}$$

$$\tilde{\vee}(a,b) \equiv \{\pi \in \mathcal{SN} | (\pi \to^* i(\pi_1) \Rightarrow \pi_1 \in a) \wedge (\pi \to^* i(\pi_2) \Rightarrow \pi_2 \in b)\}$$

$$\tilde{\bot} \equiv \mathcal{SN}$$

$$\tilde{\forall}_T(a) \equiv \{\pi \in \mathcal{SN} | \pi \to^* \lambda x\pi_1 \Rightarrow \forall t : T.\forall E \in \mathcal{M}_T.[t/x]\pi_1 \in a(E)\}$$

$$\tilde{\exists}_T(a) \equiv \{\pi \in \mathcal{SN} | \exists E \in \mathcal{M}_T.\pi \to^* (t,\pi_1) \Rightarrow \pi_1 \in a(E)\}$$

We do not detail the proof that if $A \equiv B$ then $|A|_\theta = |B|_\theta$.

In this last case, it is the presence of the quantifier $\forall$ on the right hand part of one of the rewrite schemes that is responsible for the impredicativity of the resulting logic. We can give a generic proof of cut elimination for the predicative case:

**Proposition 4.** *A quantifier-free confluent terminating rewrite systems has a pre-model, hence proofs normalize modulo such a rewrite system.*

*Proof.* To each normal closed quantifier-free proposition $A$, we associate a set of proofs $\Psi(A)$.

$$\begin{aligned}
\Psi(A) &\equiv \mathcal{SN} \text{ if } A \text{ is atomic} \\
\Psi(A \Rightarrow B) &\equiv \{\pi \in \mathcal{SN} | \pi \rightarrow^* \lambda\alpha.\pi_1 \Rightarrow \forall\pi' \in \Psi(A).[\pi'/\alpha]\pi_1 \in \Psi(B)\} \\
\Psi(A \wedge B) &\equiv \{\pi \in \mathcal{SN} | \pi \rightarrow^* (\pi_1, \pi_2) \Rightarrow \pi_1 \in \Psi(A) \wedge \pi_2 \in \Psi(B)\} \\
\Psi(A \vee B) &\equiv \{\pi \in \mathcal{SN} | \pi \rightarrow^* i(\pi_1) \Rightarrow \pi_1 \in \Psi(A) \wedge \pi \rightarrow^* i(\pi_2) \Rightarrow \pi_2 \in \Psi(B)\} \\
\Psi(\bot) &\equiv \mathcal{SN}
\end{aligned}$$

Then we define a pre-model as follows. Let $\mathcal{M}_T$ be the set of normal closed terms of sort $T$.

$$\begin{aligned}
\tilde{f}(t_1, \ldots, t_n) &\equiv f(t_1, \ldots, t_n) \downarrow \\
\tilde{P}(t_1, \ldots, t_n) &\equiv \Psi((P(t_1, \ldots, t_n)) \downarrow).
\end{aligned}$$

where let $t \downarrow$ (resp. $A \downarrow$) stand for the normal form of $t$ (resp. $A$).

Again, we leave out the proof that if $A \equiv B$ then $|A|_\theta = |B|_\theta$.

*Remark 3.* In this normalization proof we use the fact that some sets are reducibility candidates, but we never quantify on all reducibility candidates, reflecting that fact that we here deal with predicative systems.

Finally, since the interpretation $|A|_\varphi$ of an arbitrary proposition $A$ is determined by the choice of the interpretation for normal atomic propositions, it is tempting to define the latter by a fix-point construction. This is possible if the rewrite system induces a monotone interpretation function.

**Definition 10.** *Let $\mathcal{R}$ be a terminating and confluent rewrite system, rewriting atomic to non-atomic propositions. This system is said to be* positive *if the right hand side of each rewrite rule contains only positive occurrences of atomic propositions.*

**Proposition 5.** *A positive rewrite system bears a pre-model, and thus the induced deduction system enjoys proof normalization and consistency.*

We again refer to [4] for details about the fix-point construction of the pre-model.

## 5 Conclusion

We have defined generically a wide range of deductive systems. Every system is defined by a given rewrite system over first-order propositions. We have seen that the systems so defined go further than first-order logic.

We conjecture that simple combinatorial conditions on the rewrite system imply the proof elimination property and thus logical consistency. This conjecture implies the consistency of Church's higher-order logic. It is also interesting to remark that, provided this conjecture holds, its logical strength is not yet clear. In other words, we do not know which is the strongest logical system definable as a deduction modulo. We have seen though, that naive attempts to encode set theory do not succeed.

In any case, it seems that studying rewrite systems from their logical properties is a new, promising and interesting subject.

## 6 Acknowledgements

We thank an anonymous referee for pointing out an error in the normalization proof, and for helpful comments.

## References


1. S. Boutin, Réflexion sur les quotients, *Doctoral thesis*, Université de Paris 7 (1997).
2. T. Coquand and G. Huet, The Calculus of constructions, *Information and Computation*, 76 (1988) pp. 95-120.
3. G. Dowek, Th. Hardin and C. Kirchner, Theorem proving modulo, *Rapport de Recherche INRIA* 3400 (1998).
4. G. Dowek, B. Werner, Proof normalization modulo, *Rapport de recherche INRIA* 3542 (1998).
5. J. Ekman, Normal proofs in set theory, *Doctoral thesis*, Chalmers university of technology and University of Göteborg (1994).
6. J.Y. Girard, Interprétation fonctionnelle et élimination des coupures dans l'arithmétique d'ordre supérieur, *Thèse de Doctorat d'État*, Université de Paris VII (1972).
7. J.Y. Girard, Y. Lafont and P. Taylor. Proofs and Types, *Cambridge University Press* (1989).
8. L. Hallnäs, On normalization of proofs in set theory, *Doctoral thesis*, University of Stockholm (1983).
9. P. Martin-Löf, Intuitionistic type theory, *Bibliopolis*, Napoli (1984).
10. Ch. Paulin-Mohring, Inductive definitions in the system COQ, Rules and Properties, *Typed Lambda Calculi and Applications*, Lecture Notes in Computer Science 664 (1993) pp. 328-345.
11. G. Plotkin, Building-in equational theories *Machine Intelligence*, 7 (1972), pp. 73–90
12. W.W. Tait, Intensional interpretation of functionals of finite type I, *Journal of Symbolic Logic*, 32, 2 (1967) pp. 198-212.

# Proof of Imperative Programs in Type Theory

Jean-Christophe Filliâtre*

LRI, URA CNRS 410, Bât. 490, Université Paris Sud,
91405 ORSAY Cedex, FRANCE
e-mail: `Jean-Christophe.Filliatre@lri.fr`
`www.lri.fr/~filliatr`

**Abstract.** We present a new approach to certifying functional programs with imperative aspects, in the context of Type Theory. The key is a functional translation of imperative programs, based on a combination of the type and effect discipline and monads. Then an incomplete proof of the specification is built in the Type Theory, whose gaps would correspond to proof obligations. On sequential imperative programs, we get the same proof obligations as those given by Floyd-Hoare logic. Compared to the latter, our approach also includes functional constructions in a straight-forward way. This work has been implemented in the Coq Proof Assistant and applied on non-trivial examples.

## Introduction

The methods for proving programs developed in the last decades (see [4] for a survey), based on Floyd-Hoare logic [8, 6] or on Dijkstra's calculus of weakest preconditions [5], certainly experienced a great success. But the specification languages involved were usually low expressive first-order predicate logics which surely contributed to their relative failure in real case studies. More recent methods try to fill this gap, as for instance the B method [2], whose specification language includes a rather large part of first-order set-theory. Type Theory also provides expressive logics, well understood in theory and relatively easy to implement since they are based on a small set of rules. The Calculus of Inductive Constructions (CIC for short) is one of the most powerful logical framework of this kind, and the Coq Proof Assistant [1] is one of its implementations. Type Theory is naturally well-suited for the proof of purely functional programs. We show that it is also a good framework to specify and prove imperative programs.

There are already some formalizations of Floyd-Hoare logic in higher order logical frameworks, as for instance the work of T. Schreiber in LEGO [15] or M. Gordon in HOL [7]. Nevertheless, those formalizations still have the disadvantages of Floyd-Hoare logic: well-understood on small imperative languages, they appeared to be difficult to extend to real programming languages. For example, the few base datatypes (integers, booleans, ...) are usually not sufficient and the programmer quickly has to construct new datatypes using arrays, records,

* This research was partly supported by ESPRIT Working Group "Types".

pointers or a primitive notion of recursive datatypes. Then the extensions of Floyd-Hoare logic become painful (see [4], page 931).

For all those reasons, we think that we have to start with a more realistic language and to propose a more extensible method. We chose to consider a programming language with both functional features (functions as first-class objects, higher-order functions,...) and imperative ones (references, while loops,...). The base objects will be the ones of the Type Theory, which gives immediately a huge panel of datatypes (for instance lists, trees,... defined as inductive types in the CIC). References will be limited to purely functional values. Notice that such a language already includes FORTRAN, Pascal without an explicit use of pointers, and a rather large subset of ML.

In the traditional approach of Floyd-Hoare logic, programs are seen as state-transformers, where a state maps variables to values. Then the total correctness of a program $M$ can be expressed in the following way:

$$\{P\}\ M\ \{Q\} \quad\equiv\quad \forall s.\, P(s) \Rightarrow \exists s'.\ ([\![M]\!](s,s') \wedge Q(s,s'))$$

where $[\![M]\!]$ is the semantic interpretation of $M$ as a relation between input and output states. It is easy to define the type of these states when they only contain integers and booleans for instance. But this becomes difficult as soon as states may contain objects of any type. Moreover, in real case studies one has to express in post-conditions that some parts of the state are not modified by the program. This is not natural.

Thinking of a variable $x$ as an index in a global store is very close to the implementation of imperative languages, where $x$ is a pointer in the heap. It is necessary when there is possible *aliasing* in programs i.e. when two variables may point to the same object. But in practice, most programs considered do not contain aliased variables. Then we can directly represent the *contents* of a variable $x$ of the program by a variable of the logic. Predicates about the program's variables become predicates about the logic's variables, and not about some accessed values in a global store.

Consequently, we propose to express the semantics of an imperative program $M$ by *a functional program* $\overline{M}$ taking as argument a tuple $x$ of the *values* of the variables of $M$ and returning a tuple $y$ of the *values* of the variables (possibly) modified by $M$, together with the result $v$ of the evaluation. Then, the correctness may be written

$$\{P\}\ M\ \{Q\} \quad\equiv\quad \forall x.\, P(x) \Rightarrow \exists (y,v).\ \big((y,v) = \overline{M}(x) \wedge Q(x,y,v)\big) \qquad (1)$$

The functional translation relies on a static analysis of effects, following J.-P. Talpin and P. Jouvelot's *Type and Effect Discipline* [16], and on the use of *monads* [11, 17].

Then we propose a method to establish the correctness formula (1). To do that, we construct an incomplete proof $\widehat{M}$ of this proposition. By "incomplete" we mean that the proof term $\widehat{M}$ still contains gaps, whose types are known. Those gaps will give the proof obligations. Our work may be seen as an extension of the work of C. Parent [13] to imperative programs. Her approach to proving purely functional programs, based on realizability, consists in building an incomplete proof of the specification whose skeleton is the program itself. We extend this idea using a functional translation of imperative programs.

This paper is organized as follows. In the first section, we introduce a programming language with functional and imperative aspects, and we define a notion of *typing with effects* for this language. This allows us to define a functional translation of programs, which is proved to be semantically correct. In the next section, we introduce annotations in programs (pre- and post-conditions, variants) and we define an incomplete proof associated to each program, whose proof obligations establish the total correctness when proved. In the third section, we shortly describe the implementation of this work, which is already part of the Coq Proof Assistant [1]. At last, we will discuss related works and propose some possible extensions.

# 1 Effects and Functional Translation

*Preliminary definitions and notations.* In this paper we are going to consider two different kinds of programs: purely functional ones and imperative ones. Let $T$ be the type system of purely functional programs and $\Gamma \vdash e : t$ the corresponding typing judgment, where $\Gamma$ is a typing environment i.e. a mapping from variables to types. We assume that $T$ contains at least the type of booleans and a type unit which has only one value, the constant void. The type system of imperative programs will be $T_{ref} ::= T \mid T$ ref, where $T$ ref is the type of references over objects of type $T$. The corresponding typing judgment will be written $\Gamma \vdash_r e : t$. Dereferencing will be written $!x$ and assignment $x := e$, as usual in ML languages.

The abstract syntax of programs is given in Figure 1. The nonterminal symbol $E$ stands for a purely functional expression, including possible dereferencing of variables. For the moment, we only consider call-by-value application, written $(f\ e)$ — call-by-name will be considered at the end of this section. To simplify the presentation, we chose to restrict boolean expressions appearing in if and while statements to be purely functional expressions. The precise meaning of $V$ in the abstraction fun $(x : V) \rightarrow M$ will be explained in the next paragraph.

## 1.1 Effects

The functional translation of imperative programs that we are going to define relies on a keen analysis of their *effects*. We do not intend to present new ideas or results to the existing theory of static analysis and its application to effects inference. Actually, we are only interested in determining the sets of variables possibly accessed or modified by a given program. In the general case, this would require a complex analysis of *regions*, as defined by J.-P. Talpin and P. Jouvelot in [16], or some similar technique, but since we have eliminated alias possibilities in our programs, the solution is here much simpler.

$$\begin{array}{rcl} M & ::= & E \\ & | & x := M \\ & | & M \; ; \; M \\ & | & \text{if } E \text{ then } M \text{ else } M \\ & | & \text{while } E \text{ do } M \text{ done} \\ & | & \text{let } x = \text{ref } M \text{ in } M \\ & | & \text{fun } (x : V) \to M \\ & | & (M\ M) \end{array}$$

**Fig. 1.** Abstract syntax of programs

The effect $\epsilon$ of a program expression will be a pair $(R, W)$ of two sets of variables, $R$ being the set of all the references involved in the evaluation of the expression and $W$ the subset of $R$ of references which are possibly modified during this evaluation. If $\epsilon_1 = (R_1, W_1)$ and $\epsilon_2 = (R_2, W_2)$ are two effects, then $\epsilon_1 \sqcup \epsilon_2$ will denote their *union* i.e. the effect $(R_1 \cup R_2, W_1 \cup W_2)$. Finally $\epsilon \backslash x$ will denote the effect obtained by removing the occurrences of $x$ in the effect $\epsilon$.

To do type inference with effects, we introduce a new type system composed from a type system for *values*, $V$, and a type system for *computations*, $C$. They are mutually recursively defined as follows:

$$V \quad ::= \quad T \mid T \text{ ref} \mid V \to C \tag{2}$$

$$C \quad ::= \quad (V, \epsilon) \tag{3}$$

In definition (2), we express the fact that functions are first-class values and that, since we chose call-by-value semantics, functions take values as arguments to produce computations. In definition (3), we express that a computation returns a value together with an effect. Those definitions are clearly driven by the semantic and would have been different with call-by-name semantics.

To type programs with effects, we must now consider environments mapping variables to types of values, i.e. to expressions of the type system $V$. If $\Gamma$ is such an environment, then $\Gamma \vdash M : C$ will denote the typing judgment expressing that a program $M$ has the type of computation $C$. This judgment is established by the inference rules given in Figure 2. It is clear that this judgment is decidable and that the type of computation of a program is unique.

### 1.2 Functional translation

The functional translation we are going to define is based on the idea of *monads*. Monads were introduced by E. Moggi [11] and P. Wadler [17], in rather different contexts. They are used by Moggi to give semantics to programming languages. The motivations of Wadler are more pragmatic and closest to ours: he uses monads to incorporate imperative aspects (stores, exceptions, input-output, ...) in purely functional languages. A monad is composed of a type operator $\mu$ and

$$\frac{\Gamma \vdash_r E : T \quad R = \{ x \in dom(\Gamma) \mid !x \text{ in } E \}}{\Gamma \vdash E : (T, (R, \emptyset))} \text{ (EXP)}$$

$$\frac{x : T \text{ ref} \in \Gamma \quad \Gamma \vdash M : (T, (R, W))}{\Gamma \vdash x := M : (\text{unit}, (\{x\} \cup R, \{x\} \cup W))} \text{ (ASSIGN)}$$

$$\frac{\Gamma \vdash M_1 : (\text{unit}, \epsilon_1) \quad \Gamma \vdash M_2 : (V, \epsilon_2)}{\Gamma \vdash M_1 \; ; \; M_2 : (V, (\epsilon_1 \sqcup \epsilon_2))} \text{ (SEQ)}$$

$$\frac{\Gamma \vdash B : (\text{bool}, \epsilon_0) \quad \Gamma \vdash M_1 : (V, \epsilon_1) \quad \Gamma \vdash M_2 : (V, \epsilon_2)}{\Gamma \vdash \text{if } B \text{ then } M_1 \text{ else } M_2 : (V, (\epsilon_0 \sqcup \epsilon_1 \sqcup \epsilon_2))} \text{ (COND)}$$

$$\frac{\Gamma \vdash B : (\text{bool}, \epsilon_0) \quad \Gamma \vdash M : (\text{unit}, \epsilon)}{\Gamma \vdash \text{while } B \text{ do } M \text{ done} : (\text{unit}, (\epsilon_0 \sqcup \epsilon))} \text{ (LOOP)}$$

$$\frac{\Gamma \vdash M_1 : (T_1, \epsilon_1) \quad \Gamma, x : T_1 \text{ ref} \vdash M_2 : (T_2, \epsilon_2)}{\Gamma \vdash \text{let } x = \text{ref } M_1 \text{ in } M_2 : (T_2, (\epsilon_1 \sqcup \epsilon_2) \backslash x)} \text{ (LETREF)}$$

$$\frac{\Gamma, x : V \vdash M : C}{\Gamma \vdash \text{fun } (x : V) \to M : ((V \to C), (\emptyset, \emptyset))} \text{ (ABS)}$$

$$\frac{\Gamma \vdash M_1 : ((V \to (V_1, \epsilon_1)), \epsilon_0) \quad \Gamma \vdash M_2 : (V, \epsilon_2)}{\Gamma \vdash (M_1 \; M_2) : (V_1, (\epsilon_0 \sqcup \epsilon_1 \sqcup \epsilon_2))} \text{ (APP)}$$

**Fig. 2.** Typing with effects

two operators

$$\begin{aligned} &unit : A \to \mu(A) \\ &star : \mu(A) \to (A \to \mu(B)) \to \mu(B) \end{aligned}$$

satisfying three identities (which it is not necessary to give here). The main idea is that $\mu(A)$ is the type of the *computations* of type $A$. The *unit* operator is an injection of values into computations. The *star* operator takes a computation, evaluates it and passes its result to a function which returns a new computation. If we consider references, a possible monad is the one defined by $\mu(A) = S \to S \times A$, where $S$ represents the store, and where *unit* and *star* are defined by

$$\begin{aligned} unit\ v \quad &= \lambda s.(s, v) \\ star\ m\ f &= \lambda s.\text{let } (s', v) = (m\ s) \text{ in } (f\ v\ s') \end{aligned}$$

In our case, such a monad is too coarse, mainly because a global store does not allow proofs of programs to be *modular* (you have to express that some parts of the store are left unchanged by the program, which is not natural and painful). So we use *local stores* i.e. tuples of values directly representing the values of *input* and *output* variables given by the inference of effects. For instance, a computation involving the references $x$ and $y$ of type int ref which can modify the value of $x$ will be translated into a function taking the values of $x$ and $y$ as input and returning the new value of $x$ together with the result of the computation.

As noticed by Moggi, the *star* operator really acts as the let in operator of ML. In the following we will use a let in notation to make programs more readable, but the reader should have in mind the use of the monad operator to understand the generality of the discourse.

*Notations.* To define the functional translation of programs, we need to manipulate collections of values and in particular to define functions taking an $n$-tuple representing the input of a program and returning an $m$-tuple representing its output. Instead of using tuples, we will rather use *records* which are easier to manipulate. The type of a record will be written $\{ x_1 : X_1; \ldots; x_n : X_n \}$ and a particular record of that type will be written $\{ x_1 = v_1; \ldots; x_n = v_n \}$, where $x_i$ is a label, $X_i$ its type and $v_i$ a value of that type. Records will be written $\boldsymbol{x}, \boldsymbol{y}, \ldots$ for convenience and $\boldsymbol{x}.l$ will denote the field of label $l$ in record $\boldsymbol{x}$. We define the operation $\oplus$ on records as follows: the record $\boldsymbol{x} \oplus \boldsymbol{y} = \{ z_1 = w_1; \ldots; z_k = w_k \}$ contains all the labels of $\boldsymbol{x}$ and $\boldsymbol{y}$, and $w_i$ is equal to $\boldsymbol{y}.z_i$ if $z_i$ is a label of $\boldsymbol{y}$ and to $\boldsymbol{x}.z_i$ otherwise. In other words, it is the update of the record $\boldsymbol{x}$ by the record $\boldsymbol{y}$ i.e. the record made with the fields of $\boldsymbol{y}$ when they exist and of $\boldsymbol{x}$ in the other case. At last, $\boldsymbol{x} \backslash l$ will denote the record $\boldsymbol{x}$ in which the field $l$ is removed and $\boldsymbol{x}[l \leftarrow l']$ will denote the record $\boldsymbol{x}$ where the label $l$ is renamed into $l'$.

First, we give the interpretation of types with effects as purely functional types.

**Definition 1.** *The functional translation of types of values and types of computations are mutually recursively defined as follows:*

$$
\begin{array}{lll}
\textit{values} & \overline{T} & = T \\
 & \overline{V \to C} & = \overline{V} \to \overline{C} \\
\textit{computations} & \overline{(V, (R, W))} & = \overline{R} \to \overline{W} \times \overline{V} \\
\textit{effects} & \overline{\{x_1, \ldots, x_n\}} & = \{x_1 : T_1; \ldots; x_n : T_n\} \\
 & & \quad \textit{where } x_i \textit{ has type } T_i \text{ ref}
\end{array}
$$

*If $\Gamma$ is a typing environment mapping the $x_i$'s to the types $V_i$, then $\overline{\Gamma}$ will denote the environment mapping the $x_i$'s to the types $\overline{V_i}$.*

Note, there is no translation for the types $T$ ref: indeed, there is no program expression of such type and therefore there is no counterpart in the functional world. References, seen as *pointers*, do not exist anymore after the translation since we only manipulate the *values* they contain.

We are now in the position to define the functional translation itself. In the following we will use a slight abuse of notations: we will write $(\overline{M}\ \boldsymbol{x})$ even when the record $\boldsymbol{x}$ should be restricted to a subset of its fields (Another possibility is to consider that we have sub-typing on records).

**Definition 2.** *Let $M$ be a program of type $C$ in a context $\Gamma$. Then the functional translation of $M$, written $\overline{M}$, is a functional program of type $\overline{C}$ in the context $\overline{\Gamma}$, which is defined by induction on the structure of $M$ as follows:*

- $\underline{M \equiv E}$ :

$$\overline{M} = \lambda \boldsymbol{x}.(\{\}, E[!x \leftarrow \boldsymbol{x}.x])$$

- $\underline{M \equiv x_0 \ := \ M_1}$ :

$$\overline{M} = \lambda \boldsymbol{x}.\mathsf{let}\ (\boldsymbol{x_1}, v) = (\overline{M_1}\ \boldsymbol{x})\ \mathsf{in}\ (\boldsymbol{x_1} \oplus \{\, x_0 = v\, \}, \mathsf{void})$$

- $\underline{M \equiv M_1 \ ; \ M_2}$ :

$$\begin{aligned} \overline{M} = \lambda \boldsymbol{x}.\ & \mathsf{let}\ (\boldsymbol{x_1}, \_) = (\overline{M_1}\ \boldsymbol{x})\ \mathsf{in} \\ & \mathsf{let}\ (\boldsymbol{x_2}, v) = (\overline{M_2}\ (\boldsymbol{x} \oplus \boldsymbol{x_1}))\ \mathsf{in} \\ & (\boldsymbol{x_1} \oplus \boldsymbol{x_2}, v) \end{aligned}$$

- $\underline{M \equiv \mathsf{if}\ E\ \mathsf{then}\ M_1\ \mathsf{else}\ M_2}$ :

$$\begin{aligned} \overline{M} = \lambda \boldsymbol{x}.\ & \mathsf{if}\ (\overline{E}\ \boldsymbol{x})\ \mathsf{then} \\ & \quad \mathsf{let}\ (\boldsymbol{x_1}, v) = (\overline{M_1}\ \boldsymbol{x})\ \mathsf{in}\ (\boldsymbol{x} \oplus \boldsymbol{x_1}, v) \\ & \mathsf{else} \\ & \quad \mathsf{let}\ (\boldsymbol{x_1}, v) = (\overline{M_2}\ \boldsymbol{x})\ \mathsf{in}\ (\boldsymbol{x} \oplus \boldsymbol{x_1}, v) \end{aligned}$$

  It is clear now why we impose the condition on output variables to be included in the input variables: indeed, in both branches of the if we must return values for the same set of variables. So, when a variable is not modified by a branch, we have to return its initial value: therefore it must belong to the input values.

- $\underline{M \equiv \mathsf{while}\ E\ \mathsf{do}\ M_1\ \mathsf{done}}$ :
  To translate a loop, we use the following semantic equivalence:

$$M \approx (Y\ (\lambda w : \mathsf{unit} \rightarrow \mathsf{unit}.\mathsf{if}\ E\ \mathsf{then}\ (M_1\ ;\ (w\ \mathsf{void}))\ \mathsf{else}\ \mathsf{void})\ \mathsf{void})$$

  where $Y$ is a fixpoint operator. Then

$$\begin{aligned} \overline{M} = (Y\ \lambda w : \overline{C}.\lambda \boldsymbol{x}.\ & \mathsf{if}\ (\overline{E}\ \boldsymbol{x})\ \mathsf{then} \\ & \quad \mathsf{let}\ (\boldsymbol{x_1}, \_) = (\overline{M_1}\ \boldsymbol{x})\ \mathsf{in}\ \ (w\ (\boldsymbol{x} \oplus \boldsymbol{x_1})) \\ & \mathsf{else} \\ & \quad (\boldsymbol{x}, \mathsf{void})) \end{aligned}$$

  Here we assume that we have a fixpoint operator $Y$ in the Calculus of Constructions, which is not the case usually. This need will disappear when we are in position to establish termination, as it is the case in the next section.

- $\underline{M \equiv \mathsf{let}\ x_0 = \mathsf{ref}\ M_1\ \mathsf{in}\ M_2}$ :

$$\begin{aligned} \overline{M} = \lambda \boldsymbol{x}.\ & \mathsf{let}\ (\boldsymbol{x_1}, v_1) = (\overline{M_1}\ \boldsymbol{x})\ \mathsf{in} \\ & \mathsf{let}\ (\boldsymbol{x_2}, v_2) = (\overline{M_2}\ (\boldsymbol{x} \oplus \boldsymbol{x_1} \oplus \{\, x_0 = v_1\, \}))\ \mathsf{in} \\ & (\boldsymbol{x_1} \oplus (\boldsymbol{x_2} \backslash x_0), v_2) \end{aligned}$$

- $\underline{M \equiv \mathsf{fun}\ (x : V) \rightarrow M_1}$ :

$$\overline{M} = \lambda x : \overline{V}.\overline{M_1}$$

- $\underline{M \equiv (M_1\ M_2)}$

$$\begin{aligned}\overline{M} = \lambda x.\,&\text{let } (x_1, a) = (\overline{M_2}\ x) \text{ in}\\ &\text{let } (x_2, f) = (\overline{M_1}\ (x \oplus x_1)) \text{ in}\\ &\text{let } (x_3, v) = (f\ a\ (x \oplus x_1 \oplus x_2)) \text{ in}\\ &(x_1 \oplus x_2 \oplus x_3, v)\end{aligned}$$

Notice that we chose a semantics where the function is evaluated *after* its argument; therefore multiple arguments are evaluated from right to left.

□

To justify this definition, we have to prove that $\overline{M}$ preserves the semantics of $M$. We chose the formal semantics introduced by A. K. Wright and M. Felleisen in [18] to prove type soundness of SML with references and exceptions. The idea is to introduce a syntactic distinction between values and expressions and to extend the syntax of programs with a new construction $\rho\theta.M$, where $\theta$ is a mapping from variables to values representing the *store*. Then small-step reductions are introduced on extended programs, as rewriting rules driven by the syntax, and the evaluation relation $M \leadsto \rho\theta'.v$ is defined as the transitive closure of those reductions.

The preservation of the semantics can be expressed by the following theorem:

**Theorem 1.** *Let $\Gamma$ be a well-formed environment whose references are $x_1 : T_1$ ref$, \ldots, x_n : T_n$ ref and $M$ a program such that $\Gamma \vdash M : (V, (R, W))$. Let $v_i$ be values of types $T_i$ and $\theta$ the store mapping the $x_i$'s to the $v_i$'s. Then*

$$\rho\theta.M \leadsto \rho\theta'.v \qquad \Longleftrightarrow \qquad \overline{M}(\overline{\theta(R)}) = (\overline{\theta'(W)}, \overline{v})$$

*Proof.* We won't enter here the details of this proof. The *if* part is proved by induction on the derivation of the evaluation relation and the *only if* part is proved by induction on the program $M$. In both cases the proof is rather systematic since the semantic relation is driven by the syntax of programs. The reader may consult [18] to get the formal semantics of ML with references, which is greatly simplified in our case since we do not have polymorphism. □

**Call-by-variable**

Until now, we did not consider call-by-variable arguments i.e. the passing of references to functions, because their treatment is rather complex when combined with partial application (it requires the use of painful explicit coercions to re-organize elements in tuples). But if we do not allow partial application of functions doing side-effects, we can simply deal with call-by-variable. To give an idea of this method, let us consider the simple case of a function $M$ taking a first argument by-value and a second one by-variable i.e. of type $V_1 \to (x : T_2 \text{ ref}) \to (T, \epsilon)$. Its second argument is given a name, $x$, since it may appear in $\epsilon$. Then the typing rule for the application $(M\ M_1\ z)$ is the following

$$\frac{\Gamma \vdash M : ((V_1 \to (x : T_2 \text{ ref}) \to (T, \epsilon)), \epsilon_0) \quad \Gamma \vdash M_1 : (V_1, \epsilon_1) \quad z : T_2 \text{ ref} \in \Gamma}{\Gamma \vdash (M\ M_1\ z) : T, (\epsilon_0 \sqcup \epsilon_1 \sqcup \epsilon[x \leftarrow z])}$$

During the functional translation, the second argument of $M$ disappears: indeed, the functional program $\overline{M}$ does not manipulate references, but only their values, and consequently $\overline{M}$ has type $\overline{V_1} \to \overline{R} \to \overline{W} \times T$, where $\epsilon = (R, W)$. The reference $x$ now appears as a field of $\overline{R}$ and $\overline{W}$. So the functional translation of the application $(M\ M_1\ z)$ will be

$$\begin{aligned}\lambda \boldsymbol{x}.\ & \mathsf{let}\ (\boldsymbol{x_1}, v_1) = (\overline{M_1}\ \boldsymbol{x})\ \mathsf{in} \\ & \mathsf{let}\ (\boldsymbol{x_2}, f) = (\overline{M}\ (\boldsymbol{x} \oplus \boldsymbol{x_1}))\ \mathsf{in} \\ & \mathsf{let}\ (\boldsymbol{x_3}, v) = (f\ v_1\ (\boldsymbol{x} \oplus \boldsymbol{x_1} \oplus \boldsymbol{x_2})[z \leftarrow x])\ \mathsf{in} \\ & (\boldsymbol{x_1} \oplus \boldsymbol{x_2} \oplus \boldsymbol{x_3}[x \leftarrow z], v)\end{aligned}$$

This example is easily generalized to arbitrary numbers of call-by-value and call-by-variable arguments.

## 2 Program Correctness

We now come to the main point, proofs of programs, and the first thing to do is to define *how to specify* the programs. In almost all the literature about Floyd-Hoare logic and related systems, the programs are purely imperative and therefore can be seen as *sequences of statements* with separated notions of statements and expressions. Typically we have an abstract syntax of the kind

$$S \quad ::= \quad \mathsf{skip} \mid x := E \mid S\ ;\ S \mid \mathsf{if}\ E\ \mathsf{then}\ S\ \mathsf{else}\ S \mid \mathsf{while}\ E\ \mathsf{do}\ S\ \mathsf{done}$$

where $E$ is a pre-defined notion of expressions. Then it is natural to specify them by inserting logical assertions *between* the successive evaluations i.e. between the statements.

But in our case, following the tradition of functional programming languages, the notions of programs and expressions are identified. For instance, we can write programs like

$$x := (x := !x + 1\ ;\ !x)$$

$$x := (\mathsf{if}\ B\ \mathsf{then}\ \dots\ \mathsf{else}\ \dots)$$

This may appear superfluous but we claim that this is the key to deal with functions without difficulty. Take for instance a statement like

$$x := (f\ a)$$

where $f$ is a function which possibly has side-effects. Since our abstract syntax already includes statements of the form $x := M$ where $M$ is an arbitrary program, the above assignment does not change the effects. In other words, inlining the function $f$ would give a correct program, which is not the case in traditional frameworks.

Since the notions of programs and expressions are identified, we propose a more general way to specify programs, where each sub-expression of a program may be annotated with a pre- and a post-condition. A pre-condition will be a predicate over the current values of variables, as usual. For the post-conditions, we will use before-after predicates i.e. predicates referring to the current values of variables and to their values before the evaluation of the expression, as it is done in VDM. The current value of a variable $x$ will be written $x$ in both pre- and post-conditions and its value before the evaluation will be written $\overleftarrow{x}$ in a post-condition. Moreover, a post-condition must be able to express properties of the *result* of the evaluation, which will be given a name in post-conditions. The abstract syntax of programs is extended as follows:

$$
\begin{array}{lcl}
M & ::= & \{P\}\, S\, \{v \mid Q\} \\
S & ::= & E \mid x := M \mid M \ ; \ M \mid \ldots \text{(as formerly)}
\end{array}
$$

where $\{P\}$ stands for a pre-condition and $\{x \mid Q\}$ for a post-condition in which the result is referred as $x$. The type systems $V$ and $C$ for values and computations are enriched consequently:

$$
V \ ::= \ T \mid T \ \mathsf{ref} \mid (x : V) \to C \tag{4}
$$

$$
C \ ::= \ (v : V, \epsilon, P, Q) \tag{5}
$$

Note that function arguments are given names since they may now appear in annotations.

As previously, we have to give first an interpretation of types in the target language, the Calculus of Inductive Constructions. Those interpretations are written $\widehat{V}$ and $\widehat{C}$, $\widehat{C}$ being the *correctness formula.* A first idea for $\widehat{C}$ could be

$$
\forall \boldsymbol{x}.\, P(\boldsymbol{x}) \Rightarrow \exists(\boldsymbol{y}, v).\, (\boldsymbol{y}, v) = \overline{M}(\boldsymbol{x}) \wedge Q(\boldsymbol{x}, \boldsymbol{y}, v) \tag{6}
$$

But $\overline{M}$ is usually not a total function and therefore is not definable in the CIC. Thus, we choose to define $\widehat{C}$ just as

$$
\forall \boldsymbol{x}.\, P(\boldsymbol{x}) \Rightarrow \exists(\boldsymbol{y}, v).\, Q(\boldsymbol{x}, \boldsymbol{y}, v) \tag{7}
$$

and we will construct a particular proof of (7), $\widehat{M}$, which has the property to have a computational contents equal to $\overline{M}$. Therefore, the realizability theorem [14] will exactly express (6), which is the expected result.

**Definition 3.** *The interpretation in* CIC *of the types of values and the types of computations are defined as follows:*

$$
\begin{array}{llll}
\textit{if} & V = T & \textit{then} & \widehat{V} = T \\
\textit{if} & V = (x : V_0) \to C & \textit{then} & \widehat{V} = \forall x : \widehat{V_0}.\, \widehat{C}
\end{array}
$$

$$
\begin{array}{ll}
\textit{if} & C = (r : V, (R, W), P, Q) \\
\textit{then} & \widehat{C} = \forall \boldsymbol{x} : \overline{R}.\, P(\boldsymbol{x}) \Rightarrow \exists(\boldsymbol{y}, v) : \overline{W} \times \widehat{V}.\, Q(\boldsymbol{x}, \boldsymbol{y}, v)
\end{array}
$$

*If $\Gamma$ is a typing environment mapping the $x_i$'s to the types $V_i$, then $\widehat{\Gamma}$ will denote the environment mapping the $x_i$'s to the types $\widehat{V_i}$.*

Before giving the translation of the programs themselves, we have to solve a last problem: since functions in the CIC are necessarily total, a loop cannot be simply translated using a general fixpoint operator. Moreover, we are interested in proving *total correctness* and therefore we have to justify the termination of loops. Thus, loops will be annotated with a well-foundedness argument:

$$\mathsf{while}_{\phi,R}\ E\ \mathsf{do}\ M\ \mathsf{done}$$

where $\phi$ is a term and $R$ a relation over the type of $\phi$. Then such a loop will be translated using a well-founded induction over $\phi$.

In the following, an incomplete proof term of the CIC is a term where some sub-terms are still undefined and written "?". We assume that those gaps are typed, but we will not write the corresponding types for a greater clarity.

**Definition 4.** *Let $M$ be a program of type $C$ in a context $\Gamma$. Then the interpretation of a program $M$ in the* CIC, *written $\widehat{M}$, is an incomplete proof term of type $\widehat{C}$ in the context $\widehat{\Gamma}$, which is defined by induction on the structure of $M$ as follows:*

- $\underline{M \equiv \{P\}\ E\ \{Q\}}$ :

$$\widehat{M} = \lambda x.\lambda h : P.(\{\}, E[!x \leftarrow x.x], ?)$$

- $\underline{M \equiv \{P\}\ x_0 := M_1\ \{Q\}}$ :

$$\widehat{M} = \lambda x.\lambda h : P.\mathsf{let}\ (x_1, v, q_1) = (\widehat{M_1}\ x\ ?)\ \mathsf{in}\ (x_1 \oplus \{\, x_0 = v\,\}, \mathsf{void}, ?)$$

- $\underline{M \equiv \{P\}\ M_1\ ;\ M_2\ \{Q\}}$ :

$$\begin{aligned}\widehat{M} = \lambda x.\lambda h : P.\,&\mathsf{let}\ (x_1, \_, q_1) = (\widehat{M_1}\ x\ ?)\ \mathsf{in}\\ &\mathsf{let}\ (x_2, v, q_2) = (\widehat{M_2}\ (x \oplus x_1)\ ?)\ \mathsf{in}\\ &(x_1 \oplus x_2, v, ?)\end{aligned}$$

- $\underline{M \equiv \{P\}\ \mathsf{if}\ E\ \mathsf{then}\ M_1\ \mathsf{else}\ M_2\ \{Q\}}$ :

$$\begin{aligned}\widehat{M} = \lambda x.\lambda h : P.\,&\mathsf{if}\ (\widehat{E}\ x)\ \mathsf{then}\\ &\quad \mathsf{let}\ (x_1, v, q) = (\widehat{M_1}\ x\ ?)\ \mathsf{in}\ (x \oplus x_1, v, ?)\\ &\mathsf{else}\\ &\quad \mathsf{let}\ (x_1, v, q) = (\widehat{M_2}\ x\ ?)\ \mathsf{in}\ (x \oplus x_1, v, ?)\end{aligned}$$

- $\underline{M \equiv \{P\}\ \mathsf{while}_{\phi,R}\ E\ \mathsf{do}\ M_1\ \mathsf{done}\ \{Q\}}$ :
  To construct the proof term corresponding to this loop, we are going to use a well-founded induction over $\phi$. The well-founded recursor $Y_{R,\pi}$ is a higher-order term taking a relation $R$ and a proof $\pi$ that $R$ is well-founded. In our case, the proof $\pi$ is replaced by a proof obligation.

$$\begin{aligned}\widehat{M} = \lambda x.((Y_{R,?}\ \lambda w.\lambda x.\lambda\psi.\lambda h : P.\\ &\mathsf{if}\ (\widehat{E}\ x)\ \mathsf{then}\\ &\quad \mathsf{let}\ (x_1, \_, q) = (\widehat{M_1}\ x\ ?)\ \mathsf{in}\ \ (w\ (x \oplus x_1)\ \phi(x \oplus x_1)\ ?\ ?)\\ &\mathsf{else}\\ &\quad (x, \mathsf{void}, ?))\ x\ \phi(x))\end{aligned}$$

Here we have used $P$ as the loop *invariant*. There are four proof obligations related to that loop: to prove that $R$ is well-founded; to prove that $\phi$ strictly decreases in $M_1$; to prove that $M_1$ preserves $P$; and to prove that $P$ implies $Q$ when the test is negative.

- $M \equiv \{P\}\ \mathsf{let}\ x_0 = \mathsf{ref}\ M_1\ \mathsf{in}\ M_2\ \{Q\}$ :

$$\begin{aligned}\widehat{M} = \lambda x.\lambda h : P.\ & \mathsf{let}\ (\boldsymbol{x_1}, v_1, q_1) = (\widehat{M_1}\ x\ ?)\ \mathsf{in} \\ & \mathsf{let}\ (\boldsymbol{x_2}, v_2, q_2) = (\widehat{M_2}\ (x \oplus \boldsymbol{x_1} \oplus \{\, x_0 = v_1 \,\})\ ?)\ \mathsf{in} \\ & (\boldsymbol{x_1} \oplus (\boldsymbol{x_2} \backslash x_0), v_2, ?)\end{aligned}$$

- $M \equiv \{P\}\ \mathsf{fun}\ (x : V) \to M_1\ \{Q\}$ :

$$\widehat{M} = \lambda h : P.((\lambda x : \widehat{V}.\widehat{M_1}), ?)$$

Notice that here $P$ and $Q$ are the pre- and post-conditions of the *function* and not of the result of its application. Usually they are empty.

- $M \equiv \{P\}\ (M_1\ M_2)\ \{Q\}$

$$\begin{aligned}\widehat{M} = \lambda x.\lambda h : P.\ & \mathsf{let}\ (\boldsymbol{x_1}, a, q_1) = (\widehat{M_2}\ x\ ?)\ \mathsf{in} \\ & \mathsf{let}\ (\boldsymbol{x_2}, f, q_2) = (\widehat{M_1}\ (x \oplus \boldsymbol{x_1})\ ?)\ \mathsf{in} \\ & \mathsf{let}\ (\boldsymbol{x_3}, v, q_3) = (f\ a\ (x \oplus \boldsymbol{x_1} \oplus \boldsymbol{x_2})\ ?)\ \mathsf{in} \\ & (\boldsymbol{x_1} \oplus \boldsymbol{x_2} \oplus \boldsymbol{x_3}, v, ?)\end{aligned}$$

□

To justify the validity of the proof obligations we obtain, we have to prove that they apply to the right values. It directly results from Theorem 1 and from the following proposition (which is immediate by construction of $\widehat{M}$):

**Proposition 1.** *For any program $M$ the following equality holds*

$$\mathcal{E}(\widehat{M}) = \overline{M} \tag{8}$$

*where $\mathcal{E}$ is the* extraction *operator, which computes the informative contents of a proof (extraction in the Calculus of Inductive Constructions was introduced by C. Paulin in [14]).*

## Examples and comparison to Floyd-Hoare logic

*Example 1.* Let us consider the classical case of assignment where the right hand side has no effect and no annotation i.e.

$$M \quad \equiv \quad \{P\}\ x_0 := E\ \{Q\}$$

Then the proof term $\widehat{M}$ reduces to $\lambda x.\lambda h : P(x).(x \oplus \{\, x_0 = E \,\}, \mathsf{void}, ?)$ where the gap has type $Q(x, x \oplus \{\, x_0 = E \,\}, \mathsf{void})$. So we get only one proof obligation, which is the following, with some abuses of notation:

$$P \Rightarrow Q[x_0 \leftarrow E]$$

This is exactly the one we get in Floyd-Hoare logic (with the combination of the consequence rule and the assignment rule). □

*Example 2.* Let us consider again an assignment, but where the expression assigned is now the result of a function call, that is $M \equiv \{P\}\ x_0 := (f\ E)\ \{Q\}$. The function $f$ has a type $V$ of the form $V_0 \rightarrow (v : V_1, \epsilon, P_f, Q_f)$. Therefore, we can see the program $M$ as annotated this way:

$$M \quad \equiv \quad \{P\}\ x_0 := \{P_f\}\ (f\ E)\ \{v \mid Q_f\}\ \{Q\}$$

Then if we look at the proof term $\widehat{M}$, we find two gaps, the first one corresponding to the pre-condition $P_f$ and the second one to the post-condition $Q$. More precisely, the two proof obligations are the following:

$$P \Rightarrow P_f \qquad \text{and} \qquad P \Rightarrow P_f \Rightarrow Q_f \Rightarrow Q[x_0 \leftarrow v]$$

Contrary to the previous case, the expression assigned is no more substituted in the post-condition but *abstracted* through the variable $v$. □

# 3 Implementation

This work has been implemented in the Coq Proof Assistant [1] and is currently released with the system, together with a documentation and a few examples. The user gives an annotated imperative program to a tactic, and a set of proof obligations are produced, which must be proved to complete the correctness proof. As explained at the end of the first section, we have call-by-variable but without partial application (so it is closer to Pascal than ML regarding this point). The implementation also includes some additional features, namely arrays and a way to eradicate the use of auxiliary variables.

*Arrays.* When dealing with arrays, we face a potential source of aliasing problems, since $t[i]$ and $t[j]$ may refer to the same cell of an array, while it is not possible to decide statically if $i$ is equal to $j$ or not. A standard solution is to consider *the whole array* as a mutable data, like any reference (see [4], page 931). Consequently, programs manipulating arrays become functions taking arrays as arguments and returning new arrays. Arrays are axiomatized in the CIC in the very simplest way, and proof obligations are produced to check that indexes are always within the bounds of arrays.

*The case of auxiliary variables.* Auxiliary variables, sometimes called *logical variables*, are used in specifications to relate values of variables at different moments of the execution of a program. Indeed, the before-after predicates used in post-conditions are not always powerful enough to express the specifications (see for instance [4], page 940). Although it is possible to give a formal interpretation to auxiliary variables, as shown by T. Schreiber in [15], we propose another way to solve this problem. The idea is very simple: since our functional translation define names for each new value of a variable (at each application of the monad let in operator), we just have to allow the user to access those names. So we added the possibility to put labels inside programs (like the ones used for the goto statement in old programming languages), and the user may refer to the value of a given variable at a particular moment using the associated label. Then the substitution inside pre- and post-conditions is performed during the construction of $\widehat{M}$. This is a rather technical point, but it appeared to be very useful in practice, and the proof obligations generated are simpler to prove since they do not require rewriting.

*Case studies.* The first case study we did with our implementation is the program *find*, a quite complex algorithm which was proved correct by Hoare using his axiomatic logic in 1971 [9]. Applied to that annotated program, our method generated *exactly the same proof obligations* than the ones given in Hoare's paper. We also did a correctness proof of the *quicksort* algorithm and of the Knuth-Pratt-Morris string searching algorithm. Another case study is a proof of *insertion sort*, which was done recently by a novel user with the Coq system. Those case studies cover all the functionalities of the method, including loops, procedures and recursive functions.

## 4 Discussion and Future Work

We have set out in this paper a method to establish the total correctness of imperative programs in Type Theory. It shares the goals of traditional Floyd-Hoare logic, regarding programs annotations and proof obligations we expect to get, but this method uses a completely different approach, based on the construction of an incomplete proof of its correctness, itself built on top of a functional translation of the imperative program. On sequential imperative programs, we get in practice the same proof obligations as Floyd-Hoare logic, which was the expected result.

Compared to the B method of J.-R. Abrial [2], our method, even if it has not the same level of maturity, offers some benefits. First, it is based on Type Theory, a framework which is small, powerful and well-understood on a theoretical point-of-view. Secondly, we are able to express the correctness of a program and its proof in the logic, which is not the case in traditional methods where programs, their specifications and their proofs live in different worlds and where correctness depends on the correctness of the tools relating those parts. The B method was recently partly formalized in Isabelle/HOL by P. Chartier [3]. But such a formalization has the same drawbacks as Floyd-Hoare logic formalizations already mentioned [7, 15]: they may be useful to prove theoretical properties of the framework but can not be applied in practice because of painful encodings.

Closest to our approach is the one of C. Muñoz [12], who formalized the B abstract machines in PVS. As we do, he directly manipulates objects of the Type Theory, which extends the range of datatypes of B, and uses record dependent types to define the states of abstract machines (a collection of variables with a global invariant). Then operations are seen as functions on states, and the preservation of the invariant is expressed by typing, proof obligations being generated by the *type-checking conditions* mechanism of PVS.

Regarding future works, we would like to incorporate pattern-matching and exceptions to reach a more realistic language. While pattern-matching is only technical — semantically, it can be viewed as a combination of tests and access functions — the treatment of exceptions needs an extension of the notion of effects and of the specification. However, we think that our framework is well-suited for such an extension, since the only thing to do is to define the corresponding monad.

## References


1. The Coq Proof Assistant. `http://coq.inria.fr/`.
2. J. R. Abrial. *The B-Book. Assigning programs to meaning.* Cambridge University Press, 1996.
3. P. Chartier. Formalization of B in Isabelle/HOL. In *Proceedings of the Second B International Conference*, Montepellier, France, April 1998. Springer Verlag LNCS 1393.
4. P. Cousot. *Handbook of Theoretical Computer Science*, volume B, chapter Methods and Logics for Proving Programs, pages 841–993. Elsevier Science Publishers B. V., 1990.
5. E. W. Dijkstra. *A Discipline of Programming.* Prentice-Hall, 1976.
6. R. W. Floyd. Assigning meanings to programs. In J. T. Schwartz, editor, *Mathematical Aspects of Computer Science, Proceedings of Symposia in applied Mathematics 19*, pages 19–32, Providence, 1967. American Mathematical Society.
7. Mike Gordon. *Teaching and Learning Formal Methods*, chapter Teaching hardware and software verification in a uniform framework. Academic Press, 1996.
8. C. A. R. Hoare. An axiomatic basis for computer programming. *Communications of the ACM*, 12(10):576–580,583, 1969. Also in [10] 45–58.
9. C. A. R. Hoare. Proof of a program : *Find. Communications of the ACM*, 14(1):39–45, January 1971. Also in [10] 59–74.
10. C. A. R. Hoare and C. B. Jones. *Essays in Computing Science.* Prentice Hall, New York, 1989.
11. E. Moggi. Computational lambda-calculus and monads. In *IEEE Symposium on Logic in Computer Science*, 1989.
12. C. Muñoz. Supporting the B-method in PVS: An Approach to the Abstract Machine Notation in Type Theory. Submitted to FSE-98, 1998.
13. C. Parent. Developing certified programs in the system Coq – The Program tactic. Technical Report 93-29, Ecole Normale Supérieure de Lyon, October 1993. Also in Proceedings of the BRA Workshop Types for Proofs and Programs, May 93.
14. C. Paulin-Mohring. Extracting $F_\omega$'s programs from proofs in the Calculus of Constructions. In *Sixteenth Annual ACM Symposium on Principles of Programming Languages*, Austin, January 1989. ACM.
15. T. Schreiber. Auxiliary variables and recursive procedures. In *TAPSOFT'97: Theory and Practice of Software Development*, volume 1214 of *Lecture Notes in Computer Science*, pages 697–711. Springer-Verlag, April 1997.
16. J.-P. Talpin and P. Jouvelot. The type and effect discipline. *Information and Computation*, 111(2):245–296, 1994.
17. P. Wadler. Monads for functional programming. In *Proceedings of the Marktoberdorf Summer School on Program Design Calculi*, August 1992.
18. A. K. Wright and M. Felleisen. A Syntactic Approach to Type Soundness. *Information and Computation*, 115:38–94, 1994.

# An Interpretation of the Fan Theorem in Type Theory*

Daniel Fridlender

BRICS**, Department of Computer Science, University of Aarhus
Ny Munkegade, Building 540, DK-8000 Aarhus C, Denmark
e-mail: daniel@brics.dk

**Abstract.** This article presents a formulation of the fan theorem in Martin-Löf's type theory. Starting from one of the standard versions of the fan theorem we gradually introduce reformulations leading to a final version which is easy to interpret in type theory. Finally we describe a formal proof of that final version of the fan theorem.

**Keywords**: type theory, fan theorem, inductive bar.

## 1 Introduction

In informal constructive mathematics, the fan theorem is an easy consequence of the rule of bar induction. Both are about infinite objects which makes their interpretation in Martin-Löf's type theory non trivial. Bar induction can be represented in type theory, as proposed in [Mar68] and shown also in this article. But still from this interpretation it is not clear how to formulate and prove the fan theorem formally in type theory.

This is because, whereas the usual informal language to treat bar induction and the fan theorem is the same, the formal treatment of the fan theorem in type theory is technically more involved than that of bar induction. The concept of finiteness is difficult to handle simultaneously in an elegant, completely formal and constructive way; and it seems hard to avoid dealing explicitly with *fans*, whereas *spreads* are avoided in the type-theoretic interpretation of bar induction.

The fan theorem is very important in constructive mathematics since it makes possible to reconstruct large parts of traditional analysis. For explanations of the fan theorem and its role in constructive analysis see for instance [Dum77] and [TvD88].

The goal in this article is to present a formulation and a proof of the fan theorem in type theory. The type-theoretic version of the fan theorem presented here has been used in [Fri97] to interpret in type theory an intuitionistic proof of Higman's lemma which uses the fan theorem [Vel94]. However, in [Fri97] the

* Partially developed during the author's affiliation to Göteborg University, Sweden.

** Basic Research in Computer Science,
Centre of the Danish National Research Foundation.

type-theoretic fan theorem is only mentioned and the proof is omitted. The importance of the fan theorem justifies this more extended presentation.

Type theory here means Martin-Löf's type theory, of which there exist different formulations (for example, [Mar75], [Mar84], [NPS90] and [Tas97]). The exposition here should suit all of them. The proof of the fan theorem presented here has been written down in full detail with the assistance of the proof-editor ALF [Mag94] which is an implementation of the formulation of type theory given in [Tas97].

The rest of this article is organized as follows. Section 2 introduces some notations and definitions to be used in the whole article, and gives an informal presentation of bar induction and the fan theorem.

Section 3 shows a type-theoretic interpretation of bar induction and illustrates its use by proving some of its properties which are useful for the rest of the article.

Section 4 formulates and proves the fan theorem in type theory.

Finally, Section 5 presents a result by Veldman [Vel98] related to the formulations of the fan theorem given in Section 2.

The contributions of this article are the alternative informal formulations of the fan theorem in Section 2 and the formalization of the fan theorem in type theory, in Section 4.

## 2 Bar induction and the fan theorem

This section introduces the notations to be used in the whole article and gives an informal presentation of bar induction and the fan theorem. Several reformulations of the fan theorem are introduced leading to Theorem 5, which is the version that is formalized in type theory in Section 4.

### 2.1 Preliminaries

Notations:

$\mathcal{N}$ the set of the natural numbers. Variables: $n, m, k$.

$\mathcal{A}^*$ the set of the lists (finite sequences) of elements of the set $\mathcal{A}$. Variables: $\overline{u}$, $\overline{v}$, $\overline{w}$. Even $\overline{\overline{u}}$, $\overline{\overline{v}}$, $\overline{\overline{w}}$ when $\mathcal{A}$ is a set of lists.

$<a_1, \ldots, a_n>$ is the notation for lists.

$\overline{u} * \overline{v}$ is the concatenation between lists.

$\overline{u} \bullet a$ is a notation for concatenations of the form $\overline{u} * <a>$.

The variables $\alpha$, $\beta$ are used to denote infinite sequences of natural numbers. An initial segment $<\alpha(0), \ldots, \alpha(n-1)>$ of $\alpha$ is denoted $\overline{\alpha}(n)$. Given a set $\mathcal{S}$ of finite sequences of natural numbers, if $\forall n \; [\overline{\alpha}(n) \in \mathcal{S}]$, then we write $\alpha \in \mathcal{S}$. We denote by $\mathcal{S}^c$ the set $\mathcal{N}^* \setminus \mathcal{S}$.

**Definition 1 (tree).** *A* tree *is a set $\mathcal{T}$ of finite sequences of natural numbers (intuitively, a set of finite branches) which satisfy*

$$\begin{array}{ll} <> \in \mathcal{T} & \mathcal{T} \textit{ is inhabited} \\ \forall \overline{u} \ \ [\overline{u} \in \mathcal{T} \vee \overline{u} \notin \mathcal{T}] & \mathcal{T} \textit{ is decidable} \\ \forall \overline{u}, n \ \ [\overline{u} \bullet n \in \mathcal{T} \Rightarrow \overline{u} \in \mathcal{T}] & \mathcal{T} \textit{ is closed under predecessor.} \end{array}$$

**Definition 2 (finitely branching).** *A* finitely branching tree *is a tree $\mathcal{T}$ which satisfy*

$$\forall \overline{u} \in \mathcal{T} \ \exists m \ \forall n \ \ [\overline{u} \bullet n \in \mathcal{T} \Rightarrow n < m].$$

**Definition 3 (spread, fan).** *A* spread *is a tree in which every node has at least one successor, that is, a tree $\mathcal{S}$ satisfying*

$$\forall \overline{u} \in \mathcal{S} \ \exists n \ \ [\overline{u} \bullet n \in \mathcal{S}].$$

*A finitely branching spread is called a* fan.

**Definition 4 (bar).** *Given a set $\mathcal{U} \subseteq \mathcal{N}^*$ and a spread $\mathcal{S}$, $\mathcal{U}$ is a* bar on $\mathcal{S}$ *if*

$$\forall \alpha \in \mathcal{S} \ \exists n \ \ [\overline{\alpha}(n) \in \mathcal{U}].$$

When $\mathcal{S} = \mathcal{N}^*$, $\mathcal{S}$ is called the *universal spread* and $\mathcal{U}$ is said to be a *bar*.

**Proposition 1.** *Given a spread $\mathcal{S}$ and a bar $\mathcal{U}$ on $\mathcal{S}$, then $\mathcal{V} = \mathcal{U} \cup \mathcal{S}^c$ is a bar.*

We can prove that $\mathcal{V}$ is a bar by letting $\alpha$ be an arbitrary infinite sequence of natural numbers and finding $n$ such that $\overline{\alpha}(n) \in \mathcal{V}$. To this end, we determine a sequence of natural numbers $\beta$ whose initial segments are the same as those of $\alpha$ as long as they belong to $\mathcal{S}$. As soon as an initial segment of $\alpha$ does not belong to $\mathcal{S}$, $\beta$ deviates from $\alpha$. From that point, the initial segments of $\beta$ are arbitrary segments in $\mathcal{S}$. That is,

$$\beta(i) = \begin{cases} \alpha(i) & \text{if } \overline{\alpha}(i{+}1) \in \mathcal{S} \\ k & \text{if } \overline{\alpha}(i{+}1) \notin \mathcal{S}, \text{for some } k \text{ such that } \overline{\beta}(i) \bullet k \in \mathcal{S} \end{cases}$$

As $\beta \in \mathcal{S}$, and $\mathcal{U}$ is a bar on $\mathcal{S}$, we can obtain $n$ such that $\overline{\beta}(n) \in \mathcal{U}$. Now, either $\overline{\alpha}(n) \in \mathcal{S}$, in which case $\overline{\alpha}(n) = \overline{\beta}(n) \in \mathcal{U} \subseteq \mathcal{V}$, or $\overline{\alpha}(n) \notin \mathcal{S}$, hence $\overline{\alpha}(n) \in \mathcal{S}^c \subseteq \mathcal{V}$. Therefore, $\mathcal{V}$ is a bar.

## 2.2 Bar induction

*Bar induction* is the following rule, which is an axiom of intuitionistic logic

$$\frac{\begin{array}{ll} \forall \overline{u} \in \mathcal{X} \ \ \overline{u} \in \mathcal{Y} & \mathcal{X} \text{ is included in } \mathcal{Y} \\ \forall \overline{u} \in \mathcal{X} \ \ \forall n \ \ [\overline{u} \bullet n \in \mathcal{X}] & \mathcal{X} \text{ is monotone} \\ \forall \overline{u} \ \ \{[\forall n \ \ \overline{u} \bullet n \in \mathcal{Y}] \Rightarrow \overline{u} \in \mathcal{Y}\} & \mathcal{Y} \text{ is hereditary} \\ \forall \alpha \ \ \exists n \ \ [\overline{\alpha}(n) \in \mathcal{X}] & \mathcal{X} \text{ is a bar} \end{array}}{<> \in \mathcal{Y}} \ \text{BI}$$

for $\mathcal{X}, \mathcal{Y} \subseteq \mathcal{N}^*$. For other formulations of the rule of bar induction and their justification see [Dum77].

## 2.3 Fan theorem

The most important consequence of the rule of bar induction is the fan theorem.

**Theorem 1 (fan theorem).** *Given a fan $\mathcal{F}$, and a monotone bar $\mathcal{U}$ on $\mathcal{F}$, then*

$$\exists n \ \forall \alpha \in \mathcal{F} \ [\overline{\alpha}(n) \in \mathcal{U}].$$

Intuitively, the fan theorem states that for any finitely branching tree all whose branches are finite, there is an upper bound on the length of the branches. The tree, not explicit in the statement of the theorem, is the set $\mathcal{F} \setminus \mathcal{U}$ (when $\mathcal{U}$ is decidable and $<> \notin \mathcal{U}$).

The fan theorem can also be read as stating that every finitely branching tree all whose branches are finite is itself finite, that is, has a finite number of nodes. This is so, since for a finitely branching tree, the existence of an upper bound on the length of the branches is equivalent with it being finite.

A proof of the fan theorem can be obtained using the rule of bar induction with $\mathcal{X} = \mathcal{U} \cup \mathcal{F}^c$ and $\mathcal{Y} = \{\overline{u} \mid \exists n \ \forall \alpha \in \mathcal{F} \ [\alpha \text{ starts with } \overline{u} \Rightarrow \overline{\alpha}(n) \in \mathcal{U}]\}$. Proposition 1 guarantees that $\mathcal{X}$ is a bar. The monotonicity of $\mathcal{X}$ follows from those of $\mathcal{U}$ and $\mathcal{F}^c$. The inclusion of $\mathcal{X}$ in $\mathcal{Y}$ can be proved by letting $\overline{u} \in \mathcal{X}$ be arbitrary and choosing $n$ as the length of $\overline{u}$. To prove that $\mathcal{Y}$ is hereditary we assume that, for an arbitrary $\overline{u}$, $\forall k \ \ \overline{u} \bullet k \in \mathcal{Y}$ holds, and prove that $\overline{u} \in \mathcal{Y}$ also holds. If $\overline{u} \notin \mathcal{F}$, then $\overline{u} \in \mathcal{Y}$ clearly holds, since no $\alpha \in \mathcal{F}$ starts with $\overline{u}$. Otherwise, as $\mathcal{F}$ is finitely branching there exists $m$ such that for all $k$, $\overline{u} \bullet k \in \mathcal{F} \Rightarrow k < m$. As for each $k$, $\overline{u} \bullet k \in \mathcal{Y}$, it is possible to determine $n_0, \ldots n_{m-1}$ such that for each $k < m$ and $\alpha \in \mathcal{F}$ if $\alpha$ starts with $\overline{u} \bullet k$, then $\overline{\alpha}(n_k) \in \mathcal{U}$. To show that $\overline{u} \in \mathcal{Y}$, we choose $n$ to be max $\{n_k \mid k < m\}$ and use the monotonicity of $\mathcal{U}$.

## 2.4 Other formulations of the fan theorem

So far, we have used the terminology which is standard in the literature. It is possible to give alternative presentations of the fan theorem, some of which, are actually not formulated in terms of fans but in terms of arbitrary finitely branching trees.

In this section, we explore other formulations of the fan theorem with the purpose of obtaining one which is easier to represent in type theory. We shall see that there is no need to introduce notions like fan or tree in type theory, since the fan theorem can be reformulated without explicit use of those notions.

Some of the formulations that we will introduce are in terms of a special kind of tree, which we call *independent-choice trees.*

**Definition 5 (independent-choice).** *An* independent-choice tree *is a tree $\mathcal{I}$ such that for all $\overline{u}, \overline{v} \in \mathcal{I}$ of equal length,*

$$\forall n \ [\overline{u} \bullet n \in \mathcal{I} \Leftrightarrow \overline{v} \bullet n \in \mathcal{I}].$$

There is a one-to-one correspondence between independent-choice fans and infinite sequences of nonempty finite subsets of $\mathcal{N}$. An independent-choice fan $\mathcal{I}$ is uniquely determined by a sequence $\mathcal{I}_0, \mathcal{I}_1, \ldots$ of nonempty finite subsets of $\mathcal{N}$. The branches of $\mathcal{I}$ of length $n$ are obtained by choosing one element from each of the sets $\mathcal{I}_0, \mathcal{I}_1, \ldots, \mathcal{I}_{n-1}$ in that order. Every choice is independent of the other choices done to determine the branch. Similarly, there is a one-to-one correspondence between independent-choice finitely branching trees and (not necessarily infinite) sequences of nonempty finite subsets of $\mathcal{N}$.

The notion of independent-choice tree turns out to be very useful for obtaining a reformulation of the fan theorem easier to interpret in type theory.

We list first a few statements equivalent to Theorem 1.

**Theorem 2 (alternatives to fan theorem).** *The fan theorem is equivalent to the validity of*

$$\forall \text{ monotone bar } \mathcal{U} \ \ \exists n \ \ \forall \alpha \in \mathcal{T} \ \ [\overline{\alpha}(n) \in \mathcal{U}]$$

*in any of the following cases:*

1. *for all fan $\mathcal{T}$,*
2. *for all finitely branching tree $\mathcal{T}$,*
3. *for all independent-choice fan $\mathcal{T}$,*
4. *for all independent-choice finitely branching tree $\mathcal{T}$.*

The only difference between the fan theorem and item 1 is that in the latter $\mathcal{U}$ runs over bars on the universal spread, rather than over bars on the fan. With this modification, the fan theorem can be formulated for finitely branching trees as well (item 2). On the other hand, it is enough to restrict attention to independent-choice fans or trees (items 3 and 4).

To prove Theorem 2 notice that the domain on which $\mathcal{T}$ ranges in item 2 includes the one on which it ranges in item 1, and so item 2 $\Rightarrow$ item 1. Analogously, item 2 $\Rightarrow$ item 4, item 1 $\Rightarrow$ item 3, and item 4 $\Rightarrow$ item 3. Similarly, the domain on which $\mathcal{U}$ ranges in the fan theorem includes the one on which it ranges in Theorem 2, so Theorem 1 $\Rightarrow$ item 1.

To finish the proof of Theorem 2 it is enough to prove that item 3 $\Rightarrow$ item 2 and item 1 $\Rightarrow$ Theorem 1. For the former, let $\mathcal{T}$ be an arbitrary finitely branching tree and $\mathcal{U}$ an arbitrary monotone bar. Let $\mathcal{I}$ be the least independent-choice fan containing $\mathcal{T}$. Determine $n$ such that $\forall \alpha \in \mathcal{I} \ [\overline{\alpha}(n) \in \mathcal{U}]$. As $\alpha \in \mathcal{T} \Rightarrow \alpha \in \mathcal{I}$, we obtain $\forall \alpha \in \mathcal{T} \ [\overline{\alpha}(n) \in \mathcal{U}]$.

Finally, to prove that item 1 $\Rightarrow$ Theorem 1, let $\mathcal{F}$ be an arbitrary fan and $\mathcal{U}$ an arbitrary bar on $\mathcal{F}$. Define $\mathcal{V} = \mathcal{U} \cup \mathcal{F}^c$. By Proposition 1, $\mathcal{V}$ is a bar. Then, by item 1 there is an $n$ such that for all $\alpha \in \mathcal{F}$, $\overline{\alpha}(n) \in \mathcal{V}$. As $\overline{\alpha}(n) \in \mathcal{F}$, $\overline{\alpha}(n) \in \mathcal{U}$.

Observe how letting $\mathcal{U}$ run only over bars on the universal spread rather than over bars on $\mathcal{T}$, opens the possibility of a number of alternatives to the original formulation of the fan theorem. Indeed, Veldman showed that the same kind of alternatives do not hold intuitionistically if $\mathcal{U}$ is taken to be an arbitrary bar over $\mathcal{T}$. This is further explained in Section 5.

The next theorem says that more formulations can be obtained, where quantification over infinite sequences of natural numbers is avoided.

**Theorem 3 (more alternatives to fan theorem).** *The fan theorem is equivalent to the validity of*

$$\forall \textit{ monotone bar } \mathcal{U} \;\; \exists n \;\; \forall \overline{u} \in \mathcal{T} \;\; [\textit{length}(\overline{u}) = n \;\Rightarrow\; \overline{u} \in \mathcal{U}]$$

*in any of the following cases:*

5. *for all fan $\mathcal{T}$,*
6. *for all finitely branching tree $\mathcal{T}$,*
7. *for all independent-choice fan $\mathcal{T}$,*
8. *for all independent-choice finitely branching tree $\mathcal{T}$.*

Just as in the proof of Theorem 2, it is easy to obtain that item 6 $\Rightarrow$ item 5, item 6 $\Rightarrow$ item 8, item 5 $\Rightarrow$ item 7, and item 8 $\Rightarrow$ item 7. Item 6 follows from item 7 in the same way as item 2 followed from item 3 in Theorem 2.

Finally, the equivalence between item 5 and item 1 of Theorem 2 is also easy, since given a fan $\mathcal{T}$, every $\overline{u} \in \mathcal{T}$ of length $n$ is equal to $\overline{\alpha}(n)$, for some $\alpha \in \mathcal{T}$.

**Theorem 4 (one more alternative to fan theorem).** *For all monotone bar $\mathcal{U}$ and all infinite sequence $\mathcal{I}_0, \mathcal{I}_1, \ldots$ of finite subsets of $\mathcal{N}$,*

$$\exists n \;\; [\mathcal{I}_0 \times \ldots \times \mathcal{I}_{n-1} \; \subseteq \; \mathcal{U}],$$

*where $\mathcal{I}_0 \times \ldots \times \mathcal{I}_{n-1} = \{<a_0, \ldots, a_{n-1}> \;\mid\; \forall i \;\; a_i \in \mathcal{I}_i\}$.*

Theorem 4 is equivalent to the fan theorem.

Let $\mathcal{T}$ be the set $\bigcup\{\mathcal{I}_0 \times \ldots \times \mathcal{I}_{i-1} \mid \; i \in \mathcal{N}\}$. Clearly, $\mathcal{T}$ is a finitely branching tree. By item 6 of Theorem 3, there is a natural number $n$ such that all the sequences in $\mathcal{T}$ of length $n$ belong to $\mathcal{U}$. Those sequences are exactly the elements in the set $\mathcal{I}_0 \times \ldots \times \mathcal{I}_{n-1}$.

Conversely, to prove that item 8 of Theorem 3 follows from Theorem 4, let $\mathcal{T}$ be an arbitrary independent-choice finitely branching tree. Let $\mathcal{I}_i$ be the set $\{k \in \mathcal{N} \mid \; \exists \overline{u} \;\; [\text{length}(\overline{u}) = i \; \wedge \; \overline{u} \bullet k \in \mathcal{T}]\}$. Given $\overline{u} \in \mathcal{T}$ of length $n$, we have $\overline{u} \in \mathcal{I}_0 \times \ldots \times \mathcal{I}_{n-1} \subseteq \mathcal{U}$.

The advantage of the formulation of the fan theorem as in Theorem 4 is that it avoids the notions of fan and finitely branching tree. Also, if we extend the definition of *bar* to sets of finite sequences of finite subsets of natural numbers, rather than only sets of finite sequences of natural numbers, then we may write the fan theorem in the following way.

Let $\overline{\mathcal{I}}$ range over finite sequences of finite subsets of $\mathcal{N}$, and $\bigotimes$ denote the operation to obtain the Cartesian product of such a finite sequence, that is, $\bigotimes <\mathcal{I}_0, \ldots, \mathcal{I}_{n-1}> = \mathcal{I}_0 \times \ldots \times \mathcal{I}_{n-1}$.

**Theorem 5 (final reformulation of fan theorem).** *Given a monotone set $\mathcal{U}$ of finite sequences of natural numbers, if $\mathcal{U}$ is a bar, then so is $\{\overline{\mathcal{I}} \mid \bigotimes \overline{\mathcal{I}} \subseteq \mathcal{U}\}$.*

This is the formulation which is represented in type theory by Theorem 6, in Section 4.

## 3 Inductive bars

Following the Curry-Howard isomorphism ([CF58] and [How80]) every proposition is formally represented in type theory by the set of its proofs. Predicates, subsets and families of sets are identified with each other, in the sense that every predicate over the elements of a set $\mathcal{A}$, every subset of $\mathcal{A}$, and every family of sets indexed by the elements of $\mathcal{A}$, is represented by a function which when applied to an element of $\mathcal{A}$ returns a set.

Given a predicate $\mathcal{U}$ over a set $\mathcal{A}$ and a list $\overline{u}$ in $\mathcal{A}^*$, we let $\bigwedge_{\overline{u}}\mathcal{U}$ or

$$\bigwedge_{\overline{u}}\mathcal{U}$$

mean that all the elements in the list $\overline{u}$ satisfy $\mathcal{U}$. In type theory, it can be defined inductively with the following introduction rules.

$$\frac{}{\bigwedge_{<>}\mathcal{U}} \qquad \frac{\bigwedge_{\overline{u}}\mathcal{U} \quad \mathcal{U}(a)}{\bigwedge_{\overline{u}\bullet a}\mathcal{U}}$$

Notice that $\bigwedge_{\overline{u}*\overline{v}}\mathcal{U}$ is equivalent to $\bigwedge_{\overline{u}}\mathcal{U} \wedge \bigwedge_{\overline{v}}\mathcal{U}$. Associated to the definition of $\bigwedge_{\overline{u}}\mathcal{U}$ we have the following principle of induction, for every predicate $\mathcal{X}$ over $\mathcal{A}^*$.

$$\frac{\bigwedge_{\overline{u}}\mathcal{U} \quad \mathcal{X}(<>) \quad \forall\overline{v}\ [\mathcal{X}(\overline{v}) \wedge \mathcal{U}(a) \Rightarrow \mathcal{X}(\overline{v}\bullet a)]}{\mathcal{X}(\overline{u})}$$

When using this principle we refer to it as *induction on "the" proof that* $\bigwedge_{\overline{u}}\mathcal{U}$, where "the" proof is the proof of $\bigwedge_{\overline{u}}\mathcal{U}$ available at that moment.

In type theory, we formulate the definition of bar for predicates over lists of elements of an arbitrary set, rather than only for predicates over lists of natural numbers. The following definition is a variation of an idea taken from [Mar68].

**Definition 6 (inductive bars).** *Given a set $\mathcal{A}$ and a predicate $\mathcal{U}$ over $\mathcal{A}^*$, $\mathcal{U}$ is an inductive bar if $\mathcal{U} \mid <>$ (to be read $\mathcal{U}$* bars the empty sequence*), where this is inductively defined with the following introduction rules.*

$$\frac{\mathcal{U}(\overline{u})}{\mathcal{U} \mid \overline{u}} \qquad \frac{\mathcal{U} \mid \overline{u}}{\mathcal{U} \mid \overline{u}\bullet a} \qquad \frac{\forall a \in \mathcal{A}\ [\mathcal{U} \mid \overline{u}\bullet a]}{\mathcal{U} \mid \overline{u}}$$

Observe that if $\mathcal{U}(\overline{u}) \Rightarrow \mathcal{V}(\overline{u})$ for every $\overline{u} \in \mathcal{A}^*$, then also $\mathcal{U} \mid \overline{u} \Rightarrow \mathcal{V} \mid \overline{u}$ for every $\overline{u} \in \mathcal{A}^*$. Associated to the definition of $\mathcal{U} \mid \overline{u}$ we have the following principle of induction, for every predicate $\mathcal{Y}$ over $\mathcal{A}^*$.

$$\frac{\begin{array}{l} \mathcal{U} \mid \overline{u} \\ \forall\overline{v} \in \mathcal{A}^*\ \ [\mathcal{U}(\overline{v}) \Rightarrow \mathcal{Y}(\overline{v})] \\ \forall\overline{v} \in \mathcal{A}^*\ \ \forall a \in \mathcal{A}\ \ [\mathcal{Y}(\overline{v}) \Rightarrow \mathcal{Y}(\overline{v}\bullet a)] \\ \forall\overline{v} \in \mathcal{A}^*\ \ \{[\forall a \in \mathcal{A}\ \ \mathcal{Y}(\overline{v}\bullet a)] \Rightarrow \mathcal{Y}(\overline{v})\} \end{array}}{\mathcal{Y}(\overline{u})}$$

When using this principle we refer to it as *induction on "the" proof that $\mathcal{U} \mid \overline{u}$*, where "the" proof is the proof of it available at that moment.

With this principle of induction it is possible to prove in type theory that the rule BI —with inductive bars instead of bars, and arbitrary sets instead of natural numbers— is derivable. That is, that the rule $\mathrm{BI}_{\mathrm{TT}}$, below, is derivable.

$$\frac{\begin{array}{ll} \forall \overline{u} \in \mathcal{A}^* \;\; [\mathcal{X}(\overline{u}) \Rightarrow \mathcal{Y}(\overline{u})] & \mathcal{X} \text{ is included in } \mathcal{Y} \\ \forall \overline{u} \in \mathcal{A}^* \;\; \forall a \in \mathcal{A} \;\; [\mathcal{X}(\overline{u}) \Rightarrow \mathcal{X}(\overline{u} \bullet a)] & \mathcal{X} \text{ is monotone} \\ \forall \overline{u} \in \mathcal{A}^* \;\; \{[\forall a \in \mathcal{A} \;\; \mathcal{Y}(\overline{u} \bullet a)] \Rightarrow \mathcal{Y}(\overline{u})\} & \mathcal{Y} \text{ is hereditary} \\ \mathcal{X} \mid \overline{u} & \mathcal{X} \text{ bars } \overline{u} \end{array}}{\mathcal{Y}(\overline{u})} \; \mathrm{BI}_{\mathrm{TT}}$$

This rule can be derived by showing $\forall \overline{v} \in \mathcal{A}^* \;\; \mathcal{Y}(\overline{u} \hookleftarrow \overline{v})$ by induction on the proof that $\mathcal{X} \mid \overline{u}$, where $\hookleftarrow$ is a combination of the reverse and append functions, and is defined as follows.

$$\begin{array}{rcl} \overline{u} \hookleftarrow <> & = & \overline{u} \\ \overline{u} \hookleftarrow (\overline{v} \bullet a) & = & (\overline{u} \bullet a) \hookleftarrow \overline{v} \end{array}$$

Observe that whereas BI is an axiom of intuitionistic logic, $\mathrm{BI}_{\mathrm{TT}}$ can actually be proved in type theory. This is because of the definition of inductive bar, whose equivalence with the standard notion of bar in Definition 4 —in the case of sequences of natural numbers— is essentially the content of BI itself. More precisely, for any predicate $\mathcal{U}$ over $\mathcal{N}^*$, $\mathcal{U} \mid <>$ implies that $\mathcal{U}$ is a bar, but the converse is the content of the axiom BI.

In a type-theoretic context, by *bar induction* we refer to the rule $\mathrm{BI}_{\mathrm{TT}}$. When applying bar induction we will refer by *monotonicity condition* (of $\mathcal{X}$), *hereditary condition* (of $\mathcal{Y}$), and *inclusion condition* (that is, $\mathcal{X} \subseteq \mathcal{Y}$) to the instances corresponding to the premises of the rule.

**Proposition 2.** *Given a set $\mathcal{A}$, a monotone predicate $\mathcal{U}$ over $\mathcal{A}^*$ and a list $\overline{u}$ of elements of $\mathcal{A}$, then*

$$\mathcal{U} \mid \overline{u} \iff \mathcal{V}_{\overline{u}} \mid <>,$$

*where $\mathcal{V}_{\overline{u}} = \lambda \overline{v} \; \mathcal{U}(\overline{u} * \overline{v})$.*

The $\Leftarrow$ part is easy, and is left to the reader. Hint: use bar induction with $\mathcal{X} = \mathcal{V}_{\overline{u}}$ and $\mathcal{Y} = \lambda \overline{v} \; [\mathcal{U} \mid \overline{u} * \overline{v}]$; or, for another proof which does not use monotonicity of $\mathcal{U}$, by induction on the proof that $\mathcal{V}_{\overline{u}} \mid <>$.

We sketch a proof of the $\Rightarrow$ part, which is by bar induction with $\mathcal{X} = \mathcal{U}$ and $\mathcal{Y} = \lambda \overline{u} \; [\mathcal{V}_{\overline{u}} \mid <>]$. The monotonicity condition is hypothesis of the proposition and the inclusion condition is trivial. It remains to prove the hereditary condition. Assume that for all $a \in \mathcal{A}$, $\mathcal{V}_{\overline{u} \bullet a} \mid <>$. We have to show $\mathcal{V}_{\overline{u}} \mid <>$. In order to do so, we prove that for all $a \in \mathcal{A}$, $\mathcal{V}_{\overline{u}} \mid <a>$. Now, this follows from $\mathcal{V}_{\overline{u} \bullet a} \mid <>$ by bar induction with $\mathcal{X} = \mathcal{V}_{\overline{u} \bullet a}$ and $\mathcal{Y} = \lambda \overline{v} \; [\mathcal{V}_{\overline{u}} \mid <a> * \overline{v}]$.

**Proposition 3.** *Given a set $\mathcal{A}$, two monotone predicates $\mathcal{U}, \mathcal{V}$ over $\mathcal{A}^*$ and a list $\overline{u}$ of elements of $\mathcal{A}$, then*

$$\mathcal{U} \mid \overline{u} \wedge \mathcal{V} \mid \overline{u} \Longrightarrow \mathcal{W} \mid \overline{u},$$

*where $\mathcal{W} = \lambda\overline{u}\ [\mathcal{U}(\overline{u}) \wedge \mathcal{V}(\overline{u})]$.*

We sketch a proof by bar induction with $\mathcal{X} = \mathcal{U}$ and $\mathcal{Y} = \lambda\overline{u}\ [\mathcal{V} \mid \overline{u} \Rightarrow \mathcal{W} \mid \overline{u}]$. The monotonicity condition is hypothesis of the proposition. The hereditary condition follows from the facts that $\lambda\overline{u}\ [\mathcal{W} \mid \overline{u}]$ is hereditary and $\lambda\overline{u}\ [\mathcal{V} \mid \overline{u}]$ is monotone. Finally, the inclusion condition can be proved by bar induction with $\mathcal{X} = \mathcal{V}$ and $\mathcal{Y} = \lambda\overline{u}\ [\mathcal{U}(\overline{u}) \Rightarrow \mathcal{W} \mid \overline{u}]$, repeating the previous reasoning, except that the new inclusion condition is trivial.

## 4 Fan theorem in type theory

The result we present here is a type-theoretic version of the fan theorem as formulated in Theorem 5, except that it will be expressed for an arbitrary set $\mathcal{A}$ rather than only for natural numbers. Finite subsets $\mathcal{I}_i$ of $\mathcal{A}$ will be represented by lists $\overline{u}_i$ of elements of $\mathcal{A}$. Finite sequences $\overline{\mathcal{I}}$ of such subsets, by lists $\overline{\overline{u}}$ of lists. The function $\bigotimes$ occurring in the statement of Theorem 5 will be represented by a function which when applied to a list of lists $<\overline{u}_1, \ldots, \overline{u}_{n-1}>$ computes another list representing the Cartesian product $\mathcal{I}_1 \times \ldots \times \mathcal{I}_{n-1}$.

To define $\bigotimes$ we first define the binary Cartesian product $\times^f$ parametrized with a function $f$. Then, the finite Cartesian product $\bigotimes_b^f$ also parametrized. Finally we instantiate it to obtain $\bigotimes$.

Given a function $f : \mathcal{A} \rightarrow \mathcal{B}$, we denote by $\overline{f} : \mathcal{A}^* \rightarrow \mathcal{B}^*$ the function which maps $f$ on every element of its argument.

$$\overline{f}(<>) = <>$$
$$\overline{f}(\overline{u} \bullet a) = \overline{f}(\overline{u}) \bullet f(a)$$

*Example 1.* $\overline{f}(<a_0, \ldots, a_{n-1}>) = <f(a_0), \ldots, f(a_{n-1})>$.

Now, the function $\times^f$, which given a function $f : \mathcal{A} \rightarrow \mathcal{B} \rightarrow \mathcal{C}$, and two lists $\overline{u} \in \mathcal{A}^*$ and $\overline{v} \in \mathcal{B}^*$ returns a variation of the Cartesian product of $\overline{u}$ and $\overline{v}$. Instead of returning a list in $(\mathcal{A} \times \mathcal{B})^*$, it returns a list in $\mathcal{C}^*$ by applying the function $f$ to the components of each possible pair.

$$<> \times^f \ \overline{v} = <>$$
$$(\overline{u} \bullet a) \ \times^f \ \overline{v} = \overline{u} \times^f \overline{v} \ * \ \overline{f(a)}(\overline{v})$$

*Example 2.* $\overline{u} \ \times^f \ <> \ = \ <>$, for every $\overline{u}$.

*Example 3.* $<a_0, a_1> \ \times^f \ <b_0, b_1> \ = \ <f(a_0, b_0), f(a_0, b_1), f(a_1, b_0), f(a_1, b_1)>$.

The function $\bigotimes_b^f$, given a function $f : \mathcal{B} \to \mathcal{A} \to \mathcal{B}$, a base value $b \in \mathcal{B}$, and $\overline{\overline{u}} \in \mathcal{A}^{**}$, returns a list in $\mathcal{B}^*$, each of whose values is the result of iterating the function $f$ along one tuple, assigning $b$ to the empty tuple. Each tuple consists of one element from the first list of $\overline{\overline{u}}$, one from the second, etc. in the style of the Cartesian product.

$$\bigotimes_b^f(<>) = <b>$$
$$\bigotimes_b^f(\overline{\overline{u}} \bullet \overline{u}) = \bigotimes_b^f(\overline{\overline{u}}) \times^f \overline{u}$$

*Example 4.*

$$\bigotimes_b^f(\ll a_0, a_1>, <b_0, b_1\gg) \\ = <f(f(b, a_0), b_0), f(f(b, a_0), b_1), f(f(b, a_1), b_0), f(f(b, a_1), b_1)> .$$

Finally, the Cartesian product is obtained by giving $\bullet$ as the function to iterate, and $<>$ as the base value.

$$\bigotimes(\overline{\overline{u}}) = \bigotimes^{\bullet}_{<>}(\overline{\overline{u}})$$

*Example 5.* $\bigotimes(<>) = \ll\gg$.

*Example 6.* $\bigotimes(\overline{\overline{u}} \bullet <>) = <>$, for every $\overline{\overline{u}}$.

*Example 7.* $\bigotimes(\ll a_0, a_1>, <b_0, b_1\gg) = \ll a_0, b_0>, <a_0, b_1>, <a_1, b_0>, <a_1, b_1\gg$.

The set $\{\overline{\mathcal{I}} \mid \bigotimes \overline{\mathcal{I}} \subseteq \mathcal{U}\}$ in Theorem 5 can be interpreted as a predicate $\mathcal{P}$ on lists $\overline{\overline{u}}$ of lists which is true when $\bigotimes(\overline{\overline{u}})$ is "included" in $\mathcal{U}$. As $\bigotimes(\overline{\overline{u}})$ is actually not a set but a list, by it being "included" in $\mathcal{U}$ we mean that every element in the list $\bigotimes(\overline{\overline{u}})$ satisfies $\mathcal{U}$, that is, $\bigwedge_{\bigotimes(\overline{\overline{u}})} \mathcal{U}$. Thus, the predicate $\mathcal{P}$ is in fact interpreted by the function $\lambda\overline{\overline{u}}\left[\bigwedge_{\bigotimes(\overline{\overline{u}})} \mathcal{U}\right]$. Hence, in type theory Theorem 5 becomes:

**Theorem 6 (fan theorem in type theory).** *Given a set $\mathcal{A}$ and a monotone predicate $\mathcal{U}$ over $\mathcal{A}^*$, then if $\mathcal{U}$ is an inductive bar, so is the predicate*

$$\lambda\overline{\overline{u}}\left[\bigwedge_{\bigotimes(\overline{\overline{u}})} \mathcal{U}\right].$$

**Lemma 1.** *The following properties hold for every $\overline{u}$, $\overline{v}$, $\overline{w}$, and $\overline{\overline{u}}$*

1. $\overline{u} * \overline{v} \ \times^f \ \overline{w} = (\overline{u} \times^f \overline{w}) * (\overline{v} \times^f \overline{w})$
2. $<a> \times^f \ \overline{u} * \overline{v} = (<a> \times^f \overline{u}) * (<a> \times^f \overline{v})$
3. $\bigotimes(<\overline{w} \bullet a> * \overline{\overline{u}}) = \bigotimes(<\overline{w}> * \overline{\overline{u}}) * \bigotimes(\ll a\gg * \overline{\overline{u}})$
4. $\bigwedge_{\bigotimes(\overline{\overline{u}})} [\lambda\overline{u}\ \mathcal{U}(<a> * \overline{u})] \implies \bigwedge_{\bigotimes(\ll a \gg * \overline{\overline{u}})} \mathcal{U}$

Item 1 can be proved by induction on $\overline{v}$. Item 2 follows from the fact that $\overline{g}(\overline{u} * \overline{v}) = \overline{g}(\overline{u}) * \overline{g}(\overline{v})$ (letting $g$ be $f(a)$), which can also be proved by induction on $\overline{v}$. Item 3 can be proved by induction on $\overline{\overline{u}}$, using Example 6 in the base case and item 1 in the inductive case.

Though technically laborious, item 4 is intuitively clear since all the tuples in $\bigotimes(\ll a \gg * \overline{\overline{u}})$ are of the form $<a> * \overline{u}$ with $\overline{u}$ a tuple in $\bigotimes(\overline{\overline{u}})$. We omit that proof here.

For the proof of Theorem 6, we define, for $\overline{u} \in \mathcal{A}^*$,

$$\mathcal{V}_{\overline{u}} = \lambda\overline{\overline{u}} \left[ \bigwedge_{\bigotimes(\overline{\overline{u}})} (\lambda\overline{v}\, \mathcal{U}(\overline{u} * \overline{v})) \right].$$

We present a proof by bar induction with $\mathcal{X} = \mathcal{U}$ and $\mathcal{Y} = \lambda\overline{u}\ \{\mathcal{V}_{\overline{u}} \mid <>\}$.

The inclusion condition is $\mathcal{U}(\overline{u}) \Rightarrow \mathcal{V}_{\overline{u}} \mid <>$, which is easy, since when $\mathcal{U}(\overline{u})$ holds, even $\mathcal{V}_{\overline{u}}(<>)$ holds because $\bigotimes(<>) = \ll<>\gg$ by Example 5. The monotonicity condition is hypothesis of the theorem. The hereditary condition is $(\forall a \in \mathcal{A}\ [\mathcal{V}_{\overline{u}\bullet a} \mid <>]) \Rightarrow \mathcal{V}_{\overline{u}} \mid <>$. We assume

$$\forall a \in \mathcal{A}\ [\mathcal{V}_{\overline{u}\bullet a} \mid <>] \tag{1}$$

and given an arbitrary $\overline{v}$ we prove $\mathcal{V}_{\overline{u}} \mid\ <\overline{v}>$ by induction on $\overline{v}$.

If $\overline{v} = <>$, then $\mathcal{V}_{\overline{u}} \mid\ \ll<>\gg$ is direct since $\mathcal{V}_{\overline{u}}(\ll<>\gg)$ holds because of the facts that $\bigotimes(\ll<>\gg) = <>$ holds by Example 6 and that $\bigwedge_{<>}$ is trivially true regardless of the predicate.

If $\overline{v} = \overline{w} \bullet a$ for some $\overline{w} \in \mathcal{A}^*$ (such that $\mathcal{V}_{\overline{u}} \mid\ <\overline{w}>$) and $a \in \mathcal{A}$, then we know by (1) that

$$\mathcal{V}_{\overline{u}\bullet a} \mid <> \quad \text{and} \quad \mathcal{V}_{\overline{u}} \mid\ <\overline{w}>$$

and still have to prove

$$\mathcal{V}_{\overline{u}} \mid\ <\overline{w} \bullet a>.$$

By Proposition 2 it can be written like this: we know

$$\mathcal{V}_{\overline{u}\bullet a} \mid <> \quad \text{and} \quad [\lambda\overline{\overline{u}}\ \mathcal{V}_{\overline{u}}(<\overline{w}> * \overline{\overline{u}})] \mid <>,$$

(hence, by Proposition 3 we know also that

$$[\lambda\overline{\overline{u}}\ [\mathcal{V}_{\overline{u}\bullet a}(\overline{\overline{u}}) \wedge \mathcal{V}_{\overline{u}}(<\overline{w}> * \overline{\overline{u}})]] \mid <> \tag{2}$$

holds) and have to prove

$$[\lambda\overline{\overline{u}}\ \mathcal{V}_{\overline{u}}(<\overline{w} \bullet a> * \overline{\overline{u}})] \mid <>. \tag{3}$$

To prove that (2) $\Rightarrow$ (3), it is enough to prove that for every $\overline{\overline{u}} \in \mathcal{A}^{**}$,

$$\mathcal{V}_{\overline{u}\bullet a}(\overline{\overline{u}}) \wedge \mathcal{V}_{\overline{u}}(<\overline{w}> * \overline{\overline{u}}) \implies \mathcal{V}_{\overline{u}}(<\overline{w} \bullet a> * \overline{\overline{u}})$$

holds, because of the observation made after Definition 6. By the definition of $\mathcal{V}_{\overline{u}}$ and item 3 of Lemma 1, the right-hand side is equivalent to

$$\mathcal{V}_{\overline{u}}(<\overline{w}> * \overline{\overline{u}}) \wedge \mathcal{V}_{\overline{u}}(\ll a \gg * \overline{\overline{u}})$$

which follows from the left-hand side because, by item 4 of Lemma 1, $\mathcal{V}_{\overline{u}\bullet a}(\overline{\overline{u}})$ implies $\mathcal{V}_{\overline{u}}(\ll a \gg * \overline{\overline{u}})$.

# 5 Concluding remarks

The main contribution of this article is the formalization of a version of the fan theorem in type theory. That is, the formulation of Theorem 6 and its proof.

However, obtaining a version of the fan theorem which admits a direct interpretation in type theory turned out to enrich the content of the article by presenting a variety of equivalent formulations of the fan theorem.

The key to obtain such variety was letting $\mathcal{U}$ range over bars on the universal spread rather than over bars on the fan $\mathcal{T}$, in Theorem 2. Indeed, Veldman [Vel98] showed that analogous variations do not hold intuitionistically if $\mathcal{U}$ is taken to range over bars on $\mathcal{T}$. In that case, for instance, item 2 of Theorem 2 fails to hold.

Veldman proved this by providing a counterexample which relies on the Brouwer-Kripke-principle (see for instance [Vel81] for the statement of the principle). The construction of the counterexample is as follows.

Let $\mathcal{P}$ be some unsolved problem, and *stable* that is, such that the double negation of $\mathcal{P}$ implies $\mathcal{P}$. The Brouwer-Kripke-principle, yields an infinite sequence of bits $\beta$ such that

$$\begin{aligned} \mathcal{P} &\Longleftrightarrow \exists n \;\; \beta(2n) = 1, \text{ and} \\ \neg\mathcal{P} &\Longleftrightarrow \exists n \;\; \beta(2n+1) = 1. \end{aligned}$$

Let $\overline{0}(m)$ and $\overline{1}(m)$ denote

$$\overline{0}(m) = <\overbrace{0,\ldots,0}^{m}> \qquad \overline{1}(m) = <\overbrace{1,\ldots,1}^{m}> .$$

Let $\mathcal{T}$ be the tree consisting of the following finite sequences of bits: as long as $\beta(0) = \beta(1) = \ldots = \beta(m-1) = 0$, the sequences $\overline{0}(m)$ and $\overline{1}(m)$ belong to $\mathcal{T}$. As soon as $\beta(n) = 1$ for the first time, then either such an $n$ is odd, in which case $\overline{0}(m)$ belongs to $\mathcal{T}$ for every $m > n$, or $n$ is even, in which case $\overline{1}(m)$ belongs to $\mathcal{T}$ for every $m > n$. And these are all the sequences belonging to $\mathcal{T}$.

Let $\mathcal{U}$ be the set of all finite sequences $\overline{u}$ such that there exists $n < \text{length}(\overline{u})$ such that $\beta(n) = 1$. The set $\mathcal{U}$ is clearly monotone.

Extending the notion of bar in Definition 4 in the natural way to arbitrary trees, rather than spreads, we prove first that $\mathcal{U}$ is a bar on $\mathcal{T}$. This is so since given any $\alpha \in \mathcal{T}$, either $\alpha(0) = 0$ (and $\alpha(n) = 0$ for all $n$) or $\alpha(0) = 1$ (and $\alpha(n) = 1$ for all $n$). In either case, thanks to the stability of $\mathcal{P}$, $\mathcal{P}$ is solved. Thus, $\alpha \in \mathcal{T}$ implies that $\mathcal{P}$ is solved, in which case $\mathcal{U}$ is a bar, hence $\exists n \;\; \alpha(n) \in \mathcal{U}$.

On the other hand, determining $n$ such that $\forall \alpha \in \mathcal{T} \;\; [\alpha(n) \in \mathcal{U}]$ amounts to solving $\mathcal{P}$, which by assumption is unsolved.

Therefore, this gives a counterexample to the statement

$$\mathcal{U} \text{ monotone bar on } \mathcal{T} \Longrightarrow \exists n \;\; \forall \alpha \in \mathcal{T} \;\; [\overline{\alpha}(n) \in \mathcal{U}].$$

## Acknowledgements

I am very grateful to Marc Bezem, Thierry Coquand, Monika Seisenberger, Jan Smith and Wim Veldman for fertile discussions about the fan theorem, especially to Wim Veldman for the counterexample of Section 5. This article benefited also from the comments and constructive criticism of two anonymous referees.

## References

[CF58] H. Curry and R. Feys. *Combinatory Logic*, volume I. North-Holland, 1958.

[Dum77] M. Dummett. *Elements of Intuitionism.* Clarendon Press, Oxford, 1977.

[Fri97] D. Fridlender. Higman's Lemma in Type Theory. In *Types for proofs and programs*, Lecture Notes in Computer Science 1512, 1997.

[How80] W. Howard. The Formulae-as-Types Notion of Construction. In J. Seldin and J. Hindley, editors, *To H.B. Curry: Essays on Combinatory Logic, Lambda Calculus and Formalism*, pages 479–490. Academic Press, London, 1980.

[Mag94] L. Magnusson. *The Implementation of ALF - a Proof Editor Based on Martin-Löf's Monomorphic Type Theory with Explicit Substitution.* PhD thesis, Department of Computing Science, Chalmers University of Technology and University of Göteborg, 1994.

[Mar68] P. Martin-Löf. *Notes on Constructive Mathematics.* Almqvist & Wiksell, 1968.

[Mar75] P. Martin-Löf. An Intuitionistic Theory of Types: Predicative Part. In H. E. Rose and J. C. Shepherdson, editors, *Logic Colloquium 1973*, pages 73–118, Amsterdam, 1975. North-Holland Publishing Company.

[Mar84] P. Martin-Löf. *Intuitionistic Type Theory.* Bibliopolis, Napoli, 1984.

[NPS90] B. Nordström, K. Petersson, and J. Smith. *Programming in Martin-Löf's Type Theory. An Introduction.* Oxford University Press, 1990.

[Tas97] A. Tasistro. *Substitution, Record Types and Subtyping in Type Theory, with Applications to the Theory of Programming.* PhD thesis, Department of Computing Science at Chalmers University of Technology and University of Göteborg, 1997.

[TvD88] A. Troelstra and D. van Dalen. *Constructivism in Mathematics, An Introduction, Volume I.* North-Holland, 1988.

[Vel81] W. Veldman. *Investigations in intuitionistic hierarchy theory.* PhD thesis, Katholieke Universiteit te Nijmegen, 1981.

[Vel94] W. Veldman. Intuitionistic Proof of the General non-Decidable case of Higman's Lemma. Personal communication, 1994.

[Vel98] W. Veldman. Personal communication, 1998.

# Conjunctive Types and SKInT

Jean Goubault-Larrecq*

G.I.E. Dyade, INRIA, Inria bâtiment 30, F-78153 Le Chesnay Cedex,
Jean.Goubault@inria.fr

## 1 Introduction

The $\lambda$-calculus and its typed versions are important tools for studying most fundamental computation and deduction paradigms. However, the non-trivial nature of substitution, as used in the definition of $\lambda$-reduction notably, has spurred the design of various first-order languages representing $\lambda$-terms, $\lambda$-reduction and $\lambda$-conversion, where computation is simple, first-order rewriting, and substitution becomes an easy notion again. Let us cite Curry's combinators [7], Curien's categorical combinators [5], the myriad of so-called $\lambda$-calculi with explicit substitutions, among which $\lambda\sigma$ [1], $\lambda\sigma_{\Uparrow}$ [12], $\lambda\upsilon$ [17], $\lambda\zeta$ [19], etc. Unfortunately, each one of these calculi has defects: Curry's combinators do not model $\lambda$-conversion fully, categorical combinators, $\lambda\sigma$ and $\lambda\sigma_{\Uparrow}$ do not normalize strongly in the typed case [18], $\lambda\upsilon$ is not confluent in the presence of free variables (a.k.a. meta-variables), $\lambda\zeta$ models $\lambda$-conversion but not $\lambda$-reduction, etc.

SKInT [9] is a first-order language and rewrite system that does not have these defects. In particular, SKInT models reduction in the $\lambda$-calculus, in the sense that there is a mapping $L^*$ from $\lambda$-terms to SKInT such that whenever $u$ rewrites to $v$ in the $\lambda$-calculus, then $L^*(u)$ rewrites to $L^*(v)$ in SKInT. SKInT is confluent even on open terms, i.e. terms with meta-variables; $L^*$ defines a conservative embedding of the $\lambda$-calculus inside SKInT, in that $u$ and $v$ are $\lambda$-convertible if and only if $L^*(u)$ and $L^*(v)$ are convertible in SKInT; reduction in SKInT standardizes; $L^*$ preserves weak normalization, i.e., if $u$ is a weakly normalizing $\lambda$-term, then $L^*(u)$ is a weakly normalizing SKInT-term. SKInT also enjoys a simple type discipline corresponding to that of the $\lambda$-calculus, that is, if $u$ is a $\lambda$-term of type $\tau$, then $L^*(u)$ is a SKInT-term of some type $L^*(\tau)$ easily computed from $\tau$; reduction in SKInT obeys subject reduction, and every simply-typed SKInT-term normalizes strongly [9].

The aim of this paper is to extend our result on preservation of weak normalization to show that SKInT, like $\lambda\upsilon$ and $\lambda\zeta$, also preserves strong normalization, and also solvability; this is done by showing that, just like in the $\lambda$-calculus, strongly normalizing, weakly normalizing and solvable terms are characterized as terms that are typable in various conjunctive type disciplines [20, 4].

The plan of the paper is as follows: we introduce the required notions and notations in Section 2, then we attack our goal in Section 3. We show that any reasonable translation from the $\lambda$-calculus to SKInT preserves solvability, weak

* This work has been done in the context of Dyade (Bull/Inria R&D joint venture).

normalization and strong normalization (Corollary 1), where "reasonable" means that it preserves typability in certain systems of conjunctive types; this holds in particular for the translations of [9]. In turn, this result follows from a result stating that all terms that are typable in particular systems of conjunctive types (to be defined in Section 3) have the corresponding normalization properties (Theorem 1). The converse also holds (Corollary 2), just as in the $\lambda$-calculus.

The proofs have been reduced to keep the paper short and reasonably legible. Full proofs can be found in [11].

## 2 SKInT and the $\lambda$-Calculus

Recall that the syntax of the $\lambda$-calculus is [3]:

$$t ::= x \mid tt \mid \lambda x \cdot t$$

where $x$ ranges over an infinite set of so-called variables, and terms $s$ and $t$ that are $\alpha$-equivalent are considered equal; we denote $\lambda$-terms by $s$, $t$, ..., and variables by $x$, $y$, $z$, etc. $\alpha$-equivalence is the compatible closure of $\lambda x \cdot (t[x/y]) = \lambda y \cdot t$ and $t[s/x]$ denotes the usual capture-avoiding substitution of $s$ for $x$ in $t$. We shall write $=$ for $\alpha$-equivalence; in the first-order calculi to come, $=$ will denote syntactic equality.

The basic computation rule is $\beta$-reduction, the compatible closure of:

$$(\beta) \quad (\lambda x \cdot t)s \to t[s/x]$$

The relation $\longrightarrow$ is the compatible closure of this relation, $\longrightarrow^*$ is the reflexive-transitive closure of the latter, and $\longrightarrow^+$ is its transitive closure. We shall use $\longrightarrow$, $\longrightarrow^*$, $\longrightarrow^+$ ambiguously in other calculi as well, taking care to make clear which is intended.

We shall also add the following $\eta$-reduction rule:

$$(\eta) \quad \lambda x \cdot tx \to x \quad (x \text{ not free in } t)$$

to the $\lambda$-calculus, yielding the so-called $\lambda_\eta$-calculus. The corresponding compatible closure relation will sometimes be noted $\longrightarrow_\eta$ to distinguish it from $\longrightarrow$, and similarly for the calculi to come and their respective $\eta$ rules.

The terms of SKInT, and of its companion calculus SKIn [9], on the other hand, are defined by the grammar:

$$u ::= x \mid I_\ell \mid S_\ell(u, u) \mid K_\ell(u)$$

where $\ell$ ranges over $\mathbb{N}$. This is an infinitary first-order language. The reduction rules of SKInT are shown in Figure 1, thus defining an infinite rewrite system. The semantical idea behind SKInT, or SKIn, will be made clear by stating an informal translation from SKInT (or SKIn) to the $\lambda$-calculus. Intuitively:

$$\begin{aligned} I_\ell &\sim \lambda x_0 \cdot \ldots \cdot \lambda x_{\ell-1} \cdot \lambda x_\ell \cdot x_\ell \\ S_\ell(u, v) &\sim \lambda x_0 \cdot \ldots \cdot \lambda x_{\ell-1} \cdot u x_0 \ldots x_{\ell-1}(v x_0 \ldots x_{\ell-1}) \\ K_\ell(u) &\sim \lambda x_0 \cdot \ldots \cdot \lambda x_{\ell-1} \cdot \lambda x_\ell \cdot u x_0 \ldots x_{\ell-1} \end{aligned}$$

So $I_\ell$, $S_\ell$, $K_\ell$ generalize Curry's combinators $I$, $S$ and $K$ respectively.

SKIn is defined as SKInT, except that rule $(K_\ell S_{\mathcal{L}+1})$ is replaced by $(K_\ell S_\mathcal{L})$: $K_\ell(S_{\mathcal{L}-1}(u,v)) \to S_\mathcal{L}(K_\ell(u), K_\ell(v))$; conversely, SKInT is as SKIn, except that rule $(K_\ell S_\mathcal{L})$ is restricted to the case $\ell < \mathcal{L} - 1$.

$$(SI_\ell) \quad S_\ell(I_\ell, w) \to w \qquad (SK_\ell) \quad S_\ell(K_\ell(u), w) \to u$$

$$\begin{array}{llll}
(S_\ell I_\mathcal{L}) & S_\ell(I_\mathcal{L}, w) \to I_{\mathcal{L}-1} & (K_\ell I_\mathcal{L}) & K_\ell(I_{\mathcal{L}-1}) \to I_\mathcal{L} \\
(S_\ell K_\mathcal{L}) & S_\ell(K_\mathcal{L}(u), w) \to K_{\mathcal{L}-1}(S_\ell(u, w)) & (K_\ell K_\mathcal{L}) & K_\ell(K_{\mathcal{L}-1}(u)) \to K_\mathcal{L}(K_\ell(u)) \\
(S_\ell S_\mathcal{L}) & S_\ell(S_\mathcal{L}(u, v), w) & (K_\ell S_{\mathcal{L}+1}) & K_\ell(S_\mathcal{L}(u, w)) \\
& \quad \to S_{\mathcal{L}-1}(S_\ell(u, w), S_\ell(v, w)) & & \quad \to S_{\mathcal{L}+1}(K_\ell(u), K_\ell(w))
\end{array}$$

**Fig. 1.** SKInT reduction rules (for every $0 \leq \ell < \mathcal{L}$)

Both SKIn and SKInT are confluent and standardize. (See Section 3 for the definition of standard reductions.)

We can split SKInT in two: the set of all rules $(SI_\ell)$, $\ell \geq 0$, corresponds somehow to the actual $\beta$-reduction rule of the $\lambda$-calculus, or more precisely to $\beta I$-reduction (the notion of reduction of $\lambda I$), and we shall call this group of rules $\beta I$. All other rules essentially correspond to the propagation of substitutions in the $\lambda$-calculus, and we call the set of these rules $\Sigma T$. Similarly, $\Sigma$ is SKIn minus $\beta I$. It turns out that both $\Sigma$ and $\Sigma T$ are confluent, but $\Sigma T$ terminates while $\Sigma$ only normalizes weakly (even in a typed setting, see [9]).

We shall also consider SKInT$_\eta$, which is SKInT plus the following group $\eta$:

$$(\eta S_\ell) \quad S_{\ell+1}(K_\ell(u), I_\ell) \to u \quad (\ell \geq 0)$$

SKInT$_\eta$ is also confluent, and $\eta$-reductions can be postponed after all other reductions, just like in the $\lambda$-calculus.

The natural translation from the $\lambda$-calculus to SKInT, resp. SKIn, is $t \mapsto t^*$, defined in Figure 2. Whenever $u \longrightarrow v$ in the $\lambda$-calculus, $u^* \longrightarrow^+ v^*$ in SKIn, but not in SKInT. In the case of SKInT, we have to use a more complicated translation, like $L^*$: then $u \longrightarrow v$ implies $L^*(u) \longrightarrow^+ L^*(v)$. $L^*(s)$ is defined as $(L(s))^*$, where $L(s)$ is $\lambda z \cdot L_z(s)$ with $z$ a fresh variable, and $L_z(x) =_{df} xz$, $L_z(\lambda x \cdot s) =_{df} \lambda x \cdot L_z(s)$, $L_z(st) =_{df} L_z(s)(L(t))$ (see [9] for an explanation).

The simple type discipline for the $\lambda$-calculus is defined by judgments $\Gamma \vdash t : \tau$, where $t$ is a $\lambda$-term, $\tau$ is a simple type, i.e. a term in the following language:

$$\tau ::= B \mid \tau \to \tau$$

where $B$ is a given non-empty set of so-called base types. Finally, $\Gamma$ is a context, namely a finite map from variables to types; $\Gamma, x : \tau$ denotes $\Gamma$ enriched by mapping $x$ to $\tau$, where $x$ is outside the domain of $\Gamma$.

$$
\begin{array}{llll}
 & & [x]x & = I_0 \\
x^* & = x & [x]y & = K_0(y) \qquad (y \neq x) \\
(st)^* & = S_0(s^*, t^*) & [x](I_\ell) & = I_{\ell+1} \\
(\lambda x \cdot t)^* & = [x](t^*) & [x](S_\ell(u,v)) & = S_{\ell+1}([x]u, [x]v) \\
 & & [x](K_\ell(u)) & = K_{\ell+1}([x]u)
\end{array}
$$

**Fig. 2.** Translation from the $\lambda$-calculus to SKIn

The typing rules for the $\lambda$-calculus are:

$$
\frac{}{\Gamma, x : \tau \vdash x : \tau} \qquad \frac{\Gamma \vdash s : \tau_1 \to \tau_2 \quad \Gamma \vdash t : \tau_1}{\Gamma \vdash st : \tau_2} \qquad \frac{\Gamma, x : \tau_1 \vdash s : \tau_2}{\Gamma \vdash \lambda x \cdot s : \tau_1 \to \tau_2}
$$

Those for SKInT are shown in Figure 3. Notice that in typing $K_\ell(u)$, the new type $\tau'$ is always inserted before an arrow type: this is intentional (see [9]), and is related to insights in proof systems for the modal logic S4.

$$
\frac{}{\Gamma, x : \tau \vdash x : \tau} \qquad \frac{}{\Gamma \vdash I_\ell : \tau_0 \to \ldots \to \tau_{\ell-1} \to \tau_\ell \to \tau_\ell}
$$

$$
\frac{\Gamma \vdash u : \tau_0 \to \ldots \to \tau_{\ell-1} \to \tau_\ell \to \tau \quad \Gamma \vdash v : \tau_0 \to \ldots \to \tau_{\ell-1} \to \tau_\ell}{\Gamma \vdash S_\ell(u,v) : \tau_0 \to \ldots \to \tau_{\ell-1} \to \tau} \qquad \frac{\Gamma \vdash u : \tau_0 \to \ldots \to \tau_{\ell-1} \to \tau_\ell \to \tau}{\Gamma \vdash K_\ell(u) : \tau_0 \to \ldots \to \tau_{\ell-1} \to \tau' \to \tau_\ell \to \tau}
$$

**Fig. 3.** Simple types for SKInT

Both the $\lambda$-calculus and SKInT enjoy subject reduction and normalize strongly on simply-typed terms. Moreover, we have the following meta-theorem on SKInT. Call a context $\Gamma$ *arrowed* if and only if $\Gamma$ maps every variable in its domain to an arrow type (of the form $\tau_1 \to \tau_2$); then for every arrowed context $\Gamma$, if $\Gamma, x : \tau_1 \vdash u : \tau_2$, then $\Gamma \vdash [x]u : \tau_1 \to \tau_2$. The restriction to arrowed contexts is necessary: consider the case where $u$ is a variable other than $x$.

## 3 Conjunctive Types

We now turn to the relationship between conjunctive type systems for SKInT and termination properties, à la Sallé-Coppo [20, 4]. We first recall a few notions from [9]. Define the *spines* $S$ by the grammar:

$$
S ::= x \mid I_\ell \mid S_\ell S \mid K_\ell S \qquad (\ell \geq 0)
$$

The *arity* of a spine is the number of operators of the form $S_\ell$, $\ell \geq 0$, in it. If $n$ is the arity of $S$, and $v_1, \ldots, v_n$ are $n$ SKInT-terms, then the term $S[v_1, \ldots, v_n]$

is defined by:

$$\begin{array}{ll} x[] =_{df} x & (S_\ell S)[v_1,\ldots,v_n] =_{df} S_\ell(S[v_1,\ldots,v_{n-1}],v_n) \\ I_\ell[] =_{df} I_\ell & (K_\ell S)[v_1,\ldots,v_n] =_{df} K_\ell(S[v_1,\ldots,v_n]) \end{array}$$

Every term $u$ can be written in a unique way as $S[v_1,\ldots,v_n]$: the spine $S$ is the sequence of operators occurring along the leftmost branch of $u$, read top-down. Then the terms $v_1, \ldots, v_n$ are the second arguments of operators of the form $S_\ell$, $\ell \geq 0$, on the spine, read bottom-up. The terms $v_1, \ldots, v_n$ are called the *arguments* of $u$. Iterating this decomposition of terms in spine and arguments allows us to see terms as trees of spines.

Call a *one-step spine reduction* $u \longrightarrow^s v$ any one-step reduction of a redex occurring on the spine of $u$. A *spine reduction* $u \longrightarrow^{s*} v$ is a sequence of one-step spine reductions. A term that has no one-step spine contractum is called *spine-normal*. Spine reductions play the role of head reductions in the $\lambda$-calculus. (However, spine reductions are not unique.)

Define *standard reductions* $u \longrightarrow^{std*} v$ by induction on $v$ viewed as a tree of spines, if and only if $u \longrightarrow^{s*} S[u_1,\ldots,u_n]$, and $v = S[v_1,\ldots,v_n]$, where $u_i \longrightarrow^{std*} v_i$ for each $i$, $1 \leq i \leq n$. SKInT standardizes [9], in that $u \longrightarrow^* v$ (in SKInT) implies $u \longrightarrow^{std*} v$. In particular, a SKInT-term $u$ is weakly normalizable if and only if it has a normalizing standard reduction.

**Definition 1** *$u$ is* solvable *if any of the following equivalent conditions hold:*

*(i) All* SKInT*-spine reductions starting from $u$ terminate;*
*(ii) Some* SKInT*-spine reduction starting from $u$ terminates.*

*Proof.* That $(i)$ implies $(ii)$ is clear. Conversely, write $u \Rightarrow v$ when $u$ is $\Sigma T$-normal, has a spine $\beta I$-redex $S_\ell(I_\ell, w)$, and $v$ is the unique $\Sigma T$-normal form of the spine $\beta I$-contraction of $u$. (Notice that any term has at most one spine $\beta I$-redex, hence $\Rightarrow$-reductions are unique.) By examining how rules commute, we can show that if $u \longrightarrow^{s*} v$ by using $\beta I$ $n$ times, then $\Sigma T(u) \Rightarrow^* \Sigma T(v)$ in exactly $n$ steps (see the appendices to [11]). It follows that, if $(ii)$ holds (with termination in $n$ spine $\beta I$-steps), then any $\Rightarrow$-reduction starting from $u$ terminates (in exactly $n$ steps), and therefore all spine reductions do exactly $n$ spine $\beta I$-steps; as $\Sigma T$ terminates, all these spine reductions must be finite. □

We wish to characterize solvable, weakly normalizing and strongly normalizing as terms that can be typed in some systems of conjunctive types. It will be profitable to use a simplified format for conjunctive types, due to S. van Bakel [2] (see also [21]), where the type of any given term is unique—modulo the choice of types for occurrences of variables—and has a well-defined arity: this is in contrast with the usual sort of conjunctive types (see e.g. [15, 8]). Define the *strict intersection types* $\tau$ by:

$$\tau ::= B \mid \mu \rightarrow \tau \qquad \mu ::= [\tau_1,\ldots,\tau_n] \qquad (n \geq 0)$$

where $[\tau_1, \ldots, \tau_n]$ is the multiset of types $\tau_1, \ldots, \tau_n$. Intuitively, $[\tau_1, \ldots, \tau_n]$ denotes the intersection of $\tau_1, \ldots, \tau_n$. If $n = 0$, $[]$ denotes the set of all terms. We shall also write $\omega$ for $[]$, and $\mu_1 \wedge \mu_2$ for the multiset union of $\mu_1$ and $\mu_2$.

Strongly normalizing $\lambda$-terms are those that are typable in system $\mathcal{S}$, defined as follows. Call $\mathcal{S}$-*types* the types generated by the grammar:

$$\tau ::= B \mid \mu \to \tau \qquad \mu ::= [\tau_1, \ldots, \tau_n] \qquad (n \geq 1)$$

That is, multisets of types are now restricted to be non-empty. We define system $\mathcal{S}$ as the system of Figure 4 (again), but where $\tau$ and $\mu$-types are restricted to be $\mathcal{S}$-types.

$$\frac{}{\Gamma, x : \mu \wedge \tau \vdash x : \tau} \qquad \frac{\Gamma \vdash u : [\tau_1, \ldots, \tau_n] \to \tau \quad \Gamma \vdash v : \tau_1 \quad \ldots \quad \Gamma \vdash v : \tau_n}{\Gamma \vdash uv : \tau} \qquad \frac{\Gamma, x : \mu \vdash u : \tau}{\Gamma \vdash \lambda x \cdot u : \mu \to \tau}$$

**Fig. 4.** Conjunctive types for the $\lambda$-calculus

Correspondingly, we endow SKInT with the typing rules of Figure 5, yielding a typing system that we call $\mathcal{S}\omega$ (when types are $\mathcal{S}\omega$-types), or $\mathcal{S}$ (when types are $\mathcal{S}$-types).

$$\frac{}{\Gamma, x : \mu \wedge \tau \vdash x : \tau} \qquad \frac{}{\Gamma \vdash I_\ell : \mu_0 \to \ldots \to \mu_{\ell-1} \to \mu_\ell \wedge \tau \to \tau}$$

$$\frac{\Gamma \vdash u : \mu_0 \to \ldots \to \mu_{\ell-1} \to [\tau_1, \ldots, \tau_n] \to \tau \quad \Gamma \vdash v : \mu_0 \to \ldots \to \mu_{\ell-1} \to \tau_1 \quad \ldots \quad \Gamma \vdash v : \mu_0 \to \ldots \to \mu_{\ell-1} \to \tau_n}{\Gamma \vdash S_\ell(u, v) : \mu_0 \to \ldots \to \mu_{\ell-1} \to \tau}$$

$$\frac{\Gamma \vdash u : \mu_0 \to \ldots \to \mu_{\ell-1} \to \mu_\ell \to \tau}{\Gamma \vdash K_\ell(u) : \mu_0 \to \ldots \to \mu_{\ell-1} \to \mu \to \mu_\ell \to \tau}$$

**Fig. 5.** The system of conjunctive types for SKInT

Call an $\mathcal{S}\omega$-type $\tau$ *definite positive* if and only if $\omega$ only occurs negatively in $\tau$. More formally, the definite positive types $\tau^+$ and the definite negative types $\tau^-$ are defined by the grammar:

$$\begin{array}{lll} \tau^+ ::= B \mid \mu^- \to \tau^+ & \mu^+ ::= [\tau_1^+, \ldots, \tau_n^+] & (n \geq 1) \\ \tau^- ::= B \mid \mu^+ \to \tau^- & \mu^- ::= [\tau_1^-, \ldots, \tau_n^-] & (n \geq 0) \end{array}$$

A context $\Gamma$ is *definite negative* if and only if every binding in $\Gamma$ is of the form $x : \mu^-$ with $\mu^-$ definite negative. We say that the typing judgement $\Gamma \vdash s : \tau$ is *definite positive* if and only if $\Gamma$ is definite negative and $\tau$ is definite positive.

We first have the following, which we leave to the reader to check:

**Lemma 1 (Subject Reduction).** *If $\Gamma \vdash u : \tau$ in $S\omega$, resp. $S$, and $u \longrightarrow^* v$ in* SKInT *or* SKInT$_\eta$, *then $\Gamma \vdash v : \tau$ in $S\omega$, resp. $S$.*

**Theorem 1 (Normalization).** *The following holds:*

*(i) If $\Gamma \vdash u : \tau$ is derivable in system $S\omega$, then $u$ is solvable;*
*(ii) If $\Gamma^- \vdash u : \tau^+$ is definite positive and derivable in system $S\omega$, then $u$ is weakly normalizing in* SKInT *and in* SKInT$_\eta$*;*
*(iii) If $\Gamma \vdash u : \tau$ is derivable in system $S$, then $u$ is strongly normalizing in* SKInT *and even in* SKInT$_\eta$.

*Proof.* The idea is to translate the term $u$ to a $\lambda$-term, and to use the corresponding results for the $\lambda$-calculus. We modify the $u \mapsto [\![u]\!](s_0, \ldots, s_{n_1})$ translation of [9] to map SKInT-terms to $\lambda_{\oplus\epsilon}$*-terms*: the idea is that instead of dropping some arguments (like $s_\ell$ in the definition of $[\![K_\ell(u)]\!](s_0, \ldots, s_{n-1})$ for $n \geq \ell$), we shall keep them on the left of some binary operator $\oplus$ such that $s \oplus t$ is semantically equivalent to $t$ alone.

The $\lambda_{\oplus\epsilon}$-calculus is defined by the grammar:

$$t ::= x \mid tt \mid \lambda x \cdot t \mid \epsilon t \mid t \oplus t$$

and its reduction rules are $\beta\eta$-reduction plus:

$$(\epsilon) \quad \epsilon t \to t \qquad (\oplus-) \quad t_1 \oplus t_2 \to t_2 \qquad (\oplus) \quad (t_1 \oplus t_2) \oplus t_3 \to t_1 \oplus (t_2 \oplus t_3)$$

We define type systems that we call again $\mathcal{S}\omega$, resp. $\mathcal{S}$, defined on $\mathcal{S}\omega$-types, resp. $\mathcal{S}$-types, and whose typing rules are those of Figure 4, plus:

$$\frac{\Gamma \vdash t : \tau}{\Gamma \vdash \epsilon t : \tau} \qquad \frac{[\Gamma \vdash t_1 : \tau_1] \quad \Gamma \vdash t_2 : \tau_2}{\Gamma \vdash t_1 \oplus t_2 : \tau_2}$$

where the bracketed premise $\Gamma \vdash t_1 : \tau_1$ is included in $\mathcal{S}$, but omitted in $\mathcal{S}\omega$.

There is an erasing translation $t \mapsto |t|$ from $\lambda_{\oplus\epsilon}$ to the $\lambda$-calculus (with $\beta$-reduction): $|\epsilon t| = |t|$, $|t_1 \oplus t_2| = |t_2|$, $|x| = x$, $|t_1 t_2| = |t_1|\ |t_2|$, $|\lambda x \cdot tx| = |t|$ if $x$ is not free in $t$, and $|\lambda x \cdot t| = \lambda x \cdot |t|$ if $t$ is not of the form $t'x$ with $x$ not free in $t'$. $\lambda_{\oplus\epsilon}$ has the subject reduction property, and for every $\lambda_{\oplus\epsilon}$-term $t$:

(a) If $\Gamma \vdash t : \tau$ in $\mathcal{S}\omega$, then $t$ is solvable, i.e., all head-reductions starting from $t$ terminate. We call *head-reduction* in $\lambda_{\oplus\epsilon}$ any $(\epsilon)$, $(\oplus-)$, $(\oplus)$ or $(\eta)$-step, or any $(\beta)$-reduction step $s \longrightarrow t$ such that $|s| \longrightarrow |t|$ by a head $(\beta)$-reduction step in the $\lambda$-calculus (i.e., the $\lambda_{\oplus\epsilon}$-redex does not get erased).
(b) If $\Gamma \vdash t : \tau$ in $\mathcal{S}$, then $t$ is strongly normalizing.

The proofs are by appealing to the same properties in the $\lambda$-calculus, using the erasing translation above (see [11]), or by reducibility methods (for (b)): see [10].

Define the *dimension* $\dim u$ of a SKInT-term $u$ by:

$$\dim x =_{df} -1 \qquad \dim I_\ell =_{df} \ell$$
$$\dim K_\ell(u) =_{df} \max(\ell, \dim u) + 1 \quad \dim S_\ell(u, v) =_{df} \max(\ell, \dim u) - 1$$

$$[\![u]\!]_\oplus(s_0,\ldots,s_{n-1}) =_{df} \begin{cases} xs_0\ldots s_{n-1} & \text{if } u = x \\ \epsilon(s_0 \oplus \ldots \oplus s_{\ell-1} \oplus s_\ell)s_{\ell+1}\ldots s_{n-1} & \text{if } u = I_\ell \\ [\![v]\!]_\oplus(s_0,\ldots,s_{\ell-1}, s_\ell \oplus s_{\ell+1}, s_{\ell+2},\ldots,s_{n-1}) & \text{if } u = K_\ell(v) \\ [\![v]\!]_\oplus(s_0,\ldots,s_{\ell-1}, \\ \quad [\![w]\!]_\oplus(s_0,\ldots,s_{\ell-1}), s_\ell,\ldots,s_{n-1}) & \text{if } u = S_\ell(v,w) \end{cases}$$

when $n > \dim u$

$$[\![u]\!]_\oplus(s_0,\ldots,s_{n-1}) =_{df} \lambda x_n \cdot \ldots \cdot \lambda x_{m-1} \cdot [\![u]\!]_\oplus(s_0,\ldots,s_{n-1},x_n,\ldots,x_{m-1})$$

when $n < m = \dim u + 1$

**Fig. 6.** Interpretation of SKInT-terms as $\lambda_{\oplus\epsilon}$-terms

The new translation $u \mapsto [\![u]\!]_\oplus(s_0,\ldots,s_{n-1})$, parameterized by a list $s_0$, ..., $s_{n-1}$ of $\lambda_{\oplus\epsilon}$-terms, is described in Figure 6.

By abuse of language, say that $\Gamma \vdash s : \mu$ is derivable in $\mathcal{S}\omega$, resp. $\mathcal{S}$, where $\mu = [\tau_1,\ldots,\tau_k]$, if and only if $\Gamma \vdash s : \tau_i$ is derivable in $\mathcal{S}\omega$, resp. $\mathcal{S}$, for every $i$, $1 \leq i \leq k$. An easy structural induction on $u$ (see [11]) shows that, if $\Gamma \vdash u : \mu_0 \to \ldots \to \mu_{n-1} \to \tau$ in $\mathcal{S}\omega$, resp. $S$, and $\Gamma \vdash s_i : \mu_i$ in $\mathcal{S}\omega$, resp. $\mathcal{S}$, for every $i$, $0 \leq i < n$, then $\Gamma \vdash [\![u]\!]_\oplus(s_0,\ldots,s_{n-1}) : \tau$ in $\mathcal{S}\omega$, resp. $\mathcal{S}$.

A tedious check now shows that whenever $u \longrightarrow v$ in SKInT$_\eta$, then for every sequence $s_0$, ..., $s_{n-1}$ of $\lambda_{\oplus\epsilon}$-terms, $[\![u]\!]_\oplus(s_0,\ldots,s_{n-1}) \longrightarrow^* [\![v]\!]_\oplus(s_0,\ldots,s_{n-1})$ in $\lambda_{\oplus\epsilon}$, resp. $\longrightarrow^+$ in the case of $(SI_\ell)$, $(\eta S_\ell)$ and a few other rules (see [11]).

By (b), any reduction $R$ in SKInT, resp. SKInT$_\eta$, starting from a typable term in system $S$ uses only finitely many instances of rules $(SI_\ell)$ and $(\eta S_\ell)$, $\ell \geq 0$. But since $\Sigma T$ terminates, there are finitely many reduction steps (in $\Sigma T$) inbetween two $(SI_\ell)$ or $(\eta S_\ell)$-steps. So $R$ is finite, proving (*iii*).

To show (*i*), first notice that if $u \longrightarrow^s v$ in SKInT (or SKInT$_\eta$), then $[\![u]\!]_\oplus(s_0,\ldots,s_{n-1}) \longrightarrow^* [\![v]\!]_\oplus(s_0,\ldots,s_{n-1})$ (resp. $\longrightarrow^+$ if $u \longrightarrow^s v$ by $(SI_\ell)$, $(\eta S_\ell)$ and a few other rules) by head-reductions in $\lambda_{\oplus\epsilon}$. By (a), any spine-reduction step in SKInT, resp. SKInT$_\eta$, starting from a typable term in $S\omega$ has only spine-reductions that use finitely many instances of $(SI_\ell)$ or $(\eta S_\ell)$, $\ell \geq 0$. Since $\Sigma T$ terminates, (*i*) follows.

To show (*ii*), we would like to use a similar argument, but any $\lambda_{\oplus\epsilon}$-term with a definite positive typing normalizes only weakly, and then we need to show that we can lift back the given normalization strategy in $\lambda_{\oplus\epsilon}$ to some normalization strategy in SKInT; this is not easy. Instead, we observe the following. Let $u'$ be a spine-normal SKInT-term, and write $u'$ as $S[u_1,\ldots,u_k]$. We may then write $S$ as a word of the form $K_{i_{01}}\ldots K_{i_{0n_0}} S_{j_1} K_{i_{11}}\ldots K_{i_{1n_1}} S_{j_2} K_{i_{21}}\ldots K_{i_{2n_2}}\ldots S_{j_k} K_{i_{k1}}\ldots K_{i_{kn_k}} L$, with $L = I_j$ or $L$ a variable (in which case we let $j =_{df} -1$), with:

$$i_{01} > \ldots > i_{0n_0} \geq j_1 > i_{11} > \ldots > i_{1n_1} \geq j_2 > \ldots \geq j_k > i_{k1} > \ldots > i_{kn_k} > j \geq -1$$

and $k \geq 0$, $n_0 \geq 0$, $n_1 \geq 0$, ..., $n_k \geq 0$, and when $n_i = 0$, the notation $j_i > i_{i1} > \ldots > i_{in_i} \geq j_{i+1}$ means $j_i \geq j_{i+1}$. If $n > \dim u'$, then we have:

$$
\begin{aligned}
&|[\![u']\!]_\oplus(s_0, \ldots, s_{n-1})| \qquad (1)\\
&= L'|s_{j+1}| \ldots |\widehat{s_{i_{kn_k}}}| \ldots |\widehat{s_{i_{k1}}}| \ldots |s_{j_k-1}|\\
&\quad |[\![u_1]\!]_\oplus(s_0, \ldots, s_{j_k-1})||s_{j_k}| \ldots |\widehat{s_{i_{(k-1)n_{k-1}}}}| \ldots |\widehat{s_{i_{(k-1)1}}}| \ldots |s_{j_{k-1}-1}|\\
&\quad |[\![u_2]\!]_\oplus(s_0, \ldots, s_{j_{k-1}-1})| \ldots\\
&\quad \ldots\\
&\quad |[\![u_k]\!]_\oplus(s_0, \ldots, s_{j_1-1})||s_{j_1}| \ldots |\widehat{s_{0n_0}}| \ldots |\widehat{s_{01}}| \ldots s_{n-1}
\end{aligned}
$$

where $L' = |s_j|$ if $L = I_j$, or $L' = x$ if $L$ is a variable $x$, and $s_i \ldots \hat{s}_{i_1} \ldots \hat{s}_{i_p} \ldots s_j$ denotes the sequence of terms $s_i$, …, $s_j$ from which the terms $s_{i_1}$, …, $s_{i_p}$ have been omitted. If $n \leq \dim u'$, then $|[\![u']\!]_\oplus(s_0, \ldots, s_{n-1})|$ is the $\eta$-normal form of $\lambda s_n \cdot \ldots \cdot \lambda s_{\dim u'} \cdot |[\![u']\!]_\oplus(s_0, \ldots, s_{\dim u'})|$, and is therefore of the form $\lambda s_n \cdot \ldots \cdot \lambda s_{m-1} \cdot |[\![u']\!]_\oplus(s_0, \ldots, s_{m-1})|$.

As far as types are concerned, let $u'$ have a definite positive typing. Any (definite positive) $S\omega$-type of $u'$ must be of the form $\mu_0 \to \ldots \to \mu_{i_{01}} \to \mu_{i_{01}+1} \to \tau$, and the typing derivation leading to this type must map each $u_i$, $1 \leq i \leq k$, to the types $\mu_0 \to \ldots \to \mu_{j_{n+1-i}-1} \to \tau_{ip}$, $1 \leq p \leq m_i$, for some types $\tau_{ip}$. Let $\mu'_i$ be $[\tau_{i1}, \ldots, \tau_{im_i}]$. Then this typing derivation also gave $L$ the type:

$$
\begin{aligned}
&\mu_0 \to \ldots \to \hat{\mu}_{i_{kn_k}} \to \ldots \to \hat{\mu}_{i_{k1}} \to \ldots \to \mu_{j_k-1} \qquad (2)\\
&\to \mu'_1 \to \mu_{j_k} \to \ldots \to \hat{\mu}_{i_{(k-1)n_{k-1}}} \to \ldots \to \hat{\mu}_{i_{(k-1)1}} \to \ldots \to \mu_{j_{k-1}-1}\\
&\to \ldots\\
&\to \mu'_{k-1} \to \mu_{j_2} \to \ldots \to \hat{\mu}_{i_{1n_1}} \to \ldots \to \hat{\mu}_{i_{11}} \to \ldots \to \mu_{j_1-1}\\
&\to \mu'_k \to \mu_{j_1} \to \ldots \to \hat{\mu}_{i_{0n_0}} \to \ldots \to \hat{\mu}_{i_{01}} \to \mu_{i_{01}+1} \to \tau
\end{aligned}
$$

If $L$ is a variable, since the typing context is definite negative, the type above must be definite negative, so in particular every $\mu'_i$, $1 \leq i \leq k$, is definite positive. Since the type of $u'$ was assumed definite positive, every $\mu_j$ is definite negative, so the types $\mu_0 \to \ldots \to \mu_{j_{n+1-i}-1} \to \tau_{ip}$ of $u_i$ are definite positive. Similarly, if $L$ is $I_j$, then recall that $j < i_{kn_k}$ (if $n_k \neq 0$) or $j < j_k$ (if $n_k = 0$ and $k \neq 0$), and by the form of the typing rule for $I_j$, every $\mu'_i$, $1 \leq i \leq k$ must occur negatively in $\mu_\ell$, hence is definite positive (if $k \neq 0$; this is trivial if $k = 0$), hence again the types assigned to $u_i$ are all definite positive.

Having made these remarks, let $u$ be a SKInT-term with a definite positive $S\omega$-typing. Then $|[\![u]\!]_\oplus(s_0, \ldots, s_{n-1})|$ is a $\lambda$-term with a definite positive $S\omega$-typing, for any sequence $s_0$, …, $s_{n-1}$ of the right types, hence it $\beta$-normalizes weakly. Recall that a weakly normalizing $\lambda$-term $t$ has a finite Böhm tree: let $h(t)$ be the height of this tree. We show that, under the assumption that $u$ has a definite positive $S\omega$-typing and that $|[\![u]\!]_\oplus(x_0, \ldots, x_{n-1})|$ normalizes weakly for some sequence of variables $x_0$, …, $x_{n-1}$, then $u$ SKInT-normalizes weakly. This is by induction on $h(t)$, where $t = |[\![u]\!]_\oplus(x_0, \ldots, x_{n-1})|$. First, by ($i$) and since $u$ has an $S\omega$-typing, $u$ is SKInT-solvable: let $u' =_{df} S[u_1, \ldots, u_k]$ be any spine-normal form of $u$. Since $u \longrightarrow^{s*} u'$, as in case ($i$), $|[\![u]\!]_\oplus(x_0, \ldots, x_{n-1})|$ head-rewrites to

$|[\![u']\!]_\oplus(x_0,\ldots,x_{n-1})|$, and the latter is head-normal, since $x_j$ is a variable (by inspection of Equation 1). By the remark on the types of spine-normal forms (Equation 2), each $u_i$, $1 \leq i \leq k$, also has a definite positive typing. Let now $t_i$ be $|[\![u_i]\!]_\oplus(x_0,\ldots,x_{j'_{k+1-i}})|$: by Equation 1, $h(t_i) < h(|[\![u']\!]_\oplus(x_0,\ldots,x_{n-1})|) = h(|[\![u]\!]_\oplus(x_0,\ldots,x_{n-1})|)$. So the induction hypothesis applies: each $u_i$ SKInT-normalizes weakly, say to some term $v_i$. Therefore $u$ SKInT-normalizes weakly to $S[v_1,\ldots,v_k]$. This proves *(ii)* in the case of SKInT-reduction.

For SKInT$_\eta$-reduction, notice that every SKInT-normalizable term is also SKInT$_\eta$-normalizable. Indeed, observe that if $u \longrightarrow v$ by the $\eta$-rule $(\eta S_\ell)$, and $u$ is SKInT-normal, then so is $v$. □

The Normalization Theorem has an important corollary. Recall that a translation from $\lambda$-terms to a given language (say, SKInT) *preserves* strong normalization (resp. weak normalization, solvability) if and only if the translation of every strongly normalizing $\lambda$-term (resp. weakly normalizing, resp. solvable) is strongly normalizing (resp. weakly normalizing, resp. solvable).

**Corollary 1 (Preservation of Normalization Properties).** *Every translation mapping $\mathcal{S}$-typable $\lambda$-terms to $S$-typable* SKInT*-terms preserves strong normalization. Every translation mapping $\mathcal{S}\omega$-typable $\lambda$-terms to $S\omega$-typable* SKInT*-terms preserves solvability. Every translation mapping $\lambda$-terms having a definite positive typing in $\mathcal{S}\omega$ to* SKInT*-terms having a definite positive typing in $S\omega$ preserves weak normalization.*

*Proof.* Notice that these translations need not map $\lambda$-terms to SKInT-terms of the same type: we just need to preserve typability, not the types themselves. Every strongly normalizing (resp. weakly normalizing, solvable) $\lambda$-term is typable in system $\mathcal{S}$ (resp. in $\mathcal{S}\omega$, in $\mathcal{S}\omega$ with a definite positive typing) [2, 21]; the result then follows from Theorem 1. □

It follows that the $L^*$ translation of [9], in particular, preserves strong normalization, weak normalization and solvability. This works also in the presence of $\eta$-rules. Also, Corollary 1 is stronger: essentially, any reasonable translation from the $\lambda$-calculus to SKInT will preserve all three normalization properties.

Corollary 1 depends on the fact that strongly normalizing, resp. weakly normalizing, resp. solvable terms in the $\lambda$-calculus are all characterized in terms of types. We end this section by showing that the same holds in SKInT.

First, define $S$, resp. *$S\omega$-type substitutions* $\theta$ as finite maps from type variables, a.k.a. base types in $B$, to $S$, resp. $S\omega$-types. For any type or context $a$, $a\theta$ denotes the result of applying $\theta$ to $a$; $[\tau/b]$ denotes the substitution mapping $b$ to $\tau$. The following is easy:

**Lemma 2.** *If $\Gamma \vdash u : \tau$ is derivable in $S$, then for every $S$-type substitution $\theta$, $\Gamma\theta \vdash u : \tau\theta$ is derivable in $S$.*

*If $\Gamma \vdash u : \tau$ is derivable in $S\omega$, then for every $S\omega$-type substitution $\theta$, $\Gamma\theta \vdash u : \tau\theta$ is derivable in $S\omega$.*

*If $\Gamma^- \vdash u : \tau^+$ is definite positive and derivable in $S\omega$, then for every $S$-type substitution $\theta$, $\Gamma^-\theta \vdash u : \tau^+\theta$ is definite positive and derivable in $S\omega$.*

**Lemma 3.** *Every* SKInT*-normal term $u$ has a typing in system $S$. Every spine-normal* SKInT*-term $u$ has a typing in $S\omega$.*

*Proof.* We first observe that every type can be written uniquely $\mu_0 \to \ldots \to \mu_{n-1} \to b$, where $b \in B$. We call $n$ the *arity* of the type. By extension, we call arity of a typing $\Gamma \vdash u : \tau$ the arity of $\tau$. We call a typing as above $S$*-normal* if $n \geq 1$ and $\mu_{n-1} = [b']$ with $b'$ a base type other than $b$; we call it $S\omega$*-normal* if $n \geq 1$ and $\mu_{n-1} = \omega$.

Let the *degree* $d(u)$ of a SKInT-term $u$ be defined by: $d(x) =_{df} 0$, $d(I_\ell) =_{df} \ell + 1$, $d(S_\ell(v, w)) =_{df} \ell$, $d(K_\ell(v)) =_{df} \ell + 1$. We show the more general claims that: $(i)$ every SKInT-normal term $u$ has a normal $S$-typing of arity $d(u) + 1$, and: $(ii)$ every spine-normal term $u$ has a normal $S\omega$-typing of arity $d(u) + 1$. This is by structural induction on $u$.

Notice first that: $(*)$ whenever a term $u$ has an $S$-normal, resp. $S\omega$-normal typing, then it also has $S$-normal, resp. $S\omega$-normal typings $\Gamma \vdash u : \tau$ of arbitrary higher arities in the same system: indeed, if $u$ has a normal typing $\Gamma \vdash u : \tau$ of arity $n$ as above (with $b$ the base type at the end), then it also has a normal typing of arity $n+1$, namely $\Gamma\theta \vdash u : \tau\theta$, by Lemma 2, with $\theta =_{df} [[b''] \to b'/b]$, $b'' \neq b'$ in the case of system $S$, $\theta =_{df} [\omega \to b'/b]$ in the case of $S\omega$. Claim $(*)$ then follows by an easy induction on $n$.

If $u$ is a variable, then the normal typing $x : [b'] \to b \vdash x : [b'] \to b$ establishes $(i)$, and $x : \omega \to b \vdash x : \omega \to b$ establishes $(ii)$. If $u$ is of the form $I_\ell$, then we can choose the typing $\vdash I_\ell : \mu_0 \to \ldots \to \mu_{\ell-1} \to [[b'] \to b] \to [b'] \to b$ with $\mu_0, \ldots, \mu_{\ell-1}$ any $S$-types and $b' \neq b$ for $(i)$, and $\vdash I_\ell : \mu_0 \to \ldots \to \mu_{\ell-1} \to [\omega \to b] \to \omega \to b$ for $(ii)$.

When $u$ is of the form $S_\ell(v, w)$, then, first, define the conjunction $\Gamma' \wedge \Gamma''$ of two contexts $\Gamma'$ and $\Gamma''$ as the collection of bindings $x : \mu' \wedge \mu''$ (when $x : \mu' \in \Gamma'$ and $x : \mu'' \in \Gamma''$), $x : \mu'$ (if $x : \mu' \in \Gamma'$ but $x$ does not appear in $\Gamma''$), and $x : \mu''$ (if $x : \mu'' \in \Gamma''$ but $x$ does not appear in $\Gamma'$). Notice also that (by examination of the reduction rules), if $u$ is spine-normal (in particular, normal), then $d(v) \leq \ell$. We show claim $(i)$ as follows: by induction, $v$ has an $S$-normal typing of arity $d(v) + 1 \leq \ell + 1$, hence by $(*)$ it has an $S$-normal typing of arity exactly $\ell + 1$, say $\Gamma' \vdash v : \mu'_0 \to \ldots \to \mu'_{\ell-1} \to [b'] \to b$; by induction hypothesis again, $w$ has an $S$-typing, hence by $(*)$ we may assume w.l.o.g. that $w$ has an $S$-typing of arity at least $\ell$, say $\Gamma' \vdash w : \mu''_0 \to \ldots \to \mu''_{\ell-1} \to \tau''$; then, we can derive $\Gamma'[\tau''/b'] \vdash v : \mu_0 \to \ldots \to \mu_{\ell-1} \to [\tau''] \to b$, where $\mu_i =_{df} \mu'_i[\tau''/b']$, $0 \leq i < n$, by Lemma 2; then $\Gamma'[\tau''/b'] \wedge \Gamma'' \vdash u : \mu_0 \to \ldots \to \mu_{\ell-1} \to b$ is an $S$-typing of arity $d(u) = \ell$; substituting $b$ for, say, $[b''] \to b'''$ (using Lemma 2), we get the required $S$-normal typing of arity $d(u) + 1$. Showing $(ii)$ is easier: by induction, $v$ has an $S\omega$-normal typing of arity $d(v) + 1 \leq \ell + 1$, hence by $(*)$ it has an $S\omega$-normal typing of arity $\ell + 1$, say $\Gamma' \vdash v : \mu'_0 \to \ldots \to \mu'_{\ell-1} \to \omega \to b$; then $\Gamma \vdash u : \mu_0 \to \ldots \to \mu_{\ell-1} \to \omega \to b'$ is the required $S\omega$-normal typing of arity $\ell + 1$, where $\Gamma =_{df} \Gamma'[\omega \to b'/b]$, and $\mu_i =_{df} \mu'_i[\omega \to b'/b]$, $0 \leq i < \ell$.

When $u$ is of the form $K_\ell(v)$, then observe that (by examination of the reduction rules), if $u$ is spine-normal (or normal), then $d(v) \leq \ell$. We show $(i)$ as follows: by induction $v$ has an $S$-normal typing of arity $d(v) + 1$, hence by $(*)$

an $S$-normal typing $\Gamma' \vdash v : \mu'_0 \to \ldots \to \mu'_{\ell-1} \to [b'] \to b$ of arity $\ell + 1$; then $\Gamma' \vdash K_\ell(v) : \mu'_0 \to \ldots \to \mu'_{\ell-1} \to \mu \to [b'] \to b$ is the required $S$-normal typing for $u$, for any $S$-type $\mu$. And (*ii*) follows by a similar construction, replacing $[b']$ by $\omega$ and letting $\mu$ be any $S\omega$-type. □

Contrarily to what happens in the $\lambda$-calculus, types in $S\omega$ are not preserved by the inverse of SKInT-reduction. However:

**Lemma 4.** *If $u \longrightarrow^* v$ in* $\text{SKInT}_\eta$, *and $\Gamma \vdash v : \tau$ in $S\omega$, then $\Gamma\theta \vdash u : \tau\theta$ for some $S$-type substitution $\theta$.*

*Proof.* More concisely, we shall say that whenever $v$ has some $S\omega$-type $\tau$, then $u$ has type $\tau\theta$ for some $S$-substitution $\theta$ (where the contexts $\Gamma$ and $\Gamma\theta$ are understood). We first show this when $u = l$, $v = r$, and $l \to r$ is any of the reduction rules. There are only three interesting rules:

- $(SI_\ell)$: $l = S_\ell(I_\ell, w)$, $r = w$. If $\tau$ has arity $n \geq \ell$, then $\tau$ is of the form $\mu_0 \to \ldots \to \mu_{\ell-1} \to \tau'$, and we can take $I_\ell$ of type $\mu_0 \to \ldots \to \mu_{\ell-1} \to [\tau'] \to \tau'$, so that $l$ has type $\tau$. If $\tau$ has arity $n < \ell$, then let $\tau$ be $\mu_0 \to \ldots \to \mu_{n-1} \to b$, and $\theta$ be $[\tau'/b]$, where $\tau'$ is any $S$-type of arity at least $\ell - n$: by Lemma 2, $r$ has type $\tau\theta$, and since $\tau\theta$ has arity at least $\ell$, then as above $l$ has type $\tau\theta$.
- $(SK_\ell)$: $l = S_\ell(K_\ell(u), w)$, $r = u$. If $\tau$ has arity $n \geq \ell + 1$, then write $\tau$ as $\mu_0 \to \ldots \to \mu_{\ell-1} \to \mu_\ell \to \tau'$: we can give $K_\ell(u)$ the $S\omega$-type $\mu_0 \to \ldots \to \mu_{\ell-1} \to \omega \to \mu_\ell \to \tau'$, and therefore $l$ has type $\tau$ as well (notice that we need not give $w$ a type). Otherwise, as in the $(SI_\ell)$ case, $r$ and $l$ have type $\tau\theta$ for some $S$-substitution $\theta$ of arity $\ell + 1 - n$.
- $(\eta S_\ell)$: $l = S_{\ell+1}(K_\ell(u), I_\ell)$, $r = u$. If the type $\tau$ of $r$ has arity $n \geq \ell + 1$, then write $\tau$ as $\mu_0 \to \ldots \to \mu_\ell \to \tau'$, and $\mu_\ell$ as $[\tau_1, \ldots, \tau_k]$. We can give $I_\ell$ all the types $\mu_0 \to \ldots \to \mu_{\ell-1} \to \mu_\ell \to \tau_i$, $1 \leq i \leq k$, and we can give $K_\ell(u)$ the type $\mu_0 \to \ldots \to \mu_{\ell-1} \to \mu_\ell \to [\tau_1, \ldots, \tau_k] \to \tau'$, so $l$ can be given type $\tau$ again. If $n < \ell + 1$, then, if $\tau$ is of the form $\mu_0 \to \ldots \to \mu_{n-1} \to b$, let $\theta$ be $[\tau'/b]$ for any $S$-type $\tau'$ of arity at least $\ell + 1 - n$: then $l$ has type $\tau\theta$.

For all the other rules, we can choose the identity substitution for $\theta$ (see [11]).

We now claim that whenever $u \longrightarrow v$—namely, when $u = \mathcal{C}[l]$, $v = \mathcal{C}[r]$, and $l \to r$ is some reduction rule—and $v$ has type $\tau$ in $S\omega$, then $u$ has some type $\tau\theta$ in $S\omega$, where $\theta$ is an $S$-substitution. This is a straightforward structural induction on $\mathcal{C}$, using Lemma 2. The Lemma then follows by induction on the length of the reduction $u \longrightarrow^* v$. □

**Theorem 2.** *Every solvable* SKInT*-term has an $S\omega$-typing. Every* SKInT*-weakly normalizing, resp.* $\text{SKInT}_\eta$*-weakly normalizing term has a definite positive $S\omega$-typing.*

*Proof.* Let $u$ be solvable. Then $u \longrightarrow^{s*} v$, where $v$ is spine-normal; by Lemma 3, $v$ has an $S\omega$-typing $\Gamma \vdash v : \tau$; by Lemma 4, $u$ has a typing of the form $\Gamma\theta \vdash u : \tau\theta$, where $\theta$ is an $S$-substitution. This is clearly an $S\omega$-typing.

On the other hand, if $u$ is weakly normalizing (in SKInT or in $\text{SKInT}_\eta$), then $u \longrightarrow^* v$ for some SKInT-normal term $v$; by Lemma 3, $v$ has a definite positive

$S\omega$-typing $\Gamma^- \vdash v : \tau^+$; by Lemma 4, $u$ has a typing of the form $\Gamma^-\theta \vdash u : \tau^+\theta$, where $\theta$ is an $S$-substitution. By Lemma 2, this typing is therefore not only an $S\omega$-typing, but is also definite positive. □

In fact, the proof even shows that every weakly normalizing term, whether in SKInT or in SKInT$_\eta$, has an $S\omega$-typing where $\omega$ does not occur at all (but $\omega$ may occur in the typing *derivation*). This is similar to [8], Theorem 6.12.

**Theorem 3.** *If $u$ is strongly normalizing in* SKInT, *resp.* SKInT$_\eta$, *then it has an $S$-typing.*

*Proof.* As $u$ is strongly normalizing, any normalization strategy terminates. Choose any *innermost* strategy, i.e. any strategy that reduces only redexes whose strict subterms are all normal. (In particular, the redex $S_\ell(K_\ell(u_1), u_2)$ can only be reduced when $u_1$ and $K_\ell(u_1)$ are normal.) Let $\nu(u)$ denote the length of the longest reduction sequence in SKInT starting from $u$ according to this strategy.

We show the claim by induction on $\nu(u)$. If $\nu(u) = 0$, then this is by Lemma 3. Otherwise, assume that $u \longrightarrow v$ (so that $\nu(v) < \nu(u)$, hence by induction $v$ has an $S$-typing $\Gamma \vdash v : \tau$). If the reduction from $u$ to $v$ is by any rule except $(SK_\ell)$, $\ell \geq 0$, then $u$ has an $S$-typing $\Gamma\theta \vdash u : \tau\theta$, where $\theta$ is an $S$-substitution: this is as in the proof of Lemma 4.

In case $u \longrightarrow v$ by $(SK_\ell)$, this does not work any longer, since we cannot use $\omega$ (not an $S$-type). Instead, observe that $u$ can be written as $\mathcal{C}[S_\ell(K_\ell(u_1), u_2)]$, and that $v = \mathcal{C}[u_1]$. By induction hypothesis, and since $\nu(u_2) < \nu(u)$, $u_2$ has an $S$-typing $\Gamma_2 \vdash u_2 : \tau_2$, and w.l.o.g. we may assume that $\tau_2$ has arity at least $\ell$, i.e. that $\tau_2 = \mu''_0 \rightarrow \ldots \rightarrow \mu''_{\ell-1} \rightarrow \tau''$. Since the chosen reduction strategy is innermost, $u_1$ is normal, and by Lemma 3 (more precisely, by Claim (*i*) in its proof), $u_1$ has an $S$-normal typing of degree exactly $d(u_1) + 1$; but since the reduction is innermost again, $K_\ell(u_1)$ is normal as well, so $d(u_1) \leq \ell$, and (by Remark (*) in the proof of Lemma 3) therefore $u_1$ has an $S$-normal typing of arity $\ell + 1$, say v $\Gamma_1 \vdash u_1 : \mu'_0 \rightarrow \ldots \rightarrow \mu'_{\ell-1} \rightarrow [b'] \rightarrow b$. So we may now derive $\Gamma \vdash S_\ell(K_\ell(u_1), u_2) : \mu_0 \rightarrow \ldots \rightarrow \mu_{\ell-1} \rightarrow b$, where $\Gamma =_{df} \Gamma_1[\tau''/b'] \wedge \Gamma_2$, $\mu_i =_{df} \mu'_i[\tau''/b'] \wedge \mu''_i$ for each $i$, $0 \leq i < \ell$. It follows that $u$ itself has an $S$-typing (which is an instance of the latter), by a straightforward induction on $\mathcal{C}$.

The case of SKInT$_\eta$-strongly normalizing terms is completely similar. □

**Corollary 2.** *The following equivalences hold, for any* SKInT*-term $u$:*

- *$u$ solvable $\Leftrightarrow$ $u$ typable in $S\omega$*
- *$u$* SKInT*-weakly normalizing $\Leftrightarrow$ $u$* SKInT$_\eta$*-weakly normalizing*
  *$\Leftrightarrow$ $u$ has a definite positive $S\omega$-typing*
- *$u$* SKInT*-strongly normalizing $\Leftrightarrow$ $u$* SKInT$_\eta$*-strongly normalizing*
  *$\Leftrightarrow$ $u$ typable in $S$.*

## 4 Conclusion

We have shown that SKInT enjoyed exactly the same properties as the $\lambda$-calculus, as far as the relationship between conjunctive types and various normalization properties is concerned. This implies that SKInT preserves solvability, weak normalization and strong normalization, for any reasonable, i.e. typability-preserving translation from the λ-calculus to SKInT, in particular for the $L^*$ translation of [9].

It is then interesting to compare SKInT with other calculi of explicit substitutions. Indeed, although SKInT was not presented as a calculus of explicit substitutions in [9], it is definitely so: $I_\ell$ is de Bruijn index $\ell \geq 0$, and the de Bruijn substitution $[0 := v_0, \ldots, n := v_n]$ applied to $u$ is $(\ldots((u \circ_0 v_0) \circ_1 v_1) \ldots) \circ_n v_n$, where the $\circ_\ell$ operator is defined by: $u \circ_\ell v =_{df} S_{\ell+1}(K_\ell(u), v)$, as the reader is invited to check. Then $\Sigma T$ plays the role of the substitution calculus, and $\beta I$ (i.e., $(SI_\ell)$) more or less plays the role of the $\beta$ rule (the connection is not as direct as in more traditional calculi of explicit substitutions, though).

Together with the results of [9], this advances the table of properties of calculi with explicit substitutions proposed by Lang and Rose [16][1] to the following ($\supseteq \beta$ means "simulates $\beta$-reduction", CRM is "is Church-Rosser in the presence of meta-variables", SSN is "has a strongly normalizing substitution subcalculus", PSN means "preserves strong normalization").

| Name | # | $\supseteq \beta$ | first-order? | unconditional? | CRM | SSN | PSN | Reference |
|---|---|---|---|---|---|---|---|---|
| $\lambda\sigma$ | 11 | yes | yes | yes | no | yes | no | [1] |
| $\lambda\sigma_\Uparrow$ | 21 | yes | yes | yes | yes | yes | no | [6] |
| $\lambda\upsilon$ | 8 | yes | yes | yes | no | yes | yes | [17] |
| $\lambda s$ | ∞ | yes | yes | yes | no | yes | yes | [13] |
| $\lambda s_e$ | ∞ | yes | yes | yes | yes | ? | no | [14] |
| $\lambda\zeta$ | 13 | no | yes | yes | yes | | yes | [19] |
| λxci | ∞ | yes | no | no | yes | yes | ? | [16] |
| $\lambda x_B$ci | ∞ | yes | yes | no | no | yes | ? | [16] |
| SKIn | ∞ | yes | yes | yes | yes | no | no | [9] |
| SKInT | ∞ | yes | yes | yes | yes | yes | yes | [9] |
| $\lambda\beta$ | ∞ | yes | no | | yes | | yes | Church, see [3] |

The only defect we know of SKInT is that it encodes the λ-calculus in a slightly complicated, and non-unique way [9]: e.g., you may wish to use the $L^*$ translation, or any other. We believe that this drawback is offset by the fact that SKInT has basically all the properties of the λ-calculus: confluence, even on open terms; standardization; strong normalization of simply-typed terms; a conservative extension of the λ-calculus with $\beta$, resp. $\beta\eta$-conversion (see [9]); preservation of solvability, weak and strong normalization; characterization of solvable, weakly and strongly normalizable terms by conjunctive typings (this paper); all this in an infinite but regular first-order equational formulation.

Further work should investigate whether easier, direct proofs of the results presented here are possible, using variants of the reducibility method [15, 8].

---

[1] F. Lang notes that some of the results of this paper are wrong, and we have followed his remarks in the table (see `http://www.ens-lyon.fr/~flang/papiers.html`).

## References


1. M. Abadi, L. Cardelli, P.-L. Curien, and J.-J. Lévy. Explicit substitutions. In *POPL'90*, pages 31–46, 1990.
2. S. van Bakel. Complete restrictions of the intersection type discipline. *Theoretical Computer Science*, 102(1):135–163, 1992.
3. H. Barendregt. *The Lambda Calculus, Its Syntax and Semantics*, volume 103 of *Studies in Logic and the Foundations of Mathematics*. North-Holland, 1984.
4. F. Cardone and M. Coppo. Two extensions of Curry's type inference system. In P. Odifreddi, editor, *Logic and Computer Science*, volume 31 of *The APIC Series*, pages 19–76. Academic Press, 1990.
5. P.-L. Curien. *Categorical Combinators, Sequential Algorithms and Functional Programming*. Pitman, London, 1986.
6. P.-L. Curien, T. Hardin, and J.-J. Lévy. Confluence properties of weak and strong calculi of explicit substitutions. *J. ACM*, 43(2):362–397, 1996.
7. H. B. Curry and R. Feys. *Combinatory Logic*, volume 1. North-Holland, 1958.
8. J. Gallier. Typing untyped $\lambda$-terms, or reducibility strikes again! *Annals of Pure and Applied Logic*, 91(2–3):231–270, 1998.
9. H. Goguen and J. Goubault-Larrecq. Sequent combinators: A Hilbert system for the lambda calculus. *Mathematical Structures in Computer Science*, 1999.
10. J. Goubault-Larrecq. On computational interpretations of the modal logic S4 IIIb. Confluence and conservativity of the $\lambda \mathbf{ev} Q_H$-calculus. Research report, Inria, 1997.
11. J. Goubault-Larrecq. A few remarks on SKInT. Research report RR-3475, Inria, 1998.
12. T. Hardin and J.-J. Lévy. A confluent calculus of substitutions. In *France-Japan Artificial Intelligence and Computer Science Symposium*, 1989.
13. F. Kamareddine and A. Ríos. A $\lambda$-calculus à la de Bruijn with explicit substitutions. In *PLILP'95*, pages 45–62. Springer Verlag LNCS 982, 1995.
14. F. Kamareddine and A. Ríos. Extending a $\lambda$-calculus with explicit substitution which preserves strong normalisation into a confluent calculus on open terms. *Journal of Functional Programming*, 7:395–420, 1997.
15. J.-L. Krivine. *Lambda-calcul, types et modèles*. Masson, 1992.
16. F. Lang and K. H. Rose. Two equivalent calculi of explicit substitution with confluence on meta-terms and preservation of strong normalization (one with names and one first-order). Presented at WESTAPP'98, 1998.
17. P. Lescanne and J. Rouyer-Degli. From $\lambda\sigma$ to $\lambda\upsilon$: a journey through calculi of explicit substitutions. In *POPL'94*, 1994.
18. P.-A. Melliès. Typed lambda-calculi with explicit substitutions may not terminate. In *TLCA'95*, pages 328–334. Springer Verlag LNCS 902, 1995.
19. C. A. Muñoz Hurtado. Confluence and preservation of strong normalization in an explicit substitutions calculus. In *LICS'96*. IEEE, 1996.
20. P. Sallé. Une extension de la théorie des types en $\lambda$-calcul. In *5th ICALP*, pages 398–410. Springer Verlag LNCS 62, 1978.
21. É. Sayag. *Types intersections simples*. PhD thesis, Université Paris VII, 1997.

# Modular Structures as Dependent Types in Isabelle

Florian Kammüller

Computer Laboratory, University of Cambridge

**Abstract.** This paper describes a method of representing algebraic structures in the theorem prover Isabelle. We use Isabelle's higher order logic extended with set theoretic constructions. Dependent types, constructed as HOL sets, are used to represent modular structures by semantical embedding. The modules remain first class citizen of the logic. Hence, they enable adequate formalization of abstract algebraic structures and a natural proof style. Application examples drawn from abstract algebra and lattice theory — the full version of Tarski's fixpoint theorem — validate the concept.

## 1 Introduction

The initial aim of this research was to find a module system for the theorem prover Isabelle where modules are first class citizens, i.e. have a representation in the logic. This seems important when we want to formalize (mathematical) theories in which abstract entities are contained. Examples for such theories are common in abstract algebra. For example, in group theory we define *groups* as abstract objects. A group can be represented by a signature and axioms, but it is at the same time a logical formula; we say "G is a group". Other examples include formal methods of computer science where we have abstract notions like *schemas* or *abstract machines*.

In classical approaches modules for theorem provers are outside the logic: they do not have a logical representation, instead serve an efficient organization of theories. Nevertheless, most of the theorem provers that have powerful module systems (*e.g.*[OSR93,FGT93,GH93]) suggest to use their modules as representations for (algebraic) structures. Although the encapsulation and abstraction achieved by packaging structures into modules is sensible, it does not constitute an adequate representation. This becomes obvious once one leaves the scope of toy examples [KP99].

We try to combine the convenience of the representation of algebraic structures as modules with a sound logical treatment of modular structures avoiding any restrictions of reasoning. Using an extension of Isabelle HOL with a notion of sets we define dependent types as sets in order to find an embedding of signatures in the logic. Using this embedding we can represent abstract algebraic structures as such dependent "types". Furthermore, we use the very recent concept of record types in Isabelle [NW98] to represent the element patterns of algebraic structures. For example, we represent a group as a record with four fields: the carrier set, the binary operation, the inverse, and the unit element. The class of all groups is represented by a HOL set over this record type.

This paper first explains our notion of algebraic structures and gives examples in Sect. 2. In Sect. 3 dependent types and their formalization as sets in Isabelle HOL are introduced. Their application to represent structures is described. Examples of abstract algebra and the full form of Tarski's fixpoint theorem validate the construction of the concept of algebraic structures in Sect. 4. Finally, we discuss some related work and draw some conclusions in Sect. 5.

# 2 Algebraic Structures

By an ***algebraic structure*** we mean a set of concrete mathematical objects that are described as an abstract object. That is, an algebraic structure is a set of concrete entities which are considered to be similar according to a bunch of characterizing rules and a general pattern of appearance, while abstracting from other concrete characteristics. Examples for algebraic structures are groups, rings, homomorphisms, etc. The algebraic structure of groups, say, is the class of all concrete examples of groups. Hence, the structure is formed by abstracting over elements of similar appearance that fulfill common properties.

We understand program specifications, definitions of formal languages, finite automata, and the like, also as algebraic structures. Certainly, logical theories can as well be seen as algebraic structures, but it is not our aim to express logics like that. In some respects our view of algebraic structures corresponds to the notion of "Little Theories" [FGT93] in IMPS, but does not try to capture the notion of a logical theory.

In this section we characterize our notion of simple algebraic structure and higher order structure. We use an informal notion of signature instead of modules because that is what the latter basically are. We do not use a separate syntactical description language for those signatures because we think that for the encoding of mathematical structures our method of direct encoding in HOL sets plus dependent types is sufficiently self explanatory.

In the following we will talk about structures as sets of objects. We are using the set notion of Isabelle HOL as a foundation for this work. This notion is defined in terms of predicates and is thus — in a set-theoretic sense — rather a notion of *classes* than sets.

## 2.1 Simple and Higher Order Structures

An algebraic structure is a set of mathematical objects. They can be syntactically represented by their signature, i.e. by the arities of their elements and the rules which hold for the elements of the structure. An object matching the arities and fulfilling the rules is an element of a structure. A syntactical description of a structure $S$ by its signature and related rules is of the form:

$$\begin{array}{l}\textbf{signature } S(x_1,\ldots,x_n)\\ \quad x_1 \in A_1\\ \quad \ldots\\ \quad x_n \in A_n\\ \quad P_1\\ \quad \ldots\\ \quad P_m\end{array}$$

where the $A_i$ are the arities of the parameters, $i \in \{1, \ldots k\}$. The $P_k$ are properties in which the parameters $x_i$ can occur, $k \in \{1, \ldots, m\}$. The arities can denote types or sets depending on the framework. This syntax is a simplified form of the style of modules as seen in other theorem provers [OSR93,FGT93,GH93].

The associated meaning of this syntactical description of signature $S$ is what we consider as an algebraic structure

$$[\![S]\!] \equiv \{(x_1, \ldots, x_n) \in A_1 \times \ldots \times A_n \mid P_1 \ \wedge\ \ldots\ \wedge\ P_m\}$$

where in $P_i$ any of $\{x_1, \ldots, x_n\}$ can occur. We call the elements $x_1, \ldots, x_n$ *parameters* of the structure $S$.

Structures may possibly be parameterized over other structures. We call such structures *higher order structures* in contrast to *simple structures.* To identify the structures that are parameters of higher order structures, we use the term *parameter structures*, and the structure, which is defined by the higher order structure itself, we call *image structure*.

For the definition of simple structures, we use sets of extensible records. Record types are used as a template for the pattern of appearance of the structure's elements. They give us the selectors, which are projection functions enabling reference to the constituents of a simple structure. Although we use extension of record types to describe how more complex types are built from simpler ones, e.g. rings from groups, we do not use the extensibility. The latter is a feature of extensible record types that enables to model "late binding" [NW98] which is not needed in the way we model structures.

The definition of higher order structures needs a device to refer to the formal parameters. Here we employ the set theoretic construction of dependent types. It enables the use of constraints on parameter structures in the definition of an image structure. The selectors of the parameter structures admit to refer to their constituents.

For the parameter tuple *par* $\equiv (x_1, \ldots, x_n)$ of a simple structure we define a record $\alpha$ *par-sig* as[1]

$$\begin{array}{lll}\textbf{record } \alpha \textit{ par-sig} & \equiv & \\ \_ .\langle x_1\rangle & :: A_1 & \text{(postfix)}\\ \ldots & \ldots & \ldots\\ \_ .\langle x_n\rangle & :: A_n & \text{(postfix)}\end{array}$$

[1] We assume here syntax definition possibilities that are planned for records though not yet available

The underscore defines the argument positions of the field selectors of this record. For example, if $T$ is a term of appropriate record type, i.e. a suitable $n$-tuple, we can select the field $x_j$ of $T$ by $T.\langle x_j \rangle$. In general, the elements of the tuple will have names like *carrier*, or *inverse*, so the naming discipline of the record field selectors that we chose, is more informative than indexing by numbers.

The representation of a simple structure is given as a set of records; the record type defines the element pattern of the structure.

## 2.2 Example: Groups and Homomorphisms

A *group* is constituted by a carrier set and a binary function $\circ$ on that set, such that the function $\circ$ is associative, and for every element $x$ in the carrier there exists an inverse $x$. The carrier set also contains a neutral element $e$. The syntactical representation of a group by a signature is

$$\begin{array}{lll} \textbf{signature} & & \text{Group}\ (cr, \circ, inv, e) \\ \circ & \in & cr \times cr \rightarrow cr \\ inv & \in & cr \rightarrow cr \\ e & \in & cr \\ \forall\ x \in cr. & & x \circ e = x \\ \forall\ x \in cr. & & x \circ (inv\ x) = e \\ \forall x, y, z \in cr. & & x \circ (y \circ z) = (x \circ y) \circ z \end{array}$$

According to Sect. 2.1, the mathematical meaning that we associate to this example is

$$\begin{array}{l} [\![\ \text{Group}\ ]\!] \equiv \{ (\!|\ cr, \circ, inv, e\ |\!) \mid \circ \in cr \times cr \rightarrow cr\ \wedge\ inv \in cr \rightarrow cr\ \wedge\ e \in cr\ \wedge \\ \qquad (\forall x \in cr.\ x \circ e = x)\ \wedge\ (\forall x \in cr.\ x \circ inv(x) = e) \wedge \\ \qquad (\forall x, y, z \in cr.\ x \circ (y \circ z) = (x \circ y) \circ z) \} \end{array}$$

The notation $(\!|\ cr, \circ, inv, e\ |\!)$ of the elements of this set stands for an extensible record term. In this context it is sufficient to understand them as products. The base type of the set Group is defined by the following record definition[2].

$$\begin{array}{lll} \textbf{record} & \alpha\ \textit{group-sig}\ \equiv & \\ \_.\langle cr \rangle & :: \alpha\ set & \text{(postfix)} \\ \_.\langle f \rangle & :: [\alpha, \alpha] \Rightarrow \alpha & \text{(postfix)} \\ \_.\langle inv \rangle & :: \alpha \Rightarrow \alpha & \text{(postfix)} \\ \_.\langle e \rangle & :: \alpha & \text{(postfix)} \end{array}$$

The structure Group is of type ( $\alpha$ *group-sig* ) *set*. In the following example of a higher order structure for group homomorphisms, we see how the field selectors are used to refer to the constituents of a group.

A homomorphism of groups is a map from one group to another group that respects group operations. The parameters of a structure Hom for homomorphisms are groups themselves, i.e. we have a higher order structure. The following syntactical form encloses the parameter structures in square brackets.

[2] In the remainder of this paper we name the group operation $f$, instead of $\circ$, because we need to refer to the group $G$ and in prefix notation $G.\langle f \rangle$ looks more natural. An improvement of syntax for such implicit references is given by *locales* (c.f. Sect. 5)

$$\begin{array}{ll} \textbf{signature}\ \mathrm{Hom}\ [\ G, H \in \mathrm{Group}\ ]\ (\Phi) & \\ \quad \Phi \in & G.\langle cr\rangle \rightarrow H.\langle cr\rangle \\ \quad \forall x, y \in & G.\langle cr\rangle.\ \ \Phi(G.\langle f\rangle\ x\ y) = H.\langle f\rangle\ \Phi(x)\ \Phi(y) \end{array}$$

In the definition of the mathematical structure we have to add "where $G$ and $H$ are elements of the structure *Group*". That is, a mathematical object representing a homomorphism between groups has to carry also the two groups in itself. It is a triple $(G, H, \Phi)$ of two groups and a homomorphism between them. The homomorphism depends on the elements $G$ and $H$. In the image structure we need to refer to the parameter structures $G$ and $H$. Hence, we choose a dependent type, the $\Sigma$-type, to define the structure for homomorphisms.

$$\begin{array}{l} Hom \equiv \Sigma_{G \in Group}\, \Sigma_{H \in Group}\ \{\Phi \mid \Phi \in G.\langle cr\rangle \rightarrow H.\langle cr\rangle\ \wedge \\ \qquad\qquad\qquad\qquad (\forall x, y \in G.\langle cr\rangle.\ \Phi(G.\langle f\rangle\ x\ y) = H.\langle f\rangle\ \Phi(x)\ \Phi(y))\} \end{array}$$

Now the parameter groups $G$ and $H$ are bound by the $\Sigma$ operator and we can refer to them, and their constituents by using the projections, e.g. $G.\langle f\rangle$. In the following section, we explain the notion of dependent types, and how we represent them using set theoretic constructions.

## 3 Dependent Types as Structure Representation

The textbook introduction to type theory [NPS90, page 52] explains the main reason for the introduction of the $\Pi$-set as the interpretation of the universal quantifier. The Heyting interpretation of this quantifier is [Hey56]

> $\forall x \in A.B(x)$ is true if we can construct a function which when applied to an element $a$ in the set $A$, yields a proof of $B(a)$.

The dependent sum $\Sigma$ enables to deal with the existential quantifier, i.e. $\exists$ can be defined as

$$\exists x \in A.B(x) \equiv \Sigma_{x \in A} B(x)$$

We use the dependent sets in the same sense, but restrict the use to the description of structures. We consider $A$ and $B$ as structures, and not general formulas. So, we use the dependent sets as type theory uses them, but in a more naïve way restricting ourselves to the statements $x \in A$ and *not* interpreting this as "$x$ is a proof of formula $A$".

The idea is to use the syntactical signature description of the structure as a set $B(x)$ — with a formal parameter $x$. This formal parameter is an element of the first set $A$. In case of more than one parameter structure the nesting of the dependent type constructors $\Sigma$ and $\Pi$ just accumulates.

We show in this section how dependent types are formalized in HOL and how this formalization can be used to represent higher order structures.

### 3.1 Isabelle Representation

The system Isabelle HOL implements a simple type theory [Chu40] and has no dependent types. The object logic HOL of Isabelle is extended by a notion of sets. Sets are here essentially predicates, rather than "built-in" by ZF-style axioms. We use this extension to define dependent types as sets in Isabelle.

**Set Representation** One can consider the $\Sigma$-type as a general form of the Cartesian Product. If we represent $\Sigma_{x\in A}B(x)$ as a set, it is thus

$$\Sigma_{x\in A}B(x) \equiv \bigcup_{x\in A}\bigcup_{y\in B(x)} \{(x,y)\}$$

This representation of the $\Sigma$-type is used in HOL.

The $\Pi$-type is the type of dependent functions. It is related to the $\Sigma$-type. We can express this type as a set by considering the subsets of $\Sigma$ which can be seen as functions

$$\Pi_{x\in A}B(x) \equiv \{f \in \mathcal{P}(\Sigma_{x\in A}B(x)) \mid \forall x \in A. \exists!\, y \in B(x). f(x) = y\} \qquad (1)$$

where $\mathcal{P}$ denotes the powerset.

**Implementation in Isabelle** In the distribution of Isabelle HOL the $\Sigma$-type is already defined in terms of HOL sets, the $\Pi$-type not.

The most natural way to define $\Pi$ seems to be to use definition 1 defining $\Pi$ in terms of $\Sigma$. But, then the functions we would get would be sets of pairs and we would develop a new domain of functions inside HOL, when there are already functions.

The existing functions in HOL are the elements of the function type $\alpha \Rightarrow \beta$, where $\alpha$ and $\beta$ indicate arbitrary types, and $\Rightarrow$ is the function type constructor. There is a notation for $\lambda$-abstraction available, which allows to define new functions. We would like to define function sets, i.e. sets of elements of the HOL type $\alpha \Rightarrow \beta$, and on top of that we want to have that the co-domain of these functions $\beta$ may depend on the input to the function. Ideally, the type $\beta$ should depend on some $x$ of type $\alpha$. Since HOL does not have dependent types, it is impossible to integrate the dependency at the level of types. But, we can define a non-dependent type for the constructor $\Pi$ as

$$[\alpha\ set, \alpha \Rightarrow \beta set] \Rightarrow (\alpha \Rightarrow \beta)set$$

Then, we can assign the above type to a constant $\Pi$ in HOL and add the idea of dependency to the definition of this constructor.

$$\Pi_{x\in A}B(x) \equiv \{f \mid \forall x.\ \text{if } x \in A \text{ then } f(x) \in B(x) \text{ else } f(x) = (@y.\text{True})\}$$

By using the more explicit language of sets we achieve that the codomain is a set which depends on the argument to the function. The "else" case is necessary to achieve extensionality for the $\Pi$-sets.

The non-dependent function sets are a special case of this definition of $\Pi$. Using Isabelle's pretty printing facilities, we get a nice syntactical representation for that and can now write $A \rightarrow B$ for the set of functions from a set $A$ to a set $B$.

What we are doing here is classification. Equality compares functions according to their behavior on the set $A$. That is, we do not care about what a function in $\Pi_{x \in A} B(x)$ does outside $A$. We want to think of all functions which behave alike on $A$ as the same function.

To reassure ourselves that the definition of $\Pi$ is sound we have established a bijection $\Pi_{Bij}$ between the classical definition from Equation 1 and the above HOL function set as

$$\Pi_{Bij} A B \equiv \lambda f \in \Pi_{x \in A} B.\ \{(x, y) \mid x \in A \ \wedge\ y = f x\}$$

We proved in Isabelle that this map is actually a bijection.

### 3.2 Algebraic Formalization with $\Pi$ and $\Sigma$

We concentrate here on the representation of higher order structures. As already pointed out in Sect. 2 we use sets of records for simple structures. We use the dependent type constructors $\Sigma$ and $\Pi$ to represent higher order structures, that is, to express structures, where the parameters are elements of structures themselves. Roughly speaking, the $\Sigma$-types are used for general relations between parameter and image structure. When this relation is a function, i.e. the construction of the image structure is unique and defined for all elements of the parameter structure, then we can construct elements of the higher order structure using the $\lambda$-notation. In that case, the higher order structure is a set of functions, i.e. a $\Pi$-type structure.

**Use of $\Sigma$** The interpretation of the $\Sigma$-type is that of a relation between parameter and image structure. Higher order structures whose image structures are defined for certain input parameters, but not necessarily for all, can be represented by $\Sigma$. So, the elements of these higher order structures are pairs of parameter and image structure elements; for a structure as $Struc \equiv \Sigma_{x \in A} B(x)$, we can write this membership as $(a, b) \in Struc$.

But, we also want to instantiate the structure By $Struc \downarrow a$ we annotate the instantiation or application of the structure. What we are interested in is to get an instance of the image structure $B$, where $a$ is substituted for the formal parameter $x$. That is, we want to derive $B(a)$ for $a \in A$, or apply the entire structure generally to an element of the parameter structure. For $a \in A$ we construct an operator $\downarrow$ such that $(\Sigma_{x \in A} B(x)) \downarrow a$ evaluates to $B(a)$. We can define $\downarrow$ in terms of the image of a relation $\mathsf{Im}$, so it reduces to

$$Struc \downarrow a \equiv (\Sigma_{x \in A} B(x)``(\{a\}) \equiv \{y \mid \exists x \in \{a\}.(x, y) \in \Sigma_{x \in A} B(x)\}$$

Then we can use the theorem

$$(a, b) \in \Sigma_{x \in A} B(x) \Rightarrow b \in B(a)$$

to derive

$$a \in A \Rightarrow Struc \downarrow a = B(a)$$

This theorem enables us now to build the instance of a higher order structure with an element $a$ of the parameter structure $A$.

**Use of $\Pi$** Elements of higher order structures which are uniquely defined — like FactGroup in Sect. 4.2 — can be represented by a function definition in the typed $\lambda$-calculus from Sect. 3.1. These $\lambda$ functions are elements of the corresponding $\Pi$-set. Let $elem \equiv (\lambda x \in A.\ t(x))$, then

$$elem \in \Pi_{x \in A} B(x) \ \text{ iff } \ \forall a \in A.\ t(a) \in B(a)$$

The function body $t$ of the element $elem$ constructs elements of the image structure of the higher order structure to which $elem$ belongs. For the application or instantiation we do not need an extra operator as for $\Sigma$. Since we have defined the $\Pi$ type as sets of functions we can use the HOL function application $elem(a)$. If $a \in A$ then this evaluates to $t(a)$.

The proof that the body $t(a)$ for $a \in A$ is actually in some image structure $B(a)$, can be nontrivial. For the examples in Sect.s 4.2 we have to show that the constructed images are groups.

In principle one can define structures that are universally applicable to parameters directly by $\Pi_{x \in A} B(x)$. For example, we may use $\Pi$ instead of $\Sigma$ to encode the structure of group homomorphisms, because for all groups $G$ and $H$ there is always a homomorphism between $G$ and $H$. This idea is discussed elsewhere. The use of $\Pi$ as general representation for higher order structures in the described sense is more complicated than $\Sigma$.

# 4 Application Examples

In this section we present some examples of abstract algebra and lattice theory which we performed in Isabelle to validate the concept introduced in this paper. We give outlines of the corresponding definitions of the algebraic structures and present the results. We do not display the proofs because they are too long.

## 4.1 Definitions

We start from the definition of groups and homomorphisms as sets of records given in Sect. 2.2. The notion of a subgroup uses dependent types. It is a higher order structure, because we define subgroups as subsets of a group which are themselves groups. This way of definition in terms of the structure Group is only possible because structures are first class citizens and can hence be used in formulas.

**consts**
subgroup :: $(\alpha\ group\text{-}sig \times \alpha set)set$
**defs**
subgroup $\equiv \Sigma_{G \in \text{Group}}\{H. H \subseteq G.\langle cr \rangle \wedge$
$(\!| H, \lambda x \in H. \lambda y \in H.\ G.\langle f \rangle\ x\ y, \lambda x \in H.\ G.\langle inv \rangle\ x, G.\langle e \rangle |\!) \in \text{Group}\}$

From this definition of the structure subgroup we can derive classical theorems about subgroups. For example, we derive that it is sufficient to show that a subset $H$ of a group $G$ is closed under the group operations, in order to infer that $H$ is a subgroup of $G$ (subgroup introduction rule). Using the pretty printing facilities of Isabelle we define the abbreviation $H$ <<= $G$ to annotate that $H$ is a subgroup of $G$.

Rings are defined in a similar manner as groups. Assuming the definition of group homomorphisms Hom from Sect. 2.2, group automorphisms can now be defined as homomorphisms from one group to the same group such that these functions are injective on the carrier of the group.

**consts**
GroupAuto :: $(\alpha\ \textit{group-sig} \times (\alpha \Rightarrow \alpha))\textit{set}$
**defs**
$$\text{GroupAuto} \equiv \Sigma_{G \in \text{Group}}.\{\Phi \mid (G, G, \Phi) \in \textit{Hom} \wedge \text{inj\_on}_{\ G.\langle cr \rangle}\Phi \wedge \Phi(G.\langle cr \rangle) = G.\langle cr \rangle\}$$

### 4.2 Proof Examples

**Group of Bijections** We define the set of bijections Bij and a record BijGroup consisting of the set of bijections over a set $S$, the composition of these bijections, the inverse of a bijection and the identical bijection.

$$\begin{aligned} \text{Bij } S &\equiv \{f \mid f \in S \to S \wedge f(S) = S \wedge \text{inj\_on}_S f\} \\ \text{BijGroup } S &\equiv (\!|\ \text{Bij}S,\ \lambda g \in \text{Bij}S.\lambda f \in \text{Bij}S.g \circ_S f, \\ &\qquad \lambda f \in \text{Bij}S.\lambda x \in S.(\textit{Inv}_S f)\ x,\ \lambda x \in S.x\ |\!) \end{aligned}$$

We can show that this record is in the set Group, i.e. that the bijections together with the listed operations on them are a group.

$$\text{BijGroup } S \in \text{Group}$$

**Group of Ring Automorphisms** We use a definition of ring automorphisms RingAuto similar to group automorphisms (c.f. Sect. 4.1) as a higher order structure. With this we show that the set of ring automorphisms is a subgroup of the group of bijections over the carrier of the ring. This proof is much simpler than showing that ring automorphisms are a group. That is, due to the subgroup introduction rule we derived in Sect. 4.1 it suffices to show closedness of the subset RingAuto $\downarrow R$ to derive

$$R \in \text{Ring} \Longrightarrow \text{RingAuto} \downarrow R \ {<<=}\ \text{BijGroup}(R.\langle cr \rangle)$$

Using the result that the set BijGroup is indeed a group, by unfolding the definition of subgroups, we obtain immediately from the former theorem that the ring automorphisms together with the appropriate operations are a group.

$$\begin{aligned} R \in \text{Ring} \Longrightarrow\ & (\!|\ \text{RingAuto} \downarrow R, \\ & \lambda x \in \text{RingAuto} \downarrow R.\lambda y \in \text{RingAuto} \downarrow R.(\text{BijGroup } (R.\langle cr \rangle).\langle f \rangle)\ x\ y, \\ & \lambda x \in \text{RingAuto} \downarrow R.(\text{BijGroup}(R.\langle cr \rangle).\langle inv \rangle)\ x, \\ & \text{BijGroup}(R.\langle cr \rangle).\langle e \rangle\ |\!) \qquad\qquad \in \text{Group} \end{aligned}$$

The Isabelle proof code that produces this result is short; the proof is a one line command connecting the previously derived results. This theorem illustrates nicely how the first class representation of structures allows the reduction of the proposition and hence improves the proof process.

**Factorization of a Group** We define the factorization of a group by one of its normal subgroups as

$$\begin{aligned}\text{FactGroup} \equiv\ & \lambda G \in \text{Group}.\lambda H \in \{H \mid H \lhd G\}.\\ & (\!|\ \text{set\_r\_cos}_G H,\\ & \quad (\lambda X \in \mathit{set\_r\_cos}_G H.\lambda Y \in \text{set\_r\_cos}_G H.\text{set\_prod}_G XY),\\ & \quad (\lambda X \in \text{set\_r\_cos}_G H.\text{set\_inv}_G X),\\ & \quad H\ |\!)\end{aligned}$$

We use the abbreviations $\text{set\_r\_cos}_G H$ for the set of all right cosets of $H$ in $G$. The terms $\text{set\_prod}_G$ and $\text{set\_inv}_G$ stand for the lifting of the group operation and inverse to functions on sets. The notation $H \lhd G$ abbreviates that $H$ is a normal subgroup of $G$. Furthermore, we define the convenient syntax $G/H$ for the factorization FactGroup $G\ H$. With these preparations, we can prove that this factorization is again a group.

$$G \in \text{Group} \wedge H \lhd G \Longrightarrow G/H \in \mathit{Group}$$

This is equivalent to the structural proposition that the factorization of a group is a function mapping a group and an element of the set of normal subgroups of this group to another group.

$$\text{FactGroup} \in (\Pi_{G \in \text{Group}}\{H \mid H \lhd G\} \to \mathit{Group})$$

**Direct Product of Groups** Similar to the previous example we define the direct product of two groups as

$$\begin{aligned}\text{ProdGroup} \equiv\ & \lambda G_1 \in \text{Group}.\lambda G_2 \in \text{Group}.\\ & (\!|\ G_1.\langle cr\rangle \times G_2.\langle cr\rangle,\\ & \quad \lambda(x_1, y_1) \in G_1.\langle cr\rangle \times G_2.\langle cr\rangle.\lambda(x_2, y_2) \in G_1.\langle cr\rangle \times G_2.\langle cr\rangle.\\ & \qquad\qquad (\ G_1.\langle f\rangle\ x_1\ x_2, G_2.\langle f\rangle\ y_1\ y_2\ ),\\ & \quad \lambda(x, y) \in G_1.\langle cr\rangle \times G_2.\langle cr\rangle.\ (\ G_1.\langle inv\rangle\ x, G_2.\langle inv\rangle\ y\ ),\\ & \quad (\ G_1.\langle e\rangle, G_2.\langle e\rangle\ )\ |\!)\end{aligned}$$

We define the syntax $(\!|\ G1, G2\ |\!)$ for this direct product of two groups and derive that it builds again a group.

$$G_1 \in \text{Group} \wedge G_2 \in \text{Group} \Longrightarrow\ (\!|\ G1, G2\ |\!) \in \mathit{Group}$$

**Full Tarski** The fixpoint theorem of A. Tarski [Tar55] is well known in computer science. Yet the form of the theorem which is usually proved is an older version from 1928. This theorem says that the least upper bound of all fixpoints $P$ of a monotonic function $f$ over a complete lattice $(A, \sqsubseteq)$ can be obtained as $\bigvee\{x \in A \mid x \sqsubseteq f(x)\}$. The dual is true for the greatest lower bound $\bigwedge$. Besides proving that, Tarski showed in the later paper that the set of all fixpoints $P$ of $f$ is itself a complete lattice. This second result is very well suited to illustrate the need for a proper structural representation, because it is proved by applying the first part of the theorem to the interval sublattice $[\bigvee Y, 1]$ for any subset $Y$

of $P$. So, our mechanized proof illustrates again the advantages of the present approach.

The proof of this full version was first formalized by R. Pollack in LEGO [Pol90]. There partial equivalence relation have to be used, which make the proof quite hard to read.

# 5 Discussion

The approach to use dependent types as modular structures is a well known one (e.g. [Mac86]), but to represent these types as sets is new. The advantage lies in the first class property of the structures. As we have seen in Sect. 3.2, we can now define operations on modular structures in the logic. Others, like forgetful functors, theory interpretations, can be expressed in terms of those. This should be further illustrated in future work.

LEGO [Bur90,LP92], an implementation of the Extended Calculus of Constructions [Luo90b] uses dependent types as theories [Luo90a]. Our work is similar to this. Since we are constructing these types as sets our approach is different.

One difference is that our dependent structures are terms of the logic not types as in ECC. The discussion section of [Luo90a, Sect. 4.4] mentions the possibility of a combination of two ideas: one is to have dependent structures as a representation of theories, done by ECC. The other idea is to have operations on theories, that is theories are values and there are operations that can be performed on those values. These concepts were examined in the specification language CLEAR [SB83]. Since the dependent types are values of the logic in our semantical embedding of theory structures, it is possible to define operations on theories as HOL functions. This has been illustrated in this paper by defining the operation of instantiation by the structure instance operation (c.f. Sect. 3.2).

The other difference is that we are following the LCF-style of not considering proof objects. Thus, the actual proof construction leading to the results is independent of the type structure of the formalization. Nevertheless, the structures we use contain enough information to produce the instances one is interested in, as is illustrated by the example proof for the group of ring automorphisms in Sect. 4.2.

Another experiment, worth examining, is to extend Isabelle's meta logic — which is a fragment of higher order logic — to the extent that the structures presented in this paper exist generically and not just for the object logic HOL.

In an earlier version of this work we used products as base type for simple structures. Due to a suggestion of P. Martin-Löf at the TYPES 98 workshop we now employ records, although only in addition to sets.

Although the syntax definition possibilities in Isabelle are remarkably good they still can be improved. For example terms like $G.\langle f\rangle\ x\ y$ should be expressible as $x \circ y$. This is nontrivial because the reference to the element $G$ is crucial. Nevertheless, we succeeded in designing a concept of *locales* for Isabelle[KW98], realizing this feature. Locales enable definitions depending on local assumptions. The additional use of locales with the structural concepts presented in this paper achieves a satisfying style of abstract algebraic reasoning. Difficulties with $\Sigma$-types as theory representation, pointed out in [Polar], are overcome by this additional feature.

## References


[Bur90] R. Burstall. Computer Assisted Proof for Mathematics: an Introduction using the LEGO Proof System. Technical Report ECS-LFCS-91-132, University of Edinburgh, 1990.

[Chu40] A. Church. A Formulation of the Simple Theory of Types. *Journal of Symbolic Logic*, pages 56–68, 1940.

[FGT93] W. M. Farmer, J. D. Guttman, and F. J. Thayer. IMPS: an Interactive Mathematical Proof System. *Journal of Automated Reasoning*, 11:213–248, 1993.

[GH93] John V. Guttag and James J. Horning, editors. *Larch: Languages and Tools for Formal Specification.* Texts and Monographs in Computer Science. Springer-Verlag, 1993. With Stephen J. Garland, Kevin D. Jones, Andrés Modet, and Jeannette M. Wing.

[Hey56] A. Heyting. *Intuitionism: An Introduction.* North Holland, Amsterdam, 1956.

[KP99] F. Kammüller and L. C. Paulson. A Formal Proof of Sylow's First Theorem – An Experiment in Abstract Algebra with Isabelle HOL. *Journal of Automated Reasoning*, 1999. To appear.

[KW98] F. Kammüller and M. Wenzel. Locales – a Sectioning Concept for Isabelle. Technical Report 449, University of Cambridge, Computer Laboratory, 1998.

[LP92] Z. Luo and R. Pollack. Lego proof development system: User's manual. Technical Report ECS-LFCS-92-211, University of Edinburgh, 1992.

[Luo90a] Z. Luo. A Higher-order Calculus and Theory Abstraction. *Information and Computation*, 90(1), 1990.

[Luo90b] Z. Luo. *An Extended Calculus of Constructions.* PhD thesis, University of Edinburgh, 1990. Also as Report CST-65-90.

[Mac86] D. B. MacQueen. Using Dependant Types to Express Modular Structures. In *Proc. 13th ACM Symp. Principles Programming Languages.* ACM Press, 1986.

[NPS90] B. Nordström, K. Petersson, and J. M. Smith. *Programming in Martin-Löf's Type Theory — An Introduction.* Oxford Science Publications. Clarendon Press, Oxford, 1990.

[NW98] W. Naraschewski and M. Wenzel. Object-oriented Verification based on Record Subtyping in Higher-Order Logic. In *11th International Conference on Theorem Proving in Higher Order Logics*, volume 1479 of *LNCS*, ANU, Canberra, Australia, 1998. Springer-Verlag.

[OSR93] S. Owre, N. Shankar, and J. M. Rushby. The PVS Specification Language (Beta Release). Technical report, SRI International, 1993.

[Pol90] R. Pollack. The Tarski Fixpoint Theorem. e-mail to: proof-sci@se.chalmers.cs, 1990.

[Polar] R. Pollack. Theories in Type Theory. Slides, available on the Web as `http://www.brics.dk/pollack`, unknown year.

[SB83] D. T. Sannella and R. M. Burstall. Structured Theories in LCF. In *CAAP'83: Trees in Algebra and Programming*, volume 159 of LNCS, pages 377–91. Springer-Verlag, 1983.

[Tar55] Alfred Tarski. A lattice-theoretical fixpoint theorem and its applications. *Pacific Journal of Mathematics*, 5:285–309, 1955.

# Metatheory of Verification Calculi in LEGO*

## To What Extent Does Syntax Matter?

Thomas Kleymann

LFCS Edinburgh, King's Buildings, Mayfield Road, Edinburgh EH9 3JZ, Scotland

**Abstract.** Investigating soundness and completeness of verification calculi for imperative programming languages is a challenging task. Incorrect results have been published in the past. We take advantage of the computer-aided proof tool LEGO to interactively establish soundness and completeness of both Hoare Logic and the operation decomposition rules of the Vienna Development Method with respect to operational semantics. We deal with parameterless recursive procedures and local variables in the context of total correctness.

In this paper, we discuss in detail the role of representations for expressions, assertions and verification calculi. To what extent is syntax relevant? One needs to carefully select an appropriate level of detail in the formalisation in order to achieve one's objectives.

## 1 Introduction

We have taken advantage of the LEGO system [1] to produce machine-checked soundness and completeness proofs for Hoare Logic and the operation decomposition rules of the Vienna Development Method (VDM). Our imperative programming language includes (parameterless) recursive procedures and local variables. We consider static binding and total correctness. This is one of the largest developments in LEGO to date. Building on a comprehensive library it additionally consists of more than 800 definitions, lemmata and theorems.

Our message to the designers and researchers of verification calculi is that conducting computer-aided soundness and completeness proofs is both a feasible and profitable task. Our fundamental contribution has been to highlight the role of auxiliary variables in Hoare Logic. Usually, assertions are interpreted as *predicates on states* where free variables denote the value of program variables in a specific state. Variables which are unaffected by the program under consideration then take on the role of auxiliary variables. They are required to relate the value of program variables in *different* states.

Our view of assertions emphasises the pragmatic importance of auxiliary variables. We have followed a proposal by Apt & Meertens to consider assertions as *relations on states and auxiliary variables* [2]. Furthermore, we stipulate a new structural rule to adjust auxiliary variables when strengthening preconditions and weakening postconditions. This rule is stronger than all previously suggested

* An earlier version appeared as LFCS Technical Report ECS-LFCS-98-393.

structural rules, including Hoare's consequence rule [3] and rules of adaptation. As a direct consequence of the new treatment of auxiliary variables,

- we were able to show that Sokołowski's calculus for recursive procedures [4] is sound and complete if one replaces Hoare's rule of consequence with ours. In particular, none of the other structural rules introduced by Apt [5] (which lead to a complete but unsound system) are required.
- We have clarified the relationship between Hoare Logic and its variant VDM. We were able to show that, contrary to common belief, VDM is more restrictive than Hoare Logic in that every derivation in VDM can be naturally embedded in Hoare Logic.

**Deep versus Shallow Embedding.** Traditionally, one defines syntax for expressions and relative to this setup, one characterises syntax of a programming language and syntax of an assertion language. Then, one describes the meaning of every syntactic construct. This approach is known as *deep embedding.* Alternatively one may shortcut this process and identify the syntactic representation with its denotation. This technique is known as *shallow embedding.*

**Related Work.** The pioneering work on machine-checked soundness for Hoare Logic by Gordon [6] rests entirely on shallow embedding. Homeier [7] extends the soundness proof to a setting with mutually recursive procedures. His encoding is based exclusively on deep embedding. Nipkow [8] has been the first to conduct a machine-checked *completeness* proof for Hoare Logic dealing with simple imperative programs in the context of partial correctness. This contains a mixture of shallow and deep embedding. Using similar representation techniques we have extended this work to recursive procedures and local variables.

### 1.1 To What Extent Does Syntax Matter?

Before deciding on the embedding technique, one ought to clarify the objectives of the machine-assisted development. This induces the level of detail in which one needs to analyse involved concepts. One of the central issues in formalising metatheory is to what extent syntax needs to be formalised. Technically, one has a choice of deep versus shallow embedding.

A shallow embedding cuts down the work load and is therefore, at least for machine-checked developments, often the preferred approach. The drawbacks of shallow embedding are that

1. one cannot exploit the inductive (syntactic) structure to prove properties.
2. The representation of concrete examples is often more difficult to comprehend.

As the main contribution of this paper, we clarify the role of deep versus shallow embedding. In the setting of Hoare Logic, the choice of the level of embedding has a major influence in the work involved in setting up an appropriate theory of substitutions. One needs substitutions on states, expressions and assertions. With a shallow embedding of expressions and assertions, substitutions can be expressed in terms of substituting the state space.

We have investigated the metatheory of verification calculi. It was *not* our aim to show that a proof tool such as the LEGO system is suitable to verify concrete programs. Therefore, the second drawback was of little concern to us. Our strategy has been to employ a shallow embedding whenever possible.

However, one needs to pursue soundness by induction on the structure of programs whereas completeness is conducted by induction of the derivation of correctness formulae. Hence, in light of the first drawback of a shallow embedding, one needs to insist on a deep embedding for programs and the notion of deriving correctness formulae. The main benefit of employing a shallow embedding for investigating the metatheory of verification calculi are that

- we did not have to worry at all about substitutions in assertions; an otherwise daunting prospect [9, 7].
- Completeness can only be established for an assertion language which is sufficiently expressive to denote all intermediate properties such as invariants. Employing a deep embedding of assertions, one would need to additionally explicitly construct syntactic representations for all possible intermediate assertions.

### 1.2 Overview

The outline of this paper is as follows. We first formalise the notion of a state space. We then sketch our embedding of expressions, assertions and imperative programs. In Sect. 7 we discuss semantics and derivability of Hoare Logic. We motivate new rules for loops and adjusting auxiliary variables. We argue that in investigating soundness and completeness of verification calculi, one should gloss over the syntactic details of expressions and assertions. Formalising substitutions is irrelevant. We will show in Sect. 6.3 that, at least for simple imperative programs, in the soundness and completeness proof, one does not need to appeal to *any* property of a substitution function.

In Sect. 7 we show that the metatheory for verification calculi dealing with local variables is more subtle. Not only is it essential to have an adequate substitution function (on the level of states), it is also necessary to employ an *extensional* notion of equality. This requires some attention, as type-theoretic systems such as Coq and LEGO are tailored to an *intensional* type theory. The case of VDM is similar and not covered in this paper.

## 2 The State Space

The state space records the value of every program variable. Let **VAR** be the type of program variables. In a type-theoretic setting, it seems natural to investigate multiple sorts. We identify the universe of data types with the universe of all types expressible in LEGO. The type of variables can be declared by providing a function

$$\mathsf{sort} : \mathbf{VAR} \to \mathbf{Type} \ .$$

A state $\sigma$ for a type environment sort is a function mapping program variables $x$ to values of type sort($x$). The state space itself is therefore a dependent function space:

**Definition 1 (State Space).** $\Sigma \stackrel{\text{def}}{=} \Pi x : \mathbf{VAR} \cdot \mathsf{sort}(x)$

We have implemented a substitution operation on *dependent* functions which satisfies the specification

$$\sigma\,[x \mapsto t]\,(y) = \begin{cases} t & \text{if } x = y, \\ \sigma(x) & \text{otherwise.} \end{cases} \tag{1}$$

This requires quite sophisticated type theory. See [10] for details.

Alternatively, one could exploit that only a finite number of a priori determined variables $x_1, \ldots, x_n$ are usually[1] employed in any concrete program. Thus, the dependent type space $\Sigma$ degenerates into the finite product sort$(x_1) \times \cdots \times$ sort$(x_n)$ [11, 12].

## 3 Expressions

Boolean expressions occur in loops and conditional statements. Other types of expressions depend on the data types expressible in the language and occur both as subexpressions of boolean expressions and in the assignment statement. One may define the syntax of expressions by a BNF grammar.

*Example 1 (Syntax of Expression).* Homeier & Martin [13] define two classes of expressions

$$e ::= n \mid x \mid {+\!+}x \mid e_1 + e_2 \mid e_1 - e_2$$
$$b ::= e_1 = e_2 \mid e_1 < e_2 \mid b_1 \wedge b_2 \mid b_1 \vee b_2 \mid \neg b$$

We will only consider expressions without side-effects[2] and do not deal with the expression $++\,x$. The semantics can thus be easily fixed denotationally and is determined by an interpretation function $I$ and a state $\sigma$. An interpretation determines the value of constants such as 0, +, $\wedge$ and (free) variables in expressions and logical formulae e.g., $[\![x]\!](I(\sigma)) \stackrel{\text{def}}{=} I\bigl(\sigma(x)\bigr)$. Whenever we come across a boolean expression in a loop or a conditional statement, we are only interested in the value it evaluates to, **true** or **false**. Similarly, in an assignment, we treat evaluation of the expression as atomic, merely a value depending on the state

[1] An exception is e.g., Lisp.

[2] Such a strict distinction between expressions and commands is one of the fundamental principles underlying idealised Algol [14].

space. We are not interested in syntactic properties such as whether one expression is a subterm of another expression. Ignoring the syntax of expressions paves the way towards a reasonable level of abstraction when investigating properties of verification calculi for imperative programs without side-effects in expressions.

Furthermore, we are only interested in the standard interpretation[3] of constants. Hence, the state space alone determines the semantics. We only consider expressions at this semantic level:

**Definition 2 (Expressions – Shallow Embedding).** *Given an arbitrary type $T$, we represent expressions by*

$$\text{expression}(T : \texttt{Type}) \stackrel{\text{def}}{=} \Sigma \to T \ .$$

*Let* $e$ : expression($T$) *be any expression. Its evaluation depends on a concrete snapshot of the state space* $\sigma : \Sigma$ *We define* $\text{eval}(\sigma)(e) \stackrel{\text{def}}{=} e(\sigma)$.

A benefit of adopting shallow embedding is that we do not have to worry about formalising the syntax in a logical framework. Working on the metatheory, one never encounters a concrete expression! Moreover, substitutions are much easier to deal with at the semantic level. It can be defined in terms of updating states:

**Definition 3 (Updating Expressions – Shallow Embedding).**

$$e\,[x \mapsto t]\,(\sigma) \stackrel{\text{def}}{=} e(\sigma\,[x \mapsto t])$$

In a deep embedding, one would need to define an interpretation and substitution function by induction on the structure of expressions and *prove* the substitution lemma

$$[\![e\,[x \mapsto t]]\!](\sigma) = [\![e]\!](\sigma\,[x \mapsto t]) \ .$$

An advantage of deep embedding is that, for concrete expressions, substitutions are more palatable. Consider the syntactic substitution $(x * y)\,[x \mapsto 3]$. Due to the recursive definition of updating, this should reduce to $3 * y$. In the shallow embedding, we would instead have

$$\lambda\sigma \cdot \Big( \underbrace{\big(\lambda\sigma \cdot \sigma(x) * \sigma(y)\big)}_{[\![x*y]\!]} (\sigma\,[x \mapsto 3]) \Big) \tag{2}$$

which ($\beta$-)reduces to $\lambda\sigma \cdot \big(\sigma\,[x \mapsto 3]\,(x) * \sigma\,[x \mapsto 3]\,(y)\big)$. This is equivalent to

$$\lambda\sigma \cdot 3 * \sigma(y) \tag{3}$$

Unfortunately, the LEGO system offers little support for reducing (2) to (3). In concrete examples, this leads to excessively large proof obligations. Computer-aided verification becomes unfeasible[4].

[3] This not only simplifies the encoding, it also avoids the problematic issue of how to axiomatise the class of acceptable interpretations. In particular, incompleteness results of Hoare Logic e.g., [15], exploit setups with *non-standard* interpretations.

[4] In a verification of the recursive algorithm Quicksort we had not manually intervened in reducing substitutions. For the correctness proof, LEGO had to run for more than

## 4 Assertions

Traditionally, assertions are considered to be simply formulae of first-order logic, which are interpreted in the usual way, except that the value of variables is determined by a state. Semantically, from a type-theoretic point of view, assertions are the particular class of expressions over propositions i.e., expression(Prop). Instead of first-order logic it is convenient to exploit the native logic of the theorem prover. This encoding has been adopted in [6, 8].

Our novel approach to Hoare Logic has been to give a more rigorous treatment of auxiliary variables. They are required at the level of specifications to relate the value of variables in different states as assertions may otherwise only relate the value of program variables in a *single* state.

At the syntactic level, one would need to (formally) distinguish between program variables and auxiliary variables. One could for example enforce that program variables have to start with a lower-case letter, whereas auxiliary variables must start with an upper-case letter. To be well-formed, programs may only refer to program variables.

Semantically, program variables are, as before, interpreted according to the state space. However, auxiliary variables are interpreted freely. Let $T$ be the domain of this interpretation.

**Definition 4 (Assertions – Shallow Embedding).**

$$\mathrm{Assertion}(T : \mathtt{Type}) \stackrel{\mathrm{def}}{=} (T \times \Sigma) \to \mathtt{Prop}$$

*Example 2.* Let $T = \{X, Y\} \to \mathtt{int}$. Relative to an interpretation $Z : T$ and a state $\sigma$, we interpret $[\![0 \leq y \wedge x = X \wedge y = Y]\!](Z, \sigma) = 0 \leq \sigma(y) \wedge \sigma(x) = Z(X) \wedge \sigma(y) = Z(Y)$.

Due to the shallow embedding we may update assertions analogue to expressions by relaying the work to updating the state space. In practice we only need to update the value of program variables but not auxiliary variables. Let $p$ be an assertion.

**Definition 5 (Updating Assertions – Shallow Embedding).**

$$p\,[x \mapsto t]\,(Z, \sigma) \stackrel{\mathrm{def}}{=} p(Z, \sigma\,[x \mapsto t]) \ .$$

Analogue to expressions, in a deep embedding, one would need to additionally represent syntax for assertions, define an interpretation and a syntactic substitution function. Then, one would need to *prove* the substitution lemma

$$[\![p\,[x \mapsto t]]\!](Z, \sigma) = [\![p]\!](Z, \sigma\,[x \mapsto t]) \ .$$

---

37 hours requiring more than 80MB on a SUN SPARC station 20 with sufficient physical memory to avoid swapping. In comparison, on the same architecture, the completeness proof for Hoare Logic dealing with recursive procedures and local variables could be dealt with in less than 15 minutes requiring less than 25MB. In both cases, we started LEGO in the empty environment.

## 5 Imperative Programs

A shallow embedding of a non-trivial imperative programs is problematic for a strongly-typed proof system such as LEGO. An imperative program $S$ may not terminate. Hence, the denotation of $S$ is a *partial* functions on the state space, $[\![S]\!] : \Sigma \rightharpoonup \Sigma$. However, LEGO only supports total functions. To avoid partiality, one may move to relational denotational semantics $[\![S]\!] : (\Sigma \times \Sigma) \to \texttt{bool}$, see [6] for an example.

In any case, to formally prove soundness within a logical framework, one needs to pursue induction on the structure of programs. Thus, one has to select a deep embedding strategy for the imperative programming language. For the purpose of this section, we consider a (very) simple imperative programming language consisting of assignments and loops.

**Definition 6 (Syntax of Imperative Programs – Deep Embedding).** *Imperative programs* $S$ : prog *are defined by the BNF grammar* $S ::= x := e \mid$ **while** $b$ **do** $S$ *where* $x$ : **VAR**, $e$ : expression(sort($x$)) *and* $b$ : expression($\texttt{bool}$).

We employ structural operational semantics which provides a clean way to specify the effect of each language constructor in an arbitrary state. It relates a program with its initial and final state.

**Definition 7 (Structural Operational Semantics).** *The operational semantics is defined as the least relation* $. \xrightarrow{\;.\;} . \subseteq \Sigma \times \texttt{prog} \times \Sigma$ *satisfying*

$$\sigma \xrightarrow{x := e} \sigma\,[x \mapsto \mathrm{eval}(\sigma)(e)] \tag{4}$$

$$\sigma \xrightarrow{\textbf{while } b \textbf{ do } S} \sigma \qquad \textit{provided } \mathrm{eval}(\sigma)(b) = \textbf{false} \ .$$

$$\frac{\sigma \xrightarrow{S} \eta \quad \eta \xrightarrow{\textbf{while } b \textbf{ do } S} \tau}{\sigma \xrightarrow{\textbf{while } b \textbf{ do } S} \tau} \qquad \textit{provided } \mathrm{eval}(\sigma)(b) = \textbf{true} \ .$$

Intuitively, $\sigma \xrightarrow{S} \tau$ denotes that the program $S$ when invoked in the state $\sigma$ will terminate in the state $\tau$.

## 6 Semantics and Derivability of Hoare Logic

Hoare Logic is a verification calculus for deriving correctness formulae of the form $\{p\}\ S\ \{q\}$ for assertions $p$, $q$ and programs $S$. We consider total correctness. Intuitively $\{p\}\ S\ \{q\}$ specifies that, provides $S$ is executed in a state such that the precondition $p$ holds, it terminates in a state $\tau$ where the postcondition $q$ is satisfied. One distinguishes between the semantics of a correctness formulae $\models_{\mathbf{Hoare}} \{p\}\ S\ \{q\}$ (which formalises the above intuition) and the notion of deriving a correctness formulae $\vdash_{\mathbf{Hoare}} \{p\}\ S\ \{q\}$ (which is employed in order to verify concrete programs) [16].

**Definition 8 (Semantics of Hoare Logic).** *Parametrised by an arbitrary type $T$, let $\models_{\text{Hoare}} \{.\}\ .\ \{.\} \subseteq \text{Assertion}(T) \times \textbf{prog} \times \text{Assertion}(T)$ be a new judgement defined in terms of the operational semantics*

$$\models_{\text{Hoare}} \{p\}\ S\ \{q\} \stackrel{\text{def}}{=} \forall Z \cdot \forall \sigma \cdot p(Z,\sigma) \Rightarrow \exists \tau \cdot \sigma \xrightarrow{\quad S \quad} \tau \wedge q(Z,\tau)\ .$$

Based on work of Floyd [17], Hoare [3] proposed a verification calculus for partial correctness, now referred to as Hoare Logic. For every constructor of the imperative programming language, Hoare Logic provides a rule which allows one to decompose a program. The precondition of the assignment axiom

$$\{p\,[x \mapsto e]\}\ x := e\ \{p\}$$

is, at least for simple imperative programs, the sole reason for having to bother about updating assertions!

Programs mentioned in the premisses are strict subprograms of the programs mentioned in the conclusions. Unlike the operational semantics, this also holds for loops.

$$\frac{\{p \wedge b\}\ S\ \{p\}}{\{p\}\ \textbf{while}\ b\ \textbf{do}\ S\ \{p \wedge \neg b\}} \tag{5}$$

One also needs a structural rule to weaken the precondition and strengthen the postcondition is a proof obligation.This is particularly useful when one wants to apply the rule for loops as the precondition must remain invariant with respect to the body of the loop.

$$\frac{\{p_1\}\ S\ \{q_1\}}{\{p\}\ S\ \{q\}} \qquad \text{provided } p \Rightarrow p_1 \text{ and } q_1 \Rightarrow q. \tag{6}$$

### 6.1 Total Correctness

To ensure termination, the rule for loops (5) needs to be modified. We introduce a termination measure $u : \text{expression}(W)$ for some well-founded structure $(W, <)$ which is decreased whenever the body is executed:

$$\frac{\forall t : W \cdot \{p \wedge b \wedge u = t\}\ S\ \{p \wedge u < t\}}{\{p\}\ \textbf{while}\ b\ \textbf{do}\ S\ \{p \wedge \neg b\}}$$

A similar rule for verification calculi where postconditions may explicitly refer to the value of program variables in the initial state e.g., VDM, has been put forward by Manna & Pnueli [18]. Variants of this rule tailored for $W = \texttt{nat}$ [19] or $W = \texttt{int}$ [20] have also been published previously. We prefer the well-founded version, because it simplifies the completeness proof without any impact on the soundness proof [10]. It is well known that in practice, it is often easier to reason about termination using well-founded sets rather than being restricted to natural numbers [21].

## 6.2 Auxiliary Variables

Furthermore, we have strengthened the rule of consequence (6) so that one may adjust auxiliary variables when strengthening preconditions and weakening post-conditions. Let $x$ be the list of all program variables and $Z$ the list of all auxiliary variables occurring in the assertions $p_1$, $q_1$, $p$ and $q$. We propose the new rule

$$\frac{\{p_1\}\ S\ \{q_1\}}{\{p\}\ S\ \{q\}}$$

$$\text{provided } \forall Z \cdot \forall x \cdot p \Rightarrow \Big(\exists Z_1 \cdot (p_1\,[Z \mapsto Z_1]) \land (\forall x \cdot (q_1\,[Z \mapsto Z_1]) \Rightarrow q)\Big).$$

*Example 3 (Auxiliary Variables).* With this rule (but not Hoare's (6)), the two correctness formulae $\{X = x\}\ S\ \{X = x\}$ and $\{X = x + 1\}\ S\ \{X = x + 1\}$, where all variables denote integer values and $X$ is an auxiliary variable, are interderivable.

The new rule of consequence plays a crucial role in deriving the Most General Formula (MGF), the key theorem to establish completeness for Hoare Logic dealing with recursive procedures [22, 10, 23].

**Definition 9 (Derivability of Hoare Logic – Deep Embedding).** *A verification calculus for Hoare Logic is defined as the least relation*

$$\vdash_{\textbf{Hoare}} \{.\}\ .\ \{.\} \subseteq \text{Assertion}(T) \times \textbf{prog} \times \text{Assertion}(T)$$

*indexed by an arbitrary type $T$ such that*

$$\vdash_{\textbf{Hoare}} \big\{\lambda(Z,\sigma)\cdot p(Z, \sigma\,[x \mapsto \text{eval}(\sigma)(e)])\big\}\ x := e\ \{p\} \tag{7}$$

$$\frac{\forall t : W \cdot \vdash_{\textbf{Hoare}} \{\lambda(Z,\sigma)\cdot p(Z,\sigma) \land \text{eval}(\sigma)(b) = \textbf{true} \land \text{eval}(\sigma)(u) = t\}\ S\ \{\lambda(Z,\tau)\cdot p(Z,\tau) \land \text{eval}(\tau)(u) < t\}}{\vdash_{\textbf{Hoare}} \{p\}\ \textbf{while}\ b\ \textbf{do}\ S\ \{\lambda(Z,\tau)\cdot p(Z,\tau) \land \text{eval}(\tau)(b) = \textbf{false}\}}$$

*where $(W, <)$ is well-founded.*

$$\frac{\vdash_{\textbf{Hoare}} \{p_1\}\ S\ \{q_1\}}{\vdash_{\textbf{Hoare}} \{p\}\ S\ \{q\}}$$

$$\textit{provided } \forall Z \cdot \forall \sigma \cdot p(Z,\sigma) \Rightarrow \Big(\exists Z_1 \cdot p_1(Z_1,\sigma) \land \big(\forall \tau \cdot q_1(Z_1,\tau) \Rightarrow q(Z,\tau)\big)\Big). \tag{8}$$

## 6.3 Soundness

Formally, one needs to show that whenever a correctness formulae $\vdash_{\mathbf{Hoare}} \{p\}\ S\ \{q\}$ is derivable, the proposition $\models_{\mathbf{Hoare}} \{p\}\ S\ \{q\}$ holds. Soundness is best pursued by induction on the derivation of the correctness formula. For the discussion of deep versus shallow embedding, the case of an assignment is of particular interest.

**Lemma 1 (Soundness of Assignment Axiom).**

$$\models_{\mathbf{Hoare}} \{\lambda(Z,\sigma)\cdot p(Z,\sigma\,[x \mapsto \mathrm{eval}(\sigma)(e)])\}\ x := e\ \{p\}$$

**Proof:** Expanding the definition of $\models_{\mathbf{Hoare}}$, given $Z$, $\sigma$, one needs to establish

$$p(Z,\sigma\,[x \mapsto \mathrm{eval}(\sigma)(e)]) \Rightarrow \exists\tau\cdot\sigma \xrightarrow{x := e} \tau \wedge p(Z,\tau)\ .$$

The operational semantics uniquely determines the final state $\tau$. Appealing to the axiom (4), it suffices to show

$$p(Z,\sigma\,[x \mapsto \mathrm{eval}(\sigma)(e)]) \Rightarrow p(Z,\sigma\,[x \mapsto \mathrm{eval}(\sigma)(e)])\ .$$

■

As expected, due to a shallow embedding, we only have one notion of substitution (on the level of states). But perhaps surprisingly, soundness holds *regardless* of the details of the actual substitution function[5].

If one is only interested in establishing soundness (and not completeness), there is no need for any deep embeddings. Induction on the structure of programs is not required. Hence, there is no need for a deep embedding of imperative programs e.g., Gordon [6] represents programs by their relational denotational semantics.

**A Shallow Embedding of Hoare Logic.** Moreover, if one externalises the induction of the soundness proof to the meta-level as opposed to the proof tool, one can give a shallow embedding for Hoare Logic. Without a notion of derivability as given in Definition 9, soundness can be established by showing that axioms are valid with respect to $\models_{\mathbf{Hoare}}$ and that all rules preserve soundness. This approach has been pursued by Gordon [6], Homeier [7], Homeier & Martin [13] and Norrish [24].

One must however be clear about the limitations of this approach. For example, Homeier & Martin [13] erroneously claim that the soundness of a (complete) Verification Condition Generator (VCG) has been established by appealing to the axioms and rules of an (incomplete) presentation of Hoare Logic[6]. But since they employ a *shallow* embedding of Hoare Logic, correctness of the VCG has instead been established by appealing to the definition of *operational* semantics.

[5] This observations has already been reported in [8].

[6] A consequence rule is missing. Thus, one can e.g. not derive $\{x = 1\}$ **skip** $\{\mathbf{true}\}$.

## 6.4 Completeness

In an incomplete formal system, one may only verify a strict subset of all true formulae. A naive definition of completeness is bound to fail in the context of verification calculi. On the one hand, if the chosen underlying logical language is too weak, e.g., pure first-order logic together with the boolean constants **false** and **true**, some intermediate assertions cannot be expressed. Hence, derivations cannot be completed. On the other hand, if the logical language is too strong, e.g. Peano Arithmetic, it itself is already incomplete and the verification calculus inherits incompleteness.

To avoid this problem, Cook has proposed that one investigates *relative completeness* in an attempt to separate the reasoning about programs from the reasoning about the underlying logical language [25]. One only considers expressive first-order logics. Furthermore, rules of the verification calculus may be applied in a derivation if the logical side-condition is valid rather than derivable. In particular, completeness no-longer compares a proof-theoretic with a model-theoretic account.

In practice, achieving relative completeness of verification calculi is highly desirable. In logic, finding valid formulae which can not be derived is often somewhat esoteric. A different story has to be told for the notion of relative completeness in verification calculi e.g., in Sokołowski's calculus [4], it is very difficult to come up with any non-contrived correctness formula of a recursive procedure which can be derived!

In a machine-checked development, it is convenient to interpret Cook's proposal by employing the native (expresssive) logic of the theorem prover to interpret assertions. A shallow embedding of assertions automatically blurs the model and proof-theoretic aspect of assertions. As an important aspect in the completeness proof, one needs to be able to formulate an assertion which expresses the weakest precondition relative to an arbitrary program and postcondition. With a shallow embedding, this is straight-forward:

**Definition 10 (Weakest Precondition – Shallow Embedding).**

$$\mathrm{wp}(S,q)(Z,\sigma) \stackrel{\mathrm{def}}{=} \exists \tau \cdot \sigma \xrightarrow{\quad S \quad} \tau \wedge q(Z,\tau)\ .$$

With a deep embedding of assertions, one would have to derive a syntactic representation which denotes the weakest precondition. This is considerably more challenging[7].

One may prove completeness directly by induction on the structure of $S$. Instead, we follow a technique developed by Gorelick, which, previously, has only been applied to the scenario of Hoare Logic dealing with recursive procedures [27]:

1. By induction on the structure of an arbitrary program $S$, one establishes that a specific correctness formula $\mathrm{MGF}_{\mathrm{Hoare}}(S)$ is derivable in the verification calculus.

[7] If the assertion language is Peano Arithmetic, this construction is not for the faint-hearted as one has to work on the level of Gödel numbers [26].

2. Given the assumption $\models_{\mathbf{Hoare}} \{p\}\ S\ \{q\}$, one may derive $\vdash_{\mathbf{Hoare}} \{p\}\ S\ \{q\}$ by applying structural rules to $\vdash_{\mathbf{Hoare}} \mathrm{MGF}_{\mathbf{Hoare}}(S)$. All side-conditions which arise will be dealt with by the assumption.

In other words, instead of directly deriving $\models_{\mathbf{Hoare}} \{p\}\ S\ \{q\} \Rightarrow \vdash_{\mathbf{Hoare}} \{p\}\ S\ \{q\}$, one considers the stronger property $\vdash_{\mathbf{Hoare}} \mathrm{MGF}_{\mathbf{Hoare}}(S)$ for which induction goes through more easily. In particular, the direct proof cannot be applied when one considers recursive procedures, because the induction hypotheses are not strong enough.

The proposition $\vdash_{\mathbf{Hoare}} \mathrm{MGF}_{\mathbf{Hoare}}(S)$ asserts that, provided that one only considers input states in which the program $S$ terminates, one may *derive* a correctness formula in which the postcondition relates all inputs with the appropriate outputs according to the underlying operational semantics of the programming language. At the semantic level, $\models_{\mathbf{Hoare}} \mathrm{MGF}_{\mathbf{Hoare}}(S)$ holds trivially.

**Definition 11 (MGF – Shallow Embedding).**

$$\mathrm{MGF}_{\mathbf{Hoare}}(S) \stackrel{\mathrm{def}}{=} \left\{\lambda(Z,\sigma)\cdot \sigma \xrightarrow{\quad S \quad} Z\right\}\ S\ \{\lambda(Z,\tau)\cdot Z = \tau\}$$

Notice that the precondition is equivalent to the weakest precondition relative to the postcondition $\lambda(Z,\tau)\cdot Z = \tau$.

Analogue to the proof of soundness, in deriving the MGF for assignment, one again encounters the phenomenon that the details of the substitution function are irrelevant.

# 7 Extensional Equality and Local Variables

In the previous section, we have seen that, for soundness (and completeness), details of substitutions can be neglected. Catering for local initialised variables **new** $x := e$ **in** $S$ is however more demanding, because one needs to reinstate the previous value of $x$ after the block. Based on an idea by Sieber [28], Olderog [29] captures the semantics of blocks by

$$\frac{\sigma\,[x \mapsto \mathrm{eval}(\sigma)(e)] \xrightarrow{\qquad S \qquad} \tau}{\sigma \xrightarrow{\ \mathbf{new}\ x := e\ \mathbf{in}\ S\ } \tau\,[x \mapsto \sigma(x)]}\ .$$

To verify programs containing blocks, we have proposed the rule

$$\frac{\forall v\cdot \{p\,[x \mapsto v] \wedge x = e\,[x \mapsto v]\}\ S\ \{q\,[x \mapsto v]\}}{\{p\}\ \mathbf{new}\ x := e\ \mathbf{in}\ S\ \{q\}}\ .$$

Taking into account a shallow embedding of assertions, this corresponds formally to

$$\frac{\forall v\cdot \vdash_{\mathbf{Hoare}} \{\lambda(Z,\sigma)\cdot p(Z,\sigma\,[x \mapsto v]) \wedge \sigma(x) = \mathrm{eval}(\sigma\,[x \mapsto v])(e)\}\ S\ \{q\,[x \mapsto v]\}}{\vdash_{\mathbf{Hoare}} \{p\}\ \mathbf{new}\ x := e\ \mathbf{in}\ S\ \{q\}} \tag{9}$$

It is an improvement over Apt's version [5] in that it deals with initialised blocks. Furthermore, no side-conditions are required[8]. In the soundness and completeness proof, we need to appeal to the following two extensional properties of substitutions:

$$\sigma\,[x \mapsto \sigma(x)] = \sigma \tag{10}$$

$$\sigma\,[x \mapsto t_1]\,[x \mapsto t_2] = \sigma\,[x \mapsto t_2] \tag{11}$$

We restrict our attention to the crucial step of the completeness proof:

**Lemma 2 (MGF for Blocks).** *Whenever one can derive* $\vdash_{\text{Hoare}} \text{MGF}_{\text{Hoare}}(S)$, *one may also establish* $\vdash_{\text{Hoare}} \text{MGF}_{\text{Hoare}}(\textbf{new } x := e \textbf{ in } S)$.

**Proof:** Given an arbitrary $v : \text{sort}(x)$, we apply the (stronger) rule of consequence (8) to the hypothesis $\vdash_{\text{Hoare}} \text{MGF}_{\text{Hoare}}(S)$ in order to derive

$$\vdash_{\text{Hoare}} \left\{ \lambda(Z,\sigma) \cdot \sigma\,[x \mapsto v] \xrightarrow{\textbf{new } x := e \textbf{ in } S} Z \wedge \sigma(x) = \text{eval}(\sigma\,[x \mapsto v])(e) \right\} \,. \\ S \\ \{\lambda(Z,\tau) \cdot Z = \tau\,[x \mapsto v]\} \tag{12}$$

From (12), the rule for blocks (9) renders the proof obligation. As a side-condition, given states $Z$ and $\sigma$ such that

$$\sigma\,[x \mapsto v] \xrightarrow{\textbf{new } x := e \textbf{ in } S} Z \tag{13}$$

$$\sigma(x) = \text{eval}(\sigma\,[x \mapsto v])(e) \tag{14}$$

we have to find a state $\tau$ such that $\sigma \xrightarrow{S} \tau$ and $Z = \tau\,[x \mapsto v]$. Inverting the derivation of (13), there must be such a state $\tau$ which satisfies

$$\sigma\,[x \mapsto v]\,[x \mapsto \text{eval}(\sigma\,[x \mapsto v])(e)] \xrightarrow{S} \tau \tag{15}$$

and $Z = \tau\,[x \mapsto \sigma\,[x \mapsto v](x)]$. Courtesy of (14), the property (15) can be simplified to $\sigma\,[x \mapsto v]\,[x \mapsto \sigma(x)] \xrightarrow{S} \tau$. To complete the proof, one needs to appeal to the substitution properties (10) and (11) in order to replace the state $\sigma\,[x \mapsto v]\,[x \mapsto \sigma(x)]$ by the extensionally equal function $\sigma$. ∎

It follows from the specification of the update operation on states (1) that we may derive the extensional counterparts of (10) and (11)

$$\sigma\,[x \mapsto \sigma(x)]\,(y) = \sigma(y)$$

$$\sigma\,[x \mapsto t_1]\,[x \mapsto t_2]\,(y) = \sigma\,[x \mapsto t_2]\,(y)$$

whereas (10) and (11) themselves do not hold for the standard equality concepts such as Leibniz or Martin-Löf equality, because they distinguish between intensionally distinct functions. We therefore need to *axiomatise* extensionality [30].

[8] Scoping of the implicitly universally quantified $p$, $S$ and $q$ ensures that $v \notin$ *free*$(p, S, q)$.

## 8 Conclusions

To prove completeness, one needs to be able to construct assertions which express semantic properties of the programming language. On paper, one usually simply assumes that the assertion language is sufficiently expressive. Both, soundness and completeness proofs can be simplified if one does not worry about the actual syntactic representation of assertions.

Moreover, a thorough treatment of syntax has the unpleasant side-effect that substantial amount of formal detail is required to deal with substitutions at the level of states, expressions and assertions. This seems redundant as far as metatheory is concerned. Specifically, for simple imperative programs, the proofs of soundness and completeness can be conducted irrespective of the chosen substitution function. Semantically, the assignment axiom in Hoare Logic simply lifts substitutions pointwise from the level of states to predicates on states.

Syntax does however matter if, instead of metatheory, one wishes to use the axioms and rules to verify concrete programs or generate verification conditions. With a shallow embedding, assertions are functions mapping states to propositions. Not only are they more difficult to comprehend than their syntactic counterpart. Without syntactic structure, the proof tool has little guidance on how to best reduce substitutions in assertions. Verifying the Quicksort algorithm based on a shallow embedding, we found that the resulting proof obligations arising from the side-condition of the rule of consequence became too large for the LEGO system to efficiently process. Having to deal with *dependent* types, type-checking involves expensive calculations.

One ought to clarify the objectives of employing a theorem prover. There are two *orthogonal* problems in verifying imperative programs.

1. Establishing soundness and completeness for verification calculi is a challenging task. Incorrect results based on doing proofs by hand have been published in the past. The metatheory relates semantics and derivability. Syntax of assertions is not an issue. In fact, the whole idea of relative completeness is to factor out the issue of semantics versus derivability of assertions.
2. Verifying concrete programs is a labour-intensive task for which computer-aided support is vital.

We feel a reasonable approach would be to employ a shallow embedding for metatheory and a deep embedding for concrete examples. The calculus for verifying concrete programs can *informally* build on the axioms and rules investigated in the meta-theoretical analysis. Relating the two formalisations centres mostly on the issue of how expressive the assertion language is. We are somewhat sceptical whether this deserves a machine-checked proof.

But perhaps, there is an alternative. Today's proof tools are equipped with a powerful native logic e.g., LEGO supports intuitionistic higher-order logic with a rich universe of data types [31]. However, this cannot be directly employed for a deep embedding because its syntax is not inductively defined at the level of the proof system. But one could consider to treat syntax at a more informal level.

Specifically, based on a shallow embedding, one could employ parsing and pretty-printing of the theorem prover to convert between the internal representation and the user interface. Moreover, one could tailor the prover's tactics engine to better deal with substitutions. At the code level of the theorem prover, it is easier to implement a suitable substitution function for a particular class of terms.

## Acknowledgements

Thanks to Martin Hofmann for helpful comments on an earlier version of this report. I would also like to acknowledge the financial support of EPSRC (Applications of a Type Theory Based Proof Assistant), the British Council (ARC Project Co-Development of Object-Oriented Programs in LEGO) and the European Commission (Marie Curie Fellowship).

## References

1. Randy Pollack. *The Theory of LEGO, A Proof Checker for the Extended Calculus of Constructions.* PhD thesis, Laboratory for Foundations of Computer Science, University of Edinburgh, 1994.
2. Krzysztof R. Apt and Lambert G. L. T. Meertens. Completeness with finite systems of intermediate assertions for recursive program schemes. *SIAM Journal on Computing*, 9(4):665–671, November 1980.
3. C. A. R. Hoare. An axiomatic basis for computer programming. *Communications of the ACM*, 12:576–580, 1969.
4. Stefan Sokołowski. Total correctness for procedures. In J. Gruska, editor, *Sixth Mathematical Foundations of Computer Science (Tatranská Lomnica)*, volume 53 of *Lecture Notes in Computer Science*, pages 475–483. Springer-Verlag, 1977.
5. Krzysztof R. Apt. Ten years of Hoare's logic: A survey – part I. *ACM Transactions on Programming Languages and Systems*, 3(4):431–483, October 1981.
6. Michael J.C. Gordon. Mechanizing programming logics in higher order logic. In G. Birtwhistle and P.A. Subrahmanyam, editors, *Current Trends in Hardware Verification and Automated Theorem Proving (Banff, Alberta)*, number 15 in Workshops in Computing, pages 387–439. Springer-Verlag, 1989.
7. Peter Vincent Homeier. *Trustworthy Tools for Trustworthy Programs: A Mechanically Verified Verification Condition Generator for the Total Correctness of Procedures.* PhD thesis, University of California, Los Angeles, 1995.
8. Tobias Nipkow. Winskel is (almost) right: Towards a mechanized semantics textbook. *Formal Aspects of Computing*, 10:171–186, 1998.
9. Ian A. Mason. Hoare's logic in the LF. Technical Report 32, Laboratory for Foundations of Computer Science, University of Edinburgh, June 1987.
10. Thomas Kleymann. Hoare Logic and VDM: Machine-checked soundness and completeness proofs. PhD thesis ECS-LFCS-98-392, Laboratory for Foundations of Computer Science, University of Edinburgh, September 1998.
11. Arnon Avron, Furio A. Honsell, and Ian A. Mason. Using typed lambda calculus to implement formal systems on a machine. Technical Report 31, Laboratory for Foundations of Computer Science, University of Edinburgh, 1987.
12. J. von Wright, J. Hekanaho, P. Luostarinen, and T. Långbacka. Mechanizing some advanced refinement concepts. *Formal Methods in System Design*, 3:49–81, 1993.

13. Peter V. Homeier and David F. Martin. Mechanical verification of mutually recursive procedures. In M. A. McRobbie and J. K. Slaney, editors, *Automated Deduction - CADE-13*, volume 1104 of *Lecture Notes in Artificial Intelligence*, pages 201–215, New Brunswick, NJ, USA, July/August 1996. Springer-Verlag. 13th International Conference on Automated Deduction.
14. John C. Reynolds. Idealized Algol and its specification logic. In D. Néel, editor, *Tools & Notions for Program Construction*. Cambridge University Press, 1982.
15. Edmund Melson Clarke Jr. Programming language constructs for which it is impossible to obtain good Hoare axiom systems. *Journal of the ACM*, 26(1):129–147, January 1979.
16. Patrick Cousot. Methods and logics for proving programs. In Jan van Leeuwen, editor, *Handbook of Theoretical Computer Science*, volume B: Formal Models and Semantics, chapter 15, pages 841–993. Elsevier, 1990.
17. Robert W. Floyd. Assigning meanings to programs. In J. T. Schwartz, editor, *Proc. Symp. in Applied Mathematics*, volume 19, pages 19–32, 1967.
18. Z. Manna and A. Pnueli. Axiomatic approach to total correctness of programs. *Acta Informatica*, 3:243–263, 1974.
19. David Harel. Proving the correctness of regular deterministic programs: A unifying survey using dynamic logic. *Theoretical Computer Science*, 12:61–81, 1980.
20. Krzysztof R. Apt and Ernst-Rüdiger Olderog. *Verification of Sequential and Concurrent Programs*. Texts and Monographs in Computer Science. Springer, New York, 1991.
21. Nachum Dershowitz and Zohar Manna. Proving termination with multiset orderings. *Communications of the ACM*, 22(8):465–475, August 1979.
22. Thomas Schreiber. Auxiliary variables and recursive procedures. In Michel Bidoit and Max Dauchet, editors, *Proceedings of TAPSOFT '97*, volume 1214 of *Lecture Notes in Computer Science*, pages 697–711, Lille, France, April 1997. Springer-Verlag.
23. Thomas Kleymann. Hoare Logic and auxiliary variables. Technical Report ECS-LFCS-98-399, Laboratory for Foundations of Computer Science, University of Edinburgh, October 1998. Submitted to Formal Aspects of Computing.
24. Michael Norrish. Derivation of verification rules for C from operational definitions. In Joakim von Wright, Jim Grundy, and John Harrison, editors, *Supplementary Proceedings of the 9th International Conference on Theorem Proving in Higher Order Logics: TPHOLs'96*, number 1 in TUCS General Publications, pages 69–75. Turku Centre for Computer Science, August 1996.
25. Stephen A. Cook. Soundness and completeness of an axiom system for program verification. *SIAM Journal on Computing*, 7(1):70–90, February 1978.
26. Jaco de Bakker. *Mathematical Theory of Program Correctness*. Prentice Hall, 1980.
27. Gerald Arthur Gorelick. A complete axiomatic system for proving assertions about recursive and non-recursive programs. Technical Report 75, Department of Computer Science, University of Toronto, 1975.
28. Kurt Sieber. A new Hoare-calculus for programs with recursive parameterless procedures. Technical Report A 81/02, Fachbereich 10 – Informatik, Universität des Saarlandes, Saarbrücken, February 1981.
29. Ernst-Rüdiger Olderog. Sound and complete Hoare-like calculi based on copy rules. *Acta Informatica*, 16:161–197, 1981.
30. Martin Hofmann. *Extensional concepts in intensional type theory*. PhD thesis, Laboratory for Foundations of Computer Science, University of Edinburgh, 1995.
31. Zhaohui Luo. *Computation and Reasoning: A Type Theory for Computer Science*. Oxford University Press, 1994.

# Bounded Polymorphism for Extensible Objects

Luigi Liquori

Dipartimento di Matematica ed Informatica, Università di Udine,
Via delle Scienze 206, I-33100 Udine, Italy
e-mail: `liquori@dimi.uniud.it`
*Current Address*: LIP, École Normale Supérieure de Lyon
46, Allée d'Italie, F-69364 Lyon Cedex 07, France
e-mail: `Luigi.Liquori@ens-lyon.fr`

**Abstract.** In the ECOOP'97 conference, the author of the present paper investigated a conservative extension, called $\mathcal{O}b^+_{1<:}$, of the first-order Object Calculus $\mathcal{O}b_{1<:}$ of Abadi and Cardelli, supporting *method extension* in presence of *object subsumption*. In this paper, we extend that work with *explicit variance annotations* and *selftypes*. The resulting calculus, called $\mathcal{O}b^+_{s<:}$, is a proper extension of $\mathcal{O}b^+_{1<:}$. Moreover it is proved to be type sound.

**Categories.** Type systems, design and semantics of object-oriented languages.

## 1 Introduction

In the last few years, the problem of designing safe and expressive type-systems for object-based languages (also called prototype-based languages) has been widely addressed. The seminal works of [US87,CU89,Mic90,Aba94,FHM94,AC96a] share the same object-oriented philosophy, where the main entity is the one of *object* instead of the one of *class*. In those papers, classes can be easily codified by appropriate objects, following the "classes-as-objects" analogy of Smalltalk-80 [GR83]. In object-based languages, objects are modified directly from other objects (the latter called *prototypes*) by adding new methods, or by rewriting old method bodies with new ones. A primitive operation of method call is given, to send a message to (i.e. invoke a method on) an object. In functional calculi, adding or rewriting a method produces a new object that inherits all the properties of the original one.

Another key issue in object-based languages is the one of *subsumption*, i.e. the capability to use an object with a longer (or more refined) interface in every context expecting objects with a smaller (or less refined) interface. This feature has been showed to be fundamental in object-oriented paradigm, since it allows a significant reuse of code. Unfortunately, as clearly stated in [FM94,AC96a], adding object subsumption in presence of object extension make the type system very often unsound.

As a simple example of this problem, let us suppose to have a diagonal point `dpoint` composed by two fields, `x` (holds 1) and `y` (holds `self.x`). The type of this object is [`x`:*nat*, `y`:*nat*]. If we "hide", by subsumption, the `x` field, and we add again `x` with a new value $-1$ of type *int*, and we call `y` on the object `dpoint`, then we lose the subject reduction property, since the evaluation of *dpoint.y*, of type *nat*, yields the value $-1$ of type *int*. Other works by [FM95,BL95,Rém95,BBDL97,Rém98,RS98], have addressed the issue of integrating object subsumption in presence of object extension.

This paper starts from the Abadi & Cardelli's (first-order) Object Calculus, called $\mathcal{O}b_{1<:}$ [AC96b]. We briefly recall its features.

- it supports "fixed size" objects (no object extension is provided);
- it supports method override;
- it supports object subsumption;
- its type system catches run-time errors such as *message-not-understood*.

In [Liq97b], the $\mathcal{O}b_{1<:}$ calculus was extended by allowing object extension compatible with object subsumption, by providing a sound static type system and a typed equational theory on objects. This (conservative) extension was called $\mathcal{O}b^{+}_{1<:}$. This paper completes the work of [Liq97b] by extending the type system of $\mathcal{O}b^{+}_{1<:}$ with selftypes and explicit variance annotations.

*Selftypes* has been showed to be fruitful in a development of flexible type-systems for object oriented programming languages (e.g. Eiffel [Mey92], PolyTOIL [BSvG95]). Selftypes allow one to give a type to methods that return `self` or an update of `self` (for instance, a `move` method of a `point` object will have type *int*→`selftype`, where `selftype` refers to the type of `self`). Adding selftypes to object-calculi is not only an exercise of style: in fact we can give a type to a considerably number of programs that are not typable within the first-order fragment of $\mathcal{O}b^{+}_{1<:}$.

*Explicit variance annotations*, instead, support flexible subtyping, and a direct protection tool from unwanted "read" or "write" operations. More precisely, an explicit variance annotation is a "label" attached to a method name and defined together with the method body; it could be one of the following: `private`, `public`, `read_only`, and `write_only`. The meaning of explicit variance annotations is straightforward: they denote the access privileges of fields/methods belonging to the object. Having explicit variance annotations inside the calculus allows a more disciplined use of methods and fields, and enforces object encapsulation.

The addition of selftypes fits well into the type system of [Liq97b], where we distinguish between two "kinds" of objects-types, namely the *saturated* object-types, and the *diamond* object-types. Shortly, if an object can be typed by a saturated object-type, then it can receive messages and override the methods that it contains. Instead, if an object can be typed by a diamond object-type, then it can receive messages, override some methods, and it can be extended by new methods. On both types, a subtyping relation is defined.

The subtyping relation on saturated object-types can be commonly found in the literature: at first approximation, an object typed with a "longer" (i.e. with more methods) object-type can be used in any context expecting an object typed with a "shorter" (i.e. with less methods) object-type. At this level, object extension is forbidden since we can first "hide", by subsumption, a method $\mathrm{m}$ of type $\sigma$, and then extend the object with the same method $\mathrm{m}$ of type $\tau$, $\sigma$ being *incompatible* with $\tau$.

For diamond object-types, instead, the subtype relation behaves as follows: it is still possible to hide a method, but its type is *recorded* in the diamond object-type. Since object extension is only allowed on objects typed with diamond object-types, the hidden methods can be re-added again only with the *same* type.

The $\mathcal{O}b^{+}_{s<:}$ calculus that we present in this paper is a conservative extension of the first-order one $\mathcal{O}b^{+}_{1<:}$. In summary, our calculus exhibits the following features:

- extendible objects with appropriate method specialization of inherited methods,
- a (*mytype-covariant*) subtyping relation compatible with object extension,
- explicit variance annotations;
- override of explicit variance annotations;
- static detection of run-time errors, such as *message-not-understood*.

This paper is organized as follows: in Section 2 we will present the Extended Object Calculus à la Curry (i.e. without type decorations). In Section 3 we will introduce the types, decorate our $\mathcal{O}b^{+}_{s<:}$ calculus with types, and present the type system. A number of examples which are meant to give an insight of the power of $\mathcal{O}b^{+}_{s<:}$ will be provided in Section 4. The last section will be devoted to a comparison with the paper of Abadi and Cardelli [AC95], the paper of Didier Rémy [Rém98], and the paper of Riecke and Stone [RS98]. Part of this material appeared in two technical reports [Liq97a], and [Liq99].

**Acknowledgement.** The author is grateful the anonymous referees to their helpful comments on this work.

## 2 The Extended Primitive Object Calculus

The untyped syntax of the Extended Object Calculus is defined by the following grammar:

$$\mathrm{o} ::= s \mid [\mathrm{m}_i \Upsilon_i = \varsigma(s_i)\mathrm{o}_i]^{i \in I} \mid \mathrm{o.m} \mid \mathrm{o.m} := \varsigma(s)\mathrm{o} \mid \mathrm{o.m} := \Upsilon \mid \mathrm{o.m} := \Upsilon\varsigma(s)\mathrm{o}$$
$$\Upsilon ::= \texttt{private} \mid \texttt{public} \mid \texttt{read\_only} \mid \texttt{write\_only}.$$

Here the := operator can be intended as an operator on objects which overrides method m in case this method is already present in the object, otherwise it extends the object with m. The grammar for $\Upsilon$ denotes *explicit variance annotations* that are introduced to support a clear form of encapsulation and protection from unwanted "read" or "write" operations. The expression $\mathrm{o.m} := \Upsilon$ modifies (i.e. overrides) the explicit variance annotation for m. The explicit variance annotations have the following intuitive meaning:

- `public`: methods that have both read/write privilege;
- `read_only`: methods that only have read privilege;
- `write_only`: methods that only have write privilege;
- `private`: methods that do not have read/write privilege, i.e. "encapsulated".

### 2.1 Small-Step and Operational Semantics

Let $\mathrm{o}\{s\}$ denote an object where the variable $s$ can freely occur, let $\mathrm{o}\{\mathrm{o}'\}$ denote the substitution of the object $\mathrm{o}'$ for every free occurrence of $s$ in o when $\mathrm{o}\{s\}$ is present in the same context, and let, for $i, j \in I$, with $i \neq j$, $\mathrm{m}_i$ and $\mathrm{m}_j$ be distinct methods. The

| | | | | | |
|---|---|---|---|---|---|
| Let $\text{o} \triangleq [\text{m}_i \Upsilon_i = \varsigma(s_i)\text{o}_i\{s_i\}]^{i \in I}$ | | | | | |
| $(Sel)$ | $\text{o.m}_j$ | $\overset{ev}{\rightarrow} \text{o}_j\{\text{o}\}$ | $(j \in I)$ | $(a)$ | $(1)$ |
| $(Over)$ | $\text{o.m}_j := \varsigma(s_j)\text{o}'$ | $\overset{ev}{\rightarrow} [\text{m}_i \Upsilon_i = \varsigma(s_i)\text{o}_i, \text{m}_j \Upsilon_j = \varsigma(s_j)\text{o}']^{i \in I \setminus \{j\}}$ | $(j \in I)$ | $(b)$ | $(2)$ |
| $(Ann)$ | $\text{o.m}_j := \Upsilon$ | $\overset{ev}{\rightarrow} [\text{m}_i \Upsilon_i = \varsigma(s_i)\text{o}_i, \text{m}_j \Upsilon = \varsigma(s_j)\text{o}_j]^{i \in I \setminus \{j\}}$ | $(j \in I)$ | $(c)$ | $(3)$ |
| $(Ext)$ | $\text{o.m}_j := \Upsilon\varsigma(s_j)\text{o}'$ | $\overset{ev}{\rightarrow} [\text{m}_i \Upsilon_i = \varsigma(s_i)\text{o}_i, \text{m}_j \Upsilon = \varsigma(s_j)\text{o}']^{i \in I}$ | $(j \notin I)$ | | $(4)$ |

**Table 1.** Small-step Untyped Operational Semantics

small-step operational semantics can be given as the reflexive, transitive and contextual closure of the reduction relation defined in Table 1. Note that the original semantics of [AC96a] was build from the reduction rules (1) and (2). As usual, we do not make error conditions explicit. Let $\overset{ev}{\twoheadrightarrow}$ be the general many-step reduction. We remark that the $(Ann)$ rule overrides the explicit variance annotation, leaving the method body unchanged; orthogonally, the $(Over)$ rule modifies the method body, leaving the explicit method annotation unchanged. The condition $(a), (b), (c)$ are the following ones:

$$
\begin{aligned}
(a) &\triangleq \Upsilon_j \in \{\texttt{public}, \texttt{read\_only}\} \\
(b) &\triangleq \Upsilon_j \in \{\texttt{public}, \texttt{write\_only}\} \\
(c) &\triangleq \Upsilon_j : v_j, \;\; \Upsilon : v, \;\text{ and }\; v_j <: v.
\end{aligned}
$$

The condition $(a)$ allows message selection only for fields/methods that are public or readable from the outside (i.e. annotated with `public`, or `read_only`). The condition $(b)$ allows overriding only for fields/methods that are public or writable from the outside (i.e. annotated with `public`, or `write_only`). The condition $(c)$ can be explained as follows. A variance annotation (or *variance type* $v$) can be assigned to an explicit variance annotation ($\Upsilon$) via a simple "type" system proving judgments of the shape $\Upsilon : v$, where $v \in \{^+, ^-, ^\circ, ^\bullet\}$. The type rules are:

$$\texttt{public} : {}^\circ \quad \texttt{private} : {}^\bullet \quad \texttt{read\_only} : {}^+ \quad \texttt{write\_only} : {}^-.$$

Given that, the $(c)$ condition assures that the new explicit variance annotation $\Upsilon$ will override the original one $\Upsilon_j$ only if their variance types are compatible. Compatibility is assured by a partial order relation $(<:)$ on variance types, given by the following "chains":

$$^\circ <: {}^+ <: {}^\bullet, \;\text{ and }\; ^\circ <: {}^- <: {}^\bullet.$$

As a remark, we observe that we could, in principle, build a simpler and more liberal small-step semantics by dropping the side conditions $(a)$, $(b)$, and $(c)$. The type system always guarantees the soundness of well-typed expressions.

For the small-step operational semantics, we can derive an untyped equational theory (whose judgment is $\vdash \text{o} \overset{ev}{=} \text{o}'$) from the reduction rules, by simply adding rules for symmetry, transitivity and congruence, and reformulating the reduction rules as equalities. We can also define quite simply a big-step operational semantics that also induces a "lazy" strategy of evaluation, via a natural proof deduction system à la Plotkin. This semantics maps every closed expression into a normal form, i.e. an irreducible term (for a presentation of the big-step semantics and of the equational theory see [Liq99]).

| | |
|---|---|
| $\sigma, \tau$ ::= | |
| $t, u$ | type-variables |
| $\omega$ | the biggest type |
| $\texttt{obj}\ t.[\mathtt{m}_i v_i : \sigma_i\{t\}]^{i \in I}$ | *saturated* object-type, $\mathtt{m}_i$ distinct |
| $\texttt{obj}\ t.[\mathtt{m}_i v_i : \sigma_i\{t\} \diamond \mathtt{m}_j v_j : \sigma_j\{t\}]^{i \in I}_{j \in J}$ | *diamond* object-type, $v_j \in \{^\circ, ^-\}, I \cap J = \emptyset$ |

**Table 2.** Syntax of Types

# 3 The Type System

In the $\mathcal{O}b^{+}_{s<:}$ type system, the set of legal types is defined by the grammar of Table 2. The type-constant $\omega$ is the supertype of every type. We omit how to encode basic data-types which can be treated as in [AC96a]. The bound type-variable $t$ can (freely) occur in the $\sigma_i, \sigma_j$'s, and it is constrained to be *covariant*. As explained in many papers, (among others [Cas95,Cas96,BCC+96,AC96a,Liq98]) the covariance of `selftype` is necessary if we want to have a statically typed calculus with subtyping. As such, *binary methods* (i.e. methods that receive as input an argument of the same type of `self`) are lost. When a method $\mathtt{m}_j$ ($j \in I$) is invoked, the result will have a type $\sigma_j\{t\}$ in which every free occurrence of $t$ is replaced with the type $\tau$ of the receiver of the message, i.e. $\sigma_j\{\tau\}$, therefore showing the "recursive" nature of that type.

**Explicit Variance Annotations.** As we have sketched in the previous section, each $v_i, v_j$ inside object-types is a variance annotation, i.e. one of the symbols $^+$, $^-$, $^\circ$, or $^\bullet$, standing, respectively, for *covariance*, *contravariance*, *public-invariance*, and *private-invariance*. Any omitted $v$'s are taken to be equal to $^\circ$. Covariant methods allow covariant subtyping, but prevent update (see [FM94,AC96a]). Symmetrically, contravariant methods allow contravariant subtyping, but prevent invocation. Public-invariant methods, instead, can be invoked and updated. By subtyping, public-invariant methods can be regarded as either covariant or contravariant. Private-invariant methods cannot be invoked nor updated: these methods are typically introduced (and hence type-checked) being public, or readable, or writable, but are later "sealed" (implicitly via subtyping, or explicitly via annotation override) as private methods that cannot be accessed nor updated from the outside. The "compatibility" relation between variance annotations is depicted below (where $v \rightarrow v'$ means $v <: v'$, i.e. a method annotated with $v$ can be also annotated with $v'$), together with all possible forms of protection from the outside of the object performed by variance annotations.

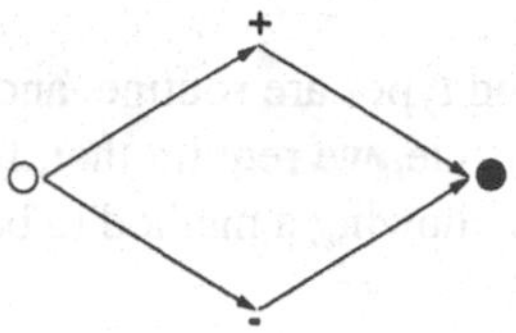


| Variance | Read? | Write? |
|---|---|---|
| ∘ | Yes | Yes |
| + | Yes | No |
| − | No | Yes |
| • | No | No |

**Saturated-types.** The saturated-types $\texttt{obj}\ t.[\mathtt{m}_i v_i : \sigma_i\{t\}]^{i \in I}$ are the ordinary object-types of [AC96a]; shortly, objects assigned to saturated-types can receive messages and can be rewritten.

**Diamond-types.** The diamond-types $\texttt{obj}\ t.[\mathtt{m}_i v_i : \sigma_i\{t\} \diamond \mathtt{m}_j v_j : \sigma_j\{t\}]^{i \in I}_{j \in J}$ are directly derived from the one of [Liq97b]. Diamond-types can be assigned to objects which can be extended and overridden. The symbol $\diamond$ distinguishes the two parts of that object-type, i.e. the *interface-part* and the *subsumption-part*; the former part describes all methods (with their types) that *may be invoked* (if not private or write-only), the latter conveys, instead, information about (the types of) methods that are subsumed in the type-checking phase. When a method is subsumed in a diamond-type it simply moves from the interface-part to the subsumption-part. This "shift" guarantees that any future addition of that method will be type-consistent with the previous one. The subsumption-part is also used as a infinite "container" of unused method types; this is important when we need to add a "fresh" method, in order to not loose the full flexibility of rapid prototyping. The shifting and the stocking of methods are performed using a suitable subtype system, presented in the Appendix.

Variance annotations are elegantly integrated within object-types. Since a method can also "migrate" from the subsumption-part to the interface-part by object extension, and since subsumed methods cannot be invoked, it follows that the occurrence of $m\upsilon : \sigma$ in the subsumption-part of a diamond-type is allowed only if $\upsilon \in \{^\circ, ^-\}$, i.e. for public or write-only methods (an object extension of a previously subsumed method behaves, operationally, as an object override).

## 3.1 Types and Judgments

The judgments we set about to prove have the forms:

$$\Gamma \vdash ok, \qquad \Gamma \vdash \sigma, \qquad \Gamma \vdash o : \sigma, \qquad \Gamma \vdash \sigma <: \tau, \qquad \Gamma \vdash \upsilon\sigma <: \upsilon\tau,$$

where $\Gamma$ is a context which gives meaning to the free variables of o, $\sigma$, and $\tau$, generated by the grammar: $\Gamma ::= \varepsilon \mid \Gamma, s : \sigma \mid \Gamma, u <: \sigma$. In contexts, we often write $s : u <: \sigma$, to denote $u <: \sigma, s : u$. By deriving the first two judgments we check the well-formation of the context $\Gamma$ and of the type $\sigma$, respectively; while with the third one, we assign a type $\sigma$ to the expression o. The last two judgments are the usual subtyping judgments between types (with variance annotations) of [AC96a]. As shown in Section 2, in order to override an explicit method annotation, we need the auxiliary judgment $\Upsilon : \upsilon$, that assigns a variance type $\upsilon$ to an explicit variance annotation $\Upsilon$.

**Cova/Contravariance.** Formally, $\sigma\{t^+\}$ stands for a type where the type-variable $t$ occurs only covariantly. Intuitively, $\sigma\{u^+\}$ means that $u$ occurs *at most* positively in $\sigma$; similarly, $\sigma\{u^-\}$ means that $u$ occurs *at most* negatively in $\sigma$. The formal definition of covariance follows in Table 3.

The type rules for well-formed contexts and types are routine, and can be found in Appendix. We only remark that in the $(T{-}\diamond)$ rule, we require that, for all $j \in J$, the type annotations $\upsilon_j$, must belong to $\{^\circ, ^-\}$, so allowing a method to be "writable".

## 3.2 Subtyping

The more important subtyping rules are presented in Table 4; the full set can be found in Appendix. The subtyping rules that deal with diamond-types and variance types are the same as in [Liq97b], and [AC95], respectively (see Appendix). Moreover we need some extra rules, for instance the rules $(S{-}Var_\diamond)$ and $(S{-}Var)$ to deal with variance

| | | |
|---|---|---|
| **Covariance** | | |
| $t\{u^+\}$ | always | |
| $\omega\{u^+\}$ | always | |
| $\mathtt{obj}\ t.[\mathrm{m}_i v_i : \sigma_i\{t\}]^{i \in I}\{u^+\}$ | if $t = u$ or for all $i \in I$: | $\begin{cases} \text{if } v_i \equiv^+, \text{then } \sigma_i\{u^+\} \\ \text{if } v_i \equiv^-, \text{then } \sigma_i\{u^-\} \\ \text{if } v_i \equiv^\circ, \text{then } u \notin FV(\sigma_i) \\ \text{if } v_i \equiv^\bullet, \text{always} \end{cases}$ |
| **Contravariance** | | |
| $t\{u^-\}$ | if $t \neq u$ | |
| $\omega\{u^-\}$ | always | |
| $\mathtt{obj}\ t.[\mathrm{m}_i v_i : \sigma_i\{t\}]^{i \in I}\{u^-\}$ | if $t = u$ or for all $i \in I$: | $\begin{cases} \text{if } v_i \equiv^+, \text{then } \sigma_i\{u^-\} \\ \text{if } v_i \equiv^-, \text{then } \sigma_i\{u^+\} \\ \text{if } v_i \equiv^\circ, \text{then } u \notin FV(\sigma_i) \\ \text{if } v_i \equiv^\bullet, \text{always} \end{cases}$ |
| **Private/Public Invariance** | | |
| $\sigma\{u^\bullet\}$ | if $\sigma\{u^+\}$ or $\sigma\{u^-\}$ | |
| $\sigma\{u^\circ\}$ | if neither $\sigma\{u^+\}$ nor $\sigma\{u^-\}$ nor $\sigma\{u^\bullet\}$ | |
| **Variance & ◇-types** | | |
| $\mathtt{obj}\ t.[\mathrm{m}_i v_i : \sigma_i\{t\} \diamond \mathrm{m}_j v_j : \sigma_j\{t\}]^{i \in I}_{j \in J}\{u^v\}$ | if $\mathtt{obj}\ t.[\mathrm{m}_i v_i : \sigma_i\{t\}]^{i \in I}\{u^v\}$ and $\mathtt{obj}\ t.[\mathrm{m}_j v_j : \sigma_j]^{j \in J}\{u^v\}$ | |

**Table 3.** Variance Occurrences

types for object-types of the same length, and the rule $(S{-}Inv_2)$ to say that a read-only or write-only component can be regarded as a private one. The rule $(S{-}Inv_1)$ is simply a reformulation of reflexivity. As a side remark, observe that the condition $\forall\, k \in I \cup J$ in rule $(S{-}Var_\diamond)$ allows to apply this rule also in the subsumption-part of the diamond-type. This condition is more liberal than the simpler $\forall\, k\ \in I$, since it allows one to re-add a forgotten method with a type different from the one we have forgotten (in accordance to its variance type), without losing type soundness.

## 3.3 Type Rules

We decorate our Extended Object Calculus with types as follows:

$$\begin{aligned} \mathrm{o} \ ::= \ & s \mid [\mathrm{m}_i \Upsilon_i = \varsigma(s_i{:}u <: \tau_i)\mathrm{o}_i]^{i \in I} \mid \mathrm{o.m} \mid \mathrm{o.m} := \varsigma(s{:}u <: \tau)\mathrm{o} \mid \\ & \mathrm{o.m} := \Upsilon \mid \mathrm{o.m} := \Upsilon\varsigma(s{:}u <: \tau)\mathrm{o}. \end{aligned}$$

The $\varsigma$-binder scopes over the object-variable $s$, referring to `self`, and the type-variable $u$, referring to the type of `self` (i.e. `selftype`). The method bodies could be intended, in the $F_{<:}$ jargon, as the polymorphic lambda abstraction $\Lambda u <: \sigma_i.\lambda s{:}u.\mathrm{o}_i$. We analyze in detail the most important type rules of $\mathcal{O}b^{+}_{\varsigma<:}$ (presented in Table 5); see Appendix for the full set of rules.

[$(V{-}Sel)$] This rule gives a type for a message send; in order for a message send to be type correct, the host object o must contain the method name $\mathrm{m}_k$ in its type. Moreover, the substitution of $t$ with $\tau$ reflects the recursive nature of object-types. The host object o can also be an object-variable $s$: in this case the type $\tau$ will be a type-variable $u$. Method selection is permitted only on public-invariant or covariant components.

$(S{-}Var_\diamond)$

$$\frac{\Gamma, u <: \mathtt{obj}\, t.[\mathrm{m}_i v_i : \sigma_i\{t\} \diamond \mathrm{m}_j v_j : \sigma_j\{t\}]_{j\in J}^{i\in I} \vdash v_k\sigma_k\{u\} <: v'_k\sigma'_k\{u\} \quad \forall k \in I \cup J}{\Gamma \vdash \mathtt{obj}\, t.[\mathrm{m}_i v_i : \sigma_i\{t\} \diamond \mathrm{m}_j v_j : \sigma_j\{t\}]_{j\in J}^{i\in I} <: \mathtt{obj}\, t.[\mathrm{m}_i v'_i : \sigma'_i\{t\} \diamond \mathrm{m}_j v'_j : \sigma'_j\{t\}]_{j\in J}^{i\in I}}$$

$(S{-}Var)$

$$\frac{\Gamma, u <: \mathtt{obj}\, t.[\mathrm{m}_i v_i : \sigma_i\{t\}]^{i\in I} \vdash v_k\sigma_k\{u\} <: v'_k\sigma'_k\{u\} \quad \forall k \in I}{\Gamma \vdash \mathtt{obj}\, t.[\mathrm{m}_i v_i : \sigma_i\{t\}]^{i\in I} <: \mathtt{obj}\, t.[\mathrm{m}_i v'_i : \sigma'_i\{t\}]^{i\in I}}$$

$$\frac{\Gamma \vdash \sigma \quad v \in \{^\circ, ^\bullet\}}{\Gamma \vdash v\sigma <: v\sigma}\ (S{-}Inv_1) \qquad \frac{\Gamma \vdash \sigma \quad v \in \{^+, ^-\}}{\Gamma \vdash v\sigma <: {}^\bullet\sigma}\ (S{-}Inv_2)$$

**Table 4.** Some Subtyping Rules

$[(V{-}Over)]$ This rule overrides the method $\mathrm{m}_k$ provided that $\mathrm{m}_k$ belongs to the interface of the object o, (i.e. $k \in I$), and that the new body for $\mathrm{m}_k$ uses the methods already present in o; this last condition is ensured by the second subtyping judgment of the premises, and corresponds to say that those methods are present in the interface-part of the type $\tau$. Object override is allowed only on public-invariant or contravariant components. We also observe that $\tau$ can also be a type-variable, and, as such, method override is allowed inside method bodies.

$[(V{-}Ann_1)]$ This rule overrides the explicit variance annotation for method $\mathrm{m}_k$ (already present in the type of o), only if the new annotation $\Upsilon$ has a variance type compatible with the variance type of $\mathrm{m}_k$ present in the object-type assigned to o. In this rule, the type of the object o is a saturated-type but can be a diamond-type as well, as in rule $(V{-}Ann_2)$. The second premise guarantees the presence of method m and the compatibility of its variance type with the new one.

$[(V{-}Ext)]$ This rule extends an object o with a method $\mathrm{m}_k$. Firstly, one can see that we cannot extend an object whose object-type is saturated. Secondly, this rule extends an object with a new (fresh) method if and only if that method is present in the subsumption-part of the diamond-type assigned to the object to be extended. But this condition can always be satisfied by a diamond-type thanks to the subtyping rule $(S{-}Ext_\diamond)$. Of course we have $\Upsilon : v_k$. The condition $H \subseteq I$ guarantees that the methods which are essential to type the body o′ are already present in the interface-part of the type $\mathtt{obj}\, t.[\mathrm{m}_i v_i : \sigma_i\{t\} \diamond \mathrm{m}_j v_j : \sigma_j\{t\}]_{j\in J}^{i\in I}$.

Note that this rule can also be applied when the method belongs to o but has been already subsumed via an application of a subtyping rule $(S{-}Shift_\diamond)$. In this case, operationally, is a method override. Moreover observe that, since object extension modifies from the outside the object, it follows that we can extend an object only with public or write only components. In fact, by looking at the subtyping rules, we can see that all variance annotations inside the subsumption-part are public-invariant or contravariant. As minor remarks on object extension, observe that:

- a "self-extension" operation is forbidden inside method bodies: in other words, the object $\mathrm{o} \triangleq [\mathrm{m} = \varsigma(s)s.\mathrm{n} := \varsigma(s)1]$, where n does not belong to o, cannot be type-decorated, because we are not able to give any correct type for the method m.

$$\frac{\Gamma \vdash \mathrm{o} : \tau \quad \Gamma \vdash \tau <: \mathtt{obj}\, t.[\mathrm{m}_k v_k : \sigma_k\{t\}] \quad v_k \in \{^\circ, ^+\}}{\Gamma \vdash \mathrm{o.m}_k : \sigma_k\{\tau\}} \; (V\text{-}Sel)$$

$$\frac{\begin{array}{l}\Gamma \vdash \mathrm{o} : \tau \quad \Gamma \vdash \tau <: \mathtt{obj}\, t.[\mathrm{m}_i v_i : \sigma_i\{t\}]^{i\in I} \quad k \in I \\ \Gamma, s_k : u <: \mathtt{obj}\, t.[\mathrm{m}_i v_i : \sigma_i\{t\}]^{i\in I} \vdash \mathrm{o}' : \sigma_k\{u\} \quad v_k \in \{^\circ, ^-\}\end{array}}{\Gamma \vdash \mathrm{o.m}_k := \varsigma(s_k{:}u <: \mathtt{obj}\, t.[\mathrm{m}_i v_i : \sigma_i\{t\}]^{i\in I})\mathrm{o}' : \tau} \; (V\text{-}Over)$$

$$\frac{\begin{array}{l}\Gamma \vdash \mathrm{o} : \mathtt{obj}\, t.[\mathrm{m}_i v_i : \sigma_i\{t\}]^{i\in I} \\ \Gamma \vdash \mathtt{obj}\, t.[\mathrm{m}_i v_i : \sigma_i\{t\}]^{i\in I} <: \mathtt{obj}\, t.[\mathrm{m}_k v : \sigma_k\{t\}] \quad \Upsilon : v\end{array}}{\Gamma \vdash \mathrm{o.m}_k := \Upsilon : \mathtt{obj}\, t.[\mathrm{m}_i v_i : \sigma_i\{t\}, \mathrm{m}_k v : \sigma_k\{t\}]^{i\in I\setminus\{k\}}} \; (V\text{-}Ann_1)$$

(Let $\tau_k \triangleq \mathtt{obj}\, t.[\mathrm{m}_h v_h : \sigma_h\{t\}]^{h\in H\cup\{k\}}$).

$$\frac{\begin{array}{l}\Gamma \vdash \mathrm{o} : \mathtt{obj}\, t.[\mathrm{m}_i v_i : \sigma_i\{t\} \diamond \mathrm{m}_j v_j : \sigma_j\{t\}]_{j\in J}^{i\in I} \quad k \in J \\ \Gamma, s_k : u <: \tau_k \vdash \mathrm{o}' : \sigma_k\{u\} \quad \Upsilon : v_k \quad H \subseteq I\end{array}}{\Gamma \vdash \mathrm{o.m}_k := \Upsilon\varsigma(s_k{:}u <: \tau_k)\mathrm{o}' : \mathtt{obj}\, t.[\mathrm{m}_i v_i : \sigma_i\{t\} \diamond \mathrm{m}_j v_j : \sigma_j\{t\}]_{j\in J\setminus\{k\}}^{i\in I\cup\{k\}}} \; (V\text{-}Ext)$$

**Table 5.** Some Term Typing Judgments

- inside method bodies, the $\varsigma$-bound variables $s_i$ (referring to `self`) in the same object o have different bound object-types. As an example consider the object $[\mathrm{m} = \varsigma(s{:}u <: [\mathrm{m}{:}int])1, \mathrm{n} = \varsigma(s'{:}u <: [\mathrm{m}{:}int, \mathrm{n}{:}int])s'.\mathrm{m}]$ of type $[\mathrm{m}{:}int, \mathrm{n}{:}int]$. This fits well with the semantics of the message send thanks to the presence of the subtyping rule $(S\text{-}Width)$.
- if we override the method n of o′ with a new body (e.g. $\varsigma(s{:}u <: [\mathrm{n}{:}int])1$), the new bound for $u$ in n does not need to be related with the older one; this is sound because the bound depends on the methods useful to type the new body.
- thanks to our sophisticated subtyping system we are not obliged to know "a priori" (in advance) all the future extensions of an object; in fact, the saturated-part of a diamond-type can always be filled with fresh methods thanks to the rule $(S\text{-}Ext_\diamond)$.

The type system enjoy the subject reduction property.

**Theorem 1 (Subject Reduction for $\mathcal{O}b^+_{s<:}$).**
*If $\Gamma \vdash \mathrm{o} : \sigma$ and $\mathrm{o} \overset{ev}{\to} \mathrm{o}'$, then $\Gamma \vdash \mathrm{o}' : \sigma$.*

## 4 Applications

In this section, we present a number of examples that help to illustrate the features of $\mathcal{O}b^+_{s<:}$. Any unspecified $\Upsilon$ and $v$ are taken to be equal to `public` and $^\circ$ respectively.

**Method Specialization.** The following extendible point

$$\mathtt{point} \triangleq [\mathrm{x} = \varsigma(s{:}u <: \sigma_1)1,\ \mathtt{plus1} = \varsigma(s{:}u <: \sigma_2)s.\mathrm{x} := \varsigma(s'{:}u' <: \sigma_1)s.\mathrm{x} + 1],$$

is typable with $\mathtt{obj}\, t.[\mathrm{x}{:}int, \mathtt{plus1}{:}t\,\diamond]$, being $\sigma_1 \equiv [\mathrm{x}{:}int]$, and $\sigma_2 \equiv \mathtt{obj}\, t.[\mathrm{x}{:}int, \mathtt{plus1}{:}t]$.

**Subtyping.** Let point be as before, and let c_point be obtained by extending point with a col field. By an inspection of the typing rules for $\mathcal{O}b^{+}_{s<:}$ we derive $\vdash$ point : $P_\diamond$, and $\vdash$ c_point : $CP_\diamond$, where

$$\begin{array}{llll} P & \triangleq \texttt{obj}\ t.[\texttt{x}{:}int, \texttt{plus1}{:}t] & CP & \triangleq \texttt{obj}\ t.[\texttt{x}{:}int, \texttt{col}{:}colors, \texttt{plus1}{:}t] \\ P_\diamond & \triangleq \texttt{obj}\ t.[\texttt{x}{:}int, \texttt{plus1}{:}t\ \diamond] & CP_\diamond & \triangleq \texttt{obj}\ t.[\texttt{x}{:}int, \texttt{col}{:}colors, \texttt{plus1}{:}t\ \diamond]. \end{array}$$

Now consider the following programs and related (derivable) types, where we introduce $\lambda$-binders to denote functions:

$$\begin{array}{lll} f_1 & \triangleq \lambda(s{:}P)s.\texttt{x} & : P{\to}int \\ f_2 & \triangleq \lambda(s{:}P)s.\texttt{x} := \varsigma(s'{:}u <: [\texttt{x}{:}int])2 & : P{\to}P \\ f_3 & \triangleq \lambda(s{:}P_\diamond)s.\texttt{col} := \varsigma(s'{:}u <: [\texttt{col}{:}colors])\texttt{red} & : P_\diamond{\to}CP_\diamond. \end{array}$$

Again, by inspecting the typing rules, we find that the following judgments are derivable:

$$\begin{array}{llll} \vdash & f_1\,(\texttt{point}) : int & \vdash & f_1\,(\texttt{c\_point}) : int \\ \vdash & f_2\,(\texttt{point}) : P & \vdash & f_2\,(\texttt{c\_point}) : P \\ \vdash & f_3\,(\texttt{point}) : CP_\diamond & (\not\vdash & f_3\,(\texttt{c\_point}) : CP_\diamond). \end{array}$$

The last judgment is correctly false since $CP_\diamond \not<: P_\diamond$.

**Method Annotations for Encapsulation.** Consider an object p with a field x and two methods, namely set and get, invokable from the outside which, respectively, return and modify the value of x. It is natural to give the following saturated-type to p:

$$Point \triangleq \texttt{obj}\ t.[\texttt{x}^\circ : int, \texttt{get}^\circ : int, \texttt{set}^\circ : int{\to}t].$$

Then, in order to make the local field x protected against external access, and the get and set methods not writable, we could override p as follow:

$$\texttt{prot\_p} \triangleq ((\texttt{p.x} := \texttt{private}).\texttt{get} := \texttt{read\_only}).\texttt{set} := \texttt{read\_only},$$

of type

$$ProtPoint \triangleq \texttt{obj}\ t.[\texttt{x}^\bullet : int, \texttt{get}^+ : int, \texttt{set}^+ : int{\to}t],$$

being that $Point <: ProtPoint$. So, the x variable becomes protected from the outside, and the get and set methods can be only invoked but not updated. As such, we obtain a neat distinction between public messages (i.e. the interface visible outside the object) and private variables (i.e. variables or local methods not accessible from the outside).

**Classes as Collection of Pre-methods.** In [Liq97b] a first-order encoding of classes-as-objects was given. As the $\mathcal{O}b^{+}_{s<:}$ is an extension of [Liq97b], it clearly follows that it also permit the building of classes and class instances. However, other encoding of classes are possible, provided that we increase our $\mathcal{O}b^{+}_{s<:}$ with polymorphic types. By polymorphic types we are able to build classes as a collection of parametric pre-methods[1]. A "pre-methods" is a polymorphic procedure that can be later used to construct a method parametric in the type of `self`. As an example, let the following object mem $\triangleq$ [get $=\varsigma(s)$true, set $=\varsigma(s)\lambda(b)s.$get :=$\varsigma(s')b$] of type $Mem \triangleq$ obj $t.$[get : $bool$, set : $bool{\to}t$], and consider the "class" memClass of [AC95] (for the sake of simplicity, all type-decorations are omitted, and $\lambda(\,)$ stands for polymorphic type-abstraction)

$$\begin{aligned}\texttt{memClass} \;\triangleq\; [&\texttt{new} = \varsigma(s)[\texttt{get} = \varsigma(s')s.\texttt{pre-get}(\,)(s'),\\ &\qquad\qquad\qquad \texttt{set} = \varsigma(s')s.\texttt{pre-set}(\,)(s')],\\ &\texttt{pre-get} = \varsigma(s)\lambda(\,)\lambda(s')\texttt{false}\\ &\texttt{pre-set} = \varsigma(s)\lambda(\,)\lambda(s')\lambda(b)s'.\texttt{get} := \varsigma(s'')b],\end{aligned}$$

of type $Class(Mem) \triangleq$ [new : $Mem$, pre-get:$\forall(u <: Mem)u{\to}bool$, pre-set: $\forall(u <: Mem)u{\to}bool{\to}u$]. The pre-get and pre-set methods of memClass are parametric pre-methods that do not use the `self` of memClass; they are used inside the bodies of get and set of the class instances generated by the new method of memClass. An instance mem of memClass will be generated by sending the message new to the class, i.e.: mem $\triangleq$ memClass.new : $Mem$. More generally, if a class instance can be typed with $Type \triangleq$ obj $t.[\mathrm{m}_i v_i : \sigma_i\{t\}\diamond]^{i\in I}_,$ then the type of the class whose instances can be typed with $Type$ is $Class(Type) \triangleq$ [new : $Type$, pre-m$_i$ : $\forall(u <: Type)u{\to}\sigma_i\{u\}]^{i\in I}_.$ As an interesting remark, we note that the type of class instances is a diamond-type: as such, all class instances can be dynamically extended by new methods (in pure prototype-based style).

**Modelling Inheritance.** Given an object-type $Type'$ (we consider a diamond-type, but we can consider a saturated-type as well) of the shape obj $t.[\mathrm{m}_i v_i : \tau_i\{t\}\diamond]^{i\in I\cup J}_,$ and a class type $Class(Type') \triangleq$ [new:$Type'$, pre-m$_i$ : $\forall(u <: Type')u{\to}\tau_i\{u\}]^{i\in I\cup J}_,$ we can say that forall $i \in I$, a pre-method pre-m$_i$ is inheritable from $Class(Type)$ to $Class(Type')$ if and only if $u <: Type'$ implies $\sigma_i\{u\} <: \tau_i\{u\}$. As in [AC95], the above condition hold for invariant and contravariant components, but not necessarily for covariant components. We overcome this restriction on covariant components using object extension. A detailed treatment of inheritance can be found in [AC95].

## 5 Related Work

This section is devoted to a comparison between some interesting and related works appeared in the literature in the last few years.

**[Rém98]** A calculus very close to $\mathcal{O}b^{+}_{s<:}$ is the one of Didier Rémy. In this calculus, objects have the shape $\zeta(\chi,\tau)[\mathrm{m}_i = \varsigma(s_i)o_i]^{i\in I}$, where $\zeta$ is a binder for types, $\tau$ denotes the type of the whole object, i.e `selftype`, $\chi$ is a type-variable that also denotes `selftype` (being that in the type rules $s_i$:$\chi$), m$_i$ are the methods contained in the object with relative bodies $\varsigma(s_i)o_i$.

[1] If one want to play with $\mathcal{O}b^{+}_{s<:}$, one may add polymorphic types and type abstraction/application, following Section 4 of [AC95].

Let $o \triangleq \zeta(\chi, \tau)[m_i = \varsigma(s_i)o_i]^{i \in I}$. Also in the calculus of Rémy, it is possible to extend objects with new methods; when we extend an object with a method m (in our notation $o.m := \varsigma(s{:}u <: \tau)o'$) this reduces to $\zeta(\chi, \tau \leftarrow \tau')[m_i{=}\varsigma(s_i)o_i, m{=}\varsigma(s)o]^{i \in I}$, where $\tau'$ is the type of `self` in the body of m, and $\tau \leftarrow \tau'$ is the new type of `self` obtained by suitable type reduction rules, necessary to maintains programs both well-formed and well-typed (but the operational semantics is still not type-driven). While there are similarities with our proposal and the one of [Rém98] - notably the use of subtyping for dealing with object extension - the two calculi have some fundamental differences:

- in [Rém98] after an object update, the type of `self` must be "recompiled" using the $\leftarrow$ function, since the type of `self` is factorised by all methods; this is not the case in $\mathcal{O}b^{+}_{s<:}$ because of a "redundancy" of type annotations inside method bodies;
- the [Rém98] calculus have the, so called, `virtual` methods (absent in $\mathcal{O}b^{+}_{s<:}$);
- the $\mathcal{O}b^{+}_{s<:}$ calculus have override of explicit annotations (absent in [Rém98]);
- variance annotations are the same in both calculi, but private-invariant annotation is absent in [Rém98].
- in $\mathcal{O}b^{+}_{s<:}$ we distinguish between two shape of objects, namely extendible objects, and "fixed-size" objects, while in [Rém98] all object are taken to be extendible;
- in [Rém98], object-types are interpreted as total functions from method labels to types, while in $\mathcal{O}b^{+}_{s<:}$ we rely on the more conventional interpretation of object-types as partial functions.

**[RS98]** The paper of Riecke and Stone describes a functional Object Calculus à la Abadi and Cardelli that allows unrestricted object extension in presence of object subsumption. The novelty of this paper is that we can forget a method with type $\sigma$ and later re-add it with a type $\tau$ *incompatible* with $\sigma$. This can be done by distinguish "external" method names by "internal" ones. A proper "dictionary" is attached to each object in order to"link" external labels to internal labels. Private fields can be hidden from the outside by subsumption.

One of the novelty of this paper is the operational semantics that at each step manipulates method dictionaries. This manipulation has a run-time cost that can slowly the running of the program, although some optimization techniques are proposed by the authors. Moreover the style of programming induced by adding dictionaries has an impact on the style of programming, since after a while of extensions and subsumptions steps one must reconstruct the correct behaviour of some methods.

**[AC95]** This paper is the "father" of the present paper; many of the ideas present in this paper have stimulated our development. The *Imperative Object Calculus* is to our knowledge the first object calculus with an imperative semantics, a sound type system with `selftypes`, subtyping and variance annotations.

## References


[Aba94] M. Abadi. Baby Modula–3 and a Theory of Objects. *Journal of Functional Programming*, 4(2):249–283, 1994.

[AC95] M. Abadi and L. Cardelli. An Imperative Object Calculus. In *Proc. of TAPSOFT/FASE*, Lecture Notes in Computer Science, pages 471–485. Springer-Verlag, 1995. Also in *Theory and Practice of Object Systems* 1(3):151-166, 1995.

[AC96a] M. Abadi and L. Cardelli. *A Theory of Objects*. Springer-Verlag, 1996.

[AC96b] M. Abadi and L. Cardelli. A Theory of Primitive Objects: Untyped and First Order Systems. *Information and Computation*, 125(2):78–102, 1996.

[BBDL97] V. Bono, M. Bugliesi, M. Dezani-Ciancaglini, and L. Liquori. Subtyping Constraint for Incomplete Objects. In *Proc. of TAPSOFT/CAAP*, volume 1214 of *Lecture Notes in Computer Science*, pages 465–477. Springer-Verlag, 1997.

[BCC+96] K. Bruce, L. Cardelli, G. Castagna, The Hopkins Object Group, G. Leavens, and B. Pierce. On Binary Methods. *Theory and Practice of Object Systems*, 1(3), 1996.

[BL95] V. Bono and L. Liquori. A Subtyping for the Fisher-Honsell-Mitchell Lambda Calculus of Objects. In *Proc. of CSL*, volume 933 of *Lecture Notes in Computer Science*, pages 16–30. Springer-Verlag, 1995.

[BSvG95] K.B. Bruce, A. Shuett, and R. van Gent. Polytoil: a Type-safe Polymorphic Object Oriented Language. In *Proc. of ECOOP*, volume 952 of *Lecture Notes in Computer Science*, pages 16–30. Springer-Verlag, 1995.

[Cas95] G. Castagna. Covariance and contravariance: conflict without a cause. *ACM Transactions on Programming Languages and Systems*, 17(3):431–447, 1995.

[Cas96] G. Castagna. *Object-Oriented Programming: A Unified Foundation*. Progress in Theoretical Computer Science. Birkäuser, Boston, 1996.

[CU89] C. Chambers and D. Ungar. Customization: Optimizing Compiler Technology for Self, a Dinamically-typed Object-Oriented Programming Language. In *SIGPLAN-89 Conference on Programming Language Design and Implementation*, pages 146–160, 1989.

[FHM94] K. Fisher, F. Honsell, and J. C. Mitchell. A Lambda Calculus of Objects and Method Specialization. *Nordic Journal of Computing*, 1(1):3–37, 1994.

[FM94] K. Fisher and J. C. Michell. Notes on Typed Object-Oriented Programming. In *Proc. of TACS*, volume 789 of *Lecture Notes in Computer Science*, pages 844–885. Springer-Verlag, 1994.

[FM95] K. Fisher and J. C. Mitchell. A Delegation-based Object Calculus with Subtyping. In *Proc. of FCT*, volume 965 of *Lecture Notes in Computer Science*, pages 42–61. Springer-Verlag, 1995.

[GR83] A. Goldberg and D. Robson. *Smalltalk-80: the Language and its Implementation*. Addison-Wesley, 1983.

[Liq97a] L. Liquori. Bounded Polymorphism for Extensible Objects. Technical Report CS-24-96, Computer Science Department, University of Turin, Italy, 1997.

[Liq97b] L. Liquori. An Extended Theory of Primitive Objects: First Order System. In *Proc. of ECOOP*, volume 1241 of *Lecture Notes in Computer Science*, pages 146–169. Springer-Verlag, 1997.

[Liq98] L. Liquori. On Object Extension. In *Proc. of ECOOP*, volume 1445 of *Lecture Notes in Computer Science*, pages 498–552. Springer-Verlag, 1998.

[Liq99] L. Liquori. Bounded Polymorphism for Extensible Objects. Technical Report RR 1999-16, École Normale Supérieure de Lyon, France, 1999.

[Mey92] B. Meyer. *Eiffel:The language*. Prentice Hall, 1992.

[Mic90] J. C. Michell. Toward a Typed Foundation for Method Specialization and Inheritance. In *Proceedings of POPL*, pages 109–124. The ACM Press, 1990.

[Rém95] D. Rémy. Refined Subtyping and Row Variables for Record Types. Draft, 1995.

[Rém98] D. Rémy. From Classes to Objects via Subtyping. In *Proc. of ESOP*, volume 1381 of *Lecture Notes in Computer Science*, pages 200–220. Springer-Verlag, 1998.

[RS98] J.G. Riecke and C. Stone. Privacy via Subsumption. In *Electronic proceedings of FOOL-98*, 1998.

[US87] D. Ungar and B. Smith, R. Self: The Power of Simplicity. In *Proc. of OOPSLA*, pages 227–241. The ACM Press, 1987.

# A The Extended Object Calculus

**Well-formed Contexts**

$$\frac{}{\varepsilon \vdash ok}\ (C{-}\varepsilon) \qquad \frac{\Gamma \vdash \sigma \quad s \notin dom(\Gamma)}{\Gamma, s : \sigma \vdash ok}\ (C{-}s) \qquad \frac{\Gamma \vdash \sigma \quad t \notin dom(\Gamma)}{\Gamma, t <: \sigma \vdash ok}\ (C{-}t)$$

**Well-formed Types**

$$\frac{\begin{array}{l}\Gamma, t <: \omega \vdash \sigma_i\{t^+\} \quad \forall i \in I \quad I \cap J = \emptyset \\ \Gamma, t <: \omega \vdash \sigma_j\{t^+\} \quad \forall j \in J \quad v_j \in \{^\circ, ^-\}\end{array}}{\Gamma \vdash \mathtt{obj}\, t.[\mathtt{m}_i v_i : \sigma_i\{t\} \diamond \mathtt{m}_j v_j : \sigma_j\{t\}]^{i \in I}_{j \in J}}\ (T{-}\diamond) \qquad \frac{\Gamma, t <: \sigma, \Gamma' \vdash ok}{\Gamma, t <: \sigma, \Gamma' \vdash t}\ (T{-}Var)$$

$$\frac{\Gamma, t <: \omega \vdash \sigma_i\{t^+\} \quad \forall i \in I}{\Gamma \vdash \mathtt{obj}\, t.[\mathtt{m}_i v_i : \sigma_i\{t\}]^{i \in I}}\ (T{-}Sat) \qquad \frac{\Gamma \vdash ok}{\Gamma \vdash \omega}\ (T{-}\Omega)$$

**Subtyping Judgments with Variance Annotations**

$$\frac{\Gamma \vdash \sigma <: \sigma' \quad v \in \{^\circ, ^+\}}{\Gamma \vdash v\sigma <:{}^+\sigma'}\ (S{-}Cova) \qquad \frac{\Gamma \vdash \sigma' <: \sigma \quad v \in \{^\circ, ^-\}}{\Gamma \vdash v\sigma <:{}^-\sigma'}\ (S{-}Contra)$$

$$\frac{\Gamma \vdash \sigma \quad v \in \{^\circ, ^\bullet\}}{\Gamma \vdash v\sigma <: v\sigma}\ (S{-}Inv_1) \qquad \frac{\Gamma \vdash \sigma \quad v \in \{^+, ^-\}}{\Gamma \vdash v\sigma <:{}^\bullet\sigma}\ (S{-}Inv_2)$$

**Standard Subtyping Judgments**

$$\frac{\Gamma \vdash \sigma}{\Gamma \vdash \sigma <: \sigma}\ (S{-}Refl) \qquad \frac{\Gamma \vdash \sigma <: \tau \quad \Gamma \vdash \tau <: \rho}{\Gamma \vdash \sigma <: \rho}\ (S{-}Trans) \qquad \frac{\Gamma \vdash \sigma}{\Gamma \vdash \sigma <: \omega}\ (S{-}\Omega)$$

**Subtyping Judgments for Object-Types**

$(S{-}Var_\diamond)$

$$\frac{\Gamma, u <: \mathtt{obj}\, t.[\mathtt{m}_i v_i : \sigma_i\{t\} \diamond \mathtt{m}_j v_j : \sigma_j\{t\}]^{i \in I}_{j \in J} \vdash v_k\sigma_k\{u\} <: v'_k\sigma'_k\{u\} \quad \forall k \in I \cup J}{\Gamma \vdash \mathtt{obj}\, t.[\mathtt{m}_i v_i : \sigma_i\{t\} \diamond \mathtt{m}_j v_j : \sigma_j\{t\}]^{i \in I}_{j \in J} <: \mathtt{obj}\, t.[\mathtt{m}_i v'_i : \sigma'_i\{t\} \diamond \mathtt{m}_j v'_j : \sigma'_j\{t\}]^{i \in I}_{j \in J}}$$

$$\frac{\Gamma, u <: \mathtt{obj}\, t.[\mathtt{m}_i v_i : \sigma_i\{t\}]^{i \in I} \vdash v_k\sigma_k\{u\} <: v'_k\sigma'_k\{u\} \quad \forall k \in I}{\Gamma \vdash \mathtt{obj}\, t.[\mathtt{m}_i v_i : \sigma_i\{t\}]^{i \in I} <: \mathtt{obj}\, t.[\mathtt{m}_i v'_i : \sigma'_i\{t\}]^{i \in I}}\ (S{-}Var)$$

$(S{-}Shift_\diamond)$

$$\frac{\Gamma \vdash \mathtt{obj}\, t.[\mathtt{m}_i v_i : \sigma_i\{t\} \diamond \mathtt{m}_j v_j : \sigma_j\{t\}]^{i \in I \cup K}_{j \in J} \quad v_k \in \{^\circ, ^-\} \quad \forall k \in K}{\Gamma \vdash \mathtt{obj}\, t.[\mathtt{m}_i v_i : \sigma_i\{t\} \diamond \mathtt{m}_j v_j : \sigma_j\{t\}]^{i \in I \cup K}_{j \in J} <: \mathtt{obj}\, t.[\mathtt{m}_i v_i : \sigma_i\{t\} \diamond \mathtt{m}_j v_j : \sigma_j\{t\}]^{i \in I}_{j \in J \cup K}}$$

$(S{-}Ext_\diamond)$

$$\frac{\Gamma \vdash \mathtt{obj}\, t.[\mathtt{m}_i v_i : \sigma_i\{t\} \diamond \mathtt{m}_j v_j : \sigma_j\{t\}]^{i \in I}_{j \in J \cup K} \quad v_k \in \{^\circ, ^-\} \quad \forall k \in K}{\Gamma \vdash \mathtt{obj}\, t.[\mathtt{m}_i v_i : \sigma_i\{t\} \diamond \mathtt{m}_j v_j : \sigma_j\{t\}]^{i \in I}_{j \in J} <: \mathtt{obj}\, t.[\mathtt{m}_i v_i : \sigma_i\{t\} \diamond \mathtt{m}_j v_j : \sigma_j\{t\}]^{i \in I}_{j \in J \cup K}}$$

$$\frac{\Gamma \vdash \mathtt{obj}\, t.[\mathrm{m}_i v_i : \sigma_i\{t\} \diamond \mathrm{m}_j v_j : \sigma_j\{t\}]^{i\in I}_{j\in J}}{\Gamma \vdash \mathtt{obj}\, t.[\mathrm{m}_i v_i : \sigma_i\{t\} \diamond \mathrm{m}_j v_j : \sigma_j\{t\}]^{i\in I}_{j\in J} <: \mathtt{obj}\, t.[\mathrm{m}_i v_i : \sigma_i\{t\}]^{i\in I}} \quad (S{-}Sat_\diamond)$$

$$\frac{\Gamma \vdash \mathtt{obj}\, t.[\mathrm{m}_i v_i : \sigma_i\{t\}]^{i\in I\cup J}}{\Gamma \vdash \mathtt{obj}\, t.[\mathrm{m}_i v_i : \sigma_i\{t\}]^{i\in I\cup J} <: \mathtt{obj}\, t.[\mathrm{m}_i v_i : \sigma_i\{t\}]^{i\in I}} \quad (S{-}Width)$$

**Type Rules for Objects**

$$\frac{\Gamma, s : \sigma, \Gamma' \vdash ok}{\Gamma, s : \sigma, \Gamma' \vdash s : \sigma} \quad (V{-}Proj) \qquad \frac{\Gamma \vdash \mathrm{o} : \sigma \quad \Gamma \vdash \sigma <: \tau}{\Gamma \vdash \mathrm{o} : \tau} \quad (V{-}Sub)$$

$$\frac{\Gamma \vdash \mathrm{o} : \tau \quad \Gamma \vdash \tau <: \mathtt{obj}\, t.[\mathrm{m}_k v_k : \sigma_k\{t\}] \quad v_k \in \{^\circ, ^+\}}{\Gamma \vdash \mathrm{o.m}_k : \sigma_k\{\tau\}} \quad (V{-}Sel)$$

(Let $\tau_i \triangleq \mathtt{obj}\, t.[\mathrm{m}_h v_h : \sigma_h\{t\}]^{h\in H_i\cup\{i\}}$).

$$\frac{\Gamma, s_i : u <: \tau_i \vdash \mathrm{o}_i : \sigma_i\{u\} \quad H_i \subseteq I \quad \Upsilon_i : v_i \quad \forall i \in I}{\Gamma \vdash [\mathrm{m}_i \Upsilon_i = \varsigma(s_i{:}u <: \tau_i)\mathrm{o}_i]^{i\in I} : \mathtt{obj}\, t.[\mathrm{m}_i v_i : \sigma_i \diamond]^{i\in I}} \quad (V{-}Obj)$$

$$\frac{\begin{array}{l}\Gamma \vdash \mathrm{o} : \tau \qquad \Gamma \vdash \tau <: \mathtt{obj}\, t.[\mathrm{m}_i v_i : \sigma_i\{t\}]^{i\in I} \qquad k \in I \\ \Gamma, s_k : u <: \mathtt{obj}\, t.[\mathrm{m}_i v_i : \sigma_i\{t\}]^{i\in I} \vdash \mathrm{o}' : \sigma_k\{u\} \quad v_k \in \{^\circ, ^-\}\end{array}}{\Gamma \vdash \mathrm{o.m}_k := \varsigma(s_k{:}u <: \mathtt{obj}\, t.[\mathrm{m}_i v_i : \sigma_i\{t\}]^{i\in I})\mathrm{o}' : \tau} \quad (V{-}Over)$$

$$\frac{\begin{array}{l}\Gamma \vdash \mathrm{o} : \mathtt{obj}\, t.[\mathrm{m}_i v_i : \sigma_i\{t\}]^{i\in I} \\ \Gamma \vdash \mathtt{obj}\, t.[\mathrm{m}_i v_i : \sigma_i\{t\}]^{i\in I} <: \mathtt{obj}\, t.[\mathrm{m}_k v : \sigma_k\{t\}] \quad \Upsilon : v\end{array}}{\Gamma \vdash \mathrm{o.m}_k := \Upsilon : \mathtt{obj}\, t.[\mathrm{m}_i v_i : \sigma_i\{t\}, \mathrm{m}_k v : \sigma_k\{t\}]^{i\in I\setminus\{k\}}} \quad (V{-}Ann_1)$$

$$\frac{\begin{array}{l}\Gamma \vdash \mathrm{o} : \mathtt{obj}\, t.[\mathrm{m}_i v_i : \sigma_i\{t\} \diamond \mathrm{m}_j v_j : \sigma_j\{t\}]^{i\in I}_{j\in J} \\ \Gamma \vdash \mathtt{obj}\, t.[\mathrm{m}_i v_i : \sigma_i\{t\} \diamond \mathrm{m}_j v_j : \sigma_j\{t\}]^{i\in I}_{j\in J} <: \mathtt{obj}\, t.[\mathrm{m}_k v : \sigma_k\{t\}] \quad \Upsilon : v\end{array}}{\Gamma \vdash \mathrm{o.m}_k := \Upsilon : \mathtt{obj}\, t.[\mathrm{m}_i v_i : \sigma_i\{t\}, \mathrm{m}_k v : \sigma_k\{t\} \diamond \mathrm{m}_j v_j : \sigma_j\{t\}]^{i\in I\setminus\{k\}}_{j\in J}} \quad (V{-}Ann_2)$$

(Let $\tau_k \triangleq \mathtt{obj}\, t.[\mathrm{m}_h v_h : \sigma_h\{t\}]^{h\in H\cup\{k\}}$).

$$\frac{\begin{array}{l}\Gamma \vdash \mathrm{o} : \mathtt{obj}\, t.[\mathrm{m}_i v_i : \sigma_i\{t\} \diamond \mathrm{m}_j v_j : \sigma_j\{t\}]^{i\in I}_{j\in J} \quad k \in J \\ \Gamma, s_k : u <: \tau_k \vdash \mathrm{o}' : \sigma_k\{u\} \qquad \Upsilon : v_k \qquad H \subseteq I\end{array}}{\Gamma \vdash \mathrm{o.m}_k := \Upsilon\varsigma(s_k{:}u <: \tau_k)\mathrm{o}' : \mathtt{obj}\, t.[\mathrm{m}_i v_i : \sigma_i\{t\} \diamond \mathrm{m}_j v_j : \sigma_j\{t\}]^{i\in I\cup\{k\}}_{j\in J\setminus\{k\}}} \quad (V{-}Ext)$$

# About Effective Quotients in Constructive Type Theory *

Maria Emilia Maietti

School of Computer Science, University of Birmingham
Edgbaston, Birmingham B15 2TT, United Kingdom
e-mail: mem@cs.bham.ac.uk

**Abstract.** We extend Martin-Löf's constructive set theory with effective quotient sets and the rule of uniqueness of propositional equality proofs. We prove that in the presence of at least two universes $U_0$ and $U_1$ the principle of excluded middle holds for small sets. The key point is the combination of uniqueness of propositional equality proofs with the effectiveness condition that allows us to recover information on the equivalence relation from the equality on the quotient set.

## 1 Introduction

Within the framework of Martin-Löf's Intuitionistic Type Theory [Mar84,NPS90], in order to generate some formal topologies [Sam87], the quotient sets are also desirable [NV97]. But some care is necessary in extending Martin-Löf's set theory with quotient sets if we want to keep constructivity.

Here, we consider the extension of intensional Martin-Löf's set theory (*MLTT*) with quotient sets as formulated in [Hof95] and we want to explore the possibility to make quotients effective. Intuitively, effectiveness for quotient sets means that if two elements of a set are in the same "equivalence class" as represented by an element of the quotient set, then the two elements satisfy the equivalence relation. A property with this name can be found in category theory as referred to an equivalence relation (see e.g. [MR77]). The usual constructions of quotients in classical set theory, in categorical universes like toposes and in the setoids made out of type theory enjoy this property.

In this paper we give an answer to the question of extending *MLTT* with effective quotients, if we also add the rule of uniqueness of equality proofs [Hof95]. Indeed, even if the rule of uniqueness of equality proofs is not provable in the intensional version of Martin-Löf's set theory as proved by M. Hofmann and T. Streicher [HS95], however it is definable by pattern-matching [Coq92], which is a very useful tool for implementations of type theory.

To formulate effectiveness we need to pass to the extension of Martin-Löf's type theory, here called $iTT$, augmented with the true judgement $A\ true$ (see [Mar84], [Val95]). According to the paradigm in [Val95], the rules of $iTT$ about

* This work has been done at the Department of Mathematics, University of Padova, Italy

true judgements, called admissible, are exactly those obtained from *MLTT* such that we can prove at the level of the metalanguage the following preservation property: ***the judgement "A true" is derivable in iTT iff there is a proof-term "a" such that "a ∈ A" is derivable in MLTT.***
We call $iTT^Q$ the extension with true judgements corresponding to $MLTT^Q$, that is *MLTT* augmented with intensional quotients and the uniqueness of equality proofs. Now, in $iTT^Q$ we express the effectiveness condition in terms of true judgements as follows

$$\frac{a \in A \quad b \in A \quad \mathsf{Id}(A/R, [a], [b]) \ true}{R(a, b) \ true}$$

and we call $iTT^{EQ}$ the extension of $iTT^Q$ with this condition. We add effectiveness as a condition on true judgements, because we are not able to think of a constructive type theory with only the four kinds of judgements

$$A \ set \qquad A = B \qquad a \in A \qquad a = b \in A$$

that extends $MLTT^Q$ and whose extension with true judgements makes the effectiveness condition admissible. Indeed, in order to admit the effectiveness condition in the corresponding extension with true judgements, this claimed type theory should allow to derive the following rule

$$\textbf{eff} \ \frac{a \in A \quad b \in A \quad p \in \mathsf{Id}(A/R, [a], [b])}{?(a, b, p) \in R(a, b)}$$

for some proof-term $?(a, b, p)$.

$$MLTT \xrightarrow{\ preservative\ } iTT$$

$$MLTT^Q \xrightarrow{\ preservative\ } iTT^Q$$

$$MLTT^Q + \textbf{eff}(?) \xrightarrow{\ preservative\ } iTT^{EQ} + \textbf{eff}(?)$$

Actually, we will show here that we can not have such a theory where **eff** can be derived, since even in the extension $iTT^{EQ}$ the principle of excluded middle holds for small sets. Indeed, in the presence of quotient sets with the effectiveness condition, the rule of uniqueness of propositional equality proofs and at least two universes $U_0$ and $U_1$, to which the codes of quotient sets are added, we can reproduce for small sets the proof of Diaconescu [Dia75] made within topos theory that the axiom of choice implies the principle of excluded middle. Therefore, to be clearer, if a constructed type theory including $MLTT^Q$ + **eff** existed, then its preservative extension with true judgements would admit the effectiveness condition. Hence, as shown here, we would be able to prove the principle of excluded middle for small sets at the level of true judgements and as a consequence of the preservation property in the pure type theory itself against its claimed constructivity.

In the framework of set theory the proof reproduced here shows the incompatibility, from the intuitionistic point of view, between the extensionality axiom and the axiom of choice. In the framework of topos theory it makes use of extensional powersets. Here, we will see that to reproduce extensionality in the context of intensional type theory, where the axiom of choice holds because of the presence of a strong existential quantifier, it is sufficient to have general effective quotients to be used on the first two universes and the rule of uniqueness of equality proofs at the propositional level. In fact, in the proof we mimic powersets by quotienting the first two universes under the relation of equiprovability. Then, we need the effectiveness condition to decode the extensional equality related to the quotients on the universes into the equiprovability relation. Finally, the rule of uniqueness of equality proofs seems crucial to identify the values of the choice function applied to two suitable extensionally equal subsets.

Of course, an analogous proof can be reproduced in the extensional version of Martin-Löf's set theory with the quotient sets as given in Nuprl [Con86] and only with the addition of the effectiveness condition.

We know that the effectiveness condition is surely derivable for decidable equivalence relations. But in general effectiveness is problematic, because it restores information that has been forgotten in the introduction rule for the equality of equivalence classes. This is confirmed by the proof given here.

The interest in the effectiveness condition arises from the mathematical practice of quotient sets. In order to keep effectiveness for quotient sets in the presence of uniqueness of equality proofs, an alternative strategy could be to let quotient sets based only on a proof-irrelevant equivalence relation, as it is in the type theory of Heyting pretoposes [Mai97].

## 2 The idea of the proof: axiom of choice versus extensionality

We describe the idea behind the proof that in the extension of Martin-Löf set theory with effective quotient sets and the uniqueness of equality proofs the axiom of choice yields classical logic on small sets. We think that this proof can go through any other possible extension with analogous extensional constructors. The idea of the proof originally due to Diaconescu [Dia75] can be clearly understood in the framework of an intuitionistic set theory with basic axioms, as the empty axiom, the pair axiom and the comprehension axiom, also only for restricted formulas as in CZF [Acz78] (see e.g. [GM78], [Bel97]). In this framework we can see how the axiom of choice is incompatible with the extensionality axiom from the constructive point of view, as we show in the following.
Let us consider a set $A$ and the following subsets of the set $\{0,1\}$, where $0 \equiv \emptyset$ and $1 \equiv \{\emptyset\}$:

$$V_0 \equiv \{x \in \{0,1\} : x = 0 \vee \exists y\, y \in A\} \qquad V_1 \equiv \{x \in \{0,1\} : x = 1 \vee \exists y\, y \in A\}$$

Now, if we apply the axiom of choice to the system of sets $\{V_0, V_1\}$ we get that the following proposition is true:

$$\forall z \in \{V_0, V_1\}\ \exists y \in \{0,1\}\ y \in z \longrightarrow$$

$$\exists f \in \{V_0, V_1\} \to \{0,1\}\ \ \forall z \in \{V_0, V_1\}\ \ f(z) \in z$$

Then we know that the premise of this implication is true by substituting $y$ with 0 in the case of $V_0$ and with 1 in the case of $V_1$. Therefore we derive by modus ponens

$$\exists f \in \{V_0, V_1\} \to \{0,1\}\ \ \forall z \in \{V_0, V_1\}\ \ f(z) \in z$$

Then, applying the elimination of the existential quantifier, we can derive

$$(f(V_0) = 0 \vee \exists y\ y \in A)\ \ \wedge\ \ (f(V_1) = 1 \vee \exists y\ y \in A)$$

from which by distributivity we get

$$(f(V_0) = 0 \wedge f(V_1) = 1) \vee \exists y\ y \in A$$

Now we are going to prove by $\vee$-elimination from the above proposition the principle of excluded middle for $A$. So, at first we assume $f(V_0) = 0 \wedge f(V_1) = 1$. Then note that if we also assume $\exists y\ y \in A$, from this by *extensionality* we get that $V_0 = V_1$, which combined with our first assumption yields $0 = 1$, which is falsum and lets us conclude $\neg\exists y\ y \in A$ and also $\exists y\ y \in A \ \vee\ \neg\exists y\ y \in A$. Since by assuming the second disjunct $\exists y\ y \in A$ we also get $\exists y\ y \in A \ \vee\ \neg\exists y\ y \in A$, by $\vee$-elimination applied on $(f(V_0) = 0 \wedge f(V_1) = 1) \vee \exists y\ y \in A$ the principle of excluded middle for any set $A$

$$\exists y\ y \in A \ \ \vee\ \ \neg\exists y\ y \in A$$

is now derived. We can adapt the outline of this proof to the extension of Martin-Löf's set theory with effective quotient sets and the uniqueness of equality proofs, as we will show in the next sections. The uniqueness of equality proof seems crucial to reproduce the proof together with the extensionality captured by effective quotient sets.

## 3 Extension of *iTT* with quotient sets

In order to investigate the possibility of an extension with effective quotient sets, firstly we extend the intensional version of Martin-Löf's Intuitionistic Type Theory [NPS90], here called *MLTT*, with quotient sets and the rule of uniqueness of proofs for the intensional propositional equality as in [Hof95] (page 111) and we call this extension $MLTT^Q$. Then we consider its preservative extension $iTT^Q$ with true judgements. Lastly we extend $iTT^Q$ with the effectiveness condition and we call this extension $iTT^{EQ}$. As said in the introduction the meaning of a *true* judgement is the following: *A true* holds if and only if there exists a proof-element $a$ such that $a \in A$ holds (for an account of this see [Mar84], [Val95]). This is meaningful, since we identify *propositions* and *sets*. We call *iTT* the extension of *MLTT* with true judgements. The rules of *iTT* ( $iTT^Q$) about true judgements are precisely those admissible by the rules of *MLTT* ($MLTT^Q$) according to the explained semantics, to which we add the following introduction rule

$$\text{(True Introduction)}\ \frac{a \in A}{A\ true}$$

such that *iTT* ($iTT^Q$) turns out to be a preservative extension of *MLTT* ($MLTT^Q$) in the sense stated in [Val95] and recalled in the introduction. For instance, among the admissible rules of *iTT*, we recall the case of the set of intensional propositional equality Id. The propositional equality is the internalization of the definitional equality between elements of a set at the level of propositions, considering two objects definitionally equal if they evaluate to the same normal form. Actually, there are two kinds of propositional equality characterizing intensional and extensional type theories: Id, which is intensional (see the rules below), and Eq, which is extensional (see [NPS90] and the section 5). Intensional propositional equality is entailed by definitional equality, that is two objects are propositionally equal if they are definitionally equal, but the other way around does not hold. On the contrary, extensional propositional equality is equivalent to definitional equality. The main difference is that in the presence of intensional propositional equality, definitional equality and type checking are decidable, but this is no longer true in the presence of extensional propositional equality.

The formation, introduction, elimination and conversion rules for the set Id are the following

**Intensional equality set**

$$\frac{A\ set \quad a \in A \quad b \in A}{\mathsf{Id}(A, a, b)\ set}$$

**I-Id**

$$\frac{a \in A}{\mathsf{id}(a) \in \mathsf{Id}(A, a, a)}$$

**E- Id**

$$\frac{d \in \mathsf{Id}(A, a, b) \quad c(x) \in C(x, x, \mathsf{id}(x)))\ [x : A]}{\mathsf{idpeel}(d, c) \in C(a, b, d)}$$

**C-Id**

$$\frac{a \in A \quad c(x) \in C(x, x, \mathsf{id}(x))\ [x : A]}{\mathsf{idpeel}(\mathsf{id}(a), c) = c(a) \in C(a, a, \mathsf{id}(a))}$$

In particular, the admissible rules corresponding to the elimination rule are the following:

$$\frac{d \in \mathsf{Id}(A, a, b) \quad \begin{array}{c}[x : A] \\ | \\ C(x, x, \mathsf{id}(x))\ true\end{array}}{C(a, b, d)\ true} \qquad \frac{\mathsf{Id}(A, a, b)\ true \quad \begin{array}{c}[x : A] \\ | \\ C(x, x)\ true\end{array}}{C(a, b)\ true}$$

Now, we extend $iTT$ with quotient sets as formulated in [Hof95][1]:
**Intensional Quotient set**

$$\frac{\begin{array}{l} R(x,y)\ set\ [x \in A, y \in A] \\ c_1 \in R(x,x)[x \in A], \qquad c_2 \in R(y,x)[x \in A, y \in A, z \in R(x,y)] \\ c_3 \in R(x,z)[x \in A, y \in A, z \in A, w \in R(x,y), w' \in R(y,z)] \end{array}}{A/R\ set}$$

**I-int.quotient**

$$\frac{a \in A \quad A/R\ set}{[a] \in A/R}$$

**eq-int.quotient**

$$\frac{a \in A \quad b \in A \quad d \in R(a,b)}{\mathsf{Qax}(d) \in \mathsf{Id}(A/R, [a], [b])}$$

**E-int.quotient**

$$\frac{\begin{array}{l} s \in A/R \quad l(x) \in L([x])[x \in A] \\ h \in \mathsf{Id}(L([y]),\ \mathsf{sub}(\mathsf{Qax}(d), l(x)),\ l(y))\ [x \in A, y \in A, d \in R(x,y)] \end{array}}{\mathsf{Q}(l,h,s) \in L(s)}$$

where the term $\mathsf{sub}(c,d) \equiv \mathsf{idpeel}(c,(x)\lambda y.y)(d)$ for $c \in \mathsf{Id}(A,a,b)$ and $d \in L(a)$ (see also [NPS90] page 64) expresses substitution with equal elements;
**C-int.quotient**

$$\frac{\begin{array}{l} a \in A \quad l(x) \in L([x])[x \in A] \\ h \in \mathsf{Id}(L([y]),\ \mathsf{sub}(\mathsf{Qax}(d), l(x)),\ l(y))\ [x \in A, y \in A, d \in R(x,y)] \end{array}}{\mathsf{Q}(l,h,[a]) = l(a) \in L([a])}$$

We also want to make quotients effective and we require:
**Effectiveness condition**

$$\frac{a \in A \quad b \in A \quad \mathsf{Id}(A/R, [a], [b])\ true}{R(a,b)\ true}$$

Effectiveness expresses the fact that, as usual, every equivalence relation on a set $A$ is the kernel of the function which maps an element of $A$ into its equivalence class.

Note that effectiveness is expressed only as a condition in terms of true judgements, since we are not able to exhibit type-theoretical rules that make this effectiveness condition admissible, like for the rules of $iTT^Q$ on true judgements, where by a type-theoretical rule we mean a rule expressed using judgements only of the following four kinds: $A\ set \quad A = B \quad a \in A \quad a = b \in A$. Indeed, in $iTT^{EQ}$ we will prove a non-constructive principle, that is the principle of excluded middle on small sets, which lets us conclude that there are

[1] But we restrict the formation rule to quotient sets based on equivalence relations. In $A/R$ we should record the proof terms $c_1$, $c_2$, $c_3$ and then the corresponding equality rule should say that varying $c_1$, $c_2$, $c_3$, the set $A/R$ is the same.

no type-theoretical rules that make the effectiveness condition on quotient sets admissible and that in the same time follow the Heyting constructive semantics of connectives.

Finally, we add the rule of uniqueness of propositional equality proofs:
**Id-Uni I**

$$\frac{a \in A \quad p \in \mathsf{Id}(A,a,a)}{\mathsf{iduni}(a,p) \in \mathsf{Id}(\mathsf{Id}(A,a,a),p,\mathsf{id}(a))}$$

The corresponding conversion rule is the following:
**Id-Uni conv**

$$\frac{a \in A}{\mathsf{iduni}(a,\mathsf{id}(a)) = \mathsf{id}(\mathsf{id}(a)) \in \mathsf{Id}(\mathsf{Id}(A,a,a),\mathsf{id}(a),\mathsf{id}(a))}$$

By using Id-Uni and the elimination rule of the propositional equality on the proposition

$$\Pi_{w \in \mathsf{Id}(A,x,y)} \mathsf{Id}(\mathsf{Id}(A,x,y),w,z)\ [x \in A, y \in A, z \in \mathsf{Id}(A,x,y)]$$

Streicher proved that (see [Hof95] page 81) the set

$$\mathsf{Id}(\mathsf{Id}(A,x,y),w,z)\ \ [x \in A, y \in A, z \in \mathsf{Id}(A,x,y), w \in \mathsf{Id}(A,x,y)]$$

is inhabited by the proof-term

$$\mathsf{idpeel}(z,(x)\lambda w' \in \mathsf{Id}(A,x,x).\mathsf{iduni}(x,w'))(w)$$

Hence, the uniqueness of proofs of propositional equality set, called UIP, holds.

*Remark 1.* As we said in the introduction, the uniqueness of proofs of the propositional equality set is definable by pattern-matching [Coq92], but it is not derivable in the intensional version of Martin-Löf's set theory, as showed by M. Hofmann and T. Streicher (see [HS95]), who built a model where UIP is not valid.

Finally, we consider the first universe $U_0$, whose elements are called small sets [NPS90], and the second universe $U_1$, whose elements are called large sets and where $U_0$ is also coded (see [Mar84] and [Dyb97], but note that we do not give a new code to terms of the first universe into the second one to make formulas more readable in the following). We have also to add the following introduction rules for the codes of the quotient sets into the universes for $i = 0, 1$
**UQ-I**

$$\frac{\begin{array}{ll} a \in U_i & r(x,y) \in U_i\ [x \in T_i(a), y \in T_i(a)] \\ \multicolumn{2}{l}{c_1 \in T_i(r(x,x))\ [x \in T_i(a)],\ c_2 \in T_i(r(y,x))\ [x \in T_i(a), y \in T_i(a), z \in T_i(r(x,y))]} \\ \multicolumn{2}{l}{c_3 \in T_i(r(x,z))\ [x \in T_i(a), y \in T_i(a), z \in T_i(a), w \in T_i(r(x,y)), w' \in T_i(r(y,z))]} \end{array}}{\widehat{a/r} \in U_i}$$

with the corresponding conversion rules

$$T_i(\widehat{a/r}) = T_i(a)/(x,y)T_i(r(x,y))$$

This extension of $iTT$, called $iTT^{EQ}$, is consistent because there is an interpretation of $iTT^{EQ}$ into classical set theory (ZFC) with two strongly inaccessible cardinals. Indeed, we interpret the quotient sets in classical quotient sets and the first two universes respectively in the set of small sets and in the set of large sets, proved to be actual sets by the presence of the two strongly inaccessible cardinals.

## 4 Small sets are classical

We are going to prove that for small sets in $iTT^{EQ}$ the principle of excluded middle holds, i.e. for any element $a$ of the first universe $U_0$, the judgement $T_0(a) \vee \neg T_0(a)$ *true* holds. This is a consequence of a particular application of the axiom of choice (AC). In topos theory the fact that AC implies the principle of excluded middle was first proved by Diaconescu [Dia75]. The same result is obtained in [MV99] within an extension of $iTT$ with a powerset constructor by adapting the logical proof of [Bel88] about Diaconescu's theorem. Also Hofmann in [Hof95] claimed that the same result can be obtained in the Calculus of Constructions by adding proof-irrelevance at the level of propositions, equiprovability as equality between propositions and extensionality as equality between dependent propositions.

Here, we show that we can recover this proof in a predicative setting with effective quotient sets instead of an impredicative one like a topos. The key point is to simulate the powerset, by quotienting the first two universes under the relation of equiprovability among their elements.
Also in $iTT^{EQ}$, the so called ***intuitionistic axiom of choice***

$$((\forall x \in A)(\exists y \in B)\ C(x,y)) \to ((\exists f \in A \to B)(\forall x \in A)\ C(x, f(x)))\ \mathit{true}$$

is proved by disjoint union sets, exactly as in [Mar84], concluding by true introduction.

We are going to use the axiom of choice on the quotients made out of the first two universes under the equivalence relation of equiprovability, i.e.

$$T_0(x) \leftrightarrow T_0(y)\ \mathit{set}\ [x \in U_0, y \in U_0] \qquad\qquad T_1(x) \leftrightarrow T_1(y)\ \mathit{set}\ [x \in U_1, y \in U_1]$$

Let us put the following abbreviations for $i = 0, 1$

$$\Omega_i \equiv U_i /\ (x,y)T_i(x) \leftrightarrow T_i(y)$$

Since there is a code for $U_0$ in $U_1$, i.e. $\widehat{U_0} \in U_1$, then there is inside $U_1$ the code $\widehat{\Omega_0}$ for $\Omega_o$ such that

$$T_1(\widehat{\Omega_0}) = \Omega_0$$

The reason to use the two universes is due to the possibility of deriving

$$\hat{\mathsf{Id}}(\hat{\Omega}_o, z, [\hat{\top}]) \in U_1\ [z \in \Omega_0]$$

where $\mathsf{T}$ is the singleton set (see [NPS90]). We use the abbreviation $a =_A b$ for $\mathsf{Id}(A, a, b)$, when it is not coded in a universe.
Moreover, if $A$ is a set, we will often write $A$ to mean the judgement $A$ *true*.

We also recall (see [NPS90]) that, in the presence of $U_0$, we can derive

$$\neg(\mathsf{true} =_{\mathsf{Bool}} \mathsf{false})$$

Now, we go on to show the claimed proof of the principle of excluded middle on small sets. As in [MV99], one of the key points is to internalize the truth of sets within the quotients on the universes, simulating the powersets. This is expressed by the following lemma, which is provable by the introduction equality rule on the quotient set in terms of true judgements and by the effectiveness condition.

**Lemma 1.** *For $i = 1, 2$ and any set $a \in U_i$, $[a] =_{\Omega_i} [\widehat{\mathsf{T}}]$ iff $T_i(a)$ true.*

**Proof.** From $[a] =_{\Omega_i} [\widehat{\mathsf{T}}]$ *true* by effectiveness of quotient sets we get $T_i(a) \leftrightarrow T_i(\widehat{\mathsf{T}})$ *true*, but $T_i(\widehat{\mathsf{T}}) = \mathsf{T}$ so $T_i(a)$ *true*. On the other hand, from $T_i(a)$ *true*, we get $T_i(a) \leftrightarrow T_i(\widehat{\mathsf{T}})$ and by the true version of the equality rule on the quotient set we conclude $[a] =_{\Omega_i} [\widehat{\mathsf{T}}]$.
∎

Now, we consider the following abbreviations: for $z \in \Omega_0$

$$E(z) \equiv \mathsf{Id}(\Omega_0, z, [\widehat{\mathsf{T}}])$$

Hence, we prove:

**Proposition 1.** *In $iTT^{EQ}$ the following proposition*

$$(\forall z \in \Sigma_{w \in \Omega_0 \times \Omega_0}\, [\widehat{E(\pi_1(w))} \hat{\vee}\, \widehat{E(\pi_2(w))}] =_{\Omega_1} [\widehat{\mathsf{T}}])$$
$$(\exists x \in \mathsf{Bool})\ (x =_{\mathsf{Bool}} \mathsf{true} \rightarrow E(\pi_1(\pi_1(z)))) \wedge (x =_{\mathsf{Bool}} \mathsf{false} \rightarrow E(\pi_2(\pi_1(z))))$$

*is true.*

**Proof.** Suppose $z \in \Sigma_{w \in \Omega_0 \times \Omega_0}\, [\widehat{E(\pi_1(w))} \hat{\vee}\, \widehat{E(\pi_2(w))}] =_{\Omega_1} [\widehat{\mathsf{T}}]$. Then $\pi_1(z) \in \Omega_0 \times \Omega_0$ and $\pi_2(z)$ is a proof of $[\widehat{E(\pi_1(\pi_1(z)))} \hat{\vee}\, \widehat{E(\pi_2(\pi_1(z)))}] =_{\Omega_1} [\widehat{\mathsf{T}}]$. Thus, by lemma 1 and by the conversion rules for $U_1$, $E(\pi_1(\pi_1(z))) \vee E(\pi_2(\pi_1(z)))$. The result can now be proved by $\vee$-elimination, by putting for example $x = \mathsf{true}$ in the case $E(\pi_1(\pi_1(z)))$ *true*.
∎

Thus, we can use the intuitionistic axiom of choice to obtain:

**Proposition 2.** *In $iTT^{EQ}$ the following proposition*

$$(\exists f \in \Sigma_{w \in \Omega_0 \times \Omega_0}\, [\widehat{E(\pi_1(w))} \hat{\vee}\, \widehat{E(\pi_2(w))}] =_{\Omega_1} [\widehat{\mathsf{T}}] \rightarrow \mathsf{Bool})$$
$$(\forall z \in \Sigma_{w \in \Omega_0 \times \Omega_0}\, [\widehat{E(\pi_1(w))} \hat{\vee}\, \widehat{E(\pi_2(w))}] =_{\Omega_1} [\widehat{\mathsf{T}}])$$
$$(f(z) =_{\mathsf{Bool}} \mathsf{true} \rightarrow E(\pi_1(\pi_1(z)))) \wedge (f(z) =_{\mathsf{Bool}} \mathsf{false} \rightarrow E(\pi_2(\pi_1(z))))$$

*is true.*

Suppose, now, that $a \in U_0$ is the code of a small set; then

$$\langle\langle [a], [\hat{\top}]\rangle, \mathsf{Qax}(\langle \lambda y.\star, \lambda y'.\mathsf{inr}(\mathsf{id}([\hat{\top}]))\rangle)\rangle$$

is an element of the set

$$\Sigma_{w \in \Omega_0 \times \Omega_0}\ [\widehat{E(\pi_1(w))} \hat{\vee}\ \widehat{E(\pi_2(w))}] =_{\Omega_1} [\hat{\top}]$$

where $\star \in \top$ is the only element of the singleton set. In fact, $\langle [a], [\hat{\top}]\rangle \in \Omega_0 \times \Omega_0$ and

$$\langle \lambda y.\star, \lambda y'.\mathsf{inr}(\mathsf{id}([\hat{\top}]))\rangle \in \mathsf{Id}(\Omega_0, [a], [\hat{\top}]) \vee \mathsf{Id}(\Omega_0, [\hat{\top}], [\hat{\top}]) \leftrightarrow \top$$

from which, since

$$\mathsf{Id}(\Omega_0, [a], [\hat{\top}]) \vee \mathsf{Id}(\Omega_0, [\hat{\top}], [\hat{\top}]) \leftrightarrow \top \ = \ T_1(\widehat{E([a])} \hat{\vee}\ \widehat{E([\hat{\top}])}) \leftrightarrow T_1(\hat{\top})$$

by the equality rule on the quotient set we get

$$\mathsf{Qax}(\langle \lambda y.\star, \lambda y'.\mathsf{inr}(\mathsf{id}([\hat{\top}]))\rangle) \in [\widehat{E([a])} \hat{\vee}\ \widehat{E([\hat{\top}])}] =_{\Omega_1} [\hat{\top}]$$

Analogously,

$$\langle\langle [\hat{\top}], [a]\rangle, \mathsf{Qax}(\langle \lambda y.\star, \lambda y'.\mathsf{inl}(\mathsf{id}([\hat{\top}]))\rangle)\rangle$$

is an element of the set

$$\Sigma_{w \in \Omega_0 \times \Omega_0}\ [\widehat{E(\pi_1(w))} \hat{\vee}\ \widehat{E(\pi_2(w))}] =_{\Omega_1} [\hat{\top}]$$

Let us put for $w \in \Omega_0$

$$\mathsf{q}_1(w) \equiv \langle\langle w, [\hat{\top}]\rangle, \mathsf{Qax}(\langle \lambda y.\star, \lambda y'.\mathsf{inr}(\mathsf{id}([\hat{\top}]))\rangle)\rangle$$

and

$$\mathsf{q}_2(w) \equiv \langle\langle [\hat{\top}], w\rangle, \mathsf{Qax}(\langle \lambda y.\star, \lambda y'.\mathsf{inl}(\mathsf{id}([\hat{\top}]))\rangle)\rangle$$

Now, let $f$ be the choice function obtained by $\exists$-elimination rule on the judgement in the proposition 2; then $f(\mathsf{q}_1([a])) =_{\mathsf{Bool}} \mathsf{true} \to E([a])$. But

$$(f(\mathsf{q}_1([a])) =_{\mathsf{Bool}} \mathsf{true}) \ \vee \ (f(\mathsf{q}_1([a])) =_{\mathsf{Bool}} \mathsf{false})$$

since the set Bool is decidable (for a proof see [NPS90], page 177), and hence, by $\vee$-elimination, lemma 1 and a little intuitionistic logic, one gets that

$$(1) \quad T_0(a) \ \vee \ (f(\mathsf{q}_1([a])) =_{\mathsf{Bool}} \mathsf{false})$$

and in an analogous way

$$(2) \quad T_0(a) \ \vee \ (f(\mathsf{q}_2([a])) =_{\mathsf{Bool}} \mathsf{true})$$

Thus, by using distributivity on the conjunction of (1) and (2), one finally obtains

**Proposition 3.** *For any small set $a \in U_0$ in $iTT^{EQ}$ the following proposition*

$$(\exists f \in \Sigma_{w \in \Omega_0 \times \Omega_0} [\widehat{E(\pi_1(w))} \hat{\vee} \widehat{E(\pi_2(w))}] =_{\Omega_1} [\hat{\top}] \to \mathsf{Bool}) \\ T_0(a) \vee (f(\mathsf{q}_1([a])) =_{\mathsf{Bool}} \mathsf{false}) \wedge f(\mathsf{q}_2([a])) =_{\mathsf{Bool}} \mathsf{true})$$

*is true.*

Now, we proceed by $\exists$-elimination assuming for some proof-term $f$

$$T_0(a) \vee (f(\mathsf{q}_1([a])) =_{\mathsf{Bool}} \mathsf{false}) \wedge f(\mathsf{q}_2([a])) =_{\mathsf{Bool}} \mathsf{true})$$

on which we are going to apply $\vee$-elimination to prove the principle of excluded middle for $T_0(a)$.
But, first of all, note that if we assume $T_0(a)$ *true* then $[a] =_{\Omega_0} [\hat{\top}]$ *true* by lemma 1 and hence

$$\mathsf{q}_1([a]) =_{\Sigma(\Omega_0 \times \Omega_0, \ldots)} \mathsf{q}_1([\hat{\top}])$$

by the elimination rule of the intensional propositional equality with respect to the proposition

$$\mathsf{q}_1(x) =_{\Sigma(\Omega_0 \times \Omega_0, \ldots)} \mathsf{q}_1(y) \; [x \in \Omega_0, y \in \Omega_0]$$

Thus, $f(\mathsf{q}_1([a])) =_{\mathsf{Bool}} f(\mathsf{q}_1([\hat{\top}]))$ and in a similar way from the same assumption we can also prove

$$f(\mathsf{q}_2([a])) =_{\mathsf{Bool}} f(\mathsf{q}_2([\hat{\top}]))$$

Hence, since by the uniqueness of propositional equality proofs UIP we get a proof-term of

$$\pi_2(\mathsf{q}_1([\hat{\top}])) =_{[\widehat{E([\hat{\top}])} \hat{\vee} \widehat{E([\hat{\top}])}] =_{\Omega_1} [\hat{\top}]} \pi_2(\mathsf{q}_2([\hat{\top}]))$$

as $\pi_1(\mathsf{q}_1([\hat{\top}])) = \langle [\hat{\top}], [\hat{\top}] \rangle = \pi_1(\mathsf{q}_2([\hat{\top}]))$, we conclude by the elimination rule of the propositional equality that

$$\mathsf{q}_1([\hat{\top}])\rangle =_{\Sigma(\Omega_0 \times \Omega_0, \ldots)} \mathsf{q}_2([\hat{\top}])$$

and therefore by transitivity

$$f(\mathsf{q}_1([a])) =_{\mathsf{Bool}} f(\mathsf{q}_2([a]))$$

Then if we also assume

$$(f(\mathsf{q}_1([a])) =_{\mathsf{Bool}} \mathsf{false}) \wedge (f(\mathsf{q}_2([a])) =_{\mathsf{Bool}} \mathsf{true}) \; true$$

we conclude $\mathsf{true} =_{\mathsf{Bool}} \mathsf{false}$ *true*. But we know that we can derive an element of $\neg(\mathsf{true} =_{\mathsf{Bool}} \mathsf{false})$. Hence, under the assumption

$$(f(\mathsf{q}_1([a])) =_{\mathsf{Bool}} \mathsf{false}) \wedge (f(\mathsf{q}_2([a])) =_{\mathsf{Bool}} \mathsf{true}),$$

the judgement $\neg T_0(a)$ *true* holds. So, from proposition 3, by $\exists$-elimination and by $\vee$-elimination applying $\vee$-introduction when the first disjunct is assumed and using the above argument when the latter disjunct is assumed, we can conclude $(T_0(a) \vee \neg T_0(a))$ *true* and

$$\Pi_{a \in U_0} T_0(a) \vee \neg T_0(a) \; true$$

To sum up the key points to reproduce the proof of the principle of excluded middle on small sets are the following:

- we use the axiom of choice, by quantifying on

$$\Sigma_{w \in \Omega_0 \times \Omega_0} [\widehat{E(\pi_1(w))} \hat{\vee} \widehat{E(\pi_2(w))}] =_{\Omega_1} [\hat{\top}]$$

  instead of $\Sigma_{w \in \Omega_0 \times \Omega_0} E(\pi_1(w)) \vee E(\pi_2(w))$ in order to forget the proof-term of the disjunction and hence we need the second universe to encode

$$E(z) \equiv \mathsf{Id}(\hat{\Omega}_o, z, [\hat{\top}]) \; [z \in \Omega_0]$$

  and to express at the propositional level when it is true;
- we exhibit a proof-term $\mathsf{q}_1$ by means of the equality rule on the quotient set such that for $a \in U_0$

$$\mathsf{q}_1([a]) \in \Sigma_{\Omega_0 \times \Omega_0} [\widehat{E(\pi_1(w))} \hat{\vee} \widehat{E(\pi_2(w))}] =_{\Omega_1} [\hat{\top}]$$

  in order to prove under the assumption $[a] =_{\Omega_0} [\hat{\top}]$ *true*

$$\mathsf{q}_1([a]) =_{\Sigma_{w \in \Omega_0 \times \Omega_0} \cdots} \mathsf{q}_1([\hat{\top}]) \; true \quad \text{and} \quad \mathsf{q}_2([a]) =_{\Sigma_{w \in \Omega_0 \times \Omega_0} \cdots} \mathsf{q}_2([\hat{\top}]) \; true$$

- we use the uniqueness of propositional equality proofs in order to prove

$$\mathsf{q}_1([\hat{\top}]) =_{\Sigma_{w \in \Omega_0 \times \Omega_0} \cdots} \mathsf{q}_2([\hat{\top}])$$

In conclusion, if we had type-theoretical rules that make all the rules of $iTT^{EQ}$ admissible such that we can prove that $C$ *true* holds in $iTT^{EQ}$ if and only if there exists a proof element for the proposition $C$, then we would have a proof element for the proposition $\Pi_{a \in U_0} T_0(a) \vee \neg T_0(a)$, which is expected to fail for small sets, according to an intuitionistic explanation of connectives.

## 5 Extensional quotient sets in extensional set theory

The proof that effectiveness of quotient sets yields classical logic for small sets can also be done within the extensional version of Martin-Löf's Intuitionistic Type Theory with true judgements, called *eTT*, extended with the rules for quotient sets, as in Nuprl [Con86], to which we add the effectiveness condition and the introduction and conversion rules of the codes for quotient sets into the first two universes.

About the rules of true judgements, we only recall the case of the set of the extensional propositional equality Eq (see [NPS90]). The formation, introduction, elimination and conversion rules are the following:

**Extensional Equality set**

$$\text{Eq)}\ \frac{C\ set\quad c \in C\quad d \in C}{\mathsf{Eq}(C,c,d)\ set} \qquad \text{I-Eq)}\ \frac{c \in C}{\mathsf{eq_C}(c) \in \mathsf{Eq}(C,c,c)}$$

$$\text{E-Eq)}\ \frac{p \in \mathsf{Eq}(C,c,d)}{c = d \in C} \qquad \text{C-Eq)}\ \frac{p \in \mathsf{Eq}(C,c,d)}{p = \mathsf{eq_C}(c) \in \mathsf{Eq}(C,c,d)}$$

In particular the elimination rule yields the admissibility of the following rule on true judgements:

$$\frac{\mathsf{Eq}(A,a,b)\ true}{a = b \in A}$$

We extend $eTT$ with the rules of extensional quotient sets:

**Quotient set**

$$\frac{\begin{array}{l} R(x,y)\ set\ [x \in A, y \in A] \\ c_1 \in R(x,x)[x \in A], \qquad c_2 \in R(y,x)[x \in A, y \in A, z \in R(x,y)] \\ c_3 \in R(x,z)[x \in A, y \in A, z \in A, w \in R(x,y), w' \in R(y,z)] \end{array}}{A/R\ set}$$

**I-quotient**

$$\frac{a \in A\quad A/R\ set}{[a] \in A/R}$$

**eq-quotient**

$$\frac{a \in A\quad b \in A\quad d \in R(a,b)}{[a] = [b] \in A/R}$$

**E-quotient**

$$\frac{s \in A/R\quad l(x) \in L([x])\ [x \in A]\quad l(x) = l(y) \in L([x])\ [x \in A, y \in A, d \in R(x,y)]}{\mathsf{Q}(l,s) \in L(s)}$$

**C-quotient**

$$\frac{a \in A\quad l(x) \in L([x])\ [x \in A]\quad l(x) = l(y) \in L([x])\ [x \in A, y \in A, d \in R(x,y)]}{\mathsf{Q}(l,[a]) = l(a) \in L([a])}$$

Then we make extensional quotients effective through the following condition in terms of true judgements:

**Effectiveness condition**

$$\frac{a \in A\quad b \in A\quad [a] = [b] \in A/R}{R(a,b)\ true}$$

We also add the codes of quotient sets in the introduction rules of the first two universes and their corresponding conversion rules, as in section 3. Note that, like for the intensional propositional equality set, the introduction of equality on quotient sets yields the admissibility of the following rule:

$$\frac{a \in A \quad b \in A \quad R(a,b)\ true}{[a] = [b] \in A/R}$$

This extension of *eTT*, called $eTT^{EQ}$, is consistent, because there exists an interpretation in classical set theory (ZFC) with two strongly inaccessible cardinals. In the presence of the extensional propositional equality set, the rules for intensional quotient sets become equivalent to those of extensional quotient sets and the same holds with respect to the effectiveness condition. So, we can reproduce in $eTT^{EQ}$ the proof of the previous section to derive

$$\Pi_{a \in U_0} T_0(a) \vee \neg T_0(a))\ true$$

which is expected to fail for small sets.

Note that this proof can not be recovered in the extensional version of set theory with effective quotient sets restricted to mono equivalence relations, that is equivalence relations inhabited by at most one proof. This kind of quotients is operating in the extensional type theory of Heyting pretoposes [Mai97] and also of toposes [Mai98], where even effectiveness can be type-theoretically expressed.

I would like to thank Silvio Valentini, Peter Aczel and Giovanni Sambin for helpful discussions that stimulated the investigation on this topic, Peter Dybier for his comments on a preliminary version of this paper and lastly the referees for their valuable suggestions.

## References

[Acz78] P. Aczel. The type theoretic interpretation of constructive set theory. In L. Paris MacIntyre, A. Pacholski, editor, *Logic Colloquium '77*. North Holland, Amsterdam, 1978.

[Bel88] J.L. Bell. *Toposes and Local Set Theories: an introduction*. Claredon Press, Oxford, 1988.

[Bel97] J.L. Bell. Zorn's lemma and complete boolean algebras in intuitionistic type theories. *The Journal of Symbolic Logic.*, 62:1265–1279, 1997.

[Con86] R. Constable et al. *Implementing mathematics with the Nuprl Development System*. Prentice Hall, 1986.

[Coq92] T. Coquand. Pattern matching with dependent types. In *Workshop on logical frameworks*, Baastad, 1992. Preliminary Proceedings.

[Dia75] R. Diaconescu. Axiom of choice and complementation. *Proc. Amer. Math. Soc.*, 51:176–178, 1975.

[Dyb97] P. Dybier. A general formulation of simultaneous inductive-recursive definitions in type theory. 1997. To appear in *Journal of Symbolic Logic*.

[GM78] N. Goodman and J. Myhill. Choice implies excluded middle. *Z. Math. Logik Grundlag. Math.*, 24:461, 1978.

[Hof95] M. Hofmann. *Extensional concept in intensional type theory*. PhD thesis, University of Edinburgh, July 1995.

[HS95] M. Hofmann and T. Streicher. The groupoid interpretation of type theory. In J. Smith G. Sambin, editor, *Twenty Five Years of Constructive Type Theory*, pages 83–111. Oxford Science Publications, Venice, 1995.

[Mai97] M.E. Maietti. The internal type theory of an Heyting Pretopos. In E. Gimenez and C.Paulin-Mohring, editors, *Proceedings of Types '96*, LNCS, 1997.

[Mai98] M.E. Maietti. *The type theory of categorical universes.* PhD thesis, University of Padova, February 1998.

[Mar84] P. Martin-Löf. *Intuitionistic Type Theory, notes by G. Sambin of a series of lectures given in Padua, June 1980.* Bibliopolis, Naples, 1984.

[MR77] M. Makkai and G. Reyes. *First order categorical logic.*, volume 611 of *Lecture Notes in Mathematics.* Springer Verlag, 1977.

[MV99] M.E. Maietti and S. Valentini. Can you add power-sets to Martin-Löf intuitionistic type theory? 1999. To appear in *Mathematical Logic Quarterly.*

[NPS90] B. Nordström, K. Peterson, and J. Smith. *Programming in Martin Löf's Type Theory.* Clarendon Press, Oxford, 1990.

[NV97] S. Negri and S. Valentini. Tychonoff's theorem in the framework of formal topologies. *Journal of Symbolic Logic*, 62:1315–1332, 1997.

[Sam87] G. Sambin. Intuitionistic formal spaces - a first communication. *Mathematical logic and its applications*, pages 187–204, 1987.

[Val95] S. Valentini. The forget-restore principle: a paradigmatic example. In J. Smith G. Sambin, editor, *Twenty Five Years of Constructive Type Theory*, pages 275–283. Oxford Science Publications, Venice, 1995.

# Algorithms for Equality and Unification in the Presence of Notational Definitions

Frank Pfenning and Carsten Schürmann *

Carnegie Mellon University
School of Computer Science
fp@cs.cmu.edu carsten@cs.cmu.edu

## 1 Introduction

Notational definitions are pervasive in mathematical practice and are therefore supported in most automated theorem proving systems such as Coq [B+98], PVS [ORS92], Lego [LP92], or Isabelle [Pau94]. Semantically, notational definitions are transparent, that is, one obtains the meaning of an expression by interpreting the result of expanding all definitions. Pragmatically, however, expanding all definitions as they are encountered is unsatisfactory, since it can be computationally expensive and complicate the user interface.

In this paper we investigate the interaction of notational definitions with algorithms for testing equality and unification. We propose a syntactic criterion on definitions which avoids their expansion in many cases without losing soundness or completeness with respect to $\beta\delta$-conversion. Our setting is the dependently typed $\lambda$-calculus [HHP93], but, with minor modifications, our results should apply to richer type theories and logics.

The question when definitions need to be expanded is surprisingly subtle and of great practical importance. Most algorithms for equality and unification rely on decomposing a problem

$$c\, M_1 \ldots M_n \doteq c\, N_1 \ldots N_n$$

into

$$M_1 \doteq N_1, \ldots, M_n \doteq N_n.$$

However, if $c$ is defined this is not necessarily complete. For example, if $k = \lambda x.\, c'$ then

$$k\, M \doteq k\, N$$

for *every* $M$ and $N$. Always expanding definitions is computationally expensive, especially when they duplicate their arguments. Expanding them only when the equality between the arguments fails, often performs much redundant computation, and, moreover, is incomplete in the presence of meta-variables. For example, with the same definition for $k$,

$$k\, X \doteq k\, c'$$

* This work was supported by NSF Grant CCR-9619584

would succeed without expanding $k$ with the substitution $X = c'$, even though the most general unifier leaves $X$ uninstantiated.

We identify a class of definitions (called ***strict***) for which decomposition is complete. It also solves a related problem with the completeness of the so-called *occurs-check* during unification by generalizing Huet's ***rigid path*** criterion [Hue75]. Fortunately, most notational definitions are strict in the sense we define. We do not deal with recursive definitions, for example, which require different considerations and have been treated in the literature on functional logic programming [Han94]. Other aspects of notational definitions in mathematical practice have been studied by Griffin [Gri88].

We have implemented a strictness checker and unification algorithm in Twelf [PS98], an implementation of the logical framework LF which supports type reconstruction, logic programming, and theorem proving. It has been applied to a variety of examples from the area of logics and programming languages. The Twelf system is freely available from the Twelf homepage `http://www.cs.cmu.edu/~twelf`.

This paper is organized as follows. In Section 2 we describe a spine formulation of LF with definitions, and in Section 3 a small logic as running example. In Section 4 we describe the strictness criterion and show its correctness. We generalize our results from conversion to unification in Section 5 and conclude and describe future work in Section 6.

## 2 Language

The type theory underlying the logical framework LF [HHP93] is divided into three levels: objects, types, and kinds. We deviate from standard formulations by adopting a spine notation for application [CP97] and by adding definitions. In spine notation, we write $c \cdot M_1; ...; M_n; \mathrm{nil}$ for a term $c\ M_1\ ...\ M_n$ to make its head explicit. It contributes significantly to the concise presentation of the theory in Section 4 and corresponds closely to the implementation in Twelf. We use $a$ for constant type families, $x$ for object-level variables, and $c$ for constructors (that is, declared constants without a definition) and $d$ for defined constants. For simplicity, we only allow definitions at the level of objects, but the results also apply to definitions at the level of types.

$$
\begin{array}{ll}
\text{Kinds:} & K ::= \mathrm{type} \mid \Pi x{:}A.\, K \\
\text{Types:} & A ::= a \cdot S \mid \Pi x{:}A_1.\, A_2 \\
\text{Objects:} & M ::= H \cdot S \mid \lambda x{:}A.\, M \mid M \cdot S \\
\text{Heads:} & H ::= x \mid c \mid d \\
\text{Spines:} & S ::= \mathrm{nil} \mid M; S \\
\text{Signature:} & \Sigma ::= \cdot \mid \Sigma, a : K \mid \Sigma, c : A \mid \Sigma, d : A = M \\
\text{Contexts:} & \Gamma ::= \cdot \mid \Gamma, x : A
\end{array}
$$

$a \cdot S$ and $H \cdot S$ are our notation for the application of a variable or constant to arguments given as a *spine*. Such terms are in weak head-normal form unless the constant at the head is defined. For the sake of readability, we omit the trailing nil from spines, and if the spine is empty, we also omit the "$\cdot$". $\Pi x : A_1 . A_2$ is a function type, which we may write as $A_1 \to A_2$ if $x$ does not occur free in $A_2$. In the examples we sometimes omit types and write definitions as $d = M$.

As in [CP97] we assume throughout that all objects are in $\eta$-long form. Note that $\eta$-long forms are preserved under $\beta\delta$-conversion. Working only with $\eta$-long forms simplifies the presentation of the formal judgments and proofs, but is not essential. Our results still hold if we drop this assumption, both with and without $\eta$-conversion. The notion of definitional equality is then based on $\beta\delta$-conversion where $\delta$-reduction expands definitions.

$$\begin{aligned} M \cdot \mathrm{nil} &\longrightarrow_\beta M \\ (\lambda x : A.\, M) \cdot (N; S) &\longrightarrow_\beta ([N/x]M) \cdot S \\ d \cdot S &\longrightarrow_\delta M \cdot S \qquad\qquad \text{where } d : A = M \in \Sigma \end{aligned}$$

A *$\beta$-redex* has the form $M \cdot S$, a *$\delta$-redex* the form $d \cdot S$.

We assume that constants and variables are declared at most once in a signature and context, respectively. As usual we apply tacit renaming of bound variables to maintain this assumption and to guarantee capture-avoiding substitution.

The LF type theory is defined by a number of mutually dependent judgments which define valid objects, types, kinds, contexts, and signatures, and, in our case, also heads and spines. We will not reiterate the rules here (see [HHP93,CP97]). The main typing judgments are of the form $\Gamma \vdash_\Sigma M : A$ — expressing that object $M$ has type $A$ in context $\Gamma$ — and $\Gamma \vdash_\Sigma S : A > A'$ — expressing that the spine $S$ acts as a vector of well-typed arguments to a head of type $A$ returning a result of type $A'$. A definition $d : A = M$ is well-formed in a signature $\Sigma$ if $\cdot \vdash_\Sigma M : A$.

We generally assume that signature $\Sigma$ is valid and fixed and therefore omit it from the typing and other related judgments introduced below. We take $\beta\delta$-conversion as our notion of definitional equality which guarantees that every well-typed object has an equivalent *normal form*. Since we also assume that every object is in $\eta$-long form these normal forms are long $\eta\beta\delta$-normal forms. We write $M \xrightarrow{\text{whr}} M'$ for weak head reduction which applies local $\beta$- or $\delta$-reductions.

We write $\Gamma \vdash M_1 \equiv M_2$ to express that two well-typed objects $M_1$ and $M_2$ are equivalent modulo $\beta\delta$-conversion. Similarly, for spines, we write $\Gamma \vdash S_1 \equiv S_2$.

Since all validity judgments are decidable with well-understood algorithms, we tacitly assume that all objects, types, kinds, spines, heads, contexts, and signatures are valid and, for equalities, that both sides have the same type or kind.

Our proofs exploit the following standard properties of definitional equality based on $\beta\delta$-conversion.

*Property 1 (Equivalence).*

1. $\Gamma \vdash M \equiv M$.

2. For all $H_1$, $H_2$ of the form $x$ or $c$,
   $\Gamma \vdash H_1 \cdot S_1 \equiv H_2 \cdot S_2$ iff $H_1 = H_2$ and $\Gamma \vdash S_1 \equiv S_2$
3. $\Gamma \vdash a_1 \cdot S_1 \equiv a_2 \cdot S_2$ iff $a_1 = a_2$ and $\Gamma \vdash S_1 \equiv S_2$
4. $\Gamma \vdash \lambda y{:}A_1.\, M_1 \equiv \lambda y{:}A_2.\, M_2$ iff $\Gamma \vdash A_1 \equiv A_2$ and $\Gamma, y : A_1 \vdash M_1 \equiv M_2$
5. $\Gamma \vdash \Pi y{:}A_1.\, B_1 \equiv \Pi y{:}A_2.\, B_2$ iff $\Gamma \vdash A_1 \equiv A_2$ and $\Gamma, y : A_1 \vdash B_1 \equiv B_2$
6. For all $M_1$, $M_2$ in which $y$ does not occur free,
   $\Gamma, y : A \vdash M_1 \cdot y \equiv M_2 \cdot y$ iff $\Gamma \vdash M_1 \equiv M_2$
7. $\Gamma \vdash M_1; S_1 \equiv M_2; S_2$ iff $\Gamma \vdash M_1 \equiv M_2$ and $\Gamma \vdash S_1 \equiv S_2$
8. If $M_1 \xrightarrow{\text{whr}} M_1'$ and $M_2 \xrightarrow{\text{whr}} M_2'$ then $\Gamma \vdash M_1 \equiv M_2$ iff $\Gamma \vdash M_1' \equiv M_2'$

For a well-typed definition $d : A = M$ the head-normal form of $M$ must always exist and have the shape $M = \lambda x_1 : A_1. \ldots \lambda x_n : A_n. H \cdot S$. We call $x_1, \ldots, x_n$ ***argument parameters***, and all other parameters in the body $H \cdot S$ ***local parameters***.

## 3 Example

To illustrate our algorithms we use the encoding of a small fragment of propositional intuitionistic logic in LF [HHP93].

$$\text{Formulas: } F ::= \top \mid \bot \mid F_1 \supset F_2$$

Formulas are represented as a type and each connective as a constant.

$$\begin{array}{llll} & & \text{o} & : \text{type} \\ \ulcorner \top \urcorner & = \text{true} & \text{true} & : \text{o} \\ \ulcorner \bot \urcorner & = \text{false} & \text{false} & : \text{o} \\ \ulcorner F_1 \supset F_2 \urcorner & = \text{imp} \cdot (\ulcorner F_1 \urcorner; \ulcorner F_2 \urcorner) & \text{imp} & : \text{o} \to \text{o} \to \text{o} \end{array}$$

This simple logic can now be extended by negation in the usual way, by defining $\neg F \overset{\text{def}}{=} F \supset \bot$, which leads to a definition of the constant *not* in terms of the other constants.

$$\text{not} : \text{o} \to \text{o} = \lambda F{:}\text{o}.\, \text{imp} \cdot (F; \text{false})$$

We write $\vdash F$ to express that the formula $F$ has a natural deduction, using the following four rules:

$$\frac{}{\vdash \top}\top I \qquad \frac{\vdash \bot}{\vdash F}\bot E \qquad \frac{\begin{array}{c}\overline{\vdash F}^{\,u} \\ \vdots \\ \vdash G\end{array}}{\vdash F \supset G}\supset I^u \qquad \frac{\vdash F \supset G \quad \vdash F}{\vdash G}\supset E$$

As shown in [HHP93], there is an adequate encoding of this calculus in LF. The judgment $\vdash F$ is represented as a dependent type family, and the four rules as object constants.

$$\begin{array}{ll} \mathrm{nd} & : \mathrm{o} \to \mathrm{type} \\ \mathrm{truei} & : \mathrm{nd} \cdot \mathrm{true} \\ \mathrm{falsee} & : \Pi F{:}\mathrm{o}.\, \mathrm{nd} \cdot \mathrm{false} \to \mathrm{nd} \cdot F \\ \mathrm{impi} & : \Pi F{:}\mathrm{o}.\, \Pi G{:}\mathrm{o}.\, (\mathrm{nd} \cdot F \to \mathrm{nd} \cdot G) \to \mathrm{nd} \cdot (\mathrm{imp} \cdot (F; G)) \\ \mathrm{impe} & : \Pi F{:}\mathrm{o}.\, \Pi G{:}\mathrm{o}.\, \mathrm{nd} \cdot (\mathrm{imp} \cdot (F; G)) \to \mathrm{nd} \cdot F \to \mathrm{nd} \cdot G \end{array}$$

The usual introduction and elimination rules of $\neg F$ can then be formulated as derived rules of inference.

$$\dfrac{\begin{array}{c} \overline{\vdash F}^{\,u} \\ \vdots \\ \vdash \bot \end{array}}{\vdash \neg F}\neg I^u \qquad \dfrac{\vdash \neg F \quad \vdash F}{\vdash \bot}\neg E$$

Clearly, $\neg I^u$ is a restriction of $\supset I^u$ and $\neg E$ is a restriction of $\supset E$. We represent these rules as defined constants in LF. This is an example of a notational definition at the level of derivations.

$$\begin{array}{rl} \mathrm{noti} & : \Pi F{:}o.\, (\mathrm{nd} \cdot F \to \mathrm{nd} \cdot \mathrm{false}) \to \mathrm{nd} \cdot (\mathrm{not} \cdot F) \\ & = \lambda F{:}o.\, \lambda u{:}(\mathrm{nd} \cdot F \to \mathrm{nd} \cdot \mathrm{false}).\, \mathrm{impi} \cdot (F; \mathrm{false}; u) \\ \mathrm{note} & : \Pi F{:}o.\, \mathrm{nd} \cdot (\mathrm{not} \cdot F) \to \mathrm{nd} \cdot F \to \mathrm{nd} \cdot \mathrm{false} \\ & = \lambda F{:}o.\, \lambda u_1{:}\mathrm{nd} \cdot (\mathrm{not} \cdot F).\, \lambda u_2{:}\mathrm{nd} \cdot F.\, \mathrm{impe} \cdot (F; \mathrm{false}; u_1; u_2) \end{array}$$

# 4 Definitions and Algorithms for Equality

In this paper we study only notational definitions. We do not explicitly treat other forms of definitions, such as recursive definitions, but our techniques are applicable in more general circumstances. For example, in MLF [HP98] — an implementation of LF extended with a module system — definitions are used to express logical interpretations.

Semantically, definitions are transparent, that is, the meaning of any term can be determined by expanding all definitions. But from a pragmatic point of view expanding all definitions is unsatisfactory for several reasons. First of all, even if the definitions are simple, their expansion is likely to be required frequently, in the core of an implementation. Secondly, definitions can duplicate their arguments, leading to a potential explosion size unless special implementation techniques are employed. Thirdly, expanding all definitions means that error messages and other output are often rendered illegible.

In this section we characterize a class of definitions whose expansion can frequently be avoided when comparing terms for equality. Based on these results, we show in the next section that the same criterion can be used to even greater benefit in unification.

### 4.1 Injectivity

Most algorithms for equality and unification rely on decomposing a problem

$$H \cdot S_1 \equiv H \cdot S_2 \tag{1}$$

into

$$S_1 \equiv S_2 \tag{2}$$

but if $H = d$ and $d : A = M$ is a notational definition, then (1) stands for

$$M \cdot S_1 \equiv M \cdot S_2. \tag{3}$$

Since $\equiv$ is a congruence, it follows trivially that (2) always implies (3). But the reverse does not necessarily hold, for example, if $M$ ignores an argument. We call those terms $M$ for which (3) implies (2) *injective*. For definitions which are injective, decomposition is complete. Recall that we assume all signatures, context, objects, equations, *etc.* to be valid.

**Definition 1 (Injectivity).** *A definition $d : A = M$ is* injective *iff for all contexts $\Delta$ and spines $S_1$ and $S_2$,*

$$\Delta \vdash M \cdot S_1 \equiv M \cdot S_2 \quad \textit{implies} \quad \Delta \vdash S_1 \equiv S_2.$$

### 4.2 Strictness

Many algorithms for equality avoid expanding definitions in equations of the form $d \cdot S_1 \equiv d \cdot S_2$ until the equality of the arguments $S_1 \equiv S_2$ fails. If that happens, definitions are expanded, and the algorithm continues with the expanded terms, probably redoing much previous computation. Without further improvements such an algorithm could be exponential for first-order terms and worse at higher types. In contrast, if we know that $d$ is injective, the algorithm can fail immediately.

Since injectivity is a semantic criterion, we have developed a syntactic criterion called ***strictness*** which guarantees injectivity and which can be easily checked. Informally, a notational definition is said to be strict, if each argument parameter occurs at least once in a ***rigid position*** [Hue75], applied only to pairwise distinct local parameters. If there are no defined constants, the rigid positions in a $\beta$-normal form are those resulting from erasing the spines following argument parameters. If there are defined constants we distinguish (inductively) between strict and non-strict ones: the former are treated like constructors, the latter are expanded. We also do not consider the head of a definition to be a rigid position (see Example 2). Our notion of strictness is a crude approximation of the notion of strictness found in functional programming.

The definition of *not*, for example, is strict, because $F$ appears in a rigid position. *noti* is also strict, because its argument parameters $F$ and $u$ occur in rigid positions. The same holds for *note*, because $F$, $u_1$, and $u_2$ occur in rigid positions.

In the following we analyze some counterexamples to illustrate strictness and its relation to injectivity.

*Example 1 (Universal quantification).* The logic presented in Section 3 can be extended to first order by introducing terms $T$ and a universal quantifier

$$F ::= \ldots \mid \forall x.F$$

In LF, terms are represented by objects of a new type i, and the universal quantifier by a new constructor

$$\mathrm{forall} : (\mathrm{i} \to \mathrm{o}) \to \mathrm{o}.$$

The (true) formula $(\forall x.F(x)) \supset F(t)$ can be defined as

$$\mathrm{allinst} = \lambda F{:}\mathrm{i} \to \mathrm{o}.\, \lambda T{:}\mathrm{i}.\, \mathrm{imp} \cdot (\mathrm{forall} \cdot F; F \cdot T)$$

allinst is not strict because $T$ does not occur in a rigid position, even though $F$ does. Indeed, if $F(x)$ does not actually depend on $x$, then $t$ is not uniquely determined and

$$\mathrm{allinst} \cdot (F; T) \equiv \mathrm{allinst} \cdot (F; T')$$

holds even if $T$ and $T'$ are different.

*Example 2 (Identity).* The definition of the identity at function type, $\mathrm{id} = \lambda F{:}\, \mathrm{o} \to \mathrm{o}.\, \lambda G{:}\mathrm{o}.\, F \cdot G$, is not strict for two reasons: the only occurrence of $F$ is at the head of the definition, and the only occurrence of $G$ is as an argument to $F$. It is also not injective, because

$$\mathrm{id} \cdot (\lambda F{:}\mathrm{o}.\, \mathrm{true}; \mathrm{false}) \equiv \mathrm{id} \cdot (\lambda F{:}\mathrm{o}.\, \mathrm{true}; \mathrm{true})$$

can be reduced to

$$\mathrm{true} \equiv \mathrm{true}.$$

*Example 3 (Identity at base type).* The definition $\mathrm{id}' = \lambda F : \mathrm{o}.\, F$ is not strict since $F$ occurs at the head of the definition. However, the identity at base type is injective. We must rule it out for different reasons (see the discussion of the occurs-check in unification in Section 5).

*Example 4 (Application to constant).* Consider $\mathrm{at} = \lambda F{:}\mathrm{o} \to \mathrm{o}.\, \mathrm{not} \cdot (F \cdot \mathrm{true})$. Note, that the argument to $F$ is not a local parameter but a constant. The definition is hence not strict. The equality problem

$$\mathrm{at} \cdot (\lambda F{:}\mathrm{o}.\, F) \equiv \mathrm{at} \cdot (\lambda F{:}\mathrm{o}.\, \mathrm{true})$$

can be expanded to

$$\begin{aligned}&(\lambda F{:}\mathrm{o} \to \mathrm{o}.\, \mathrm{not} \cdot (F \cdot \mathrm{true})) \cdot (\lambda F{:}\mathrm{o}.\, F)\\ &\quad \equiv (\lambda F{:}\mathrm{o} \to \mathrm{o}.\, \mathrm{not} \cdot (F \cdot \mathrm{true})) \cdot (\lambda F{:}\mathrm{o}.\, \mathrm{true})\end{aligned}$$

which holds because $\mathrm{not} \cdot \mathrm{true} \equiv \mathrm{not} \cdot \mathrm{true}$. Hence, the definition is not injective.

The first part in the definition of strictness formalizes the requirement that arguments to rigid occurrences of argument parameters must be pairwise distinct local parameters. This is exactly the requirement imposed on *higher-order patterns* [Mil91]. In the judgments below we generally use $\Gamma$ for a context consisting of argument parameters to a definition, and $\Delta$ consisting of local parameters.

**Definition 2 (Pattern spine).** *Let $\Delta$ be a context, $S$ be a spine. $S$ is a* pattern spine *iff $\Delta \vdash S$ pat holds which is defined by the following rules:*

$$\frac{}{\Delta \vdash \text{nil } pat}\text{ps\_nil} \qquad \frac{\Delta_1, \Delta_2 \vdash S \; pat}{\Delta_1, x : A, \Delta_2 \vdash x; S \; pat}\text{ps\_cons}$$

The formal system for strictness is defined by four mutually dependent judgments. The central judgment of *local strictness*, $\Gamma; \Delta \vdash_x M$, enforces that the argument parameter $x$ occurs in a rigid position in $M$ where it is applied to a pattern spine. Every argument parameter must be locally strict, which is enforced by *global strictness*, $\Gamma \Vdash M$. As an auxiliary judgment we use *relative strictness*, $\Gamma \Vdash_x M$ where the leading abstractions in $M$ are treated as argument parameters. $\beta$-redices and $\delta$-redices involving non-strict defined constants are reduced by $M \longrightarrow M'$.

**Definition 3 (Strictness).** *Let $\Gamma$ be a context of argument parameters, and $\Delta$ a context of local parameters. We define*

| | |
|---|---|
| $M \longrightarrow M'$ | *$M$ weak head-reduces to $M'$* |
| $\Gamma; \Delta \vdash_x M$ | *$x$ is locally strict in $M$* |
| $\Gamma \Vdash_x M$ | *$x$ is strict in $M$* |
| $\Gamma \Vdash M$ | *$M$ is strict* |

*by the rules in Figure 1. We say that the definition $d : A = M$ is strict if $\cdot \Vdash M$ holds.*

The main technical contribution of this paper is that strict definitions are injective. The proof is non-trivial and requires a sequence of properties sketched below.

**Lemma 1 (Pattern spines).** *Let $S$ be a spine s.t. $\Delta \vdash S$ pat and $M_1$ and $M_2$ be objects valid in $\Gamma$ disjoint from $\Delta$.*

*If $\Gamma, \Delta \vdash M_1 \cdot S \equiv M_2 \cdot S$ then $\Gamma \vdash M_1 \equiv M_2$*

*Proof.* By induction over the derivation of $\Delta \vdash S$ pat.

Using inductions over local, relative, and global strictness, we can then show the completeness direction of our claim for strict $d : A = M$:

$$\Gamma \vdash M \cdot S_1 \equiv M \cdot S_2 \;\text{ implies }\; \Gamma \vdash S_1 \equiv S_2.$$

We cannot prove this directly by induction, but must generalize to the following lemma which requires substitutions $\sigma$. We use standard notation for substitutions, which must always be the identity on local parameters (usually declared

$$\frac{d : A = M \in \Sigma \quad \cdot \nVdash M}{d \cdot S \longrightarrow M \cdot S}\ \mathsf{nr\_delta} \qquad \frac{M \cdot S \longrightarrow_{\beta} M'}{M \cdot S \longrightarrow M'}\ \mathsf{nr\_beta}$$

$$\frac{\Gamma; \Delta \vdash_x A}{\Gamma; \Delta \vdash_x \lambda y : A. M}\ \mathsf{ls\_ld} \qquad \frac{\Gamma; \Delta, y : A \vdash_x M}{\Gamma; \Delta \vdash_x \lambda y : A. M}\ \mathsf{ls\_lb}$$

$$\frac{\Gamma; \Delta \vdash_x A_1}{\Gamma; \Delta \vdash_x \Pi y : A_1. A_2}\ \mathsf{ls\_pd} \qquad \frac{\Gamma; \Delta, y : A_1 \vdash_x A_2}{\Gamma; \Delta \vdash_x \Pi y : A_1. A_2}\ \mathsf{ls\_pb}$$

$$\frac{M \longrightarrow M' \quad \Gamma; \Delta \vdash_x M'}{\Gamma; \Delta \vdash_x M}\ \mathsf{ls\_red} \qquad \frac{d : A = M \in \Sigma \quad \cdot \Vdash M \quad \Gamma; \Delta \vdash_x S}{\Gamma; \Delta \vdash_x d \cdot S}\ \mathsf{ls\_d}$$

$$\frac{\Gamma; \Delta \vdash_x S}{\Gamma; \Delta \vdash_x c \cdot S}\ \mathsf{ls\_c} \qquad \frac{\Gamma; \Delta \vdash_x S}{\Gamma; \Delta \vdash_x a \cdot S}\ \mathsf{ls\_a}$$

$$\frac{\Delta \vdash S \ \mathrm{pat}}{\Gamma; \Delta \vdash_x x \cdot S}\ \mathsf{ls\_pat} \qquad \frac{y : A \in \Delta \quad \Gamma; \Delta \vdash_x S}{\Gamma; \Delta \vdash_x y \cdot S}\ \mathsf{ls\_var}$$

no rule for $\Gamma; \Delta \vdash_x y \cdot S$ for $x \neq y$, $y : A \in \Gamma$

$$\frac{\Gamma; \Delta \vdash_x M}{\Gamma; \Delta \vdash_x M; S}\ \mathsf{ls\_hd} \qquad \frac{\Gamma; \Delta \vdash_x S}{\Gamma; \Delta \vdash_x M; S}\ \mathsf{ls\_sp}$$

$$\frac{M \longrightarrow M' \quad \Gamma \Vdash_x M'}{\Gamma \Vdash_x M}\ \mathsf{rs\_red} \qquad \frac{d : A = M \in \Sigma \quad \cdot \Vdash M \quad \Gamma; \cdot \vdash_x d \cdot S}{\Gamma \Vdash_x d \cdot S}\ \mathsf{rs\_d}$$

$$\frac{\Gamma; \cdot \vdash_x c \cdot S}{\Gamma \Vdash_x c \cdot S}\ \mathsf{rs\_c} \qquad \frac{\Gamma, y : A \Vdash_x M}{\Gamma \Vdash_x \lambda y : A. M}\ \mathsf{rs\_lam}$$

$$\frac{M \longrightarrow M' \quad \Gamma \Vdash M'}{\Gamma \Vdash M}\ \mathsf{gs\_red} \qquad \frac{d : A = M \in \Sigma \quad \Gamma \Vdash M \cdot S}{\Gamma \Vdash d \cdot S}\ \mathsf{gs\_d}$$

$$\frac{}{\Gamma \Vdash c \cdot S}\ \mathsf{gs\_c} \qquad \frac{\Gamma, x : A \Vdash_x M \quad \Gamma, x : A \Vdash M}{\Gamma \Vdash \lambda x : A. M}\ \mathsf{gs\_lam}$$

**Fig. 1.** A formal system for strictness

in $\Delta$). Because of possible dependencies, a substitution which maps variables in $\Gamma$ to objects with variables in $\Gamma'$ will map a parameter context $\Delta$ to a context $\Delta'$ where each declaration $y : A$ in $\Delta$ is mapped to $y : A[\sigma]$. We write $\Gamma'; \Delta' \vdash \sigma : \Gamma; \Delta$ for valid substitutions.

**Lemma 2 (Completeness).** *Let $\sigma_1, \sigma_2$ by substitutions which satisfy $\Gamma'; \Delta' \vdash \sigma_1 : \Gamma; \Delta$ and $\Gamma'; \Delta' \vdash \sigma_2 : \Gamma; \Delta$, respectively.*

1. *If $\Gamma; \Delta \vdash_x M$ and $\Gamma', \Delta' \vdash M[\sigma_1] \equiv M[\sigma_2]$ then $\Gamma' \vdash \sigma_1(x) \equiv \sigma_2(x)$.*
2. *If $\Gamma; \Delta \vdash_x S$ and $\Gamma', \Delta' \vdash S[\sigma_1] \equiv S[\sigma_2]$ then $\Gamma' \vdash \sigma_1(x) \equiv \sigma_2(x)$.*
3. *If $\Gamma \Vdash_x M$ and $\Gamma' \vdash M[\sigma_1] \cdot S \equiv M[\sigma_2] \cdot S$ then $\Gamma' \vdash \sigma_1(x) \equiv \sigma_2(x)$.*
4. *If $\Gamma \Vdash M$ and $\Gamma' \vdash M[\sigma_1] \cdot S_1 \equiv M[\sigma_2] \cdot S_2$ then $\Gamma' \vdash S_1 \equiv S_2$.*

*Proof.* The four parts are proven by simultaneous induction over the given strictness derivations, using Lemma 1 and Property 1.

As an immediate corollary, strictness is a sufficient criteria for injectivity.

**Theorem 1 (Injectivity).** *If $d : A = M$ is strict, that is, $\cdot \Vdash M$, then $d : A = M$ is injective.*

*Proof.* Using Lemma 2, part 4, for $\sigma_1 = \sigma_2 = id$

The rules of strictness implicitly define an algorithm to decide if a definition is strict or not. The algorithm traverses the structure of a term visiting all rigid positions. If it finds at least one occurrence of every argument parameter of the definition applied to a pattern spine (ls_pat), it stops and signals success. If the algorithm comes to a defined and strict constant, it applies ls_d or rs_d, otherwise it expands the definition using ls_red or rs_red, respectively. The algorithm terminates for ls_red and rs_red, because definitions cannot be recursive. In an implementation of this algorithm, one would annotate each definition with strictness information, and hence no redundant computation is necessary for ls_d, rs_d, and nr_delta. A minor variant of this algorithm has been implemented in the Twelf system [PS98].

It is easy to verify that all definitions from Section 3 satisfy the strictness condition. Definitions at base type are always strict. Definitions in normal form whose argument parameters are of base type are strict if each argument parameters occurs and it is not the identity. Most notational definitions of these two forms are thus accepted by our criterion.

At higher types, one more frequently encounters definitions which are not injective. Consequently, they cannot be strict according to our definition. A more accurate extension would have to analyze the structure of functional arguments to higher-order definitions, as in the case of strictness analysis for functional programming languages (see, for example, [HM94]). However, we suspect one quickly reaches the point of diminishing returns for this kind of complex analysis.

## 5 Results for Unification

So far we have shown how algorithms for testing equality (that is, $\beta\delta$-convertibility) can be improved by using strictness. In the presence of meta-variables these observations can be generalized to unification. We write $\Psi; \Delta \vdash M_1 \approx M_2$ for a unification problem, where $M_1$, $M_2$ are well-typed objects of the same type which can contain meta-variables declared in $\Psi$. All other parameters which are not subject to instantiation are declared in $\Delta$. So this corresponds to a $\exists\forall$ prefix of a unification problem.

Deciding when to expand definitions is in this setting more subtle than for plain equality algorithms. Expanding them only in the case of failure may return a unifier which is not most general and hence renders the algorithm incomplete. Not expanding them may cause an unnecessary occurs-check failure, yet another source of incompleteness. The following two examples show these situations.

*Example 5 (Most-general unifier).* Let $\mathrm{tr} : \mathrm{o} \to \mathrm{o} = \lambda F{:}\mathrm{o}.\,\mathrm{true}$ a definition, and $X$ a meta variable. The unification problem $X : \mathrm{o}; \cdot \vdash \mathrm{tr} \cdot \mathrm{false} \approx \mathrm{tr} \cdot X$ has as solution $\Theta = \mathrm{false}/X$ if tr is not expanded. Obviously, this solution is not most general, since the most general solution leaves $X$ uninstantiated.

*Example 6 (Occurs-check).* Let tr be the same definition as above, and $X$ a meta variable. The unification problem $X : \mathrm{o}; \cdot \vdash X \approx \mathrm{tr} \cdot X$ has no solution if tr is not expanded, because $X$ occurs on its left-hand side and as an argument to tr. But obviously the problem has a solution, $\Theta = \mathrm{true}/X$.

Most unification algorithms decompose a unification problem of the form

$$\Psi; \Delta \vdash H \cdot S_1 \approx H \cdot S_2 \tag{4}$$

into

$$\Psi; \Delta \vdash S_1 \approx S_2 \tag{5}$$

where $H$ is not a defined constant, otherwise they expand the definition. The unification algorithm for the higher-order pattern fragment [DHKP96] which is employed in Twelf follows the same technique. But strict definitions do not need to be be expanded since, because of injectivity, every unifier $\Theta$ of (4) is also a unifier of (5) and vice versa. This is expressed in the following theorem.

**Theorem 2 (Most general unifiers).** *Let $d : A = M$ be a strict definition. Then the unification problems*

$$\Psi; \Delta \vdash d \cdot S_1 \approx d \cdot S_2$$

*and*

$$\Psi; \Delta \vdash S_1 \approx S_2$$

*have the same set of solutions.*

*Proof.* Let $\Theta$ be a unifier, satisfying $\Psi'; \Delta' \vdash \Theta : \Psi; \Delta$.

$$\begin{array}{rl} & \Psi', \Delta' \vdash (d \cdot S_1)[\Theta] \equiv (d \cdot S_2)[\Theta] \\ \text{iff} & \Psi', \Delta' \vdash d \cdot (S_1[\Theta]) \equiv d \cdot (S_2[\Theta]) \\ \text{iff} & \Psi', \Delta' \vdash S_1[\Theta] \equiv S_2[\Theta] \end{array}$$

This guarantees that the unifier determined by the unification algorithm which does not expand strict definitions unless the two heads differ, is most general.

In addition, we can extend this algorithm to also treat the occurs-check problem correctly: We say that $\Psi; \Delta \vdash X\ y_1\ ..\ y_k \approx M$, where $X$ is defined in $\Psi$ and $y_1, .., y_k$ are parameters in $\Delta$, fails the *occurs-check* if $X$ has a strict occurrence in $M$ (not to be confused with a locally strict one). This is a generalization of Huet's original ***rigid path*** criterion for non-unifiability by allowing some arguments to $X$. Note also that this definition of occurs-check does not need to expand strict definitions. We show that unification problems which fail the occurs-check do not have a unifier.

Informally, one assumes a solution $\Theta$ for $X$ and then counts the number of constructor and parameter occurrences in the normal form of $(X\ y_1\ ..\ y_k)[\Theta]$ and $M[\Theta]$ to arrive at a contradiction, a similar argument as in [Pfe91]. In addition, we make use of two further properties. First, rigid positions in the arguments are preserved under normalization, and second, meta-variables can never occur in the head position of these normal forms.

The proof of the first property is rather difficult because definitions can be nested. In our proof we resolve this problem by first showing the admissibility of eliminating definitions and then inductively normalize each defined constant starting from the inside out. We write $nf(M)$ for the normal form of an object $M$, based on $\beta\delta$-conversion.

**Lemma 3 (Admissibility of eliminating definitions).** *Let $\sigma$ be substitution satisfying $\Gamma'; \Delta' \vdash \sigma : \Gamma; \Delta$. Furthermore, let $x$ be in $\Gamma$, $y$ in $\Gamma'$, and $M, S, \sigma$ in normal form.*

1. *If $\Gamma; \Delta \vdash_x M$, and $\Gamma'; \Delta' \vdash_y \sigma(x)$ then $\Gamma'; \Delta' \vdash_y nf(M[\sigma])$.*
2. *If $\Gamma; \Delta \vdash_x S$ and $\Gamma'; \Delta' \vdash_y \sigma(x)$ then $\Gamma'; \Delta' \vdash_y nf(S[\sigma])$.*
3. *If $\Gamma \Vdash_x M$ and $\Gamma'; \Delta' \vdash_y \sigma(x)$ then $\Gamma'; \Delta' \vdash_y nf(M[\sigma] \cdot S)$.*
4. *If $\Gamma \Vdash M$ and $\Gamma'; \Delta' \vdash_y S$ then $\Gamma'; \Delta' \vdash_y nf(M[\sigma] \cdot S)$.*

*Proof.* The four parts are proven by simultaneous induction over the given strictness derivations.

A direct consequence of the admissibility of eliminating definitions is that the property of being strict is preserved under normalization.

**Lemma 4 (Eliminating definitions).**

1. *If $\Gamma; \Delta \vdash_x M$ then $\Gamma; \Delta \vdash_x nf(M)$.*

*2. If $\Gamma;\Delta \vdash_x S$ then $\Gamma;\Delta \vdash_x nf(S)$ .*
*3. If $\Gamma \Vdash_x M$ then $\Gamma \Vdash_x nf(M)$.*
*4. If $\Gamma \Vdash M$ then $\Gamma \Vdash nf(M)$.*

*Proof.* The proof proceeds by simultaneous induction over the given strictness derivations, using Lemma 3.

To arrive at the contradiction described above, we must ensure that the head of a definition is never a meta-variable (the head of a $\lambda$-term is defined as the head of its body). We call such objects *rigid.*

**Definition 4 (Rigid objects).** *An object $M$ defined in $\Psi, \Delta$, where parameters in $\Delta$ are not subject to instantiation, is called a* rigid object *iff $head(nf(M))$ is either a constant or a parameter defined in $\Delta$.*

The head of a definition, no matter to which arguments it is applied, cannot be a meta-variable.

**Lemma 5 (Head).** *If $d : A = M$ is a strict definition ($\Gamma \Vdash M$), and $\sigma$ a substitution with domain $\Gamma$, then $M[\sigma] \cdot S$ is a rigid object.*

*Proof.* By induction over the strictness derivation of $\Gamma \Vdash M$.

The other part of the argument involves counting the number of parameter and constructor occurrences in a term $M$ which we write as $|M|$. It can be easily shown that this measure satisfies the following property on the unification problem in question.

**Lemma 6 (Size).** *Let $\Psi;\Delta \vdash X\ y_1 \ldots y_k \approx M$ be a unification problem, where $M$ is strict in $X$ ($\Psi;\Delta \vdash_X M$), and $\Theta$ be a unifier. Then*

$$|nf((X\ y_1 \ldots y_k)[\Theta])| \leq |nf(M[\Theta])|$$

*Proof.* By induction over the strictness derivation $\Psi;\Delta \vdash_X M$, using Lemma 4.

The third technical result of our paper can now be stated and proven: If a unification problem fails the occurs-check, it cannot have any unifiers.

**Theorem 3 (Occurs-check).** *Let $M$ be a rigid object, and $\Psi$ a context of free variables. Furthermore, let $X$ occur strictly in $M$ ($\Psi;\Delta \vdash_X M$). Then the unification problem*

$$\Psi, \Delta \vdash X\ y_1 \ldots y_k \approx M$$

*has no unifiers.*

*Proof.* Assume the unification problem fails the occurs-check and has the unifier $\Theta$. By Lemma 6, it follows that

$$|nf((X\ y_1 \ldots y_k)[\Theta])| \leq |nf(M[\Theta])|$$

but because of Lemma 5 we can show, that

$$|nf((X\ y_1 \ldots y_k)[\Theta])| < |nf(M[\Theta])|$$

contradicting the assumption that $\Theta$ is a unifier.

Hence, a unification problem which fails the occurs-check does not have any unifiers. The occurs-check is also the reason why identity functions are not considered strict. An equation $X \equiv \mathrm{id}' \cdot X$ would fail the occurs-check but have a solution (where $X$ is uninstantiated).

Therefore, strict definitions can be treated mostly as constructors in a unification algorithm. They must be expanded only in the case of a constant clash at the head during decomposition of so-called rigid-rigid equations. The unification algorithm remains sound and complete. Note that this observation is independent of whether one uses an algorithm based on Miller's higher-order patterns or Huet's original algorithm for higher-order unification.

## 6 Conclusion

We have identified a class of strict notational definitions and analyzed the way they interact with algorithms for equality and unification. Notational definitions must be expanded only in the case of constant clash. This property can be exploited to make many implementations of these algorithms more efficient, while preserving completeness and soundness with respect to $\beta\delta$-conversion. We also presented an algorithm to efficiently check definitions for strictness.

Many theorem provers rely on an *ad hoc* treatment of definitions. We believe that these systems can benefit from the results in this paper in terms of efficiency and robustness.

In future work we plan to evaluate the concept of strictness empirically in our implementation. If warranted by the results, we may investigate *partially* strict definitions, that is, definitions, where some of the argument parameters are locally strict and others are not. In such a situation definitions may only need to be "partially expanded", comparing the strict and reducing the non-strict argument positions.

## References

[B+98] Bruno Barras et al. *The Coq Proof Assistant, Reference Manual, Version 6.2.* INRIA, CNRS, France, 1998.

[CP97] Iliano Cervesato and Frank Pfenning. A linear spine calculus. Technical Report CMU-CS-97-125, CMU, 1997.

[DHKP96] Gilles Dowek, Thérèse Hardin, Claude Kirchner, and Frank Pfenning. Unification via explicit substitutions: The case of higher-order patterns. In *Joint International Conference and Symposium on Logic Programming (JICSLP'96), Bonn, Germany*, 1996.

[Gri88] Timothy G. Griffin. Notational definition — a formal account. In *Third Annual Symposium on Logic in Computer Science, Edinburgh, Scotland*, pages 372–383. IEEE, July 1988.

[Han94] M. Hanus. The integration of functions into logic programming: From theory to practice. *Journal of Logic Programming*, 19&20:583–628, 1994.

[HHP93] Robert Harper, Furio Honsell, and Gordon Plotkin. A framework for defining logics. *Journal of the Association for Computing Machinery*, 40(1):143–184, January 1993.

[HM94] Chris Hankin and Daniel Le Métayer. Deriving algorithms from type inference systems: Application to strictness analysis. In *Proceedings of the Twenty-First Annual ACM Symposium on Principles of Programming Languages, Portland*, pages 202–212. ACM, January 1994.

[HP98] Robert Harper and Frank Pfenning. A module system for a programming language based on the LF logical framework. *Journal of Logic and Computation*, 8(1):5–31, 1998. A preliminary version is available as Technical Report CMU-CS-92-191, September 1992.

[Hue75] Gérard Huet. A unification algorithm for typed $\lambda$-calculus. *Theoretical Computer Science*, 1:27–57, 1975.

[LP92] Zhaohui Luo and Robert Pollack. The LEGO proof development system: A user's manual. Technical Report ECS-LFCS-92-211, University of Edinburgh, May 1992.

[Mil91] Dale Miller. A logic programming language with lambda-abstraction, function variables, and simple unification. *Journal of Logic and Computation*, 1(4):497–536, 1991.

[ORS92] S. Owre, J. M. Rushby, and N. Shankar. PVS: A prototype verification system. In Deepak Kapur, editor, *11th International Conference on Automated Deduction (CADE)*, volume 607 of *Lecture Notes in Artificial Intelligence*, pages 748–752, Saratoga, NY, June 1992. Springer-Verlag.

[Pau94] Lawrence C. Paulson. *Isabelle: A Generic Theorem Prover*. Springer-Verlag LNCS 828, 1994.

[Pfe91] Frank Pfenning. Unification and anti-unification in the Calculus of Constructions. In *Sixth Annual IEEE Symposium on Logic in Computer Science*, pages 74–85, Amsterdam, The Netherlands, July 1991.

[PS98] Frank Pfenning and Carsten Schürmann. *Twelf User's Guide*, 1.2 edition, September 1998. Available as Technical Report CMU-CS-98-173, Carnegie Mellon University.

# A Preview of the Basic Picture: A New Perspective on Formal Topology

Giovanni Sambin - Silvia Gebellato

Dipartimento di Matematica Pura ed Applicata,
Università di Padova
via Belzoni, 7 - 35131 Padova
sambin,silvia@math.unipd.it

***Abstract.*** If the classical definition of topological space is analysed at the light of an intuitionistic and predicative foundation as Martin-Löf's type theory, one is lead to the notion of basic pair: a pair of sets, concrete points and observables (or formal neighbourhoods), linked by a binary relation called forcing. The new discovery is that this is enough to introduce the topological notions of open and closed subsets, both in the concrete (pointwise) and in the formal (pointfree) sense. Actually, a new rich structure arises, consisting of a symmetry between concrete and formal and of a logical duality between open and closed. Closed subsets are defined primitively, as universal-existential images of subsets along the forcing relation, while open subsets are existential-universal images. So, in the same way as logic gives a theory of subsets as the extension of unary propositional functions over a given set, now logic is seen to produce topology if we pass to two sets linked by a relation, that is a propositional function with two arguments.

Usual topological spaces are obtained by adding the condition that the extensions of observables form a base for a topology, which is seen to be equivalent to distributivity. Formal topologies are then obtained by axiomatizing the structure induced on observables, with some improvements on previous definitions. A morphism between basic pairs is essentially a pair of relations producing a commutative square: this is thus the essence of continuity. Usual continuous functions become a special case.

This new perspective, which is here called basic picture, starts a new phase in constructive topology, where logic and topology are deeply connected and where the pointwise and the pointfree approach to topology can live together. It also brings to the development of topology in a more general, nondistributive sense.

***Introduction.*** If the aim is to develop mathematics within a constructive set theory, topology seems to be a good test since it is a field in which foundational problems are particularly evident. This is a fortiori true if constructivity is meant in a stricter sense to include predicativity, like in Martin-Löf's constructive type theory [6]. In fact, the usual definition of topological space involves a kind of quantification over subsets, which has to be justified predicatively. Moreover, in many well known topological spaces the definition of points requires an infinite amount of information (one example is given by real numbers) and thus it is not a priori granted that the collection of points form a set.

Such problems are solved in formal topology (see [9] and [11]), which is strictly constructive since it is developed fully within Martin-Löf's type theory (henceforth simply type theory). To support intuition, type theory is equipped with a notation for subsets (as introduced and justified in [13]); in particular, for any set $S$, $U \subseteq S$ means that $U$ is a propositional function over $S$ and $a \epsilon U$ means that $a \in S$ and $U(a)$ is true.

For our present purposes, the definition of formal topology can be motivated as follows. Assume that a topology $\Omega X$ on a set of points $X$ is given by means of a base. This is expressed in type theory as a family of subsets of $X$ indexed on a set $S$, that is a function $ext : S \to \mathcal{P}X$; and this is the same (cf. [13]) as a binary relation $x \Vdash a$ which, for $x \in X$ and $a \in S$, says that $a$ is a formal neighbourhood of $x$. The main idea is then to transfer the structure of $\Omega X$ onto the set $S$, and to this aim $S$ is equipped with some new primitives. A natural choice is to add a binary operation $\cdot$ satisfying $x \Vdash a \cdot b$ iff $x \Vdash a$ and $x \Vdash b$ and thus called formal intersection, a distinguished element $1 \in S$ satisfying $x \Vdash 1$ for any $x \in X$, and an infinitary relation $a \lhd U$ for $a \in S$ and $U \subseteq S$, satisfying $a \lhd U$ iff $(\forall x \in X)(x \Vdash a \to (\exists b \epsilon U)(x \Vdash b))$ and thus called formal cover. A unary predicate $\mathsf{Pos}(a)$ *prop* $(a \in S)$ is also added, satisfying $\mathsf{Pos}(a)$ iff $(\exists x \in X)(x \Vdash a)$ and called the positivity predicate.

The definition of formal topology is then obtained by expressing the above situation in pointfree terms, that is by requiring the structure $\mathcal{A} = (S, \cdot, 1, \lhd, \mathsf{Pos})$ to satisfy all the properties of the new primitives $\cdot, 1, \lhd, \mathsf{Pos}$ which can be formulated without any mention of points of $X$. This leads to (cf. [9] and [10]):

$\mathcal{A} = (S, \cdot, 1, \lhd, \mathsf{Pos})$ is a formal topology if:

$(S, \cdot, 1)$ is a commutative monoid;

$\lhd$ satisfies

$$\text{reflexivity } \frac{a \epsilon U}{a \lhd U} \qquad \text{transitivity } \frac{a \lhd U \quad (\forall b \epsilon U)(b \lhd V)}{a \lhd V}$$

$$\cdot \text{ - left } \frac{a \lhd U}{a \cdot b \lhd U} \qquad \cdot \text{ - right } \frac{a \lhd U \quad a \lhd V}{a \lhd \{b \cdot c : b \epsilon U, c \epsilon V\}}$$

$\mathsf{Pos}$ satisfies

$$\text{monotonicity } \frac{\mathsf{Pos}(a) \quad a \lhd U}{(\exists b \epsilon U)\mathsf{Pos}(b)} \qquad \text{positivity } \frac{\mathsf{Pos}(a) \to a \lhd U}{a \lhd U}$$

(for an analytic explanation of such conditions see [11]).

Any infinitary relation $\lhd$ is equivalently presented as an operator on subsets $\mathcal{A}U \equiv \{a \in S : a \lhd U\}$; then it can be shown that $\lhd$ is a cover if and only if $\mathcal{A}$ is a closure operator which moreover satisfies distributivity in the form $\mathcal{A}(U \cdot V) = \mathcal{A}(U) \cap \mathcal{A}(V)$ (where $U \cdot V \equiv \{b \cdot c : b \epsilon U, c \epsilon V\}$). Then a *formal open* can be defined as a subset $U$ of $S$ such that $U = \mathcal{A}U$.

The presence of the positivity predicate Pos (which does not appear explicitly in the usual theory of locales, or pointless topology, see e.g. [4]) has sometimes been felt as a redundancy; from the above considerations, we see that Pos$(a)$ is the only primitive corresponding to an existential quantification over points, and it thus becomes a positive pointfree way to express that $ext(a)$ is inhabited. Its presence was due (apart from the convenience in the definition of formal points and in the treatment of Scott domains [14]) to the expectation of obtaining a good definition of formal closed subsets. As we will see here, to obtain this not only Pos must be kept, but the way it expresses existential quantification over points must be strengthened, thus reaching a binary predicate which is as relevant as the formal cover and dual to it, in a sense to be specified below.

What is the point of the move to pointfree terms? An ideological rejection of points altogether is not a far reaching motivation in our opinion; on the contrary, we believe that when points form a set, this information should by no means be thrown away (two examples: rational numbers and all finite sets). The trouble is that in the most interesting examples there is no simple way to generate inductively all the points one would like to have. In the case of real numbers, this problem was overcome by Dedekind with the introduction of Dedekind cuts and by Brouwer with choice sequences. Formal topology allows to solve the same problem in more general terms by introducing the abstract notion of formal point. Like formal topologies are defined axiomatically by requiring all the properties which can be expressed in the pointfree language with $\cdot, 1, \lhd$ and Pos, now formal points of a formal topology are *defined* to be those subsets of $S$ which cannot be distinguished, in such language, from subsets of the form $\alpha_x \equiv \{a \in S : x \Vdash a\}$. Note that this idea is exactly the same which led Dedekind from rational numbers to cuts, and to the definition of real numbers as cuts (cf. [2]). Using the notation adopted above, in a topological space a point $x$ satisfies the conditions:

$$x \Vdash 1 \qquad\qquad x \Vdash a \cdot b \text{ iff } x \Vdash a \text{ and } x \Vdash b$$

$$\frac{x \Vdash a \quad a \lhd U}{(\exists b \in U)(x \Vdash b)} \qquad \frac{x \Vdash a}{\mathsf{Pos}(a)}$$

So, a subset $\alpha$ of $S$ is said to be a formal point if, after writing $\alpha \Vdash a$ in place of $\alpha \ni a$ (that is $a \in \alpha$), all the above conditions are satisfied with $\alpha$ replacing $x$; we reach in this way the same definition as that given in [9].

The collection of formal points over a formal topology $\mathcal{A}$ is denoted by $Pt(\mathcal{A})$. The structure $(Pt(\mathcal{A}), \ni, \mathcal{A})$ is called a formal space. It is type theory which gives a precise foundational meaning to the distinction between topological spaces and formal spaces, since it refrains from considering $Pt(\mathcal{A})$ a set like any other, and in this sense it has favoured the emergence of formal topology itself.

In a similar way, we now see how a new quite rich structure emerges after rejection of the identification of closed subsets with complements of open subsets (which, as we shall see, is an example of the identification of $\exists\neg$ with $\neg\forall$). To this aim, we have to go back to the simple structure $(X, \Vdash, S)$ we met above and take it as our main object of study. It will be rewarding, mainly from a conceptual point of view: it leads to a new perspective on formal topology, which we have called basic picture and of which this paper gives a preview.

The discovery (by Sambin) of binary Pos and hence much of the basic picture in December '95 was indirectly stimulated by discussions with Per Martin-Löf on the notion of formal closed subset; morphisms and a correct appreciation of symmetry came later (and are due to both authors). The basic picture has been presented in several occasions, mainly at Types '96, Aussois, December 1996, at the First Workshop on Formal Topology, Padova, October 1997 and at WoLLIC '98, Sao Paulo, July 1998.

It is a pleasure for us to thank Per Martin-Löf, both for his interest in formal closed subsets, which is almost as old as formal topology itself, and for more recent discussions, in particular on some of the topics in the last paragraph here. We also thank Bernhard Reus for his questions during his visit to Padova in Autumn '98, which helped us to improve exposition.

***Basic pairs.*** A structure $\mathcal{X} \equiv (X, \Vdash, S)$, where $X$ and $S$ are arbitrary sets and $\Vdash$ is an arbitrary binary relation between them, is here called a *basic pair*. To help the intuition, we may (as in the introduction above) think of $X$ as a set of concrete points and $S$ as a set of basic formal opens (or observables); $x \Vdash a$ can be read as "$a$ is a formal neighborhood of $x$" or more neutrally as "$x$ forces $a$" and then the relation $\Vdash$ itself is called forcing. This way of reading introduces a distinction between the left side, which is called concrete side, and the right one, which is called formal side. The relation $\Vdash$ is the way to pass from the concrete to the formal side, and conversely. For any $a \in S$, the *extension* of $a$ is the subset of $X$ of all concrete points forcing $a$, that is $ext\, a \equiv \{x \in X : x \Vdash a\}$. In topological terms, the family of subsets $(ext\, a)_{a \in S}$ is of course a sub-base for a topology on $X$, like any family of subsets of $X$. In general it is not a base for a topology, since we do not require that it covers all the set $X$, that is $(\forall x)(\exists a)(x \Vdash a)$, and that the intersection of its members is open, that is $(\forall x)(\forall a, b)(x \Vdash a \,\&\, x \Vdash b \rightarrow (\exists c)(x \Vdash c \,\&\, ext\, c \subseteq ext\, a \cap ext\, b))$ (cf. [3], p. 26).

In the other direction, any element $x \in X$ on the concrete side determines a subset $\Diamond x \equiv \{a \in S : x \Vdash a\}$ on the formal side, which is called the system of neighborhoods (or approximations) of $x$. The picture we have in mind is something like:

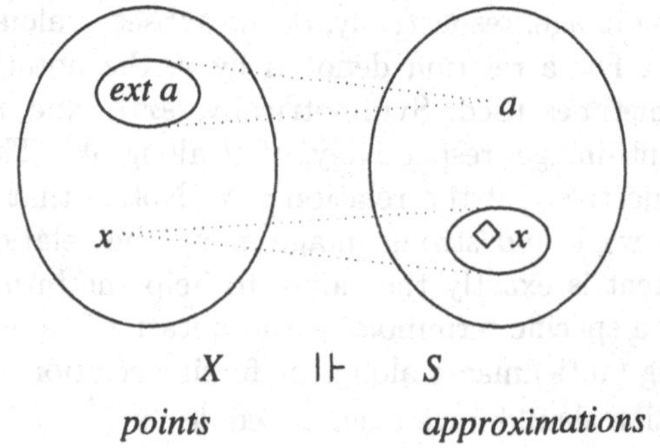

The definition of $\Diamond$ is immediately extended to any subset $A \subseteq X$ by defining as usual $\Diamond A \equiv \bigcup_{x \epsilon A} \Diamond x$. Spelling out the definition of union of subsets (see [13]), we see that $\Diamond A$ is just the image of $A$ along $\Vdash$ through an existential quantification:

$$\Diamond A \equiv \{a \in S : (\exists x \in X)(x \Vdash a \,\&\, x \,\epsilon\, A)\}.$$

Because of the option for intuitionism, the image of $A$ obtained through a universal quantification is not definable in terms of $\Diamond$ and we thus are lead to put

$$\Box A \equiv \{a \in S : (\forall x \in X)(x \Vdash a \rightarrow x \,\epsilon\, A)\}.$$

So both $\Diamond$ and $\Box$ are operators on subsets, that is functions from $\mathcal{P}(X)$ to $\mathcal{P}(S)$. The fact that they are given by an existential and universal quantification respectively is immediately visible by adopting a notation for quantification relativized to subsets (as justified in [13]):

$$\Diamond A \equiv \{a \in S : (\exists x \,\epsilon\, ext\, a)(x \,\epsilon\, A)\}$$
$$\Box A \equiv \{a \in S : (\forall x \,\epsilon\, ext\, a)(x \,\epsilon\, A)\}$$

Also the intuition of $\Diamond A$ and $\Box A$ is now clear: in fact $a \,\epsilon\, \Diamond A$ means that $ext\, a$ meets the subset $A$, while $a \,\epsilon\, \Box A$ means that $ext\, a \subseteq A$. In the other direction, also $ext$ is extended to any subset $U \subseteq S$ by putting $ext\, U \equiv \bigcup_{a \epsilon U} ext\, a$; $ext\, U$ is the existential image of $U$ along the inverse of $\Vdash$, and is called the *extension* of $U$. As above, also the universal image $rest\, U$ has to be considered, and is called the *restriction* of $U$. Using quantifiers relativized to $\Diamond x$, the formal definitions are:

$$ext\, U = \{x \in X : (\exists a \,\epsilon\, \Diamond x)(a \,\epsilon\, U)\}$$
$$rest\, U = \{x \in X : (\forall a \,\epsilon\, \Diamond x)(a \,\epsilon\, U)\}$$

A glance at the definitions shows that the definition of the operators $ext$ and $rest$ could be obtained from that of $\Diamond$ and $\Box$, respectively, just by switching the role of the sets $X$ and $S$. In fact, writing as usual $\Vdash^-$ for the inverse of the relation $\Vdash$, we see that $\mathcal{X}^- \equiv (S, \Vdash^-, X)$ is still a basic pair, perfectly as good as $\mathcal{X} \equiv (X, \Vdash, S)$; we call $\mathcal{X}^-$ the symmetric of $\mathcal{X}$. So the operators $ext$ and $rest$ in $\mathcal{X}$ are just the same thing as $\Diamond$ and $\Box$, respectively, but in its symmetric $\mathcal{X}^-$.

In purely mathematical terms, $\Diamond A$ and $\Box A$ give what is sometimes called the weak and strong image, respectively, of the subset $A$ along a relation, which in this case is $\Vdash$. For a relation denoted by $r$, the notation $rA$ and $r^{-*}A$, respectively, is sometimes used. Symmetrically, $ext\, U$ and $rest\, U$ are just the weak and strong anti-image, respectively, of $U$ along $\Vdash$. They are denoted by $r^-U$ and $r^*U$, respectively, if the relation is $r$. Notice that $r^-U$ and $r^*U$ are the same thing as weak and strong image along the relation $r^-$. Even if the mathematical content is exactly the same, to help the intuition we here have preferred to adopt a specific terminology and notation, namely $\Diamond$, $\Box$, *ext*, *rest*, for weak and strong (anti-)images along the forcing relation $\Vdash$, which according to a uniform notation should have been called $\Vdash$, $\Vdash^{-*}$, $\Vdash^-$, $\Vdash^*$ respectively.

Beside the geometrical symmetry between the left side $X$ and the right side $S$, there is also a logical duality clearly present: the definition of $\Diamond$ and $\Box$ are obtained one from the other by interchanging the roles of $\forall$ with $\exists$ and $\rightarrow$ with &. The same of course holds for *ext* and *rest*. So a picture could be:

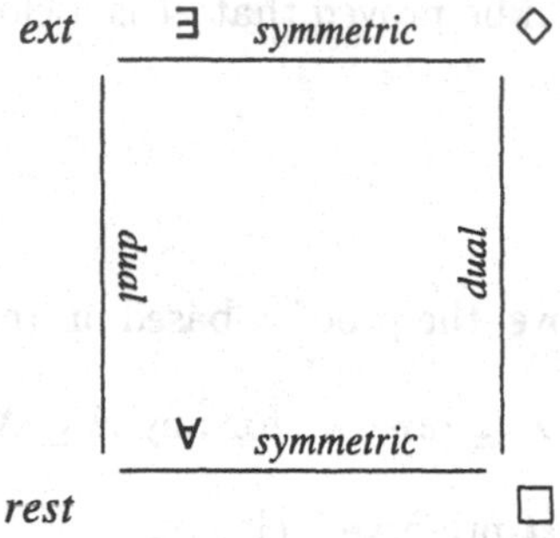


What is the use of all this structure? We begin by seeing that the topological notions of interior and closure are immediately obtained by combinations of the four operators $\Diamond, \Box, ext, rest$. The symmetry of the picture will then produce also their pointfree, or formal, versions.

***Interior and closure.*** The interior of a subset $A$ of $X$ is usually defined as the set of points of $X$ with a neighborhood all contained in $A$ (see for instance [5], pp. 42, 44). In our notation, this definition becomes

$$int A \equiv \{x \in X : (\exists a \,\epsilon\, \Diamond x)(\forall y \in X)(y \Vdash a \rightarrow y \,\epsilon\, A)\},$$

and then it is clear that such combination of quantifiers is just the composition of *ext* after $\Box$, that is $int A \equiv ext \Box A$. To our knowledge, this simple and basic fact had not been noticed before.

As usual we say that $A$ is *open* if $A = int A$; but, of course, we cannot expect *int* so defined to be a topological interior operator, since nowhere it has been assumed anything telling that the intersection of two open subsets is open. However, it can be proved that *int* is an interior operator, that is

i. $int A \subseteq A$,
ii. if $A \subseteq B$ then $int A \subseteq int B$,
iii. $int A \subseteq int\, int A$,

for any $A, B \subseteq X$. Condition i. follows immediately from the adjunction

$$ext U \subseteq A \ \text{ iff } \ U \subseteq \Box A, \quad \text{for any } U \subseteq S \text{ and } A \subseteq X \tag{1}$$

by taking $U$ to be $\Box A$, condition ii. follows from the fact that the operators *ext* and $\Box$ preserve inclusion of subsets and iii. is a consequence of

$$\Box\, ext \Box A = \Box A, \quad \text{for any } \ A \subseteq X$$

which follows easily from (1) above.

Quite similarly, the usual definition of the closure $cl A$ of a subset $A$ of $X$ says that $x \epsilon cl A$ if any neighborhood of $x$ intersects $A$. In our notation,

$$cl A \equiv \{x \in X : (\forall a \epsilon \Diamond x)(\exists y \epsilon ext\, a)(y \epsilon A)\}$$

that is $cl A \equiv rest \Diamond A$. It can be proved that $cl$ is a closure operator, that is

i. $A \subseteq cl A$,
ii. if $A \subseteq B$ then $cl A \subseteq cl B$,
iii. $cl\, cl A \subseteq cl A$,

for any $A, B \subseteq X$. Like above, the proof is based on the adjunction

$$\Diamond A \subseteq U \quad \text{iff} \quad A \subseteq rest U, \quad \text{for any } A \subseteq X \text{ and } U \subseteq S \tag{2}$$

and the fact that $\Diamond$ and *rest* preserve inclusion.

Like we did above with open subsets, we say that $A$ is *closed* if $A = cl A$, even if $cl$ is not a closure operator in the sense of topology (since the union of two closed subsets is not necessarily closed).

***Formal open and formal closed subsets.*** Because of the symmetry between the left and the right side of a basic pair $X \xrightarrow{\Vdash} S$, the above definitions of $int \equiv ext \Box$ and $cl \equiv rest \Diamond$ also have symmetric definitions, obtained by replacing each operator with its symmetric: $\mathcal{C} \equiv \Diamond rest$ and $\mathcal{A} \equiv \Box\, ext$. By symmetry, it is immediate that $\mathcal{C}$ is an interior operator and $\mathcal{A}$ is a closure operator. We now see that actually $\mathcal{A}$ is something already known, while $\mathcal{C}$ is in a sense what we were looking for. In fact, spelling out the definition of $\mathcal{A}$, we see that

$$a \epsilon \mathcal{A} U \equiv (\forall x \in X)(x \Vdash a \rightarrow (\exists b \epsilon U)(x \Vdash b))$$

that is, $a \epsilon \mathcal{A} U$ if all concrete points forcing $a$ also force $U$, which is the relation between $a$ and $U$ which was meant to be expressed by the formal cover $a \lhd U$. So, as in formal topology, we say that $U$ is formal open if $U = \mathcal{A} U$, even if in the wider generality of basic pairs the closure operator $\mathcal{A}$ does not necessarily satisfy distributivity since $X$ is not equipped with a topology in the traditional sense. Such generality, however, allows us to see that $\mathcal{A}$ is symmetric to $cl$, which means that the notion of "$a$ being covered by $U$", that is $a \epsilon \mathcal{A} U$, is just the symmetric of $x \epsilon cl A$, that is "$x$ is an adherence point of $A$"; that is, the formula defining one notion can be obtained from the other by interchanging points and opens. Also this simple fact was, apparently, not noticed before.

More interesting is the second operator $\mathcal{C}$, which is the novelty emerged, by symmetry with *int* or equivalently by duality with $\mathcal{A}$, from the general study of basic pairs. Spelling out its definition, we have

$$a \epsilon \mathcal{C} F \equiv (\exists x \in X)(x \Vdash a \,\&\, (\forall b \in S)(x \Vdash b \rightarrow b \epsilon F))$$

which we can now recognize as a strengthening of the intuitive pointwise interpretation of the positivity predicate. In fact, since $(\forall b \in S)(x \Vdash b \rightarrow b \epsilon F)$

is just $\Diamond x \subseteq F$, we see that $a \epsilon \mathcal{C}F$ means not only that $a$ is inhabited by a concrete point $x$, but also that $\Diamond x \subseteq F$, that is all neighborhoods of such point $x$ are elements of $F$. As we write $a \lhd U$ for $a \epsilon \mathcal{A}U$, we also will write $\mathsf{Pos}(a, F)$ for $a \epsilon \mathcal{C}F$, for any $a \in S$ and $F \subseteq S$, and call Pos a binary positivity predicate. The previous unary positivity predicate is now obtained as a special case, by putting $\mathsf{Pos}(a) \equiv \mathsf{Pos}(a, S)$.

The relevance of binary Pos is that it allows to define by symmetry the notion of formal closed: we say that a subset $F$ of $S$ is *formal closed* if $F = \mathcal{C}F$, or equivalently $a \epsilon F$ iff $\mathsf{Pos}(a, F)$.

In this way we see that the notions of concrete and formal, open and closed subsets are all defined by means of a couple of relativized quantifiers of the form $\exists\forall$ or $\forall\exists$ (see the picture below). The logical structure is so evident that one could even reverse the perspective and conceive of such topological notions as conceptual tools to treat combinations of quantifiers in an intuitive way.

***The isomorphism theorem.*** By definition of *int*, any concrete open subset $A$ is of the form $ext\, U$ for some $U \subseteq S$. Conversely, any subset of $X$ of the form $ext\, U$, for any $U \subseteq S$, is concrete open, because $ext\, U = ext \Box\, ext\, U = int\, ext\, U$. Therefore:

$A \subseteq X$ is concrete open iff $A = ext\, U$ for some $U \subseteq S$

Quite similarly, one can prove that:

$A \subseteq X$ is concrete closed iff $A = \boldsymbol{rest}\, U$ for some $U \subseteq S$
$U \subseteq S$ is formal open iff $U = \Box A$ for some $A \subseteq X$
$F \subseteq S$ is formal closed iff $F = \Diamond A$ for some $A \subseteq X$.

It is then easy to see that, when restricted to open subsets (either concrete or formal), the operators *ext* and $\Box$ are bijective, and one inverse of the other. Similarly for closed subsets, with ***rest*** and $\Diamond$.

It follows from the fact that *int* is an interior operator that an arbitrary union of concrete open subsets is concrete open. Symmetrically, an arbitrary union of formal closed subsets is formal closed. Dually, an arbitrary intersection of concrete closed (formal open) subsets is concrete closed (formal open). We can as usual define the meet of an arbitrary family of concrete open subsets $int\, A_i$ as the interior of the intersection, that is $\bigwedge_{i \in I} int\, A_i \equiv int\,(\bigcap_{i\in I} int\, A_i)$; dually, the join of an arbitrary family of formal open subsets is defined by $\bigvee_{i\in I} \mathcal{A}U_i \equiv \mathcal{A}(\bigcup_{i\in I} \mathcal{A}U_i)$. So concrete and formal open subsets form two complete lattices. Quite similarly for closed subsets. Then one can prove that:

*Theorem.* The operator *ext* is an isomorphism between the lattice of formal open and that of concrete open subsets. Dually, the operator ***rest*** is an isomorphism between the lattices of formal closed and of concrete closed subsets.

This theorem gives further evidence of the correctness of our definitions. In particular, it shows that a binary positivity predicate $\mathsf{Pos}(a, F)$, or equivalently an interior operator $\mathcal{C}$, is necessary to obtain a predicative notion of formal closed subset which corresponds well, as in the case of open subsets, to that of concrete closed subset.

The following picture summarizes most of the information about open and closed subsets:

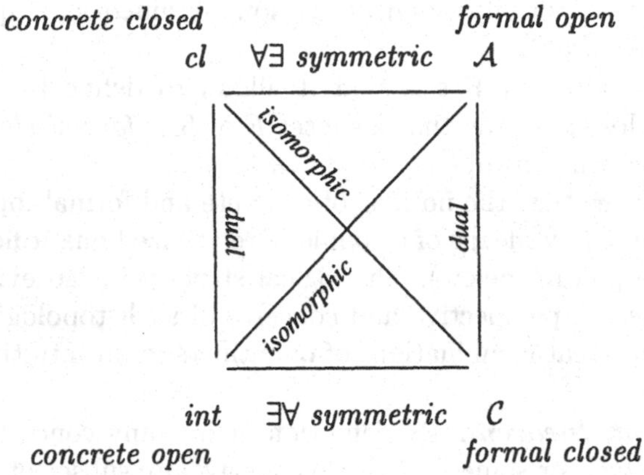


Of course, the vertical line at the right refers to the formal side, and at the left to the concrete side. Also, the top horizontal line refers to closure operators, and the bottom one to interior operators. One diagonal refers to open subsets, the other to closed subsets.

***Continuity.*** What we have seen so far could be summarized by saying that topology begins with basic pairs. They are the simplest extension of the notion of set, that is two sets linked in the weakest possible way, namely by a relation. We are now going to see that continuity begins with the weakest possible way to link two basic pairs, namely a pair of relations giving rise to a commutative square.

Given two basic pairs $\mathcal{X} \equiv X \xrightarrow{\Vdash} S$ and $\mathcal{Y} \equiv Y \xrightarrow{\Vdash'} T$, we say that a pair of relations $r : X \to Y$ and $s : S \to T$ is a *morphism*, or a *relation-pair*, from $\mathcal{X}$ to $\mathcal{Y}$ if the diagram

$$\begin{array}{ccc} X & \xrightarrow{\Vdash} & S \\ \downarrow{\scriptstyle r} & & \downarrow{\scriptstyle s} \\ Y & \xrightarrow{\Vdash'} & T \end{array}$$

is commutative. Here we assume that composition of relations is defined as usual; then, writing $rx$ for $r\{x\}$, commutativity of the above diagram is expressed by the equation

$$\Diamond rx = s\Diamond x \quad \text{for any } x \in X. \tag{3}$$

Several motivations lead to consider relations rather than functions and then to adopt the above definition of morphisms between basic pairs. First of all, relations are more general than functions and they allow to grasp better the essence of continuity. Secondly, on one hand we obtain the usual definition of continuity for functions as a particular case, but on the other hand we will also be able to give a natural constructive definition of topological Kripke structures.

A third good reason for considering relations is that the inherent symmetry of basic pairs is somehow preserved: if $(r,s):\mathcal{X}\to\mathcal{Y}$ is a morphism, also the inverse $(s^-,r^-)$ is a morphism, from $\mathcal{Y}^-$ into $\mathcal{X}^-$. This statement would be impossible with functions.

Given a relation $r:X\to Y$, a simple minded extension of the usual definition of continuity for functions is to require that $r^-$ is open. Since any open subset of $Y$ is of the form $ext\,U$ for some $U\subseteq T$, this amounts to

$$r^-(ext\,U) = int(r^-\,ext\,U) \quad \text{for any } U\subseteq T.$$

Since $ext$ distributes arbitrary unions, it is enough to require that

$$r^-(ext\,b) = int(r^-\,ext\,b) \quad \text{for any } b\in T. \tag{4}$$

One can see that, putting $asb \equiv ext\,a \subseteq r^-(ext\,b)$, such requirement is equivalent to (3) above. So, (3) is satisfied when $r^-$ is open, for a suitable choice of $s$. On the other hand, it can easily be proved that if $(r,s)$ is a morphism, then $r^-$ is open and $s$ is essentially uniquely determined by $r$; in fact, if $(r,s')$ is any other morphism, then $s$ and $s'$ coincide "topologically", that is $\mathcal{A}(s'^-b) = \mathcal{A}(s^-b)$ for any $b\in T$. In this sense (3) is equivalent to $r^-$ being open; we prefer the former for aesthetic reasons.

An equivalent characterization is reached through a different path. Assume we express the fact that $r^-$ is open as:

$$\text{for any } U\subseteq T, \text{ there is } V\subseteq S \text{ such that } r^-(ext\,U) = ext\,V.$$

More constructively, this can be expressed by requiring the existence of a family of subsets $V_b\subseteq S$ for $b\in T$ such that

$$r^-(ext\,b) = ext\,V_b \quad \text{for any } b\in T. \tag{5}$$

But as we have seen already, the family of subsets $(V_b)_{b\in T}$ is equivalently represented as a relation $asb\equiv a\,\epsilon\,V_b$, and then (5) becomes

$$r^-(ext\,b) = ext(s^-b) \quad \text{for any } b\in T. \tag{6}$$

It is a matter of fact that (6) is equivalent to (3). Actually, one can prove that also

$$r^*(rest\,F) = rest(s^*F) \text{ for any } F\subseteq T,$$
$$\Box(r^{-*}A) = s^{-*}(\Box A) \text{ for any } A\subseteq X$$

are equivalent formulations of morphisms.

***The category of basic pairs and related notions.*** Basic pairs and relation-pairs form a category, which we call **BP**. **BP** is closely related to the category $\mathbf{Rel}^2$, that is the category whose objects are arrows in **Rel**, the category of sets and relations, and morphisms are indeed defined as commutative squares. So, objects of $\mathbf{Rel}^2$ are what we called basic pairs, and morphisms what we called relation-pairs. However, the notion of equality of arrows is not the same, since two arrows in **BP** are defined to be equal when they behave in the same way "topologically". So we say that two relation-pairs $(r, s)$ and $(r', s')$ are equal when

$$\begin{array}{ll} s\Diamond x = s'\Diamond x & \text{for any } x \in X \\ r^{-} ext\, b = r'^{-} ext\, b & \text{for any } b \in T \end{array}$$

It can be proved that $(r, s)$ is equal to $(r', s')$ exactly when weak and strong anti-images along $r$ and $r'$ behave equally on open and on closed subsets of $Y$, respectively (that is, $r^{-} ext U = r'^{-} ext U$ and $r^{*} rest U = r'^{*} rest U$ for any $U \subseteq T$) and $s$ and $s'$ behave equally on open and on closed subsets of $S$ (that is, $s\Diamond A = s'\Diamond A$ and $s^{-*}\Box A = s'^{-*}\Box A$ for any $A \subseteq X$). One can show that such equality is indeed an equivalence relation and that it is respected by composition; in other terms, one can think of **BP** as a quotient of $\mathbf{Rel}^2$. So, the usual nice tricks with diagrams are possible in **BP** as they were in $\mathbf{Rel}^2$. For instance, the commutative square of the definition of a morphism $(r, s)$ can be read also as a morphism $(\Vdash, \Vdash')$ from the basic pair $X \xrightarrow{r} Y$ into the basic pair $S \xrightarrow{s} T$.

A basic pair is technically also the same thing as a boolean Chu space (see [8]); we have chosen to adopt the new name of basic pair to recall that topology is now involved and that the underlying set theory is constructive type theory. The category **BP** strictly generalizes the category of boolean Chu spaces, because morphisms of Chu spaces are defined as pairs of functions, and in opposite directions. It also provides it with a new topological taste. One can therefore expect from **BP** an even wider range of applications than those developed and foreseen by V. Pratt for Chu spaces (see his www page [7]).

The notion of continuity for relations (sometimes euphemistically called "many-valued functions") has been considered by various authors, particularly in the past; a textbook is [1]. Two more recent references are [16], especially section 4.4 where some bibliographic references can also be found, and [17], which generalizes[1] the notion of continuous relation as introduced in [12].

When $X$ and $Y$ are topological spaces, a relation $r : X \to Y$ is said to be lower semi-continuous if $r^*$ is closed, that is $r^* A$ is closed in $X$ whenever $A$ is closed in $Y$, and upper semi-continuous if $r^*$ is open (see [16]). Lower semi-continuity is classically equivalent to $r^-$ open, and hence to our (4), which does not need any free variable on subsets, while the free variable on subsets which is used to express upper semi-continuity is not eliminable. This is why we have adopted the former as our definition (while continuous relations of [1] are required to satisfy both).

Note that our definition is still sufficient to give the usual definition of continuity for functions as a special case when the relation $r$ is actually a function.

***Topological Kripke structures.*** In textbooks on modal logic, a Kripke structure is usually defined as a set $X$ together with a relation $r : X \to X$. Clearly,

[1] Note that the generalization of [12] given by M. B. Smyth in [17] is in the opposite direction of that presented here.

it is a special case of basic pair (in which $S = X$). We are more interested however in the fact that basic pairs allow to introduce a constructive definition of topological Kripke structure in a natural way. In fact, we say that $(\mathcal{X}, r)$ is a topological Kripke structure if $X \xrightarrow{\Vdash} S$ is a basic pair, so that $X$ is topologized by $S$ through $\Vdash$, and $r : X \to X$ is a relation whose inverse $r^-$ is open. In other terms, a topological Kripke structure is essentially nothing but a morphism from a basic pair into itself. Then also the notion of p-morphism (called contraction in [12]) can now be generalized, and described simply as a commutative cube, of which one face is $(\mathcal{X}, r)$ and the opposite face is $(\mathcal{Y}, s)$.

***Extending formal topology.*** To conclude this preview, we can repeat the process described in the introduction as a motivation for the definition of formal topology, but now starting from a more general situation, given by a basic pair $(X, \Vdash, S)$. The unfolding of the basic picture in the previous pages has shown that to describe in the best possible way the concrete topological structure of $X$ by means only of the formal side, we have to adopt two primitive relations $\lhd$ and $\mathsf{Pos}$ or equivalently two operators $\mathcal{A}$ and $\mathcal{C}$, which will be assumed to be a closure operator and an interior operator respectively. When $\mathcal{A}$ and $\mathcal{C}$ are defined by means of the relation $\Vdash$ in a basic pair, the link between them is automatically given by the fact that $\mathcal{A} \equiv \Box\, ext$ and $\mathcal{C} \equiv \Diamond\, rest$ with respect to *the same* forcing relation. We now have to add a condition expressing this with no mention of $X$, and hence of $\Vdash$. We thus arrive at

$$\text{compatibility} \quad \frac{a \in \mathcal{A}U \quad a \in \mathcal{C}V}{(\exists b \in U)(b \in \mathcal{C}V)}$$

which is easily seen to hold in any basic pair. We thus reach the following definition, which we express in the perfectly equivalent notation with $\lhd$ and $\mathsf{Pos}$ to underline the relation with the previous definition of formal topology:

*Definition of basic (formal) topology.* A triple $\mathcal{S} \equiv (S, \lhd, \mathsf{Pos})$ is called a basic formal topology if $S$ is a set, $\lhd$ and $\mathsf{Pos}$ are infinitary relations satisfying:

$$\text{reflexivity} \quad \frac{a \in U}{a \lhd U} \qquad \text{transitivity} \quad \frac{a \lhd U \quad (\forall b \in U)(b \lhd V)}{a \lhd V}$$

$$\text{antirefl.} \quad \frac{\mathsf{Pos}(a, F)}{a \in F} \qquad \text{trans.} \quad \frac{\mathsf{Pos}(a, F) \quad (\forall b \in S)(\mathsf{Pos}(b, F) \to b \in G)}{\mathsf{Pos}(a, G)}$$

$$\text{compatibility} \quad \frac{a \lhd U \quad \mathsf{Pos}(a, F)}{(\exists b \in U)(\mathsf{Pos}(b, F))}$$

Due to the complete symmetry of a basic pair, if we transfer the structure of a basic pair onto its left-concrete side, rather than conversely as we did above, we reach a definition which differs from the above only in notation and terminology.

That is, we say that $(X, cl, int)$ is a basic concrete topology if $X$ is a set, $cl$ is a closure operator and $int$ an interior operator, linked by the condition

$$\frac{x \in cl A \quad x \in int B}{(\exists y \in A)(y \in int B)}$$

which now has an immediate intuitive content since it characterizes the closure of a subset when opens are given by an interior operator. This is a quite simple but rich structure, which never came to life before because it was hidden under the equalities of classical logic.

The notion of basic formal topology strictly generalizes the previous definition of formal topology in two ways. Since no condition expressing that $(ext\, a)_{a \in S}$ is a base is present in a basic pair, basic topologies have no condition guaranteeing that formal opens form a frame. Since they *do* form a complete lattice in any case, the difference is distributivity. This was previously expressed by the requirement $\mathcal{A}(U \cdot V) = \mathcal{A}U \cap \mathcal{A}V$, or equivalently $\cdot$ - left and $\cdot$ - right. Taking up an idea in [15], distributivity can be expressed, even in absence of the primitive operation $\cdot$ of formal intersection, by adding the requirement that $\mathcal{A}(U{\downarrow}V) = \mathcal{A}U \cap \mathcal{A}V$ where $U{\downarrow}V \equiv \{a \in S : (\exists b \in U)(a \lhd \{b\}) \,\&\, (\exists c \in V)(a \lhd \{c\})\}$. In the equivalent notation with $\lhd$, $\mathcal{A}(U{\downarrow}V) = \mathcal{A}U \cap \mathcal{A}V$ is expressed by

$$\downarrow\text{-right} \quad \frac{a \lhd U \quad a \lhd V}{a \lhd U{\downarrow}V}$$

which is sufficent to prove that formal opens form a frame. This offers a simpler formulation of formal topologies, obtained from the definition given in the introduction by suppressing $\cdot$ and 1 and by replacing $\cdot$ - left and $\cdot$ - right with $\downarrow$-right. A considerable advantage of this new formulation is that it includes in an easier way those examples where a preorder rather than a binary operation is immediately available (two examples: the power of a set and trees).

However, we are more interested at the moment in the presence of a binary, rather than unary, positivity predicate Pos, and this is the second generalization. In fact, it can be proved that a unary Pos is essentially (apart from the condition of positivity, which can be added at will) the same thing as a trivial binary Pos; Pos is said to be trivial if $\mathsf{Pos}(a, F) \to (\forall b)(\mathsf{Pos}(b, S) \to b \in F)$ holds, which is a constructive way to express that $\emptyset$ and $\mathcal{C}S$ are the only formal closed subsets. Thus the new version of formal topology, with a binary Pos, includes the previous one as a special case. It also includes the theory of locales, simply as the special case with an improper Pos, that is one for which $\mathsf{Pos}(a, F)$ is always false.

In our opinion, what we have presented here is sufficient to conclude that the basic picture is indeed the basic perspective for a very general approach to constructive topology. The control of distributivity (that is, the fact that it can be added on top, in the form of $\downarrow$-right) opens the way to the development of nondistributive topology, in which the formal and the concrete approach seem to be mathematically equivalent. The presence of binary Pos permits a predicative treatment of formal closed subsets, which now have a primitive definition parallel to that of formal open subsets, just as the combination of quantifiers $\exists\forall$ is parallel to ∀∃. Of course, much work is still to be done to reach a solid development (we have so far extended to the general case, that is nondistributive and with binary Pos, a portion of previous formal topology; as an example, arrows between basic topologies can be obtained by taking as defining conditions exactly the properties of the second component in a relation-pair). Given the novelty of the underlying ideas, however, we would not be very surprised if it will lead to some unexpected new applications.

## References


1. C. BERGÈ, *Espace topologiques - functions multivoques*, Dunod, Paris, 1959.
2. R. DEDEKIND, *Stetigkeit und irrationale Zahlen*, Vieweg, 1872. also in Gesammelte mathematische Werke, vol III, Vieveg 1932.
3. R. ENGELKING, *Outline of general topology*, North-Holland, Amsterdam, 1968.
4. P. T. JOHNSTONE, *Stone Spaces*, Cambridge studies in advanced mathematics 3, Cambridge University Press, 1982.
5. J. L. KELLEY, *General topology*, Van Nostrand, Toronto, New York, London, 1955.
6. P. MARTIN-LÖF, *"Intuitionistic type theory", notes by Giovanni Sambin of a series of lectures given in Padua, June 1980*, Bibliopolis, Naples, 1984.
7. V. PRATT, *A guide to Chu spaces.* page of the World Wide Web with address: http://boole.stanford.edu/chuguide.html.
8. ——, *Chu spaces and their interpretation as concurrent objects*, in Computer Science Today: Recent Trends and Developments, J. van Leeuwen, ed., Springer Lecture Notes in Computer Science 1000, 1995, pp. 392–405.
9. G. SAMBIN, *Intuitionistic formal spaces - a first communication*, in Mathematical Logic and its Applications, D. Skordev, ed., Plenum, New York - London, 1987, pp. 187–204.
10. ——, *Intuitionistic formal spaces vs. Scott domains*, in Atti del Congresso "Temi e prospettive della logica e della filosofia della scienza contemporanee", Cesena, January 7-10 1987, C. Cellucci and G. Sambin, eds., vol. 1, Bologna, 1988, CLUEB, pp. 159–163.
11. ——, *Formal topology - state of the art.* in preparation.
12. G. SAMBIN AND V. VACCARO, *Topology and duality in modal logic*, Annals of Pure and Applied Logic, 37 (1988), pp. 249–296.
13. G. SAMBIN AND S. VALENTINI, *Building up a toolbox for Martin-Löf's type theory: subset theory*, in Twenty-five Years of Constructive Type Theory, Proceedings of the Congress held in Venice, October, 1995, G. Sambin and J. Smith, eds., Oxford Logic Guides 36, Oxford U. P., 1998, pp. 221–244.
14. G. SAMBIN, S. VALENTINI, AND P. VIRGILI, *Constructive domain theory as a branch of intuitionistic pointfree topology*, Theoretical Computer Science, 159 (1996), pp. 319–341.
15. I. SIGSTAM, *Formal spaces and their effective presentations*, Archive for Mathematical Logic, 34 (1995), pp. 211–246.
16. M. B. SMYTH, *Topology*, in Handbook of Logic in Computer Science, S. Abramsky, D. Gabbay, and T. Maibaum, eds., Oxford U. P., 1992.
17. ——, *Semi-metrics, closure spaces and digital topology*, Theoretical computer science, 151 (1995), pp. 257–276.

# Lecture Notes in Computer Science

For information about Vols. 1–1616
please contact your bookseller or Springer-Verlag

Vol. 1618: J. Bézivin, P.-A. Muller (Eds.), The Unified Modeling Language. Proceedings, 1998. IX, 443 pages. 1999.

Vol. 1619: M.T. Goodrich, C.C. McGeoch (Eds.), Algorithm Engineering and Experimentation. Proceedings, 1999. VIII, 349 pages. 1999.

Vol. 1620: W. Horn, Y. Shahar, G. Lindberg, S. Andreassen, J. Wyatt (Eds.), Artificial Intelligence in Medicine. Proceedings, 1999. XIII, 454 pages. 1999. (Subseries LNAI).

Vol. 1621: D. Fensel, R. Studer (Eds.), Knowledge Acquisition Modeling and Management. Proceedings, 1999. XI, 404 pages. 1999. (Subseries LNAI).

Vol. 1622: M. González Harbour, J.A. de la Puente (Eds.), Reliable Software Technologies – Ada-Europe'99. Proceedings, 1999. XIII, 451 pages. 1999.

Vol. 1623: T. Reinartz, Focusing Solutions for Data Mining. XV, 309 pages. 1999. (Subseries LNAI).

Vol. 1625: B. Reusch (Ed.), Computational Intelligence. Proceedings, 1999. XIV, 710 pages. 1999.

Vol. 1626: M. Jarke, A. Oberweis (Eds.), Advanced Information Systems Engineering. Proceedings, 1999. XIV, 478 pages. 1999.

Vol. 1627: T. Asano, H. Imai, D.T. Lee, S.-i. Nakano, T. Tokuyama (Eds.), Computing and Combinatorics. Proceedings, 1999. XIV, 494 pages. 1999.

Col. 1628: R. Guerraoui (Ed.), ECOOP'99 - Object-Oriented Programming. Proceedings, 1999. XIII, 529 pages. 1999.

Vol. 1629: H. Leopold, N. García (Eds.), Multimedia Applications, Services and Techniques - ECMAST'99. Proceedings, 1999. XV, 574 pages. 1999.

Vol. 1631: P. Narendran, M. Rusinowitch (Eds.), Rewriting Techniques and Applications. Proceedings, 1999. XI, 397 pages. 1999.

Vol. 1632: H. Ganzinger (Ed.), Automated Deduction – Cade-16. Proceedings, 1999. XIV, 429 pages. 1999. (Subseries LNAI).

Vol. 1633: N. Halbwachs, D. Peled (Eds.), Computer Aided Verification. Proceedings, 1999. XII, 506 pages. 1999.

Vol. 1634: S. Džeroski, P. Flach (Eds.), Inductive Logic Programming. Proceedings, 1999. VIII, 303 pages. 1999. (Subseries LNAI).

Vol. 1636: L. Knudsen (Ed.), Fast Software Encryption. Proceedings, 1999. VIII, 317 pages. 1999.

Vol. 1637: J.P. Walser, Integer Optimization by Local Search. XIX, 137 pages. 1999. (Subseries LNAI).

Vol. 1638: A. Hunter, S. Parsons (Eds.), Symbolic and Quantitative Approaches to Reasoning and Uncertainty. Proceedings, 1999. IX, 397 pages. 1999. (Subseries LNAI).

Vol. 1639: S. Donatelli, J. Kleijn (Eds.), Application and Theory of Petri Nets 1999. Proceedings, 1999. VIII, 425 pages. 1999.

Vol. 1640: W. Tepfenhart, W. Cyre (Eds.), Conceptual Structures: Standards and Practices. Proceedings, 1999. XII, 515 pages. 1999. (Subseries LNAI).

Vol. 1641: D. Hutter, W. Stephan, P. Traverso, M. Ullmann (Eds.), Applied Formal Methods - FM-Trends 98. Proceedings, 1998. XI, 377 pages. 1999.

Vol. 1642: D.J. Hand, J.N. Kok, M.R. Berthold (Eds.), Advances in Intelligent Data Analysis. Proceedings, 1999. XII, 538 pages. 1999.

Vol. 1643: J. Nešetřil (Ed.), Algorithms – ESA '99. Proceedings, 1999. XII, 552 pages. 1999.

Vol. 1644: J. Wiedermann, P. van Emde Boas, M. Nielsen (Eds.), Automata, Languages, and Programming. Proceedings, 1999. XIV, 720 pages. 1999.

Vol. 1645: M. Crochemore, M. Paterson (Eds.), Combinatorial Pattern Matching. Proceedings, 1999. VIII, 295 pages. 1999.

Vol. 1647: F.J. Garijo, M. Boman (Eds.), Multi-Agent System Engineering. Proceedings, 1999. X, 233 pages. 1999. (Subseries LNAI).

Vol. 1648: M. Franklin (Ed.), Financial Cryptography. Proceedings, 1999. VIII, 269 pages. 1999.

Vol. 1649: R.Y. Pinter, S. Tsur (Eds.), Next Generation Information Technologies and Systems. Proceedings, 1999. IX, 327 pages. 1999.

Vol. 1650: K.-D. Althoff, R. Bergmann, L.K. Branting (Eds.), Case-Based Reasoning Research and Development. Proceedings, 1999. XII, 598 pages. 1999. (Subseries LNAI).

Vol. 1651: R.H. Güting, D. Papadias, F. Lochovsky (Eds.), Advances in Spatial Databases. Proceedings, 1999. XI, 371 pages. 1999.

Vol. 1652: M. Klusch, O.M. Shehory, G. Weiss (Eds.), Cooperative Information Agents III. Proceedings, 1999. XI, 404 pages. 1999. (Subseries LNAI).

Vol. 1653: S. Covaci (Ed.), Active Networks. Proceedings, 1999. XIII, 346 pages. 1999.

Vol. 1654: E.R. Hancock, M. Pelillo (Eds.), Energy Minimization Methods in Computer Vision and Pattern Recognition. Proceedings, 1999. IX, 331 pages. 1999.

Vol. 1655: S.-W. Lee, Y. Nakano (Eds.), Document Analysis Systems: Theory and Practice. Proceedings, 1998. XI, 377 pages. 1999.

Vol. 1656: S. Chatterjee, J.F. Prins, L. Carter, J. Ferrante, Z. Li, D. Sehr, P.-C. Yew (Eds.), Languages and Compilers for Parallel Computing. Proceedings, 1998. XI, 384 pages. 1999.

Vol. 1657: T. Altenkirch, W. Naraschewski, B. Reus (Eds.), Types for Proofs and Programs. Proceedings, 1998. VIII, 207 pages. 1999.

Vol. 1661: C. Freksa, D.M. Mark (Eds.), Spatial Information Theory. Proceedings, 1999. XIII, 477 pages. 1999.

Vol. 1662: V. Malyshkin (Ed.), Parallel Computing Technologies. Proceedings, 1999. XIX, 510 pages. 1999.

Vol. 1663: F. Dehne, A. Gupta. J.-R. Sack, R. Tamassia (Eds.), Algorithms and Data Structures. Proceedings, 1999. IX, 366 pages. 1999.

Vol. 1664: J.C.M. Baeten, S. Mauw (Eds.), CONCUR'99. Concurrency Theory. Proceedings, 1999. XI, 573 pages. 1999.

Vol. 1666: M. Wiener (Ed.), Advances in Cryptology – CRYPTO '99. Proceedings, 1999. XII, 639 pages. 1999.

Vol. 1667: J. Hlavička, E. Maehle, A. Pataricza (Eds.), Dependable Computing – EDCC-3. Proceedings, 1999. XVIII, 455 pages. 1999.

Vol. 1668: J.S. Vitter, C.D. Zaroliagis (Eds.), Algorithm Engineering. Proceedings, 1999. VIII, 361 pages. 1999.

Vol. 1671: D. Hochbaum, K. Jansen, J.D.P. Rolim, A. Sinclair (Eds.), Randomization, Approximation, and Combinatorial Optimization. Proceedings, 1999. IX, 289 pages. 1999.

Vol. 1672: M. Kutylowski, L. Pacholski, T. Wierzbicki (Eds.), Mathematical Foundations of Computer Science 1999. Proceedings, 1999. XII, 455 pages. 1999.

Vol. 1673: P. Lysaght, J. Irvine, R. Hartenstein (Eds.), Field Programmable Logic and Applications. Proceedings, 1999. XI, 541 pages. 1999.

Vol. 1674: D. Floreano, J.-D. Nicoud, F. Mondada (Eds.), Advances in Artificial Life. Proceedings, 1999. XVI, 737 pages. 1999. (Subseries LNAI).

Vol. 1675: J. Estublier (Ed.), System Configuration Management. Proceedings, 1999. VIII, 255 pages. 1999.

Vol. 1976: M. Mohania, A M. Tjoa (Eds.), Data Warehousing and Knowledge Discovery. Proceedings, 1999. XII, 400 pages. 1999.

Vol. 1677: T. Bench-Capon, G. Soda, A M. Tjoa (Eds.), Database and Expert Systems Applications. Proceedings, 1999. XVIII, 1105 pages. 1999.

Vol. 1678: M.H. Böhlen, C.S. Jensen, M.O. Scholl (Eds.), Spatio-Temporal Database Management. Proceedings, 1999. X, 243 pages. 1999.

Vol. 1679: C. Taylor, A. Colchester (Eds.), Medical Image Computing and Computer-Assisted Intervention – MICCAI'99. Proceedings, 1999. XXI, 1240 pages. 1999.

Vol. 1680: D. Dams, R. Gerth, S. Leue, M. Massink (Eds.), Theoretical and Practical Aspects of SPIN Model Checking. Proceedings, 1999. X, 277 pages. 1999.

Vol. 1682: M. Nielsen, P. Johansen, O.F. Olsen, J. Weickert (Eds.), Scale-Space Theories in Computer Vision. Proceedings, 1999. XII, 532 pages. 1999.

Vol. 1683: J. Flum, M. Rodríguez-Artalejo (Eds.), Computer Science Logic. Proceedings, 1999. XI, 580 pages. 1999.

Vol. 1684: G. Ciobanu, G. Păun (Eds.), Fundamentals of Computation Theory. Proceedings, 1999. XI, 570 pages. 1999.

Vol. 1685: P. Amestoy, P. Berger, M. Daydé, I. Duff, V. Frayssé, L. Giraud, D. Ruiz (Eds.), Euro-Par'99. Parallel Processing. Proceedings, 1999. XXXII, 1503 pages. 1999.

Vol. 1687: O. Nierstrasz, M. Lemoine (Eds.), Software Engineering – ESEC/FSE '99. Proceedings, 1999. XII, 529 pages. 1999.

Vol. 1688: P. Bouquet, L. Serafini, P. Brézillon, M. Benerecetti, F. Castellani (Eds.), Modeling and Using Context. Proceedings, 1999. XII, 528 pages. 1999. (Subseries LNAI).

Vol. 1689: F. Solina, A. Leonardis (Eds.), Computer Analysis of Images and Patterns. Proceedings, 1999. XIV, 650 pages. 1999.

Vol. 1690: Y. Bertot, G. Dowek, A. Hirschowitz, C. Paulin, L. Théry (Eds.), Theorem Proving in Higher Order Logics. Proceedings, 1999. VIII, 359 pages. 1999.

Vol. 1691: J. Eder, I. Rozman, T. Welzer (Eds.), Advances in Databases and Information Systems. Proceedings, 1999. XIII, 383 pages. 1999.

Vol. 1692: V. Matoušek, P. Mautner, J. Ocelíková, P. Sojka (Eds.), Text, Speech and Dialogue. Proceedings, 1999. XI, 396 pages. 1999. (Subseries LNAI).

Vol. 1693: P. Jayanti (Ed.), Distributed Computing. Proceedings, 1999. X, 357 pages. 1999.

Vol. 1694: A. Cortesi, G. Filé (Eds.), Static Analysis. Proceedings, 1999. VIII, 357 pages. 1999.

Vol. 1695: P. Barahona, J.J. Alferes (Eds.), Progress in Artificial Intelligence. Proceedings, 1999. XI, 385 pages. 1999. (Subseries LNAI).

Vol. 1696: S. Abiteboul, A.-M. Vercoustre (Eds.), Research and Advanced Technology for Digital Libraries. Proceedings, 1999. XII, 497 pages. 1999.

Vol. 1697: J. Dongarra, E. Luque, T. Margalef (Eds.), Recent Advances in Parallel Virtual Machine and Message Passing Interface. Proceedings, 1999. XVII, 551 pages. 1999.

Vol. 1698: M. Felici, K. Kanoun, A. Pasquini (Eds.), Computer Safety, Reliability and Security. Proceedings, 1999. XVIII, 482 pages. 1999.

Vol. 1699: S. Albayrak (Ed.), Intelligent Agents for Telecommunication Applications. Proceedings, 1999. IX, 191 pages. 1999. (Subseries LNAI).

Vol. 1701: W. Burgard, T. Christaller, A.B. Cremers (Eds.), KI-99: Advances in Artificial Intelligence. Proceedings, 1999. XI, 311 pages. 1999. (Subseries LNAI).

Vol. 1702: G. Nadathur (Ed.), Principles and Practice of Declarative Programming. Proceedings, 1999. X, 434 pages. 1999.

Vol. 1703: P. Laurence, T. Kropf (Eds.), Correct Hardware Design and Verification Methods. Proceedings, 1999. XI, 366 pages. 1999.

Vol. 1704: Jan M. Żytkow, J. Rauch (Eds.), Principles of Data Mining and Knowledge Discovery. Proceedings, 1999. XIV, 593 pages. 1999. (Subseries LNAI).

Vol. 1705: H. Ganzinger, D. McAllester, A. Voronkov (Eds.), Logic for Programming and Automated Reasoning. Proceedings, 1999. XII, 397 pages. 1999. (Subseries LNAI).

Vol. 1707: H.-W. Gellersen (Ed.), Handheld and Ubiquitous Computing. Proceedings, 1999. XII, 390 pages. 1999.